HARD LESSONS IN CORPORATE GOVERNANCE

How should corporations be run? Who should get a say, and what results can we expect? *Hard Lessons in Corporate Governance* provides an accessible introduction to the various failed attempts at using corporate governance to improve society. It introduces the record of these failures and illuminates hard lessons spread across thousands of empirical studies. If we look at the outcomes generated by various corporate governance "best" practices, we find that none of the practices work. If we look at the theories and assumptions that support modern corporate governance, we find they are likely wrong. And if we look at the prospect of corporate governance to improve political, environmental, and social outcomes, we find ample evidence that governance will fail us here too. After documenting these failures, Bryce Tingle K.C. turns to the most important lesson: How to fix this important, but broken, system.

Bryce C. Tingle, K.C. is Professor and N. Murray Edwards Chair in Business Law in the Faculty of Law at the University of Calgary. He is a member of one of the Securities Commissions in Canada, serves as the Chair for various business corporations, and spent decades advising boards, including as the General Counsel of several international corporate groups.

Hard Lessons in Corporate Governance

BRYCE C. TINGLE

University of Calgary

CAMBRIDGE
UNIVERSITY PRESS

CAMBRIDGE
UNIVERSITY PRESS

Shaftesbury Road, Cambridge CB2 8EA, United Kingdom

One Liberty Plaza, 20th Floor, New York, NY 10006, USA

477 Williamstown Road, Port Melbourne, VIC 3207, Australia

314–321, 3rd Floor, Plot 3, Splendor Forum, Jasola District Centre, New Delhi – 110025, India

103 Penang Road, #05–06/07, Visioncrest Commercial, Singapore 238467

Cambridge University Press is part of Cambridge University Press & Assessment, a department of the University of Cambridge.

We share the University's mission to contribute to society through the pursuit of education, learning and research at the highest international levels of excellence.

www.cambridge.org
Information on this title: www.cambridge.org/9781009170611

DOI: 10.1017/9781009170628

First published 2024

A catalogue record for this publication is available from the British Library

Library of Congress Cataloging-in-Publication Data
NAMES: Tingle, Bryce C. (Bryce Cyril), 1967– author.
TITLE: Hard lessons in corporate governance / Bryce C. Tingle, University of Calgary.
DESCRIPTION: Cambridge, United Kingdom ; New York, NY : Cambridge University Press, 2024. | Includes bibliographical references and index.
IDENTIFIERS: LCCN 2023044210 | ISBN 9781009170611 (hardback) | ISBN 9781009170628 (ebook)
SUBJECTS: LCSH: Corporate governance – Law and legislation.
CLASSIFICATION: LCC K1327 .T56 2024 | DDC 338.5–dc23/eng/20231003
LC record available at https://lccn.loc.gov/2023044210

ISBN 978-1-009-17061-1 Hardback
ISBN 978-1-009-17063-5 Paperback

To the people I love most in the world:

Rebecca, Miranda, Afton, Aubrey, and Winston.

You stopped me from talking about corporate governance at the dinner table, but nothing was said about dragging you all into the subject through a book dedication.

Contents

Acknowledgments   *page* ix

Editorial Note   xi

Introduction   1

1   Our Corporate Governance Experiment   17

PART I   WHAT DO WE KNOW ABOUT CORPORATE
GOVERNANCE PRACTICES?

2   Best Practices for Boards of Directors   37

3   Can We Measure Corporate Governance?   56

4   Do We Understand Executive Compensation Best Practices?   70

5   What Explains Shareholder Voting?   93

6   Shareholder Activism   118

7   Proxy Advisors   143

PART II   WHAT CAN WE CONCLUDE ABOUT OUR THEORIES
OF CORPORATE GOVERNANCE?

8   Taking Stock of the Argument So Far: We Need a Better
    Theory of the Firm   169

9   How Crooked Is the Timber?   193

10 Markets and Corporate Governance   210

PART III ARE SOCIAL WELFARE OUTCOMES ANY DIFFERENT?

11 Achieving Social and Environmental Goals through Corporate
    Governance   235

12 Shareholders and ESG Disclosure   258

13 Where Do We Go from Here?   289

Index   297

Acknowledgments

There are many people who have a hand in a book like this. It gives me considerable sympathy for Oscar winners desperately wracking their brains to name every contributor to their achievement before the orchestra plays them out. Invariably, someone will be missed and the next thing you know your agent will not return your calls.

I would like to express my gratitude to a long list of research assistants over the years who have helped in the task of finding hundreds of papers on various aspects of our modern corporate governance project: Alena Storton, Ami Matthias, Charlotte Hardwicke-Brown, Colin Bartlett, Jennifer Labelle, Joel Tallerico, Julie Bogle, Manpreet Dhillon, Matt Gal, Paul Brar, Ricki-Lee Gerbrandt, Ryan Millar, Sharan Sandal, Taylor Watt, and Tyler Anthony. They were all excellent students and researchers.

I am particularly grateful to Lena Clayton (JD'25) who assisted me in getting everything organized and double-checked for publication in this book. Her intelligence, incisive edits, work ethic, and scrupulous attention to detail are of the sort found only among the best kind of lawyers. I am also grateful to John Challice for his encouragement and assistance with this project. He is a great asset to the world of those who care about books, and an even better friend.

Behind this book lies decades of advising and serving on various boards of directors. I am grateful to all the people with whom I have served. A theme of this book is that it is one of the hardest things in the world to successfully build and grow a business; I admire the people I've known who try. Insofar as there is any wisdom at all in this book, it was doubtless learned from these fellow directors and colleagues. I particularly would like to thank Bob McKenzie, from whom I learned many of the aspects of character and integrity in the boardroom that can't be taught in books.

I would also like to acknowledge Murray Edwards and Ian Holloway KC, whose mutually reinforcing generosity made my transition to academia possible. I have benefitted greatly from the unusual opportunity of going from a long career in business and law to a position that gave me the time and incentives to bring empirical research to bear on my experiences.

My wife Rebecca and I have always joked that, in the form of our family, we jointly manage the world's least impressive nonprofit. I am grateful beyond measure for her enormous contributions to that slightly disreputable organization, as well as her unfailing support for me, and hence this book.

Finally, I would like to thank world peace. Well, not "thank" world peace, but sort of urge it on everyone. It is super important, and we have to let our voices be … whoops, that's the orchestra.

Editorial Note

This book is the product of a decade of research into various aspects of our modern corporate governance project. There are thousands of empirical studies about corporate governance and an equally large secondary literature discussing these studies. Over the past decade, I published approximately two dozen peer-reviewed journal articles covering much of the ground summarized in this book. In a very real way, I learned the "hard lessons" of corporate governance – much of which came as a surprise – as I wrote these papers.

My law review articles are directed to an academic audience and have all the merits and deficiencies of academic writing, particularly the forbidding presence of hundreds of footnotes in each paper. This book, in contrast, was always intended to be an accessible summary of the most important things we have learned about corporate governance. It is aimed not just at academics, but at the legion of thoughtful professionals working in corporate governance, many of whom would naturally be deterred by a book that looked like a very, very long and boring academic article.

Whether I have avoided the prim, vaguely censorious tone of serious scholarship, can be left to the reader's judgment, but the real problem arose in connection with footnotes. The earliest drafts of this book contained more than a thousand footnotes, making up more than a third of the text. Any sensible person would flee such an ominous display, particularly the busy practical people who I hope will find this book most useful.

My solution has been to cut out footnotes as much as possible, except where they fix the source of a quotation, or where they reference the empirical literature that is core to the conclusions – large and small – in the text that follows. I have particularly cut footnotes supporting assertions that are not controversial, widely known, or can be supported by a superficial search of the Internet. I have also, reluctantly, significantly reduced the summaries of cited research that is a common feature in American law review footnotes. I hope the text of the book makes clear the cited articles' relevant conclusions, and that thanks to the Internet any interested person can simply read the abstract of any paper that catches their attention. I draw comfort that very few readers will either notice or care about the disfigurement of my precious footnotes, which are in a very real way a law professor's treasure.

Finally, my journal articles remain available for anyone seeking more detailed and enthusiastic footnoting practices. Material in this book was drawn from the following published and forthcoming articles:

INTRODUCTION

Bryce C. Tingle, "How Good Are Our 'Best Practices' When It Comes to Executive Compensation? A Review of Forty Years of Skyrocketing Pay, Regulation, and the Forces of Good Governance" (2017) 80:2 *Saskatchewan Law Review* 387–420.

CHAPTER 1

Bryce C. Tingle, "The Most Important Theory in Corporate Law Is Unhelpful: Agency Cost Theory Explains Anything and Predicts Nothing" (*Berkeley Business Law Journal*, forthcoming).
Bryce C. Tingle, "Returning Markets to the Center of Corporate Governance" (2023) 48:4 *Journal of Corporation Law* 663–718.

CHAPTER 2

Bryce C. Tingle, "What Do We Really Know about Corporate Governance Best Practices? A Review of the Empirical Research Since 2000" (2017) 59:3 *Canadian Business Law Journal* 292–331.

CHAPTER 3

Bryce C. Tingle, "What Is Corporate Governance? Can We Measure It? Can Investment Fiduciaries Rely on It?" (2018) 43:2 *Queen's Law Journal* 223–262.

CHAPTER 4

Bryce C. Tingle, "How Good Are Our 'Best Practices' When It Comes to Executive Compensation? A Review of Forty Years of Skyrocketing Pay, Regulation, and the Forces of Good Governance" (2017) 80:2 *Saskatchewan Law Review* 387–420.
Bryce C. Tingle, "Framed! The Failure of Traditional Agency Cost Explanations of Executive Pay Practices" (2017) 54:4 *Alberta Law Review* 899–928.

CHAPTER 5

Bryce C. Tingle, "Expressive Voting and Irrational Outcomes in Corporate Elections" (2021) 67:1 *McGill Law Journal* 71–118.

CHAPTER 6

Bryce C. Tingle, "Two Stories about Shareholders" (2021) 58:1 *Osgoode Hall Law Journal* 57–108.

CHAPTER 7

Bryce C. Tingle, "Bad Company! The Assumptions behind Proxy Advisors' Voting Recommendations" (2014) 37:2 *Dalhousie Law Journal* 709–748.
Bryce C. Tingle, "The Agency Cost Case for Regulating Proxy Advisory Firms" (2016) 49:2 *UBC Law Review* 725–787.

CHAPTER 8

Bryce C. Tingle, "The Most Important Theory in Corporate Law Is Useless: Agency Cost Theory Explains Anything and Predicts Nothing" (*Berkeley Business Law Journal*, forthcoming).

CHAPTER 9

Bryce C. Tingle and Eldon Spackman, "Do Corporate Fiduciary Duties Matter?" (2019) 4:4 *Annals of Corporate Governance* 272–326.
Bryce C. Tingle, "The Most Important Theory in Corporate Law Is Useless: Agency Cost Theory Explains Anything and Predicts Nothing" (*Berkeley Business Law Journal*, forthcoming).
Bryce C. Tingle, "The Limits of Corporate Governance in Contributing Solutions to Social and Environmental Problems" (forthcoming).

CHAPTER 10

Bryce C. Tingle, "Returning Markets to the Center of Corporate Law" (2023) 48:4 *Journal of Corporation Law* 663–718.

CHAPTER 11

Bryce C. Tingle, "Corporations on the Couch: Is Therapeutic Disclosure a Kind of Madness?" (2022) 22:3 *UBC Law Review* 745–801.
Bryce C. Tingle, "The Limits of Corporate Governance in Contributing Solutions to Social and Environmental Problems" (forthcoming).

CHAPTER 12

Bryce C. Tingle, "Corporations on the Couch: Is Therapeutic Disclosure a Kind of Madness?" (2022) 22:3 *UBC Law Review* 745–801.
Bryce C. Tingle, "What Do We Know About Shareholders' Potential to Solve Environmental and Social Problems?" (2023) 58:1 *Georgia Law Review* 169–247.
Bryce C. Tingle, "Review Essay: Institutional Shareholders, Short-Termism and the Odds of a Coincidence" (2020) 63:3 *Canadian Business Law Journal* 389–399.

Introduction

The year before I went to law school, I attended a late-night movie in a crowded and very noisy campus theater. I can't remember the film we were all there to see, but I do remember that for the warmup, the theater was playing classic Chuck Jones Looney Tunes cartoons. These mostly revolved around Wile E. Coyote's elaborate and painfully unsuccessful attempts to capture (and eat!) the Road Runner; whoever was playing the cartoons knew their audience – not one of whom apparently loved animals. There was a great deal of amusing commentary shouted at the movie screen, but the line I remember came when Coyote put on roller skates and strapped himself to a giant magnet, and at once we understood the logic behind feeding the Road Runner metallic birdseed. As the lunatic brilliance of the plan dawned on us, someone in the theater confidently shouted out, "It's going to work! This time, it's going to work!"

The humor of the line derives, of course, from our collective awareness that it is certainly NOT going to work, and that Coyote's plan will produce yet another elaborate and equally improbable failure, resulting in either a head injury or spinal compression so severe that he walks out of the frame like an accordion. I have increasingly come to see this moment, both the misplaced confidence and the absurdist humor, as a useful metaphor for our current corporate governance project.

This will strike some readers (but definitely not all) as a completely unfair analogy. Wile E. Coyote had remarkably poor judgment even before his multiple concussions, whereas our current corporate governance regime is the product of decades of scholarly, regulatory, and private efforts by very worthy, un-concussed people. I acknowledge the justice of this objection. But that one aspect of the analogy aside, there really is a lot of similarity between the explosions, crashes, and falls depicted in the cartoon and what has been going on in our public markets for about forty years.

An almost perfect example is provided by the modern effort to control executive compensation. Efforts to control executive pay began in a relatively modest way in the Securities Act of 1934.[1] (US Steel objected to the new disclosure rules on the grounds revealing senior executive pay "would be conducive to disturbing the morale of the organization" – not an argument that would be even attempted now.[2])

Aside from some 1978 disclosure rules around perquisites like company jets and three martini lunches, not much happened until 1992, when the Securities and Exchange Commission (SEC) introduced a greatly expanded executive pay disclosure regime and ushered in the era of compensation governance reform. Over the next two decades, there followed an all-out attack on the nature and quantum of corporate pay:

- The Omnibus Budget Reconciliation Act of 1993 provided punitive tax treatment for any payments exceeding $1 million to the CEO and four highest-paid executives of any public company, unless those payments were conditional on achieving performance targets.
- In 1998, the Financial Accounting Standards Board (FASB) announced that repricing options would result in the issuing company taking an accounting charge each year based on the appreciation of the value of the option.
- The Sarbanes–Oxley Act of 2002 forbade loans to executive officers, imposed blackout periods on executives trading, imposed compensation clawbacks in the event of earnings restatements, and generally raised the pressure on boards to increase their independence from management.
- Further changes to the Internal Revenue Code were made in 2004 to limit corporate managers' flexibility in making certain elections to defer compensation, to restrict withdrawals of certain kinds of deferred compensation, to prevent executives from receiving this compensation until six months after severance, and to prevent option backdating.
- Late in 2004, FASB announced that all firms would have to begin recognizing an accounting expense in their financial statements in relation to all stock option grants.
- In 2006, the SEC revised its disclosure rules around compensation again. Following the 1934 Act reforms, executive compensation took up less than one page of the typical three-to–five page proxy statement. By the time of the 2006 reforms, the average length of the largest company's proxy statements was forty-five pages. Following the 2006 reforms, the average length exceeded seventy pages, much of it focused on compensation.[3]
- Around this time, proxy advisory firms such as Institutional Shareholder Services (ISS) and Glass, Lewis & Co. (Glass Lewis) began to grow in importance and influence. These firms provide voting recommendations to institutional shareholders, which had grown to dominate public markets. Proxy advisory firms dedicate considerable resources to evaluating executive compensation in public companies, basing many of their voting recommendations (even in relation to board nominees) on a company's adoption of satisfactory compensation practices.
- In the wake of the 2008 financial crisis, Occupy Wall Street, a widespread protest movement, focused considerable public outrage on executive pay levels.

- Throughout the 2000s, books, newspapers, magazines, and broadcast media devoted significant resources to reporting on executive pay issues and scandals, as well as evaluating the quality of companies based, in part, on their pay practices.
- Boards responded to this negative publicity by almost universally adopting new processes for setting executive pay. This included frequent market checks, fully independent compensation committees, and employing a vast industry of compensation consultants.
- In 2011, the SEC introduced further compensation disclosure rules in obedience to various provisions of the Dodd–Frank Wall Street Reform and Consumer Protection Act.
- The Dodd–Frank legislation also introduced "say-on-pay" voting rules that gave shareholders the right to vote on executive pay arrangements every three years. The UK had adopted say-on-pay in 2002, then made shareholder votes on pay binding in 2013.[4]
- The increasing importance of executive compensation was reflected in the guidelines published by proxy advisors for the benefit of companies looking to follow best practices in their compensation decisions. By the end of this past decade, ISS, the largest of these advisors, was providing companies with fourteen pages of compensation instruction in their main voting guidelines, another twenty-six pages in a compensation FAQ, yet another twenty-six pages in an equity compensation FAQ, fifteen pages on how to measure pay-for-performance, and several other documents related to choosing peer firms for comparative pay disclosure. As there are several proxy firms that public companies need to satisfy, it is not an exaggeration that there are well over 100 pages of strictures that must be examined from this source alone. Large institutional investors like CalPERS generate their own compensation-inflected proxy voting guidelines which must be consulted.

What was the result of all this activity? Whereas between the 1940s and 1970s, median CEO pay had remained relatively constant, it grew 125 percent through the 1990s.[5] Between 1978 and 2012, average CEO pay of the 350 largest US companies increased by a whopping 875 percent.[6] During this time, the ratio of CEO compensation to that of the average worker rose 900 percent from 29:1 in 1978 to 273:1 in 2012.[7] In fact, CEO pay growth has doubled the rise in the Standard & Poor's Index (S&P) over the past thirty years.[8] This is what an escaping roadrunner looks like in the corporate governance context.

What makes Road Runner cartoons funny? It isn't that the Road Runner always escapes. On its own, that would be annoying (in some of the same ways that overly generous executive pay packages are annoying). Rather, the humor arises from the behavior of Coyote. He just never gives up. In one cartoon episode, Coyote enthusiastically puts together a total of *thirteen* different attempts to capture the

Road Runner and is absolutely undeterred by his steadily mounting failures. The cumulative effect of doggedly persisting, failure after failure, is to turn Coyote from a potentially dangerous predator into an object of sympathy because he is clearly delusional. Interestingly, the list above includes *fourteen* different strategies for constraining executive pay tried since 1992.

Coyote's persistence is not a matter of character. He isn't like the British nation holding on through the terrible year following Dunkirk or, for that matter, Gandhi holding on despite the British. Coyote's persistence is the persistence of someone whose grasp on reality is so skewed that he keeps trying his elaborate plans because he genuinely believes they are certain to work. That is why we generally do not come out of a Road Runner cartoon feeling inspired by the potentialities of the human spirit. We come out laughing at the absurd Rube Goldberg devices constructed by Coyote with an apparently limitless credit account with the Acme Corporation. Only someone truly delusional would attempt a plan to catch the Road Runner with roller skates and a giant magnet – especially near a busy railway.

In exactly the same way, we are missing an opportunity to enjoy a fine display of absurdity if we ignore the Rube Goldberg aspect of the devices we have been deploying in the corporate governance sphere. What, for example, is CalPERS thinking when they produce their own proxy voting guide to offer suggestions about executive compensation? Do they believe there is something to add to the literally hundreds of pages of guidance produced by proxy advisors, academics, law firms, compensation consultants, and other institutional investors? Do they expect their modest contribution will be the thing that finally tips the scales on executive pay?

Possibly even more absurd are the frequent regulatory expansions of compensation disclosure. When Dodd–Frank was being passed, was there anyone who believed shareholders were not getting enough information in the seventy-odd pages of compensation disclosure that existed following the 2006 reforms? Was something vital missing? Who is reading all this disclosure? A typical institutional fund manager owns a portfolio of dozens to hundreds of different companies, nearly all of which produce their proxy materials at about the same time each year. How is adding more paper to the unread pile ever going to work? This approach seems crazy even if we are unfamiliar with the well-established research finding that the quality of peoples' decisions is *inversely* related to the quantity of information available to them.[9]

The absurdity of these strategies is enhanced by the fact that, unlike Coyote, we, the audience, have known for most of the past several decades that these Rube Goldberg devices are going to fail. We are precisely in the position of a raucous student audience enjoying the pretended confidence of someone shouting, "this time it's going to work!" Executive perks actually increased after the 1978 disclosure reforms, as managers began copying what was being done at other companies.[10] After a 1984 attempt by Congress to use the Tax Code to restrict the use of golden parachutes, these devices both proliferated and increased in value as the new tax rules took on an unwelcome aspirational aspect.[11] The performance pay tax changes in 1993 resulted in compensation structures that paid out much more than the old, boring steady paycheck-and-bonus arrangements of earlier generations of managers.[12] To induce executives to enter a risky lottery, companies had to offer a chance of lottery-level winnings. Say-on-pay had been accompanied by faster pay increases in Britain during the decade before it was introduced to America.[13]

Early in this century, it should have been clear, even to someone completely unfamiliar with the academic research, that the previous decade's spectacular growth in executive compensation suggested the tools we were using were not fit for purpose. But, like Coyote, we just doubled down, using the same materials in increasingly complex and rickety ways. (In another cartoon, Coyote once again uses metallic birdseed and a giant magnet, but this time he attracts a large metal container of TNT. This is an interesting parallel to the say-on-pay voting reforms.)

One important feature of Road Runner cartoons is that Wile E. Coyote's injuries are not the fault of the Road Runner. If they were inflicted by a flightless bird, the cartoons would take on the slightly sour flavor of sadism. (This is why the "Itchy and Scratchy" parodies in *The Simpsons* are seldom very funny once the audience gets the single-note joke about the violence of children's cartoons.) Instead, Coyote is almost always the architect of his own misfortunes as he runs afoul of cannons, anvils, rockets, and explosives that were only introduced into the delicate southwestern desert ecosystem by himself. (He does admittedly also have an academically understudied series of product liability claims against Acme Corp.)

There is widespread agreement among scholars that most, if not all, of the steps we took to control the rise of executive compensation actually had the effect of *increasing* executive pay. For example, our new disclosure rules operated like a ratchet, driving pay relentlessly upwards, as no company wanted to pay its executives in ways that suggested they were below average, and as the disclosure about other companies provided negotiation resources useful for executives feeling left behind. The tax changes pushed companies into using increasing amounts of equity incentives. Shareholders used their new power over compensation to strike deals that former Delaware Supreme Court Chief Justice Leo Strine described as, "pay packages well out of line with other corporate managers, but in exchange CEOs must focus intently on stock price growth and be willing to treat other corporate constituencies callously if that is necessary."[14] As for the major interventions of the US Government, pay levels actually increased 29 percent following Sarbanes–Oxley and 21 percent following Dodd–Frank, "above what can be explained by size, firm performance and time."[15] This the equivalent of the magnet you are holding accidentally attracting a train.

The final parallel between our serious work on executive compensation and Road Runner cartoons is the bitter irony that the Road Runner nearly always gets to eat the birdseed. In fact, the Road Runner lives in an ecosystem where the apparent role of Coyote is to ensure the bird is fed. In 1993, the year the modern fixation on executive compensation began, payments to the five highest-paid senior executives of a US corporation absorbed, on average, 5 percent of its profits; by 2003, this had increased to 10 percent.[16] This, finally, is the moment that shareholders and the corporate governance industry, surrounded by the wreckage of their own trap, smoking gently from an explosion and clutching a magnet that has been twisted into a pretzel, get to hear the captains of American industry say a cheerful "beep-beep" before speeding away.[17]

1 CORPORATE GOVERNANCE IS ABOUT TO BECOME MUCH LESS AMUSING

In modern corporate governance, cartoonishly simple stories have always triumphed over more cautious appraisals of the evidence. For example, the rising use of equity incentives and pay-for-performance schemes outlined in this Introduction was accompanied by constant expressions of concern from researchers examining the evidence. Right at the beginning, in 1980, one scholar observed that the empirical evidence on the relationship between executive equity holdings and firm performance was "quite mixed."[18] By 1986, another scholar noted that "no consensus has developed" among empirical researchers about the impact of managerial exposure to equity.[19] In 1994, a scholar observed on this subject, "the results of the studies are inconclusive."[20] In 1995, two other researchers noted there was a "singular lack of consistency in the empirical results reported."[21] In 1999, one of the leading researchers in the area of executive compensation, Kevin Murphy observed, "[u]nfortunately, although there is a plethora of evidence on dysfunctional consequences of poorly designed pay programs, there is surprisingly little direct evidence that higher pay-performance sensitivities lead to higher stock-price performance."[22] Yet, during this period, the use of equity and pay-for-performance schemes went from being extremely rare to universal. These sorts of scholarly reservations were no match against the simple and intuitive story that managers are untrustworthy, and so it is wise to align their economic interests with those of the shareholders.

Executive pay is not an outlier. Virtually every governance practice we have adopted over the past thirty years has been accompanied by widespread concern among those familiar with the empirical literature that the practice in question would either not work or that it would work in ways we did not want. Sarbanes–Oxley and Dodd–Frank have the distinction of both being accompanied by articles from well-respected corporate law scholars with the impolite phrase "quack corporate governance" in their titles.[23] These papers pointed out that there was plenty of pre-existing evidence that the practices enjoined by those statutes would not work in the ways reformers hoped.

This striking feature of the modern corporate governance project – its willful blindness – is about to become a real problem. When the focus was just on maximizing shareholder returns, corporate governance's absurdities didn't seem that important. They were probably at best a waste of time; at worst, the governance practices only adversely impacted the shareholders, who were usually among those most loudly advocating for them. Now, however, corporate governance is being seriously suggested as a solution to very important social problems and that doesn't seem nearly as funny.

There are a bewildering range of terms used to describe this turn in corporate governance: "corporate social responsibility" or "CSR," "Environmental, Social, Governance" or "ESG," "sustainability," "triple bottom-line," "stakeholderism," a concern for "constituencies," "charity," "EESG" (adding "employees" to ESG), and when applied to investors, "stewardship," "socially responsible investing," or "SRI." The precise differences between these terms don't matter that much; they mostly act as synonyms, and their conceptual ambiguity is often deliberate.

This book is not about the merits of the social, environmental, and economic outcomes hoped for by various participants in the corporate governance industry. It is self-evidently valuable to reduce discrimination, inequality, pollution, and other social harms. It is also inescapable that if a corporation does not generate profits, it will eventually go out of business, which, among other tragedies, defeats the point of making it an agent for improving the world. Rather, this book, at its core, is about the limits of our corporate governance system to produce all kinds of corporate outcomes. If our governance interventions cannot even manage the basic task of holding down executive pay to improve shareholder returns, it is going to be surprising if they can solve much more complex, long-term social problems. Wile E. Coyote may be a diligent guy, and arguably some of his failures are a function of bad luck and shoddy workmanship at Acme Corp., but still, most of us would hesitate to put him in the cockpit of a passenger jet.

Yet that is where he appears to be headed. Very serious people in Washington are investing significant amounts of effort to use corporate governance to solve some of our biggest problems. Elizabeth Warren, the closest thing American politics has to a corporate governance professional, has legislation amending various aspects of the corporate contract that she expects will solve the problems of declining American competitiveness, income inequality, campaign finance, and serious anti-social behavior.[24] Her office's description of the benefits of her Accountable Capitalism Act forcibly reminds of one of the exhaustive claims made by certain brands of laundry detergent.

Outside of politics, a recent joint statement by more than seventy law professors and other academics argued: "With less than a decade left in which to address the catastrophic threat of climate change, and with investors, companies, accountants, policymakers and academics expressing a shared sense of urgency, now is the time to act to reform corporate governance."[25] The Business Roundtable, a group of CEOs of very large companies, issued a joint statement in 2019 that claimed future corporate activities would reflect a "fundamental commitment to all our stakeholders."[26]

The 2020 World Economic Forum said something similar.[27] (I am not quoting it because, honestly, who cares what self-congratulatory nonsense gets announced at Davos each year?) It is estimated that more than $30 trillion of investment capital globally is driven by ESG data.[28] As we will see later, most "ESG investing" is just wishful thinking and marketing – but not all of it. For example, there is now apparently a market for proxy voting advice predicated on environmental and social outcomes rather than financial returns.[29]

If corporate governance channels lack the power to effect meaningful social welfare reforms, then all the time and energy reformers are putting into corporate governance is wasted. The resources of those striving for a better world would be better invested in other methods of accomplishing it. Sophisticated observers of corporate governance, like law professors Kahan and Rock, already argue that corporate governance reforms are primarily useful to politicians and other interested parties as a way to seem to do something without actually impacting the real interests of those who benefit from the current political and social order.[30]

Another problem is that if corporate governance reforms are not capable of producing the desired results, failure will breed cynicism. We have already seen this in relation to executive compensation. The advocates of modern corporate governance are committed to the dual propositions that most of what happens in corporations is the product of managerial self-interest, and that the various governance devices we have implemented should be sufficient to constrain managerial behavior. The fact that these practices consistently fail to hold down executive pay is, therefore, interpreted as powerful evidence of the greed and dishonesty of managers and the corruption and apathy of corporate directors. This has a strongly negative impact on our society. At this point in our history, do we need more cynicism about the trustworthiness of our institutions?

Reforms to corporate governance are not costless. They waste resources and opportunities. Just acquiring ESG data will cost investors more than $1 billion this year.[31] Corporations spend millions of dollars to provide disclosure of all types, with nonfinancial governance-related disclosure making up most of the paper being produced. There are more than seventy different rating agencies that produce more than 600 ESG ratings, and some companies complain they are asked to respond to as many as 250 different surveys to describe how they include ESG factors in disclosure and decision-making.[32] All this is fine if some social good is being secured, but if the governance activity is ineffective, the costs in time, resources, and attention represent a dead weight loss to society.

It is not the thesis of this book that corporate governance reforms have no effects. That would be stupid. Even though the Road Runner seems mostly unaffected by the Coyote's schemes, Acme Corp.'s balance sheet swells, the desert becomes littered with blackened craters, and Coyote's hopeful family goes hungry. In the case of our modern corporate governance regime, it has been accompanied by several concerning trends: companies are investing less in their businesses, they are less resilient to economic shocks, the flow of capital has been changed in ways that seem problematic, some groups like corporate executives and shareholders may have been benefited relative to others, and our public markets have become places to avoid if possible. In particular, the market activities of bargaining and experimentation have been replaced by one-size-fits-all solutions. This, in turn, has eliminated any scope for innovation or experimentation, as well as damaging the production of social capital that, it turns out (somewhat surprisingly), market activities generate better than any other institution we have tested.[33]

2 THE THESIS OF THIS BOOK

This book argues that nearly everything we have done to change corporate governance in the past forty years is a mistake. Specifically, it attempts to persuade readers that:

- Virtually none of our corporate governance best practices turn out to positively affect anything we care about, particularly firm performance.
- Corporate governance practices cannot be usefully generalized across heterogeneous companies.
- The "monitoring board," characterized by an emphasis on independent directors checking managerial self-interest, generally fails to accomplish its objects and ignores many of the best ways directors add value to a corporation.
- Governance interventions by shareholders (proposals, proxy fights, and takeovers) have nothing to do with reducing agency costs and often lead to corporate underperformance.
- The increase in executive pay was not caused by greedy managers encountering apathetic boards but by the good faith efforts of companies to adopt the pay practices commanded by the governance industry and institutional shareholders.
- For entirely rational reasons, shareholder voting is irrational and poorly suited to contribute positively to corporate governance outside of the limited role it was given traditionally in corporate law.
- Proxy advisors generate their voting advice in deeply flawed ways that impair the quality of corporate governance and, ironically, suggest serious agency problems in their own market.
- The quality of a firm's corporate governance is virtually impossible for outsiders to measure or rank, outside of its effects on financial performance.
- Agency cost theory is not a useful way of looking at corporate governance, and while it is true in a banal sense, it has consistently failed to generate successful hypotheses.
- The best evidence we have is that managers are, on average, faithful fiduciaries of their companies.

- The focus of modern corporate governance reforms on after-the-fact welfare outcomes has seriously damaged the core market activities that historically generated corporate governance. This has produced a variety of social and economic harms.
- Nearly all corporations in America are embedded in competitive product, labor, capital, and resource markets, which both gives them little slack for management misbehavior and denies them the capacity to engage in material voluntary ESG activities.
- Disclosure has no therapeutic effects on managers, meaning they don't learn anything from it, and it does not change their behavior. The disclosure does, however, teach *outsiders* things that cause them to behave in ways that often defeat the objectives of the disclosure. We saw this in relation to executive compensation disclosure reforms, but it is also true of environmental disclosure.
- Because institutional shareholders face competitive markets for investment advice, and because they have only crude legal and financial tools at their disposal, public market ESG investing is not capable of producing meaningful changes to corporate behavior.

Fundamentally, this book argues that the most important feature of business corporations is that they are in *business*. Corporate governance practices that don't directly address a firm's specific competitive challenges are either irrelevant or harmful. Many of us feel a natural attraction to corporate governance imperatives that don't necessitate a deep engagement with a firm's particularities. For one thing, it allows outsiders like us to have an opinion. If the market activities that make up a business are taken seriously, only insiders and industry experts who have carefully studied the firm in question are liable to have anything useful to contribute. The rest of us would just have to shut up – and we hate that. Like university students watching late night cartoons in a campus movie theater, we love yelling our opinions at the screen.

The other thing we hate is the hard work and compromise involved in legislating stuff. If corporate governance won't work to produce the economic and social changes we want, then the alternative is that we will have to pass laws and regulation – the things our parents and grandparents did. America often seems incapable of that now. It's definitely a problem, but it isn't corporate governance's problem.

3 THE APPROACH

There is only one way to proceed in a book like this and that is to reference what has grown into a vast empirical literature on corporate governance. This commitment to peer-reviewed statistical regressions may sound odd coming from an author who has so far relied heavily on a children's cartoon to provide force for his arguments, but without empirical evidence, the debates around corporate governance become interminable.

Conducting empirical research on corporate governance is difficult. There are many ways the results can be misleading, chief among them the problem of determining causality. There are many potential causes for the corporate behavior examined in this literature and isolating the actual causes of the behavior is challenging. Another problem is that it is often difficult to select the right peer companies to serve as controls when examining the impact of a governance intervention. A governance outcome might look quite different if you pick control companies that are the same size, rather than if you pick companies from the same industry, companies with the same levels of free cash flow, or companies experiencing similar growth trends.

For these reasons, as well as others, it is possible to find studies that come to contradictory conclusions on most governance topics. There are legal and finance academics who have therefore concluded that empirical research is unable to tell us much about the merits of various corporate governance initiatives. In some places, this is undoubtedly true. For example, the evidence on whether our managers are pressured by public markets into managing for the short term is mixed to the point that it is very hard to say conclusively whether it is true or not. However, for most areas, the general thrust of the empirical literature is quite clear by now. Where possible, the book will rely on meta-studies and literature reviews by experts that draw their conclusions from careful examination of dozens or even hundreds of empirical studies. As we will see, in most areas, these studies tend to produce fairly clear and consistent conclusions.

Where meta-studies are unavailable (usually because the body of research is comparatively new), we will look at the most recent research, evaluating the ways it differs from earlier studies with different findings. For example, when it comes to the long-term value impact of activist shareholders, one of the earliest papers found this was positive.[34] The methods employed in this paper were strongly criticized by multiple authors and subsequent research improving on its methods came to different results.[35] There seems no reason to refer to the empirical results in this area as "mixed" but, rather, we can confidently rely on the most recent research as reflecting the current best understanding. We will also confine our investigation to studies performed in the United States (and to a much lesser extent, Canada and the UK). The legal, cultural, and economic environments of other countries are too different to feel confident that treating them the same will tell us something useful. Fortunately, most of the research on these topics makes use of American data.

There are two other aspects of the method the book will be using that may provide us with confidence concerning this book's conclusions. The first is that each chapter looks at the research on many different issues that bear on its conclusions. For example, to demonstrate that the monitoring conception of the board is a mistake, we will not only look at the research on the effect of independent directors on firm performance; we will also look at their impact on executive compensation, CEO turnover, and the firm's use of free cash flow. We will also look more generally at the impact of independence on corporate outcomes by examining the effects of independent audit and compensation committees, board diversity (which is supposed to increase independence from the old boys' networks), interlocking directorships, and splitting the CEO and board chair position. As well, the book will look outside the research on boards to determine whether research in other areas supports the importance of director independence. When shareholders (presumably independent) get involved in firm governance, do they do anything different? What happens after a proxy fight when the shareholders appoint board members over the protests of management? Is the corporate governance of private equity-backed companies better than public companies?

What we will find looking at the totality of this evidence is that the independent monitoring conception of the board, one of the central obsessions of modern corporate governance, is wrong. It is possible that this book might miss crucial research in one or two areas, or that the body of research in an area may be consistently making mistakes in the way they measure the relevant variables. But the hope is that by surveying many different bodies of research, all bearing on the same question, these sorts of errors will not impact the book's overall conclusions.

The second support for this book's method is that its thesis is relatively modest. It is proposing that modern corporate governance's normative program has consistently failed to generate positive corporate outcomes. It does not depend on demonstrating that current corporate governance has generated *negative* corporate performance outcomes (although this can be argued, at least in certain areas). Even if the empirical evidence is "mixed," this should be fatal to our top-down corporate governance regime. To serve a useful function in guiding legal understandings, regulatory reform, and corporate behavior, modern corporate governance should produce clear, positive results. There are costs to the many regulatory and governance practices we have introduced over the past forty years; those costs are automatically too high if it is challenging to find the benefits.

4 THE NATURE OF THIS BOOK

At some point in the eighteenth century, the owners of English country houses began tearing up the boxed hedges and straight walks of the rational (but slightly anal-retentive) gardens they had inherited from their ancestors. These were replaced by artificial hills, newly constructed picturesque ruins, and artfully designed wild forests. Sometimes a deliberately unkempt person was hired to inhabit the ruins as a "hermit." This change was one of the signs that the age of reason was giving way to the Romantic era. Importantly, though, both garden regimes were artificial, required a lot of work, and are a bit amusing in their monomania.

Something less than a theory, but certainly more than incremental responses to practical problems, animated these garden renovations. What the Canadian philosopher Charles Taylor calls "the social imaginary" changed, and this change, at the level of the abstract, drove a massive alteration in the character of English gardens. A similar change to the social imaginary occurred in corporate governance several decades ago. It wasn't really a new theory, since the main candidate, agency cost theory, was explicitly introduced to the world as a partial equilibrium model; it assumed the only unsolved corporate problem was agent loyalty.[36] That means that, as a theory, it did not even claim to deal with the most important problems facing business corporations, like how to make money or raise capital. Yet, the idea that corporate governance was primarily about maximizing executive loyalty somehow came to dominate discussions of corporate governance.

Because "theory" is the wrong way to describe what happened to corporate governance, this book will often use the word "story." The corporate governance story was an easily grasped moralizing narrative that ignored as much as it illuminated. For example, it tended to ignore the actual business performance of companies, measured by their external cash flows, in favor of illuminating how the corporation managed and allocated its internal cash. Like any great story, it remade the world in which corporate governance happened. Managers as agents came to appear either disloyal or always teetering on the verge of disloyalty, shareholders as principals needed to get more deeply involved in firm management, and directors became guards rather than advisors and participants in firm governance. This was as radical a recasting of the landscape of firm governance as hiring a factory worker to pretend they are a medieval monk in a garden for ten hours a day. It is in its capacity as a story, rather than a formal model or theory, that the target of this book's criticisms operates in the background of corporate governance discussions. The world the story calls into existence influences reform efforts, sets research agendas, and provides explanations for market behaviors and outcomes.

It should be clear that this book is not a "how to" manual. It will describe a great deal of the current corporate governance landscape, but not in a way focused on helping readers navigate it. It also isn't suggesting landscaping features we might try, or some grand theory about how the "right" governance landscape should look. Rather, this book proposes what we might call an environmentally progressive regime for corporate governance: stop messing about with it. Let it return to a decentralized, ad hoc affair, which may eventually pleasantly surprise us by growing wild in ways we could never have anticipated. (It will also produce a few thorns, but we can root these out without taking a bulldozer to the rest of the garden.)

This book is not interested in whether corporations are best understood as a "nexus of contracts" or some other independently existing thing. (Emphasis invariably placed by proponents on the ontological significance of "thing.") It is not interested in the question of whether business corporations are "private" and thus deserving of liberalism's benign neglect, or whether they are, in an important way, "public" with a corresponding obligation to serve the general will. It is not interested in the ways in which modern corporate governance "federalizes" corporate law. It does not particularly care whether a corporate governance approach seems to reflect a conception of the corporation established by generations of Delaware judges. This book is only concerned with whether our current practices and theories work.

The book is thus unapologetically unsophisticated. It expects corporate governance practices to make companies more profitable, shareholders richer, and employees and consumers better off. It expects governance regulations and practices to accomplish their purposes of protecting vulnerable parties, without causing unnecessary harm to companies or other constituencies. In its pragmatic unsophistication, this is a book that rightly begins with a story involving a children's cartoon.

NOTES

1 See Kevin J. Murphy, "The Politics of Pay: A Legislative History of Executive Compensation" (2011) *Marshall School of Business Working Paper No. FBE 01.11*, online: SSRN, https://ssrn.com/abstract=1916358 [Murphy, "Politics of Pay"].
2 "U.S. Steel Guards Data on Salaries: Sends Details Confidentially to SEC Head with the Request that they be Kept Secret," *The New York Times*, June 2, 1935, online: www.nytimes.com/1935/06/02/archives/us-steel-guards-data-on-salaries-sends-details-confidentially-to.html.
3 Murphy, "Politics of Pay," above at note 1 at 8.
4 Dodd–Frank Wall Street Reform and Consumer Protection Act, Pub. L. No. 111-203, 124 Stat 1376 (2010) at 1899; Directors' Remuneration Report Regulations 2002 (UK), SI 2002/1986; Enterprise and Regulatory Reform Act 2013 (UK), s. 79.
5 Carola Frydman and Dirk Jenter, "CEO Compensation" (2010) 2:1 *Annual Review of Financial Economics* 75–102 at 78–80 (Table 1 and Figures 2a and 2b).
6 Lawrence Mishel and Natalie Sabadish, "CEO Pay in 2012 Was Extraordinarily High Relative to Typical Workers and Other High Earners" (2013) 367 *Economic Policy Institute* 1–11 at 4 [Mishel and Sabadish, "CEO Pay 2012"]. See also, Lucian Bebchuk and Yaniv Grinstein, "The Growth of Executive Pay" (2005) 21:2 *Oxford Review of Economic Policy* 283–303 at 286–287 [Bebchuk and Grinstein, "Growth of Pay"]; Harwell Wells, "U.S. Executive Compensation in Historical Perspective" in Randall S. Thomas and Jennifer G. Hill (eds.), *Research Handbook on Executive Pay* (Cheltenham: Edward Elgar, 2012), p. 49; Martin J. Conyon, "Executive Compensation and Board Governance in US Firms" (2014) 124:574 *The Economic Journal* F60–F89 at F60.
7 Marc T. Moore, "Corporate Governance, Pay Equity, and the Limitations of Agency Theory" (2015) 68:1 *Current Legal Problems* 431–464; Alex Edmans and Xavier Gabaix, "Executive Compensation: A Modern Primer" (2016) 54:4 *Journal of Economic Literature* 1232–1287 at 1235. See also, Kevin J. Murphy, "Executive Compensation" in Orley Ashenfelter and David Card (eds.), *Handbook of Labor Economics* (Amsterdam: Elsevier Science B.V., 1999), vol. 3B, p. 2485 [Murphy, "Executive Compensation"].
8 Mishel and Sabadish, "CEO Pay 2012," above at note 6 at 4; Steven N. Kaplan, "Are U.S. CEOs Overpaid?" (2008) 22:2 *Academy of Management Perspectives* 5–20. See also, Carola Frydman and Raven E. Saks, "Executive Compensation: A New View from a Long-Term Perspective, 1936–2005" (2010) 23:5 *The Review of Financial Studies* 2099–2138 at 2111, Figure 3.
9 Omri Ben-Shahar and Carl Schneider, *More than You Wanted to Know: The Failure of Mandated Disclosure* (Princeton: Princeton University Press, 2014); Troy Paredes, "Blinded by the Light: Information Overload and its Consequences for Securities Regulation" (2003) 81:2 *Washington University Law Quarterly* 417–486; Susanna Kim Ripken, "The Dangers and Drawbacks of the Disclosure Antidote: Towards a More Substantive Approach to Securities Regulation" (2006) 58:1 *Baylor Law Review* 139–204.

10 Murphy, "Politics of Pay," above at note 1 at 9.

11 *Ibid* at 14.

12 Bryce C. Tingle, "How Good Are Our 'Best Practices' When It Comes to Executive Compensation? A Review of Forty Years of Skyrocketing Pay, Regulation, and the Forces of Good Governance" (2017) 80:2 *Saskatchewan Law Review* 387–420 at 395.

13 Jeffrey N. Gordon, "Say on Pay: Cautionary Notes on the UK Experience and the Case for Shareholder Opt-In" (2009) 46:2 *Harvard Journal on Legislation* 323–367 at 343–344.

14 Leo E. Strine, Jr., "Who Bleeds When the Wolves Bite? A Flesh-and-Blood Perspective on Hedge Fund Activism and Our Strange Corporate Governance System" (2017) 126:6 *Yale Law Journal* 1870–1970 at 1872.

15 Linda Hughen, Malik Mahfuja and Eunsup Daniel Shim, "The Impact of Sarbanes-Oxley and Dodd–Frank on Executive Compensation" (2019) 20:3 *Journal of Applied Accounting Research* 243–266 at 263.

16 Bebchuk and Grinstein, "Growth of Pay," above at note 6 at 286–287.

17 While closed captioning, episode titles, and the memories of many would recall the sound of the Road Runner to be "beep, beep," Warner Bros. lists "beep, beep" and "meep, meep" as the Road Runner's sound. However, Paul Julian, the artist who voiced the Road Runner's classic sounds, preferred "hmeep, hmeep" or "mweep, mweep" for the sound effect. See *Beep, beep (sound)*, Wikipedia (last modified 28 April 2023), online: https://en.wikipedia.org/wiki/Beep,_beep_(sound). Preferred pronunciations aside, all can achieve the same effect when cheerfully voiced while speeding away.

18 James L. Bothwell, "Profitability, Risk, and the Separation of Ownership from Control" (1980) 28:3 *Journal of Industrial Economics* 303–311 at 304.

19 Herbert G. Hunt, "The Separation of Corporate Ownership and Control: Theory, Evidence and Implications" (1986) 5 *Journal of Accounting Literature* 85–124 at 96.

20 Helen Short, "Ownership, Control, Financial Structure and the Performance of Firms" (1994) 8:3 *Journal of Economic Surveys* 203–249 at 206.

21 Kenneth J. Rediker and Anju Seth, "Boards of Directors and Substitution Effects of Alternative Governance Mechanisms" (1995) 16:2 *Strategic Management Journal* 85–99 at 86.

22 Murphy, "Executive Compensation," above at note 7 at 2539.

23 Roberta Romano, "The Sarbanes-Oxley Act and the Making of Quack Corporate Governance" (2005) 114:7 *Yale Law Journal* 1521–1611; Stephen M. Bainbridge, "Dodd-Frank: Quack Federal Corporate Governance Round II" (2011) 95:5 *Minnesota Law Review* 1779–1821.

24 Elizabeth Warren, *Accountable Capitalism Act*, Senator Elizabeth Warren, online (pdf): www.warren.senate.gov/imo/media/doc/Accountable%20Capitalism%20Act%20One-Pager.pdf.

25 Andrew Johnston et al., "Corporate Governance for Sustainability Statement" (2019), online: SSRN, https://ssrn.com/abstract=3502101.

26 *Business Roundtable Redefines the Purpose of a Corporation to Promote "An Economy That Serves All Americans*," Business Roundtable (August 19, 2019), online: www.businessroundtable.org/business-roundtable-redefines-the-purpose-of-a-corporation-to-promote-an-economy-that-serves-all-americans. See also, Ronald J. Gilson and Curtis J. Milhaupt, "Shifting Influences on Corporate Governance: Capital Market Completeness and Policy Channeling" (2022) 12:1 *Harvard Business Law Review* 1–54 at 6.

27 Klaus Schwab, *The Davos Manifesto: The Universal Purpose of a Company in the Fourth Industrial Revolution*, World Economic Forum (December 2, 2019), online: www.weforum.org/agenda/2019/12/davos-manifesto-2020-the-universal-purpose-of-a-company-in-the-fourth-industrial-revolution/

28 Alexander Joshua Michael Fish, D. H. Kim and Shankar Venkatraman, "The ESG
    Sacrifice" (2019), online: *SSRN*, https://ssrn.com/abstract=3488475 at 5.
29 See, for example, *Policy Supports Investors Choosing to Integrate Climate Performance
    & Disclosure into their Proxy Voting*, Institutional Shareholder Services Inc. (March 9,
    2020), online: www.issgovernance.com/iss-launches-climate-voting-policy/; *2020 Proxy
    Paper Guidelines: An Overview of the Glass Lewis Approach to Proxy Advice Canada*,
    Glass Lewis (2020), online (pdf): www.glasslewis.com/wp-content/uploads/2016/11/
    Guidelines_Canada.pdf.
30 Marcel Kahan and Edward Rock, "Symbolic Corporate Governance Politics" (2014) 94:6
    Boston University Law Review 1997–2044 at 2035.
31 Emily Chasan, "Spending on ESG Data Seen Rising to $1 Billion Amid Asset Growth,"
    Bloomberg, March 9, 2020, online: www.bloomberg.com/news/articles/2020-03-09/
    spending-on-esg-data-seen-rising-to-1-billion-amid-asset-growth.
32 *Corporate Sustainability Reporting: Past, Present, Future*, US Chamber of Commerce
    Foundation (November 2018), online (pdf): www.uschamberfoundation.org/sites/
    default/files/Corporate%20Sustainability%20Reporting%20Past%20Present%20Future
    .pdf at 29; Feifei Li and Ari Polychronopoulos, "What a Difference an ESG Ratings
    Provider Makes!" (2020), online (pdf): *Research Affiliates*, www.researchaffiliates.com/
    documents/770-what-a-difference-an-esg-ratings-provider-makes.pdf; Alexander Joshua
    Michael Fish, D. H. Kim and Shankar Venkatraman, "The ESG Sacrifice" (2019), online:
    SSRN, https://ssrn.com/abstract=3488475; Bradford Cornell and Aswath Damodaran,
    "Valuing ESG: Doing Good or Sounding Good" (2020), online: *SSRN*, https://ssrn.com/
    abstract=3557432.
33 See discussions in Bryce C. Tingle, "Returning Markets to the Center of Corporate
    Law" (2023) 48:4 *Journal of Corporation Law* 663–718; Nathan B. Oman, *The Dignity
    of Commerce: Markets and the Moral Foundations of Contract Law* (Chicago: The
    University of Chicago Press, 2017).
34 Lucian A. Bebchuk, Alon Brav and Wei Jiang, "The Long-Term Effects of Hedge Fund
    Activism" (2015) 115:5 *Columbia Law Review* 1085–1156.
35 See discussion in Bryce C. Tingle, "The Agency Cost Case for Regulating Proxy Advisory
    Firms" (2016) 49:2 *UBC Law Review* 725–787 at notes 114–118.
36 See William W. Bratton and Simone M. Sepe, "Corporate Law and the Myth of Efficient
    Market Control" (2020) 105:3 *Cornell Law Review* 675–740; Kenneth Lehn, "Corporate
    Governance and Corporate Agility" (2021) 66 *Journal of Corporate Finance* 101929.

1

Our Corporate Governance Experiment

What exactly is the governance experiment we have been pursuing over the past forty years? There have, of course, been a lot of little experiments, about whether this or that corporate governance practice or institution is useful for advancing some aim. For example, we have asked whether independent directors fire underperforming CEOs faster, or whether equity incentives improve executives' performance. These little experiments, largely ignored outside of academic journals, have added up to bigger experiments addressing the novel assumptions made by modern corporate governance about the untrustworthiness of corporate officers, the limited capacities of directors, and the superhuman competencies of institutional shareholders. These experiments are important, forming a great deal of the discussion in the following chapters, but they are not the core hypothesis that we have been testing over the past four decades.

This chapter is instead about how we came to create a governance regime resting on two beliefs so fundamental that they generally go unnoticed. The first of these beliefs is that corporate governance practices can be evaluated as "good" or "bad" without regard to their impact on a specific company's operational outcomes. The second of these beliefs is that governance coming from outside the firm, in a top-down fashion from regulators or other third parties, is generally superior to the governance arrangements that grow organically out of the interactions of various corporate constituencies. So, for example, many of the initial proponents of the modern governance regime claimed that the historical practice of corporate boards partially comprised of directors who were also employees of the company (called "inside" or "non-independent" directors), was a sign the old corporate governance system was failing. The CEO had too much power, and he liked directors who, as his subordinates, were afraid to cross him. As a result, these early governance scholars argued, companies are better off with regulators and other third parties applying pressure from outside the organization to reduce the numbers of inside directors until they are mostly eliminated.

What both beliefs have in common is a lack of regard for markets: the "product" markets that provide a referendum on corporate activities, including corporate governance, and the "governance" market made up of the various constituencies – officers, directors, investors, employees, customers, suppliers, business partners, lenders – that must agree on terms before assembling to form the productive coalition that is required for a corporation to do its work.

The dismissal of markets, in turn, was made possible in the 1970s by the introduction to corporate law of a theory about economic efficiency, and then a theory about agency costs. These theories provided the deep assumptions that gave rise to modern corporate governance's propensity to cheerfully ignore markets.

A good analogy for the various layers of belief behind modern corporate governance is provided by Doctor Frankenstein's well-known and important experiments in the early nineteenth century. The outcome of running electricity through a dead arm is interesting, but more important for what it starts to tell us about the larger question of whether life and human consciousness is merely a function of organic matter and electrical impulse. Even this, though, is not the core question that interested Mary Shelley and, to a lesser degree, Mel Brooks in *Young Frankenstein*. They were investigating the merits of the often-invisible belief that knowledge and morality are separate things. (For those unfamiliar with the story of Frankenstein, Martin Heidegger explores the same question in *Die Frage nach der Technik*, but not, it must be said, with the incisiveness of Mel Brooks.)

1.1 THE TRAGIC BIRTH OF MODERN CORPORATE GOVERNANCE

It is a cliché in corporate law scholarship to begin every discussion of corporate governance by referencing the work of Professors Adolf Berle and Merrick Dodd. This is usually the most boring part of a corporate law paper (and that is saying something). Fortunately, the debate between Berle and Dodd in the 1930s is only relevant for our purposes in the way it illustrates how far they were from our modern understanding of corporate governance.

Berle and Dodd were among the first scholars to consider the implications of the modern public corporation. Unlike most commercial enterprises that preceded it, the American public corporation of the early twentieth century was increasingly run by professional managers with only loose connections to its' largest shareholders. To Berle and Dodd, the rise of the autonomous corporate manager was as noteworthy as the transition of Doctor Frankenstein's monster from a collection of inanimate objects under the good doctor's control, to a monster very much under its own control. Like the townspeople with their pitchforks and torches, Berle and Dodd's principal concern was not the welfare of the monster, but its possible impact on the neighbors. They were more interested in the political and social implications of the separation of ownership and control, than its impact on business performance. For this reason, their analysis was pitched at such a high level of generality that they failed to distinguish between the board of directors and the CEO: one of the central power dynamics in modern understandings of the widely held corporation.[1]

In terms of outcomes, their analysis eventually led them to espouse a manageri-
alist philosophy, which understood a corporate executive as a kind of benevolent
technocrat mediating the interests of the various constituencies that make up the
modern firm.[2] In other words, their analysis led them directly away from the preoccupation with unfaithful agents found in modern corporate governance.

The character of Berle and Dodd's influence can be seen in the fact that while
those gentlemen were constantly cited, very little attention was paid to what we
call "corporate governance" in the following decades. The great economist, Ronald
Coase, who was the first to examine the economic interior of corporations in a
now famous paper published in 1937, noted at the end of his career that the paper
"had little or no influence for thirty or forty years after it was published."[3] The first
extended discussion of corporate governance was published in 1962, but the term
"corporate governance" wasn't even invented until the 1970s.[4] Until 1985, the phrase
"corporate governance" was mentioned only once in *The Times* of London and it
first appeared in *The Economist* in 1990.[5]

This isn't a case of the topic we call "corporate governance" being avidly debated
under a different name (like Mel Brooks' Doctor Frankenstein insisting his name be
pronounced "Fronckensteen"). Rather, until the 1970s, most scholars and market actors
did not share our understanding of the constellation of relationships and concerns that
make up the field of corporate governance. The poetically named Bayless Manning
famously described corporate law in the 1960s as bereft of any theoretical content, with
"nothing left but our great empty corporation statutes – towering skyscrapers of rusted
girders, internally welded together and containing nothing but wind."[6]

Law professors and finance scholars generally remained confident that managers
were faithful stewards of corporate resources and acted to maximize corporate cash
flows.[7] Eugene Fama and Merton Miller (both Nobel Prize-winning economists)
referred to this belief executives maximized the current market value of firms as "the
market value rule" and observed in 1972, that "despite many years of controversy,
[it has not] yet been demonstrated that the market value rule leads to predictions
that are so widely at variance with observed management behavior as to rule it out,
even as a first approximation."[8]

To modern market actors, this seems astonishing. When we look at corporations
now, pretty much all we see is the specter of self-interest. We evaluate every aspect
of corporate law, regulation, and practice in light of how it will incentivize corporate
managers to produce the outcomes we favor. An executive or director does not present themselves to our view without the ghostly overlay of their potential deviance
from faithfully advancing the interests of some corporate constituency. This change,
creating the field we now call "corporate governance," occurred over a surprisingly
short time. The credit (or, if I am being honest, the blame) for this change is owed
to two distinct intellectual moves.

The first of the intellectual changes arose from the law and economics movement
in the late 1960s and early 1970s. The application of economics to legal concerns

encouraged legal actors to evaluate the merits of corporate legal structures by their contributions to efficiency. This reflected a shift from corporate law's traditional concern with enforcing previously struck deals, to facilitating some preferred result – usually wealth maximization. This is to say that aim of corporate law changed from facilitating *ex ante* bargaining to advancing *ex post* outcomes. We will discuss the specific impact this had on corporate law in Chapter 11.

A logical outgrowth of the law and economics approach was the second of these intellectual changes: the adoption of agency cost theory when it arose in its modern form in the second half of the 1970s. While we will discuss agency cost theory in greater detail in Chapter 10, it is important to understand the way it came to define the field of corporate governance.

1.2 AGENCY COST THEORY

Agency cost theory is usually dated to Michael Jensen's and William Meckling's 1976 paper, *Theory of the Firm: Managerial Behavior, Agency Costs and Ownership Structure*.[9] Jensen and Meckling began their project by noting the same phenomenon observed by Bayless Manning: there was no unifying or explanatory theory about corporations as objects in their own right. They called the state of understanding about what occurred inside business corporations as constituting an "empty box"[10] and went on to note:

> While the literature of economics is replete with references to the "theory of the firm," the material generally subsumed under that heading is not a theory of the firm but actually a theory of markets in which firms are important actors. The firm is a "black box" operated so as to meet the relevant marginal conditions.... Except for a few recent and tentative steps, however, we have no theory which explains how the conflicting objectives of the individual participants are brought about into equilibrium so as to yield this result.[11]

Their solution was to examine the incentives of the various constituencies inside corporations, paying attention to the internal allocations of corporate cash flows.[12] While there were others writing in a similar vein in the 1970s, Jensen and Meckling are almost universally credited with inaugurating agency theory.[13]

Rejecting the view that the interests of managers and the firm were identical, agency theory, in Jensen and Meckling's telling, characterized shareholders as principals employing executives as agents to manage the shareholders' property: the corporation. "[T]he relationship between the stockholders and manager of a corporation fit the definition of a pure agency relationship."[14] Because managers' interests can reliably be expected to diverge from those of the shareholders, certain costs are incurred to minimize the firm resources diverted away from the shareholders. These "agency costs" were defined by Jensen and Meckling as the sum of: (1) monitoring expenses by the principal (this includes the cost of a board of directors as well as the costs incurred by shareholders in informing themselves about corporate performance and voting wisely); (2) the expense of "establishing appropriate incentives for the agents" (which are a type of monitoring expense); (3) the bonding expenditures incurred by the agent to guarantee she will not take actions that harm the shareholders, or to ensure they will be compensated if she does take those actions; and (4) the "residual loss," which is the unavoidable reduction of welfare experienced by the shareholders as a result of agents' decisions diverging from those that would maximize shareholder welfare.[15]

Agency cost theory both created the field of corporate governance and, in the same intellectual move, its implied objective: reducing agency costs as much as possible to benefit the shareholders. As Professor Edward Rock notes, "[t]heoretical and empirical finance scholarship, and the standard finance textbooks, all conceptualize the corporation as run for the benefit of the shareholders."[16] The new field also supplied the lack that had been expressed by Bayless Manning, the absence of any unifying theory for corporate law.

So long as the corporation was a "black box" with little attention paid to the incentives of internal actors and the distribution of internal cash flows, corporate law scholarship was left only with evaluating the externally visible economic performance of firms. This is what had produced Bayless Manning's empty girders containing only wind. Business corporations are extremely heterogeneous entities. They have different ownership structures, very different types of boards and executive teams, they compete in radically different product markets, and deploy an extensive variety of constantly changing business strategies. They face different types of competitors, suppliers, and customers, dissimilar regulatory regimes, and frequent changes to the macroeconomic environment that impact them differently. Even the common constituencies that form around firms are radically different. There is a vast difference, for example, between the relationship of a tech company with a small, highly paid, highly educated, mostly autonomous labor force, and a manufacturer with a vast, unionized workplace. The two sorts of firms may even want different things from their employees: creativity and independence versus discipline.

Agency cost theory allowed meaningful generalizations to be made about these companies. Notwithstanding their heterogeneity, all firms have the same internal structure, namely, boards, executives, and shareholders, and all firms could now have the same object: keeping agency costs to a minimum. This commonality, revealed by agency cost theory, permitted generalizations to be made about business corporations; it provided a field in which governance best practices might be discerned and academics and regulators were soon debating the superiority of these structures and practices.[17] Corporate governance could change from a focus on how best a company could manage its resources to succeed in various product markets (about which the average outsider could have no useful opinion) to how closely the company adhered to those best practices identified as most effective at minimizing agency costs.

The radical nature of this intellectual transition cannot be overstated. The switch from a focus on the external performance of the firm to its internal relations led to a fundamental change in how academics, regulators, and corporate critics evaluated behavior. In Melvin Eisenberg's influential book, *The Structure of the Corporation*, published in the same year as Jensen and Meckling's *Theory of the Firm*, he proposed that the board's essential function was to monitor senior executives.[18] All other functions of the board – advising the CEO, generating strategy, making introductions, authorizing major corporate decisions – were of minor importance or (he claimed) would seldom produce real value.

Even the kind of people who could enter into discussions of corporate governance changed from corporate executives or business professors with insight into the economic realities of specific firms, to academics and critics who knew nothing about business, but felt the agency cost story provided them with a clear guide by which to make judgments and propose regulatory changes.

Organizations such as proxy advisors, newspapers, think tanks, and magazines got into the business of judging and ranking firms' governance without regard for those companies' relative product market performance. These outside organizations were usually completely ignorant of much that a businessperson would regard as important about the corporation's operations, resources, competitive landscape, personalities, and strategic alternatives. But in what can only be described as a triumph of the human spirit, their vast ignorance about business didn't deter them from eventually forming what is now often referred to as the "governance industry" or even (by those especially disapproving), the "corporate governance machine."[19]

We should take a moment to contemplate the weirdness of this turn of events. The most vocal parties about what constitutes "good governance" are generally the ones most ignorant of the details of what is going on in various corporations and their markets. Corporate managers and directors who do, presumably, know something about the problems they are facing in their business, are usually the ones on the receiving end of lectures about new practices for firm governance. Those concerned about the outsized power of America's executives should consider the meekness with which they have routinely been taken to the woodshed for discipline by third parties who are often entirely unfamiliar with what those executives do all day.

An illustration of the strange nature of modern notions of corporate governance is provided by a high-profile board conflict that recently broke out in the usually somnolent environment of Canada's boardrooms. While Canada's media reveled in the drama and compared it to various Hollywood productions featuring titans of industry throwing glasses of water into each other's faces, the fight was a bit of a let-down. One of the problems was that many of the main characters seemed to resemble mid-level bureaucrats in the old Soviet Union – the kind that look like they mainly subsist on a diet of potatoes. As well, between the demands of Covid and the Canadian winter you had to discern people's emotional state from the appearance of the top third of their heads as they walked past reporters into buildings. The rest of their bodies were covered by bulky winter outerwear and firmly positioned masks. (Canadians may occasionally fight in boardrooms, but they follow public health guidance without fuss.)

The farcical nature of the dispute announced itself right at the beginning with a "butt dial" to the CEO of Rogers Communications, a large Canadian telecommunications company, during which he learned that the Chair of his board of directors was conspiring with the CFO (the butt-dialer) to replace him. The CEO reacted like you would expect: He lobbied for the support of the directors, and there was a lot of confusion and excommunications until a court resolved the matter by permitting the Chair to replace the CEO's board supporters with the equivalent of Doctor Frankenstein's submissive assistant, Igor. The Board Chair was able to do this because he controlled a family trust that held superior voting shares, and Canadian corporate legislation allows shareholders to requisition a meeting at any time and elect new directors. Purged of any hint of independence, the new board of directors followed the Chair's instructions, and the situation was resolved – with extreme prejudice to the old CEO.

The entire affair resulted in endless reams of commentary from governance experts throughout the English-speaking world. Some expressed concern for the state of "shareholder democracy" in Canadian businesses.[20] Dual-class voting shares were singled out as loathsome for the way they divorced voting power from economic interest. (It will be interesting if "one dollar, one vote" ever resonates with the general public.) Other governance authorities noted that boards should be "independent" (apparently meaning "independent of shareholders" as well as the more commonly understood "independent of the CEO" – because the new board was definitely independent in that sense). Some of the tribunes of good governance emphasized that the fundamental feature of good governance is "accountability," presumably meaning it is a problem that someone with voting control over a company is unaccountable. (Not sure what the alternative is here.)

What all of these entirely predictable reactions did not touch upon was whether the CEO ought to have been fired. Was this a good decision? Was the Board Chair right? This would strike many of the governance experts who weighed in on the drama as a fundamentally unfair question. They don't know the CEO, the CFO, the displaced directors, the new directors, or the Chair. Which of those people have the best business judgment? The governance experts don't know about Rogers' long-term strategy, or its corporate needs. To be honest, there is no evidence the experts knew anything about the discharged CEO's performance beyond the information gleaned from a stock chart. Interestingly, the stock price of the company dipped during the period of chaotic conflict, but has since recovered, suggesting the oppressed millionaires who run Canada's investing institutions are fine with the change. It goes without saying that this subsequent market judgment has proven to be irrelevant to the governance industry's evaluations of a case that so obviously violated the canons of "good governance."[21]

The gulf between how a regular person understands "good" corporate governance and the way specialists understand it is vital to the continuing success of the modern governance project. The average person understands good corporate governance to be connected with successful operational outcomes. In particular, businesspeople believe a well-governed company is one that maximizes its external cash flows and profits, usually by competing successfully in its markets. However, the meaning of "good corporate governance" for specialists now refers primarily to the adoption of certain legal structures and practices that, themselves, are not specifically connected to outcomes in the market for the corporation's products or services. These legal structures and practices are referred to as "best practices," and they constitute the core of modern corporate governance. It is generally assumed that the two definitions of "good governance" have something to do with each other, but as we shall see in Chapters 3 and 4, they do not.

1.3 THE CURRENT MOMENT IN CORPORATE GOVERNANCE

Very little blame for the current state of corporate governance should be laid at the door of Jensen and Meckling's original paper. In addition to the fact that there were a number of scholars writing in the same vein around the same time, the modern corporate governance movement systemically misunderstood or ignored aspects of their original paper. (The ways in which this was done will be discussed in Chapter 10.) Nevertheless, the general trends in how we have decided to regulate the firms at the commanding heights of our economy are easily visible.

Beginning in the late 1970s, we increasingly came to see corporate law, and even securities regulation, as the method by which agents (corporate managers) were disciplined, monitored, and directed to faithfully act in the best interests of their principals (the shareholders). In the course of this project, regulators such as Congress, the SEC, and the stock exchanges, as well as the private parties that gradually formed the governance industry, began revising the board structures, executive compensation, and historical roles and powers of shareholders, with the aim of controlling executive behavior. These developments will be discussed in detail throughout the rest of the book, but it is worth noting how straightforwardly they follow from the initial simple insight of agency cost theory.

Until the 2008 financial crisis, the focus of reformers was entirely on maximizing outcomes for shareholders. As Jensen and Meckling proposed, investors seemed to be the company's "principals," whose property had been entrusted to managerial agents. There was an energetic and inconclusive debate behind the scenes among academics concerning whether shareholders actually fit the role of "principal" either in economic reality or as a matter of law, but this debate occurred mostly out of sight of the actors influencing governance practices in America's public companies.

Following the 2008 financial crisis, however, something shifted in the general public's perception of corporations, and this previously ignored academic debate broke out into the real world. Increasing numbers of shareholders, regulators, and members of the governance industry began to argue that shareholders were not the only "principals" of corporations, other parties also deserved that status: employees, society, and even the environment. All these groups contribute something to the productive coalition, and all of them deserve to have their interests considered in firm decision-making.

In Chapters 12 and 13, we will discuss this turn to "stakeholder" or "constituency" conceptions of firm governance, but it is worth noting that this turn has so far occurred entirely within the prevailing intellectual field created by agency cost theory. The definition of "principal" may have changed, but the central problem is still conceptualized as "how do we get managerial agents to do their job of advancing the interests of their principals?" The overall approach to corporate governance has also largely stayed the same. Since the principals (however they are defined) are the same for virtually every company, and the agents are the same for every company, there must exist "best practices" that will produce better outcomes for the principals in at least most companies, allowing us to cheerfully ignore any details relating to those companies, their activities, the relevant personalities, and the state of their markets.

The new candidates for governance best practices are only slightly different from the old best practices. Shareholders continue to receive a great deal of attention as monitors and correctors of managerial malfeasance, only now the ideal shareholder is one with an explicit environmental and social focus. Boards play a key part in keeping the agents in line, only now the independent director seems less important than, say, directors appointed by the employees, or possessing expertise on environmental issues. The financial incentives of managers continue to seem quite important, but they should be less about maximizing total shareholder return, paying off instead on the achievement of other objectives, such as reducing pollution.

The details are changing, but the overall theory and practice remain identical. That is why, even for those who regard the four decades of corporate governance reforms that were designed to advance shareholder interests as a mistake, it makes sense to examine the impact of these reforms. If the wealth-maximizing governance approach shares the same theoretical approach and tools as the newer more socially oriented corporate governance, the failures of the former project may tell us something about our hopes for the latter. (As well, of course, shareholders remain important principals of corporations whatever other parties are added to the list.)

The scale and intrusiveness of modern corporate governance can come as a surprise to those unfamiliar with the field. While the highest-profile best practices are imposed by regulators, stock exchanges, and legislation, many more practices are essentially imposed by the governance industry. The scope and granularity of these interventions can be seen by examining ISS QuickScore, published by the largest proxy advisor in the United States. QuickScore rates the "quality" of a corporation's governance arrangements by determining how closely they reflect no fewer than ninety-two different best practices.[22] Similarly, the voting guidelines and FAQs published by ISS, that are regularly consulted by publicly listed issuers to understand how they should govern their companies, now run to 212 pages. There are many other lists of best practices published by other proxy advisory firms, institutional shareholders, think tanks, media outlets, and even securities regulators that must also be consulted. These lists are broadly similar to one another, but not so similar that corporate counsel feels comfortable simply ignoring them. Almost none of the practices detailed in these many lengthy documents existed back in 1976. Agency cost theory made them, and thus modern corporate governance, possible.

There is a tendency on the part of academics to overestimate the power of ideas – even dumb ideas like the ones we are discussing. (For example, as we will see in Chapter 11, there are trendy theories about corporate social responsibility and sustainable investing in today's academia that will, *of necessity*, only be honored in the real world in the ways hypocrisy honors virtue.) It would be hard, however, in the case of agency cost theory, to overestimate the idea's impact.

This influence can be clearly seen in a multitude of major changes in the governance arrangements of America's public companies. In the 1950s, only 20 percent or so of US board members were independent.[23] By 2005, it was 70 percent, and by 2021, it was 86 percent.[24] For more than 60 percent of boards today, the only non-independent director is the CEO.[25] Prior to the 1990s, executive pay largely consisted of salary plus an annual bonus. Equity incentives, designed to align the interests of managers and shareholders, quickly took off in the 1990s, and by 2010, 62 percent of the compensation received by large-company CEOs came from equity incentives alone.[26] Two decades ago, 75 percent of American public companies combined the roles of CEO and board chair, now only 41 percent do so, and those that have resisted this practice have nearly all created the position of "independent lead director" that functions much like a board chair.[27]

Even much lower-profile governance structures are replicated throughout all American public companies. In the United States, 98 percent of the S&P 500 firms had annual board performance evaluations[28]; 90 percent of boards are not staggered[29]; 89 percent have some form of majority voting[30]; 72 percent have deferred compensation plans; 91 percent don't provide meeting fees; 89 percent of boards now reject the once ubiquitous stock options[31]; 94 percent have director share ownership requirements; and 98.4 percent of the Russell 1000 don't use poison pills.[32] Large public companies all tend to have the same board committees (including committees that are not made mandatory by regulation), the same policies on things like director service on other boards, and they appear to generally hire people with the same backgrounds.[33] This monoculture is even more prevalent in other English-speaking countries.[34] The famous legal advisor, Martin Lipton, is not wrong when he observed, "[t]he governance and takeover defense profiles of U.S. public companies have been transformed by the widespread adoption of virtually all of the 'best practices.'"[35]

1.4 PUBLIC AND PRIVATE MARKET GOVERNANCE

The monoculture found in public companies, which usually face the full force of the modern corporate governance regime, can be contrasted with the livelier governance arrangements of private corporations. For startup companies in places like Silicon Valley, the question of corporate governance is almost never resolved, and their governance arrangements are almost never "finished." As founders, investors, employees, new executives, and business partners acquire shares, enter into agreements, and replace one another, board composition changes, different securities with terms impacting governance are issued, and nuanced contractual provisions related to firm control are adopted, amended, and replaced.

When teaching law students about entrepreneurial ventures, one of the hardest things to make them understand is the way that dozens of contractual and legal structures can influence the governance of companies. For example, the requirement for unanimity in a shareholder or investor rights agreement gives enormous power to any one of the parties. This power to withhold approval of, say, a financing or change of business can be leveraged to get concessions in entirely unrelated areas, like firing the CFO or increasing the stock option pool. The use of preferred shares by sophisticated investors incentivizes managers to take greater risks or their own common shares might not be worth anything. Founders may possess informal authority that exceeds what one might expect from reading the legal documents; a desirable CEO may demand scope of action that greatly exceeds the power provided by her equity position. High-powered equity incentives like "cliff" stock vesting provisions can lead to perverse strategic behavior by executives or founders desperate to avoid being terminated, such as refusing to transmit crucial information, hiring less capable people, or focusing their energy on morale-damaging firm politics.

It is also easier to see the way that the market for corporate governance in private companies embraces parties outside of the usual assumed triumvirate of "executives, directors, and shareholders." Large customers often exert considerable formal and informal influence over firm governance in order to ensure the company in question remains viable and continues to meet the customers' needs. Key suppliers often get dragged into corporate governance disputes, as do business partners and other contractual counterparties. Media outlets, the general public, consumers, and employees also all exert visible influence on the governance of private companies.

As a result of this governance "liveliness," there is enormous heterogeneity in the governance arrangements and practices among private growth companies. In many startup companies, the managers are firmly under the control of the venture capital investors. These venture capitalists deploy a range of legal devices to maintain much higher levels of control over managers than will ever exist in the public markets. However, as we have seen with some notably absurd failures like WeWork and Theranos, there are also companies with investors and boards that contribute to the corporation in ways that resemble the contributions of the human appendix.

There is also a great deal of experimentation in the private market. To take just one example, beginning early in this century, angel investments in Silicon Valley and elsewhere began to be made using convertible notes. Usually, the notes were structured to convert into equity at a discount to the price set by a subsequent arms-length investor. Because these notes could only have a one-year term (to accommodate a California law regulating lenders), angel investors often came to possess enormous power over companies that were unable, in the time available before maturity, to secure the financing that would convert the note. In 2013, Y Combinator introduced the Simple Agreement for Future Equity ("SAFE") to address these governance deficiencies.[36] By stripping out the "debt" elements and thus removing the pressures imposed by the threat of default at the end of the one-year term, the SAFE removed the governance effects of the convertible note structure while leaving its economic profile largely intact. SAFEs are now a common tool used around the country for early-stage angel investments.

The bargaining, heterogeneity, and innovation visible in the private market are precisely what have disappeared in the governance arrangements of public companies. The rest of this book will look at the interrelated questions: have we lost anything important? Have we gained anything valuable?

1.5 A PRELIMINARY ANSWER

Outside of the echo chamber of the corporate governance industry, it is hard to sustain the view that the last four decades of corporate governance reforms have improved the way companies are run. In subsequent chapters, we will look at peer-reviewed studies using suitable controls and complex regressions. But the current corporate governance regime produces a great deal of exasperation in lawyers and businesspeople who have never opened the pages of an academic finance journal.

For example, polls of directors and officers in the United States and Europe regularly find considerable skepticism about the value of many corporate governance practices.[37] Some of these poll results are extremely amusing, like the large majority of directors that don't have a high regard for dialogue with shareholders, or the majority that are skeptical about the value of risk committees. (Neither of these views would ever make it into an annual report.) Other opinions of corporate directors make a great deal more sense, such as the 93 percent of directors that feel proxy advisors have too much power, or the 96 percent that think activist investors are too focused on the short term. For their part, notwithstanding that equity incentives have made them rich beyond their predecessors' dreams, senior executives do not believe modern pay practices are effective in influencing their day-to-day decisions.[38] Even the legal profession, which has risen in importance in corporate boardrooms because of modern corporate governance, has its doubts about the regime.[39] (Surely the fact that our governance system has been an unparalleled gift to the legal profession is, itself, a reason to question its merits. Since when has "let's add more lawyers" been a reliable path to efficiency gains?)

For their part, the governance industry and securities regulators are extremely disappointed that compliance with governance best practices so often amounts to little more than a box-checking exercise.[40] But what else could it be since, as we have seen, corporate governance is expressly about something other than the corporation's operational success in its markets? Anything not closely connected to the corporation's survival and success is not going to turn into the preoccupation of a conscientious director or officer. A director focused firmly on "good corporate governance" as defined by the governance industry is a director who has made a category mistake about their job. It is possible that the directors wearily going through the formalities of adopting governance best practices are mistaken, and these practices are tightly linked to positive operational outcomes, but they clearly don't believe this. Maybe the directors and officers are wrong, but they do know a lot more about their companies than we do. In fact, as we shall see in Chapters 5 and 12, even institutional fund managers purchase and vote their shares as if many of the governance structures championed by their governance departments and proxy advisors are unimportant.

Even if we comfortably ignore the officers and directors (whose views could be the result of financial self-interest), we still have some broadly visible reasons to doubt the effectiveness of modern corporate governance practices. The *Financial Times* announced at the end of the twentieth century that "the 1990s have been the decade of corporate governance."[41] Since then, we have had two recessions that exposed considerable problems with corporate governance in America. Academics debate whether either the "dot-com" recession of the early aughts or the "great recession" that started in 2008 were "caused" by poor corporate governance.[42] No one, however, is arguing about the pretty serious governance problems that were revealed by both recessions. Some of the worst governance failures in American history occurred at ostensibly well-governed companies like Enron, Health South, WorldCom, Tyco, and a variety of financial firms that had engaged in absurdly risky or dishonest behavior.

Between those two recessions, American businesses engaged in the widespread and fraudulent practice of option backdating, while executive compensation, possibly the best litmus test of agency cost controls, exploded. Trust in large corporations has never been lower since Gallup started asking Americans the question in 1973.[43] According to Edelman, 70 percent of respondents in the developed world now "do not perceive the CEO to be a believable source of information about a company."[44] These facts, visible to any moderately well-informed observer, are why many find it reasonable to ask: where are the gains from our ostensible improvements in corporate governance?

If we look beyond frauds, scandals, and declines in reputation, it is not like supporters of the modern governance regime can point to obvious economic successes.

American productivity growth has sagged throughout the period of "good governance," aside from a few years in the mid-1990s.[45] This is probably not the fault of our corporate governance regime (though, as we shall see, R&D expenditures tend to increase when some "best practices" are avoided, while other "best practices" appear to be associated with long-term declines in corporate performance and investment). It is enough, however, to note that our current corporate governance regime has coincided with a secular slowdown in corporate growth.

Another major trend over the past four decades has been a decline in the attractiveness of our public markets, which is where our current governance regime lives. America's stock exchanges are currently less than half the size they were in the 1990s.[46] Between 1980 and 2000, an average of 310 operating companies a year went public in the United States; since then, the annual average has been less than 100.[47] The drop has been particularly severe among smaller new entrants to the stock market. At the same time, the number of US private companies backed by private equity has increased more than sixfold.[48] There are many possible explanations for the decline in public markets, but unlike our stagnating economic growth, a much stronger case can be made that our corporate governance regime bears a certain amount of the responsibility. Chapter 10 will evaluate the merits of this argument.

It is easy to see then why the average businessperson would regard much of what goes on in corporate governance as inessential or potentially problematic. You don't have to be a scientist to know that when villagers start turning up dead, maybe we've created a monster.

NOTES

1 Mariana Pargendler, "The Corporate Governance Obsession" (2016) 42:2 *Journal of Corporation Law* 359–402 [Pargendler, "Governance Obsession"].
2 Lynn A. Stout, "On the Rise of Shareholder Primacy, Signs of Its Fall, and the Return of Managerialism (in the Closet)" (2013) 36:2 *Seattle University Law Review* 1169–1186 at 1170–1171, 1182.
3 Ronald Coase, "The Nature of the Firm: Influence" (1988) 4:1 *Journal of Law, Economics and Organization* 33–48.
4 Pargendler, "Governance Obsession," at note 1 at 362; Richard Eells, *The Government of Corporations* (New York: The Free Press of Glencoe, 1962). See also Laura F. Spira and Judy Slinn, *The Cadbury Committee: A History* (Oxford: Oxford University Press, 2013) at xx.
5 Brian R. Cheffins, "The History of Corporate Governance" in Mike Wright et al. (eds.), *The Oxford Handbook of Corporate Governance* (Oxford: Oxford University Press, 2013), p. 46 at p. 57 [Cheffins, "History of Corporate Governance"].
6 Bayless Manning, "The Shareholder's Appraisal Remedy: An Essay for Frank Coker" (1962) 72:2 *Yale Law Journal* 223–265 at 245, note 37.
7 See the history in J. B. Heaton, "Corporate Governance and the Cult of Agency" (2019) 64:2 *Villanova Law Review* 201–222 at 210–211.
8 Eugene F. Fama and Merton H. Miller, *The Theory of Finance* (New York: Holt Rhinehart & Winston, 1972) at p. 75.

9 Michael C. Jensen and William H. Meckling, "Theory of the Firm: Managerial Behavior, Agency Costs and Ownership Structure" (1976) 3:4 *Journal of Financial Economics* 305–360 [Jensen and Meckling, "Theory of the Firm"].

10 *Ibid* at 306; Cheffins, "History of Corporate Governance," at note 5.

11 Jensen and Meckling, "Theory of the Firm," at note 9 at 306–307.

12 Bryce C. Tingle, "What Is Corporate Governance? Can We Measure It? Can Investment Fiduciaries Rely on It?" (2018) 43:2 *Queen's Law Journal* 223–262 at 229.

13 Melvin Aron Eisenberg, *The Structure of the Corporation: A Legal Analysis* (Washington, DC: Beard Books, 1976) [Eisenberg, *Structure*]; Bengt Holmström, "Moral Hazard and Observability" (1979) 10:1 *The Bell Journal of Economics* 74–91; Stephen A. Ross, "The Economic Theory of Agency: The Principal's Problem" (1973) 63:2 *The American Economic Review* 134–139; Michael Spence and Richard Zeckhauser, "Insurance, Information, and Individual Action" (1971) 61:2 *The American Economic Review* 380–387; Eugene F. Fama, "Agency Problems and the Theory of the Firm" (1980) 88:2 *Journal of Political Economy* 288–307.

14 Jensen and Meckling, "Theory of the Firm," at note 9 at 309.

15 Jensen and Meckling, "Theory of the Firm," at note 9 at 308. Note Jensen and Meckling's formal list of agency costs does not include incentives, but incentives are discussed in the section that immediately proceeds their formal list and they fit awkwardly as either a monitoring or bonding cost. As well, I include it explicitly because of incentives' importance in the subsequent history of agency theory and corporate governance.

16 Edward B. Rock, "For Whom Is the Corporation Managed in 2020? The Debate over Corporate Purpose" (2021) 17:2 *The Business Lawyer* 363–395.

17 Cheffins, "History of Corporate Governance," at note 5; Brian R. Cheffins, "Delaware and the Transformation of Corporate Governance" (2015) 40:1 *Delaware Journal of Corporate Law* 1–76; Anita Anand, Frank Milne and Lynnette Purda, "Voluntary Adoption of Corporate Governance Mechanisms" (2006), *Queen's Economics Department Working Paper No. 1112*, online: SSRN, https://ssrn.com/abstract=921450 at 2; Carol Liao, "A Canadian Model of Corporate Governance" (2014) 37:2 *Dalhousie Law Journal* 559–600 [Liao, "Canadian Model"].

18 Eisenberg, *Structure*, at note 13 at p. 162. It should be noted, however, that Eisenberg was a critic of agency cost theory, notwithstanding his championing of a monitoring board: see, for example, Melvin Aron Eisenberg, "New Modes of Discourse in the Corporate Law Literature" (1984) 52:4–5 *George Washington Law Review* 582–608 at 595–596.

19 Paul Rose, "The Corporate Governance Industry" (2007) 32:4 *Journal of Corporation Law* 887–926; Dorothy S. Lund and Elizabeth Pollman, "The Corporate Governance Machine" (2021) 121:8 *Columbia Law Review* 2563–2634.

20 See, for example, Ian Bickis, "Rogers Saga 'A Teachable Moment' on Canada's Out-of-Date Corporate Rules, Experts Say," *The Canadian Press*, November 7, 2021, online: www.cbc.ca/news/business/rogers-debacle-corporate-regulations-1.6240625.

21 See, for example, Jacqueline Hansen, "How Ted Rogers's Preoccupation with Family Control Planted Seeds for the Turmoil in his Empire," *CBC News*, November 5, 2021, online: www.cbc.ca/news/business/ted-rogers-family-trust-explained-1.6237088.

22 *ISS Governance QuickScore 2.0: Overviews and Updates*, Institutional Shareholder Services Inc. (January 2014), online (pdf): www.issgovernance.com/file/files/ISSGovernanceQuickScore2.0.pdf; Guhan Subramanian, "Corporate Governance 2.0" (March 2015), *Harvard Business Review*, online: https://hbr.org/2015/03/corporate-governance-2-0.

23 Jeffrey N. Gordon, "The Rise of Independent Directors in the United States, 1950–2005: Of Shareholder Value and Stock Market Prices" (2007) 59:6 *Stanford Law Review* 1465–1568 at 1474–1475.

24 *Ibid* at 1474; *2021 U.S. Spencer Stuart Board Index*, Spencer Stuart (2021), online (pdf): www
    .spencerstuart.com/-/media/2021/october/ssbi2021/us-spencer-stuart-board-index-2021.pdf.

25 Harald Baum, "The Rise of the Independent Director: A Historical and Comparative
    Perspective" (2017), *Max Planck Private Law Research Paper No. 16/20*, online: SSRN,
    https://ssrn.com/abstract=2814978; *2019 U.S. Spencer Stuart Board Index*, Spencer
    Stuart (2019), online (pdf): www.spencerstuart.com/-/media/2019/ssbi-2019/us_board_
    index_2019.pdf at 15 [Spencer Stuart, *2019 Board Index*].

26 Yvan Allaire, "Pay for Value: Cutting the Gordian Knot of Executive Compensation"
    (2012), *Institute for Governance of Private and Public Organizations – Working Group on
    Compensation of IGOPP Policy Paper*, online: SSRN, https://ssrn.com/abstract=2070766
    at 24, Figure 8. See Martin J. Conyon, "Executive Compensation and Board Governance
    in US Firms" (2014) 124:574 *The Economic Journal* F60-F89 at F74.

27 *U.S. Spencer Stuart Board Index 2021 Highlights*, Spencer Stuart (2021), online (pdf):
    www.spencerstuart.com/-/media/2021/october/ssbi2021/usbi2021-highlights.pdf   at   4;
    Spencer Stuart Board Index 2014, Spencer Stuart (2014), online (pdf): www.nyse.com/
    publicdocs/nyse/listing/Spencer_Stuart_Board_Index_2014.pdf at 8.

28 *US Spencer Stuart Board Index 2020 Highlights*, Spencer Stuart (2020), www.spencerstu
    art.com/-/media/2020/december/ssbi2020/ssbi_2020_highlights.pdf at 3.

29 Spencer Stuart, *2019 Board Index*, above at note 25 at 15.

30 *Ibid* at 15.

31 *Ibid* at 9, 29.

32 *Ibid* at 31; Ethan Klingsberg, Paul Tiger and Elizabeth Bieber, "A Look at the Data
    Behind Recent Poison Pill Adoptions" (April 24, 2020), *Harvard Law School Forum
    on Corporate Governance*, online: https://corpgov.law.harvard.edu/2020/04/24/
    a-look-at-the-data-behind-recent-poison-pill-adoptions/.

33 Spencer Stuart, *2019 Board Index*, above at note 25 at 23–24.

34 For example, *2019 Canada Spencer Stuart Board Index*, Spencer Stuart (2019), online
    (pdf): www.spencerstuart.com/-/media/2020/canada-bi-2019/canada-bi-2019-final.pdf.

35 Martin Lipton, "Some Thoughts for Boards of Directors in 2018" (November 30, 2017),
    Harvard Law School Forum on Corporate Governance, online: https://corpgov.law.har
    vard.edu/2017/11/30/some-thoughts-for-boards-of-directors-in-2018/.

36 John F. Coyle and Joseph M. Green, "Contractual Innovation in Venture Capital" (2014)
    66:133 *Hastings Law Journal* 133–182.

37 See, for example, *The Swinging Pendulum: Board Governance in the Age of Shareholder
    Empowerment – PwC's 2016 Annual Corporate Directors Survey*, PricewaterhouseCoopers
    International Limited (October 2016), online (pdf): www.pwc.com/us/en/corporate-gov
    ernance/annual-corporate-directors-survey/assets/pwc-2016-annual-corporate-directors-
    survey.pdf (59 percent of directors ranked diversity considerations not "very important" at
    4; 66 percent expressing some concern about proxy access at 9; 65 percent don't believe
    in mandatory retirement policies and 90 percent oppose term limits at 10; only small
    minorities have a high regard for dialogue with shareholders at 11; 96 percent of directors
    believe activists are too focused on the short term at 14; 93 percent believe proxy advisors
    have too much power at 14; 57 percent feel shareholders have too much say in gover-
    nance at 14; less than half of the directors indicated their boards acted on their annual
    board self-evaluations at 18; a majority don't believe risk committees are useful at 29; 72
    percent don't believe say-on-pay has reduced executive compensation levels at 33). An
    earlier study found that a variety of governance best practices supported by usually more
    than 75 percent of polled investors, failed to get support from even 25 percent of direct-
    ors: *What Matters In The Boardroom: Director and Investor Views on Trends Shaping*

Governance and the Board of the Future, PricewaterhouseCoopers International Limited (2014), online (pdf): www.pwc.pl/pl/pdf/forum-rad-nadzorczych/pwc-what-matters-in-the-boardroom-director-investor-views.pdf; Silvia Ascarelli, "Corporate Europe Is Skeptical About Tougher Governance Codes," *The Wall Street Journal*, October 7, 2004, online: www.wsj.com/articles/SB109710683845238701; Beckey Bright, "Investors Are Skeptical of Success of Sarbanes-Oxley, Poll Finds," *The Wall Street Journal*, October 14, 2005, online: www.wsj.com/articles/SB112912865268466716.

38 See, for example, Michael Beer and Nancy Katz, "Do Incentives Work? The Perceptions of a Worldwide Sample of Senior Executives" (2003) 26:3 *Human Resource Planning* 30–44 at 36.

39 Liao, "Canadian Model," above at note 17.

40 *Box-tickers beware: FRC's 2020 review of UK Governance Code reporting*, Simmons & Simmons LLP (December 23, 2020), online: www.simmons-simmons.com/en/publica tions/ckj1ibv4k1srjoa629ht6ipec/box-tickers-beware-frc-s-2020-review-of-uk-governance-code-reporting; Andrew Chamberlain, *If Your Board Isn't Adding Value, What is it Doing?* (January 29, 2021), online: www.linkedin.com/pulse/your-board-isnt-adding-value-what-doing-andrew-chamberlain/; George Serafeim, "Social-Impact Efforts That Create Real Value" (September-October 2020), *Harvard Business Review*, online: https://hbr.org/2020/09/social-impact-efforts-that-create-real-value.

41 Brian Cheffins, "The Corporate Governance Movement, Banks and the Financial Crisis" (2015) 16:1 *Theoretical Inquiries in Law* 1–44 at 5 citing Moira Conoley, "Moves to Halt Another Decade of Excess," Financial Times, August 5, 1999.

42 Grant Kirkpatrick, "The Corporate Governance Lessons from the Financial Crisis" (2009) 1 *Financial Market Trends*, online (pdf): *Organisation for Economic Co-operation and Development*, www.oecd.org/finance/financial-markets/42229620.pdf; Peter Yeoh, "Causes of the Global Financial Crisis: Learning from the Competing Insights" (2010) 7:1 *International Journal of Disclosure and Governance* 42–69 at 53–59. But see, Sidney Leung and Bertrand Horwitz, "Corporate Governance and Firm Value During a Financial Crisis" (2009) 34:4 *Review of Quantitative Finance and Accounting* 459–481 at 479; Brian R. Cheffins, "Did Corporate Governance Fail during the 2008 Stock Market Meltdown – The Case of the S&P 500" (2009) 65:1 *The Business Lawyer* 1–65.

43 *Confidence in Institutions*, Gallup Inc. (2022), online: www.gallup.com/poll/1597/confi dence-institutions.aspx. See also, 2015 *Edelman Trust Barometer*, Edelman Inc. (January 19, 2015), online: www.edelman.com/trust/2015-trust-barometer.

44 2015 *Edelman Trust Barometer Executive Summary*, Edelman Inc. (2015), online: www .scribd.com/doc/252750985/2015-Edelman-Trust-Barometer-Executive-Summary at 7.

45 *Growth in GDP per Capita, Productivity and ULC*, Organisation for Economic Co-operation and Development (March 2022), online: https://stats.oecd.org/Index .aspx?DataSetCode=PDB_GR.

46 'Where Have All the Public Companies Gone?', *Bloomberg*, April 9, 2018, online: www .bloomberg.com/opinion/articles/2018-04-09/where-have-all-the-u-s-public-companies-gone.

47 Jay R. Ritter, "Re-energizing the IPO Market" in Martin Neil Baily, Richard J. Herring and Yuta Seki (eds.), *Financial Restructuring to Sustain Recovery* (Washington, DC: Brookings Institution Press, 2013), pp. 123–146.

48 Connie Lin, "Jamie Dimon Says Big Banks and Publicly Traded Companies are Losing Their Grip over Global Finance," *Fast Company*, April 4, 2022, online: www.fastcom pany.com/90737818/jamie-dimon-says-big-banks-and-publicly-traded-companies-are-los ing-their-grip-over-global-finance.

PART I

What Do We Know about Corporate Governance Practices?

Wherein:

- We examine the central corporate governance practices involving boards of directors, shareholders, executive compensation, and proxy voting, to see if these practices work.
- We explore whether it is reasonable to assume there are practices generalizable across heterogeneous companies.
- We evaluate the merits of several crucial assumptions of the modern governance project:
  - Is the primary role of boards of directors to monitor management? If not, have we overprioritized independence as an important quality of directors?
  - Are executive performance and equity pay incentives useful for getting companies to do what we want, or are humans more complicated than the carrot-seeking donkeys we have assumed?
  - Do shareholders have the capacity and incentives for productive engagement with corporate governance?
  - Are outside third parties, such as proxy advisors and compensation consultants, in a position to usefully contribute to specific firms' corporate governance?

2

Best Practices for Boards of Directors

In the early 1990s, the UK suffered a series of embarrassing corporate fiascos. The most notorious involved Robert Maxwell, a prominent titan of industry who apparently killed himself on a private yacht vacation. This was curious because rich people rarely kill themselves on yacht vacations. However, it was subsequently found that hundreds of millions of dollars were missing from the employee pension fund of one of his companies, and that his entire business empire was insolvent. (A cheap thing to do would be to note that this corporate scandal, giving rise to the modern governance regime, was the same that apparently launched Maxwell's daughter, Ghislaine, on her path to infamy with Jeffrey Epstein. However, that is precisely the kind of spurious point that you will *not* find in this book.)

The collapse of Maxwell Communications occurred at roughly the same time that Bank of Credit and Commerce International (BCCI) went bust revealing that it was the preferred bank of criminals around the world, including the fraudsters running it. Even the innocent-sounding British company Polly Peck went bankrupt after being looted and mismanaged (not necessarily in that order) by its leadership.

The proposed solution to these scandals was the creation of the obscurely titled "Committee on the Financial Aspects of Corporate Governance" to provide recommendations on how to address what appeared to many in the UK to be a major breakdown in corporate integrity.[1] The Committee was generally referred to as the "Cadbury Committee" after its chair, Adrian Cadbury, and its subsequent report in 1992 is usually called the "Cadbury Report." This report was the first to set out a comprehensive list of governance "best practices" and suggested that companies be required to either follow those best practices or explain why they were not doing so.

The Cadbury Report was incredibly influential due to the intuitiveness of its recommendations, along with its clever use of the "comply or explain" mechanism to avoid the appearance of intruding too deeply into the substantive internal arrangements of companies. It was copied by countries around the world. As a practical matter, companies in places where this regime came into force tended to adopt nearly all the recommended best practices.[2]

The Cadbury Report mostly reflected the logic of agency cost theory, and its recommendations focused heavily on the importance of independent boards and board processes to properly monitor managers. The focus of the Report on boards of directors grew out of the fact that boards are the center of power in a corporation. As a legal matter, corporate managers are merely delegated the board's power over the business and, of course, boards retain the power to dismiss senior officers. Shareholder power in corporate arrangements was not a focus of the Report because, as we shall see in Chapters 5 through 8, and Chapter 12, shareholders confront obstacles and lack the tools needed to engage deeply with corporate governance. It was only when board-level governance interventions seemed to fail in the decade following the Cadbury Report that governance industry actors began to lean into practices designed to enhance shareholder power outside of the takeover context.

By the time the Cadbury Report arrived, its way of thinking about corporate governance was so deeply ingrained that the Report's recommendations seemed obvious. Companies were fundamentally similar enough that "best practices" could be generalized across heterogenous firms and industries, and those best practices ought to be focused on providing independent checks on managerial power. Any dissent from the corporate community was dismissed as self-interested. Indeed, the Cadbury Report generally seemed so inoffensive that it appeared serendipitous that it shared its name with a famous line of candy bars.

Over time, the formulation of governance best practices has evolved slightly, but the focus on independent, monitoring boards has been retained, along with confidence that best practices exist. The rest of this chapter will review the evidence in favor of these two assumptions.

2.1 INDEPENDENT DIRECTORS

The New York Stock Exchange (NYSE) required at least two independent directors on company boards since 1956, but it began the process of amending its listing rules in 1977 to give increasing prominence to board-level independence.[3] At the same time, the beginnings of the governance industry began agitating for control of boards to be handed over to non-executive directors.[4]

As we have seen, from 1950 to 2005, the percentage of independent directors on American corporate boards rose from constituting only a third of the board to occupying every chair in the boardroom other than the one reserved for the CEO. It is impossible to overstate the prominence of independent directors in summaries of corporate governance best practices. For example, proxy advisory firms' voting guidelines are significantly driven by director independence. While other qualities of directors, such as "experience and skills," are mentioned, they never generate voting outcomes.[5] What does generate outcomes for ISS (the market leader) is whether a director is "independent" according to 19 finely-tuned criteria.[6] Independence drives outcomes in the election of individual directors (this includes independence measured at a board, chair, and committee level) and support for shareholder proposals (e.g., to separate the CEO and chair roles, create independent board committees, enhance board diversity, or institute term limits). Independence also determines things like whether a merger or corporate restructuring will be approved and whether an executive compensation scheme is satisfactory.

Independence also plays an outsized role in both media rankings of corporate boards and institutional investor guidelines. Fortune's Modern Board 25 ranking system places importance on the "expertise and independence of board members" and "the tenure of independent directors."[7] The largest defined benefit pension plan in the United States, CalPERS, includes board independence as one of their five governance and sustainability principles, with specific attention to whether there is a majority of independent directors, if those independent directors have confidential executive sessions, if board committees are independent, whether the board chair is independent, and so on.[8]

No aspect of corporate governance has been studied as intensively as independent boards. With very few exceptions, empirical studies have found no connection between board independence and any corporate outcome we care about.

The most prominent meta-analysis conducted from fifty-four empirical studies comprising forty years of data and 40,160 observations concluded in 1999 that there is no connection between board composition and corporate performance.[9] Literature reviews performed since 2000 confirm this conclusion. In 2002, Professors Bhagat and Black concluded that, based on their review of the literature, there was no evidence that majority board independence led to better outcomes and some suggestion that super-majorities of independent directors performed worse.[10] Another literature review published by the Federal Reserve Board of New York in 2003 came to the same conclusions.[11]

A 2007 study of 254 public companies in over fifty industries found, "the worst ROE [return on equity] performers in each of fifty industries have approximately the same percentage of independent directors as the best ROE performers in each industry. No pattern emerges to suggest that it makes any difference at all to shareholders' financial return whether a board has a higher or lower percentage of independent directors."[12] A 2008 study covering more than twenty years and containing up to 20,000 samples for some of the variables found "board independence is *negatively* correlated with contemporaneous and subsequent operating performance."[13] A 2012 study of 6,000 firms over twenty two years and using more sophisticated statistical techniques to measure causal effects determined there is "no causal relation between board size or independence, and firm performance."[14]

The failure of independent boards to make a difference in company-wide outcomes is duplicated in surprising areas within the firm. For example, a 2005 meta-analytic review of research on executive compensation concluded from more than 30,000 observations that there was no evidence independent boards did better at controlling executive pay.[15] (The explosion in executive pay levels has, after all, largely coincided with the rise of the independent board since the 1980s.)

It appears as well that independent directors do no better at terminating under-performing CEOs than insider-dominated boards, and that corporate misconduct actually *increases* with board independence.[16] Again, this should not be a great sur-prise to us. The corporate excess of the dot-com era, the accounting frauds of the Enron era, the widespread stock option backdating scandals, and the governance failures that helped create the 2008 financial crisis all occurred in an environment of majority or super-majority independent boards. (Indeed, research performed on the governance of financial firms during the financial crisis of 2007–2008 found that the proportion of independent directors was inversely related to stock returns during an era that stress-tested financial businesses in America.[17])

There are at least two possible explanations for the failure of empirical evidence to establish independent directors as value-enhancing. The first is that there is some-thing wrong with the monitoring conception of the board. We will delay considering this possibility to Chapters 8 and 9 because we need more data to properly evaluate it.

For now, however, a more straightforward explanation for the failure of indepen-dent directors is that the value of independent directors varies widely over firms, industries, personalities, and corporate issues.[18] Research shows, for example, that independent directors appear to be more valuable in industries that are relatively non-technical and where the cost of acquiring information about the firm's business is low.[19] They do a better job of controlling CEO pay if their ages are further apart[20] or if they make less money.[21] Similar backgrounds shared between the CEO and an independent director (such as a common university, military service, regional ori-gin, academic, or industry background) appear to impact independent director per-formance.[22] In contrast, R&D-intensive companies benefit particularly from larger numbers of insiders on the board.[23]

These are just a few factors that can be measured and coded into a statistical model. Anyone who has actually worked with a board can think of dozens of other factors that make an effective independent director. In a letter to the Berkshire Hathaway shareholders, Warren Buffet pointed out the essential emptiness of inde-pendence as a director quality and indicated that most of the independent directors he had served with (at the time he estimated this might be as much as 250) "lacked at least one of the three qualities I value [business-savvy, interested, and shareholder-oriented]. As a result, their contribution to shareholder well-being was minimal at best and, too often, negative."[24] Other important qualities of an effective indepen-dent director not mentioned by Buffet include:

- the intestinal fortitude to challenge management or take unpopular stands;
- a sense of humor to manage conflicts;
- fierce loyalty to the organization;
- expertise relevant to the company's business operations and that complements management's skills and knowledge;

- the spirit of friendly cooperation required to get a CEO to confide and take advice from the board;
- a strong work ethic; and
- the ability to work with others in a body that mostly operates by consensus.

Thus, the value of outside directors is likely dependent on highly personal factors that are only visible to their close colleagues over time. Their value also depends on outside variables that range from the personality of the CEO to the nature of the company's industry. The quality of their performance can even vary according to the task. (For example, there are studies that show independent directors positively influence merger and acquisition outcomes.[25]) It is possible, therefore, to retain the belief that the proper role of the board is primarily to monitor management and still conclude that one-size-fits-all corporate governance best practices are not suited to accomplish effective monitoring.

Regardless of the explanation we choose for the failure of independent boards to create value for the shareholders, the empirical work of the past two decades makes it clear that the independence best practice – so central to modern conceptions of good governance – is wrong.

2.2 BOARD COMMITTEES

The board committee is a logical outgrowth of agency-inflected views of corporate governance. Audit committees, compensation committees, governance committees, risk committees, environmental committees, and many other possible subgroupings of the board of directors have three theoretical advantages over the full board. First, as the full board has some inside directors, it is tainted in a way that a committee entirely comprised of independent directors is not. Admittedly, these days most public company boards have only one inside director, but as this is the CEO (a figure ascribed tremendous powers by the governance industry), the safest thing is to move oversight of any important board task to a committee comprised of safely independent directors.

The second advantage of a board committee is that it communicates a sense of responsibility over an area of governance to specific individual directors. Ever since it was wrongly reported that thirty-eight bystanders passively witnessed the murder of Kitty Genovese in 1964, social psychology has explored the "bystander effect," commonly understood to mean that the likelihood a bystander will intervene in an emergency goes down as the number of witnesses to the emergency goes up.[26] Translated to the less dramatic environment of the boardroom, this might mean that directors may avoid concerning themselves with unpleasant tasks (such as negotiating pay with senior management) or boring tasks (such as reviewing the integrity of the financial statements) unless they are uniquely singled out as responsible.

(It should be noted that outside of laboratory experiments conducted by social psychologists, there is some question as to whether the bystander effect exists, or if it does, under what precise conditions. A 2019 study looking at over 200 real-world surveillance video recordings found little evidence that the bystander effect is common, and even concluded that increasing numbers of bystanders can increase the likelihood of intervention.[27] This may not have anything to do with the merits of delegating board responsibilities to committees, but it is reassuring to know about humans.)

The final supposed advantage of board committees is that they ensure directors deal with some important responsibilities that might otherwise be ignored. Thus, climate change campaigners, who feel boards pay insufficient attention to carbon emissions, advocate for climate-risk board committees, while the 2008 financial crisis created a demand for corporate risk committees. Depending on the business and the mood of the governance industry, companies are petitioned to create safety committees, environmental, social, and governance (ESG) committees, as well as many others. It is an area that promises full employment to governance gadflies for the indefinite future, as boards' general responsibility to oversee the corporation can be divided into infinitely smaller slices, and as corporations are encouraged to take on responsibilities that go far beyond following the law and making profits.

The best-studied of all board committees is the audit committee. The audit committee was first proposed by the American Institute of Accountants in 1939,[28] following a scandal with McKesson & Robbins, Inc., in which a twice-convicted felon and his three brothers were able to overstate the balance sheet of the company by nearly $20 million thanks to mistakes by their auditor.[29] It is the original committee proposed by governance reformers, who started advocating for its universal adoption in the 1970s. This prompted the SEC to endorse establishing the committee in all public companies in 1972, and the NYSE to require all listed companies to maintain an audit committee beginning in 1977.[30] At first, insiders were permitted on these committees, but Sarbanes-Oxley mandated only independent directors in 2003. Wholly independent audit committees are probably the least controversial best practice in corporate governance after majority independent boards. Their intuitive appeal has been entirely unaffected by a parade of empirical studies suggesting independent audit committees do nothing to improve the quality of corporate financial reporting.

An early study in this century by April Klein found the strongest case in favor of independence: companies with a majority-independent audit committee appear to have better quality earnings accruals.[31] (Earnings accruals are a common way of manipulating financial results but are detectable using a variety of models.[32]) Professor Klein did not find, however, that committees entirely comprised of independent directors experience improved results compared to committees with a simple majority of independent directors.

Following Klein's research, several studies failed to find any connection between the presence of independent directors on the audit committee and the quality of corporate financial reporting.[33] Indeed, of the seven studies looking at earnings accruals, five have failed to find any benefits of majority independent audit committees.

None of the seven studies provide any evidence in favor of the 100 percent independence requirement now found in corporate governance best practices.

Several studies use metrics other than earnings management to explore the relationship between audit committee composition and the quality of financial monitoring. For example, some studies have used third-party evaluations of financial reporting[34] or the information content of earnings announcements to evaluate audit committee performance.[35] None of them find any evidence that independent directors on the audit committee improve the quality of financial reporting.

Other studies examine the impact of independent audit committees on financial restatements. Two of these studies find no evidence that independent directors impact the likelihood of a financial restatement,[36] while the third finds there is a connection.[37] The probative value of these studies is limited because recent research suggests only three percent of restatements are due to deliberate manipulation, as opposed to causes like internal errors or misapplication of an accounting standard, which outside directors are unlikely to be in a position to catch.[38] (After all, these mistakes were missed by the auditors who have a lot more visibility on internal journal entries than even the best-informed outside director.) More useful is a study of eighty-seven firms that fraudulently manipulated their financial statements between 1982 and 2000, which found they had the same percentage of independent directors on their audit committees as the control sample.[39]

The strongest case for audit committee independence is seemingly made by two studies that found a robust correlation between audit committee independence and the likelihood of an auditor issuing a going concern note.[40] However, this may not mean the statements are more accurate. These results are also compatible with the conclusion that outside directors are risk-adverse and may be aggressive in advocating for going concern warnings when perhaps they are not warranted. Independent audit committee members may thus make statements less accurate.

Taken as a whole, the research on audit committees provides little support for majority independence in audit committees and no evidence in favor of the 100 percent requirement found in Sarbanes-Oxley. These results will come as no surprise to anyone who has actually attended audit committee meetings. An independent director generally has no source of information about the financial affairs of the company outside of what they are told by management and the auditors. The odds are negligible that they will find an error management and the auditors have missed, or that these directors will uncover a fraud that has deceived even the accounting firm that just combed through the company's internal records.

In reality, audit committees tend to focus on a limited number of judgment issues identified in advance by the auditors and management (such as whether to include a going concern note), and on a predictable line of questioning about whether the auditors had adequate levels of cooperation from the company in performing their work. This latter line of questioning only commences after members of the executive team leave the audit committee meeting. The tenor of the subsequent confidential meeting might cause a stranger to American governance to wonder how frequently auditors' families are taken hostage by corporate managers covering up fraud. Even the much-maligned Enron audits would pass these sessions with flying colors.

The research on other types of board committees is essentially similar. Compensation committees are usually regarded as the second-most important board committee, as they oversee the most direct and obvious way managers can extract agency costs. Seven different studies have found that compensation committees with a higher proportion of outside directors have no significant impact on the level of CEO compensation,[41] with several studies finding that a committee comprised entirely of independent directors actually leads to higher executive pay.[42] The mere presence of a compensation committee seems correlated with higher executive pay, holding all other things constant.[43]

There are two possible explanations for these counterintuitive findings. The first is that independent directors are not actually independent, and now see their jobs as akin to bank tellers working for a bank with only one customer. This is the explanation favored by the corporate governance industry, but as we will see in Chapter 4, it seems improbable when we consider the totality of information about how executive compensation decisions are made.

The evidence is much greater for the second possible explanation: independent directors are strongly motivated to apply the latest recommended best practice around executive compensation and, as we will also see in Chapter 4, these best practices are almost invariably linked to higher executive pay. Regardless of the explanation, the research tells us that, at a minimum, independent directors do not improve (and may worsen) corporate pay outcomes. That is, independent directors fail against the standard set by their own reason for existence.

2.3 BOARD DIVERSITY

This book is not about America's legacy of oppression of various minorities and – in the case of women – various majorities. There are a lot of reasons why governments may decide that diversity mandates for corporate boards are a good idea. This book is only interested in one reason often given for board diversity initiatives: the "business case" or "corporate governance case" for board diversity. To this point, nearly all the research on this area has been conducted on women's impact on the board; there are, of course, many other categories of under-represented groups.

The corporate governance case for gender diversity is founded on several propositions. The first is that diversity helps boards overcome tendencies to groupthink by introducing unfamiliar (gendered) perspectives. The second is that women are more independent than other independent directors because they are less socially similar to the (usually male) CEO. They are not part of the "boys' club." Finally, women bring unique capabilities and styles of decision-making to the board. Broadly speaking, all these rationales for board diversity reflect the modern corporate governance view that prioritizes independence in directors whose essential job is conceived as checking management in various ways.

The recent corporate governance reforms relating to gender diversity probably owe their impetus to a 2007 Catalyst study that ranked Fortune 500 companies according to the proportion of women on their boards, divided them into quartiles on this basis, and compared their performance between 2001 and 2004.[44] The study found that companies with boards in the top quartile massively outperformed companies with boards in the lowest quartile. A similar 2012 study by Credit Suisse Research Institute on 2,360 companies around the world found that firms with at least one woman on the board significantly outperformed all-male boards.[45]

These studies, and in particular the Catalyst study, have come under sharp criticism by scholars.[46] The principal difficulty is that with no controls, there is no way to show causation (successful businesses could be more likely to promote diversity) or whether the correlation is with financial success at all, rather than with some third factor (e.g., some types of businesses may be more likely than others to appoint women to the board). In relation to the latter point, we know from research that certain industries, such as real estate, have historically been much more likely to have female directors than other industries (such as transportation or natural resource extraction).[47] We also know that bigger companies are more likely to have diverse boards.[48] It may be these factors rather than the presence of female directors that are producing attractive financial outcomes.

Peer-reviewed academic studies of North American businesses contradict the more informal work in this area. Since 2000, three studies on North American companies have found gender diversity is positively correlated with financial performance,[49] but in two of these cases, the authors later returned to the question with better-designed studies and more sophisticated techniques to determine causality and found no connection between gender diversity and financial outcomes.[50] Explaining earlier work that found a connection between diversity and performance, both research teams found this correlation in their subsequent research, but both found the correlation disappears once "we apply reasonable procedures to tackle omitted variables and reverse causality problems."[51] One paper went on to find diversity had no effect; the other found firms perform worse as gender diversity increases.

In contrast, at least eleven peer-reviewed studies since 2000 have found no causal relationship between gender and performance, or a negative relationship.[52] These results are not a referendum on women, but on the idea that independent directors make a valuable contribution to corporate outcomes. There seems little reason to doubt that women are indeed generally more independent from the usually male CEOs. Yet this independence doesn't lead to better outcomes.

When we look at executive pay levels, the best proxy for actual agency costs, we once again find the "extra" independence produced by diverse boards has no discernible effects. In fact, gender diversity on the board apparently produces higher executive pay, just as independent directors appear to produce higher pay.[53]

2.4 SEPARATION OF THE CEO AND CHAIR ROLES

If you believe the main job of the board is to monitor the CEO and other senior executives, then it seems obvious that the historically common American practice of combining the CEO and board chair roles is a terrible idea. You can't have the board "managed" by the very person it is ostensibly monitoring. In two articles published right at the beginning of the agency cost era of corporate governance, Eugene Fama and Michael Jensen took aim at the practice as a clear mistake.[54] Since they drew attention to the issue, the corporate governance industry has increasingly targeted the practice, and American companies have slowly and somewhat reluctantly complied.

Little research has been performed since 2000 on the basic question of whether separating the CEO and chairperson roles produces positive economic benefits because the question was answered definitively during the prior decade.[55] A 1995 meta-analysis of seven previous studies found no benefits but did observe some evidence in the studies compatible with the view that combining the two positions (called "duality" in the finance literature) may be positively associated with performance in some circumstances but negatively in others.[56] A later, larger meta-analysis in 1998 of thirty one empirical studies also concluded that separating the roles produces no measurable outcomes.[57]

The studies performed since the millennium have confirmed the conclusions of these earlier papers.[58] For example, one set of researchers took advantage of the natural experiment afforded by the 2007–2008 financial crisis to evaluate whether duality impacted financial firm performance and found it did not.[59] Another paper found that separating the roles had no impact on performance, organizational risk-taking, or executive pay practices.[60] Summarizing the field of finance literature on CEO duality, one team of scholars observed in 2011, "we are not aware of a body of literature in corporate governance – or elsewhere – where null results present with such consistency."[61]

Perhaps because the central question of duality's impact on corporate performance was resolved so early, researchers interested in the area have felt free to devote themselves to more nuanced questions about the possibility that separating the roles makes sense in some situations and not in others.[62] (Limited evidence for this was identified as early as the 1995 meta-analysis discussed above.) Qualitative studies on boards in Canada, America, and the UK have produced a finely-tuned understanding of the difficulties that arise with a separate chair and CEO (such as the politics created by the blurring of responsibilities and authority) and the various personality traits necessary to make one structure or the other work effectively.[63]

For their part, quantitative studies have revealed interesting relationships between outcomes in this area and various external and internal organizational circumstances. For example, a recent paper found evidence that the informational efficiencies generated by unified leadership are associated with performance gains for companies with significant knowledge assets – measured by patent citations and R&D spending.[64] This is related to earlier research that found combining the two roles had advantages "under conditions of resource scarcity or high complexity."[65] Another study found that CEOs who are also board chairs do better in negotiating takeovers.[66]

The literature on CEO duality is useful because it is one of the few areas in corporate governance where there is virtually no evidence in favor of the relevant best practice. To the contrary, the literature actually demonstrates the way in which the value of board duality depends on firm and personality characteristics so specific that they could not be taken into account by anything as crude as a "best practice."

2.5 DIRECTOR COMMITMENTS OUTSIDE THE COMPANY

A comparatively recent trend in corporate governance involves criticizing certain activities of directors outside of the boardroom. For example, ISS has included the concept of director "busyness" or "overboarding" in its voting guidelines since at least 2010. A busy director is one who participates in too many formal roles outside of their board position. There is variety in how the condition is defined, but most members of the governance industry articulate a best practice of limiting directors to something between three and six boards. Academic research in the area tends to use three or more boards as the measure of "busyness."

More than three-quarters of the companies in the S&P 500 now have policies restricting the number of outside boards on which their directors can serve.[67] Surprisingly, however, the number of directors with extensive outside commitments has increased. In 1998, 26.8 percent of directors in the United States held two or more board positions – by 2010, this had increased to almost 40 percent.[68] This is surprising because, generally, American companies have eventually done what the governance industry told them was the best practice in a particular area. It is, therefore, telling that firms seem to be deliberately ignoring the governance industry in this one area.

The first study on overboarded directors, published in 2003, examined 3,190 US companies and found no evidence that busy directors adversely impacted firm performance or the likelihood of securities fraud lawsuits.[69] In contrast, a smaller 2006 study that looked only at the large companies making up the Forbes 500 came to the opposite conclusion: overboarded directors were associated with lower market-to-book ratios and returns on assets.[70]

Two recent studies appear to explain the conflicting early work. When larger datasets, such as the S&P 1500 are examined, director overboarding is positively correlated with performance.[71] But, if the 500 largest companies from the sample are looked at in isolation, the relationship is either negative or essentially neutral.[72] A recent study, published in 2013, is the first to try to correct for endogeneity (in other words, attempting to control for reverse causal relationships).[73] It also uses a larger sample size, looking at 14,449 firm-years of the S&P 1500 from 1996 to 2009, and at all the venture-backed IPOs from 1996 to 2008. The study found that for all types of companies, director busyness was positively correlated with operating success, but that the benefits are concentrated among younger and less established firms.[74] Newly public companies are particularly likely to have busy directors: 45 percent of them serve on more than three boards.[75] The study finds that busy directors have a strong positive impact on firm performance that declines over time as the company grows.[76]

This evidence that smaller and younger companies benefit from corporate governance arrangements that differ from larger and more established firms is also found in the area of "interlocking" directors. Interlocking directors (a term that would have occasioned blank stares from previous generations of corporate leaders) are directors on one board that sit together on other corporate boards. The mere fact of an interlocking directorship is generally sufficient to attract a "withhold" vote from proxy advisors.

There isn't as much empirical evidence on interlocking directors as one would like, but what evidence exists tends to support the conclusions visible in the director overboarding research. Interlocked boards appear to cause superior performance generally, but the advantages are disproportionately experienced by "firms that are young, or have high growth opportunities, low ROA [return on assets], or past stock momentum."[77]

The research on our current best practices around directors' outside activities is once again suggestive that our intuitions are wrong. Companies seem to benefit from the relationships and networks that attend directors who are busy or sit on boards together. Unsurprisingly, this is particularly true of younger companies that are more dependent on the networks and human capital brought by their directors. A fitting conclusion to this section is provided by one of the studies on overboarded directors:

> [O]ur paper highlights the extent to which different types of firms place different demands on their boards; optimal corporate governance is not identical across all firms.... Restrictions on the ability of directors to serve on multiple boards could pose negative externalities on firms' governance structures, in particular those of younger, less established firms. Broad-brush recommendations to reduce directorships should not be pursued.[78]

It's tough to improve on that.

2.6 SUMMARY

The hypothesis that increasing the independence of boards would lead to better outcomes – a logical result of the monitoring conception of the board in agency cost theory – is contradicted by all available evidence. This is true whether we are defining better outcomes in terms of firm performance, increasing the accuracy of firm reporting, terminating underperforming executives, or controlling the direct expropriation of value from the corporation through executive pay. We have done everything we can to improve market-wide board monitoring with no discernable improvement in anything we care about. As a group of finance scholars reviewing the literature recently concluded, "It might be time to concede that our conception of boards as all-encompassing monitors is doubtful.... Our review calls into question whether boards are really equipped to catch or stop misbehavior."[79] An alternative conclusion might be that whatever the advantages of independent directors in fulfilling the monitoring function, they are matched, and even exceeded, by the liabilities arising from independent directors' relative ignorance of the details of the business, people, and markets in which the firm operates.

Whatever the cause, survey data demonstrates that companies mainly value directors for their contributions to firm strategy and decision-making, not their monitoring role.[80] There is evidence the companies are right. Boards with directors possessing related-industry experience (suggesting they are useful sources of strategic advice) trade at higher valuations and have better operating performance.[81]

The second conclusion that we can draw from this research is that there is little evidence that generalizable "best practices" exist. Rather, there is considerable evidence that the impact of various governance structures and practices varies depending on fine-grained distinctions in personality and corporate circumstances. This is a phenomenon familiar to anyone who has sat through wedding speeches providing sincere advice to the newly married couple and thought, "that may work for you, but if I did that my spouse would divorce me."

NOTES

1   Adrian Cadbury, *Report of the Committee on the Financial Aspects of Corporate Governance* (London: Gee and Co. Ltd., 1992), online (pdf): *ECGI*, www.ecgi.global/sites/default/files/codes/documents/cadbury.pdf.

2   Brian R. Cheffins, "The History of Corporate Governance" in Mike Wright et al. (eds.), *The Oxford Handbook of Corporate Governance* (Oxford: Oxford University Press, 2013).

3   Robert B. Thompson, "Delaware, the Feds, and the Stock Exchange: Challenges to the First State as First in Corporate Law" (2004) 29:3 *Delaware Journal of Corporate Law* 779–804; New York Stock Exchange, *New York Stock Exchange Listed Company Manual*, sections 303A.01-303A.05, online: *NYSE*, https://nyseguide.srorules.com/listed-company-manual.

4   Ralph Nader, Mark J. Green and Joel Seligman, *Taming the Giant Corporation* (New York: Norton, 1976); Business Roundtable, "The Role and Composition of the Board of Directors of the Large Publicly Owned Corporation" (1978) 33:4 *The Business Lawyer* 2083–2113.

5   *United States Summary Proxy Voting Guidelines: Benchmark Policy Recommendations*, Institutional Shareholders Services Inc. (December 13, 2022), online (pdf): www.issgovernance.com/file/policy/active/americas/US-Voting-Guidelines.pdf at 77.

6   *Ibid* at 10.

7   *Methodology for Fortune Modern Board 25 (2022)*, Fortune (2022), online: https://fortune.com/franchise-list-page/modern-board-25-2022-methodology/.

 8 *CalPERS' Governance & Sustainability Principles*, California Public Employees'
    Retirement System (September 2019), online (pdf): www.calpers.ca.gov/docs/forms-pub
    lications/governance-and-sustainability-principles.pdf.
 9 Dan R. Dalton et al., "Number of Directors and Financial Performance: A Meta-analysis"
    (1999) 42:6 *Academy of Management Journal* 674–686.
10 Sanjai Bhagat and Bernard Black, "The Uncertain Relationship Between Board
    Composition and Firm Performance" (1999) 54:3 *The Business Lawyer* 921–963 at 938.
11 Benjamin E. Hermalin and Michael S. Weisbach, "Boards of Directors as an
    Endogenously Determined Institution: A Survey of the Economic Literature" (2003) 9:1
    Economic Policy Review (Federal Reserve Bank of New York) 7–26.
12 Eric Fogel and Andrew M. Geier, "Strangers in the House: Rethinking Sarbanes-Oxley
    and the Independent Board of Directors" (2007) 32:1 *Delaware Journal of Corporate Law*
    33–72 at 52.
13 Sanjai Bhagat and Brian Bolton, "Corporate Governance and Firm Performance" (2008)
    14:3 *Journal of Corporate Finance* 257–273 at 258.
14 M. Babajide Wintoki, James S. Linck and Jeffery M. Netter, "Endogeneity and the
    Dynamics of Internal Corporate Governance" (2012) 105:3 *Journal of Financial Economics*
    581–606 at 603–604.
15 Yuval Deutsch, "The Impact on Board Composition on Firms' Critical Decisions: A
    Meta-analytic Review" (2005) 31:3 *Journal of Management* 424–444 at 424. See also,
    Ronald C. Anderson and John M. Bizjak, "An Empirical Examination of the Role of the
    CEO and Compensation Committee in Structuring Executive Pay" (2003) 27:7 *Journal
    of Banking and Finance* 1323–1348.
16 Eliezer M. Fich and Anil Shivdasani, "Are Busy Boards Effective Monitors?" (2006)
    61:2 *Journal of Finance* 689–724 [Fich and Shivdasani, "Effective Monitors?"]; Nicolas
    Eugster, Oskar Kowalewski and Piotr Spiewanowski, "Internal Governance Mechanisms
    and Corporate Misconduct" (2022), *IESEG School of Management Working Paper Series
    No. 2022-ACF-05*, online: SSRN, https://ssrn.com/abstract=4390593.
17 David H. Erkens, Mingyi Hung and Pedro Matos, "Corporate Governance in the 2007–
    2008 Financial Crisis: Evidence from Financial Institutions Worldwide" (2012) 18:2
    Journal of Corporate Finance 389–411.
18 See for example, Frederick Tung, "The Puzzle of Independent Directors: New Learning"
    (2011) 91:3 *Boston University Law Review* 1175–1190 at 1177.
19 Ran Duchin, John G. Matsusaka and Oguzhan Ozbas, "When Are Outside Directors
    Effective?" (2010) 96:2 *Journal of Financial Economics* 195–214.
20 Brian G. M. Main, Charles A. O'Reilly and James Wade, "The CEO, the Board of
    Directors and Executive Compensation: Economic and Psychological Perspectives"
    (1995) 4:2 *Industrial and Corporate Change* 293–332 at 319–320.
21 Charles A. O'Reilly III, Brian G. Main and Graef S. Crystal, "CEO Compensation as
    Tournament and Social Comparison: A Tale of Two Theories" (1988) 33:2 *Administrative
    Science Quarterly* 257–274 at 261–262.
22 Byoung-Hyoun Hwang and Seoyoung Kim, "It Pays to Have Friends" (2009) 93:1 *Journal
    of Financial Economics* 138–158.
23 Jeffrey L. Coles, Naveen D. Daniel and Lalitha Naveen, "Boards: Does One Size Fit
    All?" (2008) 87:2 *Journal of Financial Economics* 329–356.
24 Warren E. Buffet, *Letter to Shareholders in Berkshire Hathaway Inc.*, Berkshire Hathaway
    Inc. (February 21, 2003), online (pdf): www.berkshirehathaway.com/letters/2002pdf.pdf at 17.
25 See James F. Cotter, Anil Shavdasani and Marc Zenner, "Do Independent Directors
    Enhance Target Shareholder Wealth During Tender Offers" (1997) 43:2 *Journal of
    Financial Economics* 195–218 at 216.

26 Rachel Manning, Mark Levine and Alan Collins, "The Kitty Genovese Murder and the Social Psychology of Helping: The Parable of the 38 Witnesses" (2007) 62:6 *American Psychologist* 555–562.

27 Richard Philpot et al., "Would I Be Helped? Cross-National CCTV Footage Shows That Intervention Is the Norm in Public Conflicts" (2020) 75:1 *American Psychologist* 66–75.

28 American Institute of Accountants, Committee on Auditing Procedure, "Extensions of Auditing Procedure; Statements on Auditing Procedure, No. 01" (1939) *American Institute of Accountants* 249, online (pdf): https://egrove.olemiss.edu/dl_aia/249.

29 Sheila D. Foster and Bruce A. Strauch, "Auditing Cases That Made a Difference: McKesson & Robbins" (2009) 5:4 *Journal of Business Case Studies* 1–16.

30 Brenda S. Birkett, "The Recent History of Corporate Audit Committees" (1986) 13:2 *The Accounting Historians Journal* 109–116.

31 April Klein, "Audit Committee, Board of Director Characteristics, and Earnings Management" (2002) 33:3 *Journal of Accounting and Economics* 375–400.

32 See discussion of these models in Jagdish Pathak et al., "Do Audit Committee and Characteristics of Boards of Directors Influence Earnings Management?" (2014), online: SSRN, https://ssrn.com/abstract=2406080.

33 Biao Xie, Wallace N. Davidson III and Peter J. DaDalt, "Earnings Management and Corporate Governance: The Roles of the Board and the Audit Committee" (2003) 9:3 *Journal of Corporate Finance* 295–316 at 305; Joon S. Yang and Jagan Krishnan, "Audit Committees and Quarterly Earnings Management" (2005) 9:3 *International Journal of Auditing* 201–219 at 215; Aloke Ghosh, Antonio Marra and Doocheol Moon, "Corporate Boards, Audit Committees, and Earnings Management: Pre- and Post-SOX Evidence" (2010) 37:9–10 *Journal of Business Finance and Accounting* 1145–1176 at 1145; David Larcker, Scott A. Richardson and Irem Tuna, "Corporate Governance, Accounting Outcomes, and Organizational Performance" (2007) 82:4 *The Accounting Review* 963–1008; Yun W. Park and Hyun-Han Shin, "Board Composition and Earnings Management in Canada" (2004) 10:3 *Journal of Corporate Finance* 431–457 at 452.

34 Andrew J. Felo, Srinivasan Krishnamurthy and Steven A. Solieri, "Audit Committee Characteristics and the Perceived Quality of Financial Reporting: An Empirical Analysis" (2003), online: SSRN, https://ssrn.com/abstract=401240 at 1.

35 Kirsten L. Anderson, Stuart Gillan and Daniel N. Deli, "Boards of Directors, Audit Committees, and the Information Content of Earnings" (2003), *Weinberg Center for Corporate Governance Paper No. 2003-04*, online: SSRN, https://ssrn.com/abstract=401240.

36 Ying Zhang, "Three Essays on Financial Restatements," PhD Thesis, Concordia University (2012), p. 54; Anup Agrawal and Sahiba Chadha, "Corporate Governance and Accounting Scandals" (2005) 48:2 *Journal of Law and Economics* 371–406.

37 Lawrence J. Abbott, Susan Parker and Gary F. Peters, "Audit Committee Characteristics and Financial Misstatement: A Study of the Efficacy of Certain Blue Ribbon Committee Recommendations" (2002), online: SSRN, https://ssrn.com/abstract=319125.

38 Marlene Plumtree and Teri Lombardi Yohn, "An Analysis of the Underlying Causes Attributed to Restatements" (2010) 24:1 *Accounting Horizons* 41–64 at 47.

39 David B. Farber, "Restoring Trust After Fraud: Does Corporate Governance Matter?" (2005) 80:2 *The Accounting Review* 539–561. See also, Dain C. Donelson, John M. McInnis and Richard D. Mergenthaler, Jr., "The Effect of Corporate Governance Reform on Financial Reporting Fraud" (2015), online: SSRN, https://ssrn.com/abstract=2138348.

40 Scott N. Bronson et al., "Are Fully Independent Audit Committees Really Necessary?" (2009) 28:4 *Journal of Accounting and Public Policy* 265–280; Joseph V. Carcello and Terry L. Neal, "Audit Committee Composition and Auditor Reporting" (2000) 75:4 *The Accounting Review* 453–467.

41 Martin J. Conyon, "Executive Compensation and Board Governance in US Firms" (2014) 124:574 *The Economic Journal* F60–F89 at F80; Martin J. Conyon and Lerong He, "Compensation Committees and CEO Compensation Incentives in US Entrepreneurial Firms" (2004) 16:1 *Journal of Management Accounting Research* 35–56 at 50–52; Catherine M. Daily et al., "Compensation Committee Composition as a Determinant of CEO Compensation" (1998) 41:2 *Academy Management Journal* 209–220 at 214; Harry A. Newman and Haim A. Mozes, "Does the Composition of the Compensation Committee Influence CEO Compensation Practices?" (1999) 28:3 *Financial Management* 41–53 at 50; Ian Gregory-Smith, "Chief Executive Pay and Remuneration Committee Independence" (2012) 74:4 *Oxford Bulletin Economics and Statistics* 510–531 at 528; Martin J. Conyon and Danielle Kuchinskas, "Compensation Committees in the United States" in Christine A. Mallin (ed.), *Handbook on International Corporate Governance: Country Analyses* (Cheltenham, UK: Edward Elgar, 2006), pp. 151–169 at p. 154; Nikos Vafeas, "Further Evidence on Compensation Committee Composition as a Determinant of CEO Compensation" (2003) 32:2 *Financial Management* 53–70 at 69; Ronald C. Anderson and John M. Bizjak, "An Empirical Examination of the Role of the CEO and the Compensation Committee in Structuring Executive Pay" (2003) 27:7 *Journal of Banking and Finance* 1323–1348 at 1326.
42 Kam-Ming Wan, "Can Boards with a Majority of Independent Directors Lower CEO Compensation?" (2009), online: *SSRN*, https://ssrn.com/abstract=1421549 at 14; Martin J. Conyon and Simon I. Peck, "Board Control, Remuneration Committees, and Top Management Compensation" (1998) 41:2 *Academy Management Journal* 146–157 at 154 [Conyon and Peck, "Top Management Compensation"].
43 Conyon and Peck, "Top Management Compensation," above at note 42.
44 Lois Joy et al., "The Bottom Line: Corporate Performance and Women's Representation on Boards" (October 15, 2007), online (pdf): *Catalyst*, www.catalyst.org/wp-content/uploads/2019/01/The_Bottom_Line_Performance_and_Womens_Representation_on_Boards.pdf.
45 Bryce C. Tingle, "What Do We Really Know About Corporate Governance Best Practices? A Review of the Empirical Research Since 2000" (2017) 59:3 *Canadian Business Law Journal* 292–331 at note 96.
46 Daniel Ferreira, "Board Diversity" in R. Anderson and H. K. Baker (eds.), *Corporate Governance: A Synthesis of Theory, Research and Practice* (Hoboken: John Wiley & Sons, 2010), pp. 225–242 at pp. 235–236, 239.
47 *Ibid* at p. 232.
48 Renee Adams and Daniel Ferreira, "Women in the Boardroom and Their Impact on Governance and Performance" (2009) 94:2 *Journal of Financial Economics* 291–309 [Adams and Ferreira, "Women in the Boardroom"].
49 Niclas L. Erhardt, James D. Werbel and Charles B. Shrader, "Board of Director Diversity and Firm Financial Performance" (2003) 11:2 *Corporate Governance: An International Review* 102–111; Renee Adams and Daniel Ferreira, "Diversity and Incentives in Teams: Evidence from Corporate Boards" in *Essays on the Economics of Organizations*, PhD Dissertation, University of Chicago (2002); David A. Carter, Betty J. Simkins and W. Gary Simpson, "Corporate Governance, Board Diversity and Firm Value" (2003) 38:1 *Financial Review* 33–53.
50 Adams and Ferreira, "Women in the Boardroom," above at note 48; David A. Carter et al., "The Gender and Ethnic Diversity of U.S. Boards and Board Committees and Firm Financial Performance" (2010) 18:5 *Corporate Governance: An International Review* 396–414 [Carter et al., "Gender and Ethnic"].

51 Adams and Ferreira, "Women in the Boardroom," above at note 48 at 292; Carter et al., "Gender and Ethnic," above at note 50 at 397.

52 Yi Wang and Bob Clift, "Is There a 'Business Case' for Board Diversity?" (2009) 21:2 *Pacific Accounting Review* 88–103; Claude Francoeur, Réal Labelle and Bernard Sinclair-Desgangé, "Gender Diversity in Corporate Governance and Top Management" (2008) 81:1 *Journal of Business Ethics* 83–95; Toyah Miller and Maria del Carmen Triana, "Demographic Diversity in the Boardroom: Mediators of the Board Diversity – Firm Performance Relationship" (2009) 46:5 *Journal of Management Studies* 755–786 at 777; Adams and Ferreira, "Women in the Boardroom," above at note 48; Kassim Hussein and Bill Kiwia, "Examining the Relationship Between Female Board Members and Firm Performance – A Panel Study of US Firms" (2009) 18:2 *African Journal of Finance and Management* 20–31; Kathleen Farrell and Philip Hersch, "Additions to Corporate Boards: The Effect of Gender" (2005) 11:1 *Journal of Corporate Finance* 85–106; Frank Dobbin and Jiwook Jung, "Corporate Board Gender Diversity and Stock Performance: The Competence Gap or Institutional Investor Bias" (2011) 89:3 *North Carolina Law Review* 809–840; Carter et al., "Gender and Ethnic," above at note 50; Charles A. O'Reilly III and Brian G. M. Main, "Women in the Boardroom: Symbols or Substance?" (2012), *The Rock Center for Corporate Governance at Stanford University Working Paper Series No. 117*, online: SSRN, https://ssrn.com/abstract=2039524 [O'Reilly and Main, "Symbols or Substance"]; Felix von Meyerinck et al., "As California Goes, So Goes the Nation? Board Gender Quotas and Shareholders' Distaste of Government Interventions" (2022), *European Corporate Governance Institute – Finance Working Paper No. 785/2021*, online: SSRN, https://ssrn.com/abstract=3303798; Daniel Greene, Vincent J. Intintoli and Kathleen M. Kahle, "Do Board Gender Quotas Affect Firm Value? Evidence from California Senate Bill No. 826" (2020) 60 *Journal of Corporate Finance* 101526. See also, Sekou Bermiss, Jeremiah Green and John R. M. Hand, "Does Greater Diversity in Executive Race/Ethnicity Reliably Predict Better Future Firm Financial Performance?" (2023) *Journal of Economics, Race, and Policy* 1–16 (looking at racial diversity).

53 O'Reilly and Main, "Symbols or Substance," above at note 52; Tasawar Nawaz, "How Much Does the Board Composition Matter? The Impact of Board Gender Diversity on CEO Compensation" (2022) 14:18 *Sustainability* 11719. But see, Sascha Strobl, Dasaratha V. Rama and Suchismita Mishra, "Gender Diversity in Compensation Committees" (2016) 31:4 *Journal of Accounting, Auditing and Finance* 415–427 (found no significant correlation between female presence on the compensation committee and CEO pay); Alex Edmans, Caroline Flammer and Simon Glossner, "Diversity, Equity, and Inclusion" (2023), *National Bureau of Economic Research Working Paper No. 31215*, online: NBER, www.nber.org/papers/w31215 (finding no correlation between board diversity and treatment of diversity in the organization).

54 Eugene F. Fama and Michael C. Jensen, "Agency Problems and Residual Claims" (1983) 26:2 *The Journal of Law and Economics* 327–349 at 331; Eugene F. Fama and Michael C. Jensen, "Separation of Ownership and Control" (1983) 26:2 *The Journal of Law and Economics* 301–325 at 314–315.

55 Eugene Kang and Asghar Zardkoohi, "Board Leadership Structure and Firm Performance" (2005) 13:6 *Corporate Governance: An International Review* 785–799 at 793 [Kang and Zardkoohi, "Board Leadership"].

56 Brian Boyd, "CEO Duality and Firm Performance: A Contingency Model" (1995) 16:4 *Strategic Management Journal* 301–312 at 309 [Boyd, "CEO Duality"].

57 See Dan R. Dalton et al., "Meta-Analytic Reviews of Board Composition, Leadership Structure, and Financial Performance" (1998) 19:3 *Strategic Management Journal* 269–290.

58 Kang and Zardkoohi, "Board Leadership," above at note 55; Sanjai Bhagat, Brian J. Bolton and Roberta Romano, "The Promise and Peril of Corporate Governance Indices" (2008) 108:8 *Columbia Law Review* 1803–1882 at 1852–1853; Sanjai Bhagat and Brian Bolton, "Director Ownership, Governance, and Performance" (2013) 48:1 *Journal of Financial and Quantitative Analysis* 105–135; Elisabeth Dedman, "CEO Succession in the UK: An Analysis of the Effect of Censuring the CEO-to-Chair Move in the Combined Code on Corporate Governance 2003" (2016) 48:3 *The British Accounting Review* 359–378; David F. Larcker, Gaizka Ormazabal and Daniel J. Taylor, "The Market Reaction to Corporate Governance Regulation" (2011) 101:2 *Journal of Financial Economics* 431–448 at 433; Raghavan Iyengar and Ernest Zampelli, "Self-Selection, Endogeneity, and the Relationship Between CEO Duality and Firm Performance" (2009) 30:10 *Strategic Management Journal* 1092–1112 at 1111; Aiyesha Dey, Ellen Engel and Xiaohui Liu, "CEO and Board Chair Roles: To Split or Not to Split?" (2011) 17:5 *Journal of Corporate Finance* 1595–1618.

59 David H. Erkens, Mingyi Hung and Pedro Matos, "Corporate Governance in the 2007–2008 Financial Crisis: Evidence from Financial Institutions Worldwide" (2012) 18:2 *Journal of Corporate Finance* 389–411.

60 Ryan Krause, Matthew Semadeni and Albert A. Cannella, "CEO Duality: A Review and Research Agenda" (2014) 40:1 *Journal of Management* 256–286 [Krause, Semadeni and Cannella, "CEO Duality"].

61 Dan R. Dalton and Catherine M. Dalton, "Integration of Micro and Macro Studies in Governance Research: CEO Duality, Board Composition, and Financial Performance" (2011) 37:2 *Journal of Management* 404–411 at 408. See also, Krause, Semadeni and Cannella, "CEO Duality," above at note 60 at 282.

62 Krause, Semadeni and Cannella, "CEO Duality," above at note 60 at 264.

63 Jay Lorsch and Andy Zelleke, "Should the CEO be the Chairman?" (2005) 46:2 *MIT Sloan Management Review* 70–74; Richard Leblanc and Katharina Pick, *Separation of Chair and CEO Roles: Importance of Industry Knowledge, Leadership Skills, and Attention to Board Process*, The Conference Board (August 2011), online (pdf): www .yorku.ca/rleblanc/publish/Aug2011_Leblanc_TCB.pdf.

64 Jinyu He and Heli Wang, "Innovative Knowledge Assets and Economic Performance: The Asymmetric Roles of Incentives and Monitoring" (2009) 52:5 *Academy of Management Journal* 919–938.

65 Boyd, "CEO Duality," above at note 56 at 309.

66 Victor A. Ghazal, "CEO Duality and Corporate Stewardship: Evidence from Takeovers" (2015), online: *SSRN*, https://ssrn.com/abstract=2616464.

67 2021 *U.S. Spencer Stuart Board Index*, Spencer Stuart (2021), online (pdf): www.spencer stuart.com/-/media/2021/october/ssbi2021/us-spencer-stuart-board-index-2021.pdf at 18.

68 Keren Bar-Hava, Feng Gu and Baruch Lev, "Busy Directors are Detrimental to Corporate Governance" (January 2013), online (pdf): *Coller School of Management, Tel Aviv University*, https://en-coller.tau.ac.il/sites/nihul.tau.ac.il/files/management/semi nars/account/gu.pdf at 1.

69 Stephen P. Ferris, Murali Jagannathan and Adam C. Pritchard, "Too Busy to Mind the Business? Monitoring by Directors with Multiple Board Appointments" (2003) 58:3 *Journal of Finance* 1087–1111 at 1111.

70 Fich and Shivdasani, "Effective Monitors?," above at note 16.

71 George D. Cashman, Stuart L. Gillan and Chulhee Jun, "Going Overboard? On Busy Directors and Firm Value" (2012) 36:12 *Journal of Banking and Finance* 3248–3259 [Cashman, Gillan and Jun, "Going Overboard"]; Laura Field, Michelle Lowry and

Anahit Mkrtchyan, "Are Busy Boards Detrimental" (2013) 109:1 *Journal of Financial Economics* 63–82 [Field, Lowry and Mkrtchyan, "Busy Boards"].

72 Cashman, Gillan and Jun, "Going Overboard," above at note 71; Field, Lowry and Mkrtchyan, "Busy Boards," above at note 71 at 68.

73 Neither Fich and Shivdasani, "Effective Monitors?," above at note 16 nor Cashman, Gillan and Jun, "Going Overboard," above at note 71 corrected for endogeneity, see Field, Lowry and Mkrtchyan, "Busy Boards," above at note 71 at 77–78.

74 Field, Lowry and Mkrtchyan, "Busy Boards," above at note 71 at 66.

75 *Ibid* at 67.

76 *Ibid* at 81.

77 David F. Larcker, Eric C. So and Charles C. Y. Wang, "Boardroom Centrality and Firm Performance" (2013) 55:2–3 *Journal of Accounting and Economics* 225–250 at 248.

78 Field, Lowry and Mkrtchyan, "Busy Boards," above at note 71 at 81.

79 Timothy Taylor, "Corporate Boards: Stop Expecting the Impossible?," *Conversable Economist,* June 30, 2016, online: https://conversableeconomist.blogspot.com/2016/06/corporate-boards-stop-expecting.html citing Steven Bovie et al., "Are Boards Designed to Fail? The Implausibility of Effective Board Monitoring" (2016) 10:1 *Academy of Management Annals* 319–307 at 335. See also, Dan R. Dalton et al., "The Fundamental Agency Problem and Its Mitigation: Independence, Equity, and the Market for Corporate Control" in James P. Walsh and Arthur P. Brief (eds.), *The Academy of Management Annals,* (New York: Lawrence Erlbaum Associates, 2007), vol. 1, pp. 1–64 at p. 39.

80 David F. Larcker and Brian Tayan, "The Evolution of Corporate Governance: 2018 Study of Inception to IPO" (November 2018), online (pdf): *Stanford Graduate School of Business,* www.gsb.stanford.edu/sites/default/files/publication-pdf/cgri-survey-2018-corporate-governance-evolution.pdf; Steven Boivie et al., "Corporate Directors' Implicit Theories of the Roles and Duties of Boards" (2021) 42:9 *Strategic Management Journal* 1662–1695. See also, Myles L. Mace, *Directors, Myth and Reality* (Boston: Harvard Business School Press, 1971) at p. 179; Ada Demb and F.-Friedrich Neubauer, *The Corporate Board: Confronting the Paradoxes* (Oxford: Oxford University Press, 1992) at p. 13.

81 Nishant Dass et al., "Board Expertise: Do Directors from Related Industries Help Bridge the Information Gap?" (2014) 27:5 *The Review of Financial Studies* 1533–1592.

3

Can We Measure Corporate Governance?

For many members of the modern governance industry, the most appealing aspect of governance best practices is that they can be counted. For example, in the modern view, to evaluate the quality of a board of directors, an outside observer only needs to count the number of independent directors. This eliminates the difficult task of learning about the company, its specific business and strategic needs, directors' individual personalities and characters, as well as the group dynamics of the board. It is simply a matter of counting a thing (independent directors) that is easily observed from outside the company. It is this feature, more than any other, which permits the corporate governance industry to flourish. The dense array of public institutions, private firms, media outlets, and academic centers get to have an opinion about corporate governance because, in the modern governance regime, "good governance" is a simple matter of addition and subtraction, producing a bottom-line "score" or assessment of the corporation in question.

These governance scores are not only predicated on the idea that what matters in corporate governance can be counted, but they also assume that what might appear as entirely incommensurate things can, in fact, be made commensurate. In other words, the modern governance industry to some extent depends on the idea that you can determine that an independent director as chair (a positive) is equal to a compensation scheme that over-relies on stock options (a negative). If this strikes you as stupid, then you are a poor candidate to work in the corporate governance industry. You have to do this kind of math in order to determine whether Volkswagen has better governance than Ford.

By the beginning of this decade, investment funds purporting to invest according to evaluations of corporate governance managed more than $16.6 trillion in US-domiciled assets.[1] Measurements of corporate governance are the leading non-financial criteria taken into account by institutional investors (after avoiding companies in the tobacco industry or associated with repressive regimes).[2]

The important (but absurd) process of calculating the governance "score" or "rating" of firms takes the form of products like ISS' Governance QualityScore, MSCI's GovernanceMetrics score, and various governance-inflected indices provided by, among others, Dow Jones or London's FTSE Group. There are many different third parties engaged in this all-important work of adding and subtracting dozens (even hundreds) of governance best practices to arrive at net governance totals. I like to imagine them all wearing green eye shades and using old-fashioned calculating machines with long paper ribbons falling in piles on the floor, and at lunch getting into fights with accountants who stupidly only measure actual financial performance.

Companies have mostly dealt with the rise of these governance measurement schemes by either ignoring them, embracing them, or engaging in light fraud to fool them. The main way companies embrace the metrics is to actively work to improve their governance scores. A large industry of consultants has arisen to assist companies in making the necessary changes to their governance arrangements and disclosure practices. Even large, successful companies like GE and Aetna have reportedly hired advisors to recommend governance changes that will "boost their ratings."[3]

The poster child for the "light fraud" approach to the governance ratings is undoubtedly Volkswagen AG. On September 18, 2015, the US Environmental Protection Agency (EPA) issued a Notice of Violation indicating that for seven years Volkswagen AG had fraudulently sold cars that emitted pollutants up to 40 times higher than the standard. It had installed software on each car that detected when it was undergoing official emissions testing and altered the normal engine performance to hide its actual emissions profile. Something like this fraud might have been expected from Volkswagen. As *Fortune* observed, "The company has a history of scandals and episodes in which it skirted the law."[4] Subsequent reporting found major problems with Volkswagen's corporate governance, including a lack of checks and balances, regulatory failures arising from its close connections to German officials, the payment of bribes to directors, a succession of imperial CEOs, structural problems arising from its "two-tier" board, an ineffective whistle-blowing system (it allegedly failed in this case), and supine independent directors.[5]

It is surprising, therefore, that the same month the EPA filed its Notice of Violation, Volkswagen was named the Industry Group Leader in the Dow Jones Sustainability Index with full marks in a variety of corporate governance-related categories.[6] It had previously also headed the tables in 2013.[7] The company was included in the FTSE4Good Index, as well, which took three months to remove it.[8] Volkswagen's corporate governance was bad, but according to the proxies for good governance used by the Dow Jones and FTSE, it appeared good – or at least adequate. This sort of thing happens all the time in corporate governance, most famously in the case of Enron, an exemplar of good governance practices right up until the end.[9]

Volkswagen's bad governance was very expensive to its shareholders. The value of Volkswagen fell by more than 30 percent in the days after the EPA announcement, it paid almost $16.6 billion in settlements with owners and regulators, and over 500 class action lawsuits were filed against it. Lawsuits from investors alone exceeded $9 billion.

Ten years ago, the financial logic behind investing in good corporate governance dominated rating firms' marketing pitches, but in a telling transition, a rating firm like ISS now only promises to measure "governance risk."[10] ISS' current marketing language is an amusing exercise of carefully *not* saying why investors should care about "governance risk," or what "governance risk" actually is, but at the same time implying that the "governance risk" ISS measures is just like the other kinds of risk that go to investment returns. This carefully constructed, self-referential, and deliberately unhelpful marketing representation is the sort of thing top legal talent recommends when what you do (count "best practices") may be unconnected with what your clients care about (generating financial returns). MCSI, in contrast, is prepared to go way out on a limb and state that their ratings measure "a company's management of financially relevant ESG risks and opportunities."[11] Ten years ago, MCSI was confidently announcing its ratings were relevant "to generating long term sustainable investment returns."[12] Now, they are – barely – claiming "financial relevance" or at least the "management" of things that are "relevant."

When you get right down to it, no one cares about "good governance" for its own sake. Activists on Twitter (or *sigh* "X") are not going to mob the lead independent director of a firm that includes an insider on its Nomination and Governance Committee. It is not intrinsically wrong, unfair, or harmful to have an insider on a board committee. The only reason to care about this stuff is if you believe "good governance" is connected to positive financial outcomes.

There are some unconvincing attempts to link things like independent directors and equity incentives to desirable non-financial outcomes (like environmental performance), but they run into the problem that for decades the governance industry has emphasized the ways its calculation of good governance is firmly linked to shareholder value maximization, presumably at the expense of other financial claimants on the company's resources like employees and various species of endangered birds.

Later in the book, we will examine the various practices that are expected to produce better social and environmental outcomes. In this chapter, we take on the straightforward question of whether good governance ratings are, in fact, connected to better financial performance. This is the core claim, and it is the one that has the oldest and most extensive empirical literature.

3.1 COMMERCIAL RATING PROVIDERS

The largest commercial ratings firms are ISS and MSCI. ISS reviews approximately 280 governance factors spread across four general categories: board structure, compensation practices, shareholder rights, and audit practices. The identity of the factors is proprietary, but from what is publicly disclosed, they appear to all revolve around relatively standard "best practices" such as independent directors, board committees, compensation decisions, the presence of say-on-pay, and the use of takeover defenses.[13] (Just a few years ago, ISS reviewed "only" 200 governance factors, suggesting a geometric growth rate of factors normally exclusively seen when chopping the heads off hydras.[14]) MSCI's governance ratings are created through a relatively straightforward examination of 100 "key metrics."[15] The key metrics are also the typical governance best practices.

In the first decade of this century, there were two studies that found strong positive correlations between a high governance ranking and subsequent corporate performance, but both suffered from significant methodological problems. The first study, published in 2009, failed to take into account the ratings of companies that failed, merged, or declared bankruptcy during the five years of the study, introducing survivorship bias.[16] As well, the risk adjustments were not consistent with those used today in finance, casting significant doubt on the conclusions.[17] The second study had bigger problems: more than half of the returns attributed to the "high-performing" companies were derived from the risk adjustments made by the researchers, not from firm performance, and virtually all the excess returns were attributable to one anomalous year, 2009.[18] In other years, the returns vanished.

The largest and most methodologically sound study on the commercial rankings was published in 2010 and examined 5,059 company ratings by ISS, 1,565 ratings by Governance Metrics International (GMI) (now part of MSCI), and 1,906 ratings from The Corporate Library.[19] With respect to each of these corporate governance rankings, the study found no correlation between a company's governance score and future accounting restatements, class-action lawsuits, accounting operating performance (return on assets), market-to-book ratio, and stock price performance. The authors concluded, "these governance ratings have either limited or no success in predicting firm performance or other outcomes of interest to shareholders."[20]

More recent research has tended to concentrate on "ESG" ratings, which purport to include corporate governance scores along with environmental and social non-financial factors. These scores are then often weighted in various ways to create indices.[21] There are a number of companies that provide ESG ratings.

Evaluating the merits of the "governance" portion of commercial ESG indices is difficult for several reasons. First, many empirical studies on the performance of ESG-driven portfolios do not decompose the various elements of the ESG indices, so it is difficult to see what role the governance ratings (as opposed to the environmental and social ratings) are playing in the overall success or failure of the portfolio. Second, the distributions in scores tend to be highly concentrated, only poorly differentiating firms.[22] Finally, the literature generally presents endogeneity issues that the research frequently does not address, for example, whether ESG practices produce better performance, or whether these practices instead follow superior performance (as success allows companies to spend more money on ESG investments).[23] Alternatively, the correlations found in some of the literature may actually be to firm size (as big companies tend to score better in ESG rankings than smaller firms) or industry composition (as companies in some industries, such as technology, do better in the rankings than, say, those in resource extraction).[24]

Nevertheless, there is some research that does cast light on the capacity of corporate governance ratings to predict corporate outcomes. Nearly all of it finds that the corporate governance scores that make up the leading ESG indices have no statistically measurable impact on performance. For example, a 2009 attempt to measure the impact of each category of ESG ratings on corporate outcomes using three different performance benchmarks found that while scores in the "community," "employee relations," and "environmental" categories had a positive relationship with performance, the impact of the "governance" score was negative.[25] A 2014 study attempting to correct for several deficiencies in earlier research found that during the period 1997–2007, the governance scores awarded by the leading ESG ratings firm (now part of MSCI) had little relationship with corporate success.[26] The authors comment, "This is in line with most of the literature regarding the effectiveness of the governance indices in predicting corporate performance."[27] Since 2000, at least six peer-reviewed academic studies have found that the corporate governance portion of ESG ratings is unconnected to corporate performance.[28] This effect persists across time, different measures of performance, and different rating agencies.

As we will see in Chapter 12, studies that compare ESG ratings awarded by different providers to the same company have very low rates of correlation. To take one example, a recent study looking at six well-established ESG ratings datasets found low convergence in their assessments of firms. Companies that were highly rated according to one system were low-rated in the others. These differences in outcome persisted even after adjusting for variations in what ratings firms claimed they were measuring. Thus, "the low agreement implies all or almost all of the ratings have low validity."[29] Helpfully for our purposes, the study broke out ESG sub-categories and found that correlations between the corporate governance scores of different firms were among the lowest of any category. The researchers point out the implications: "If the ratings are invalid, then investors do not know which firms are the most responsible and risk misallocating trillions of dollars in capital,"[30] and "if firms expend resources to achieve high scores on invalid metrics, then even well-intended attention to social metrics reduces social welfare."[31]

3.2 ACADEMIC GOVERNANCE RATINGS

Perhaps the failure of commercial governance rating schemes is not surprising. Commercial governance actors are in the business of making money, and sometimes that involves selling toys coated in lead paint. Customers of these kinds of companies are generally not expected to continue to happily ingest lead, particularly when the deficiencies in the product are pretty easy to discover. However, as we will see in Chapter 7, the market for corporate governance data is special, in that it is largely comprised of parents who don't really care that much about what happens to their children.

Academics, however, are free of commercial imperatives. They don't face the time constraints of generating ratings on thousands of companies every year, and they don't need to invent some recondite process that goes beyond simply counting independent directors and looking at whether the CEO gets free use of the corporate jet. Academics are presumably concerned only with discovering the "truth" about corporate governance and then publishing it to the acclaim of the tiny audience that cares. Unfortunately, it turns out that academic efforts to score corporate governance fail just as comprehensively.

The first large-scale academic effort to develop a model that measures governance quality appeared in 2003 and reflected data on about 1,500 US public corporations for the period between 1990 and 1999.[32] Often referred to in the literature as the "G-Index," the 24 variables used in the model consist of measuring various best practices, heavily weighted towards antitakeover protections.

The authors of the study believe the index reflects the heart of corporate governance because it reflects "the balance of power between shareholders and managers."[33] (Note this reflects the modern view that corporate governance consists of controlling agency costs rather than facilitating operational outcomes.) The study found that a strategy of buying the highest-ranking companies and shorting the lowest-ranking would earn impressive abnormal returns. The study has been enormously influential in other research where the G-Index is used, often uncritically, as a measure of the quality of companies' governance.

Several studies have been published re-evaluating the G-Index. By and large, they have had the effect of casting doubt on the merits of the G-Index as a measure of corporate governance quality.[34] One study published in 2006 found that if the time period in the analysis was extended to include 2000–2003, the G-Index failed to predict outcomes.[35] Indeed, the highest-ranked firms in the G-Index actually underperformed the lowest-ranked firms during these four years. Other studies looked at firm performance in the 1980s, before takeover defenses were adopted, and provided evidence that causation ran opposite to the G-Index authors' assumptions. Poorly performing firms adopted takeover protections (no doubt because they felt vulnerable) and this, rather than governance failures, is responsible for the association of performance with the G-Index ratings in the 1990s.[36] Finally, researchers looked into the predictive validity of the G-Index and found that it does not distinguish firms that will have major scandals from those that will not.[37]

In 2009, Harvard law professor Lucien Bebchuk and several co-authors attempted to improve the predictability of the G-Index by removing those variables in the model that had not previously been identified as correlated with corporate performance.[38] They proposed an "entrenchment" index or "E-index," that consists of a sub-set of just six factors that go to the quality of governance in a company: restrictions on the ability of shareholders to amend the bylaws and corporate charter, the requirement of a super-majority to approve a merger, the use of golden parachutes, the presence of a poison pill, and the existence of a staggered board (this is a board on which directors serve multi-year terms, so it takes a shareholder activist at least two years to elect a majority). The logic is that "entrenched management" is not subject to the disciplining effects of the market for corporate control, and a high E-Index score indicates a dismissive attitude towards the interests of shareholders as well as a possibly supine board.

Bebchuk and his co-authors ranked companies on their E-Index criteria for the period 1990–2003 and evaluated the returns that would be generated by shorting the worst-governed (high E-Index) companies while buying the best (low E-Index). Like the G-Index before them, they found this trading strategy would generate abnormal returns. This study has also been very influential among scholars. According to data on Professor Bebchuk's website, the E-Index has been used by over 1,000 studies since its publication.[39] It was also, at least for a time, the basis for commercial governance rankings provided by the proxy advisor Glass Lewis.

A lot of subsequent research has again cast doubt on the accuracy of the E-Index as a measure of governance quality.[40] A closer examination of the excess returns discovered by Bebchuk and his colleagues found these returns were actually driven by the different industry compositions of the long and short portfolios – not by differences in governance features.[41] Once industry differences in the portfolios were accounted for, neither the G-Index nor the E-Index were able to predict outcomes.

Another study found some correlation between the two indices and operating performance, but no correlation at all with future stock market performance.[42] Firms ranking as better governed under the two indices turned out to be *less* likely to experience management turnover in cases of poor performance.[43] (So much for the assumptions about what signals managerial "entrenchment.") Finally, a recent paper looked at both the E-Index and the G-Index and after correcting for measurement errors in the underlying data, concluded neither was associated with statistically significant investment outcomes.[44]

The failure of the two most prominent academic indices to differentiate well-governed firms from their opposites has concerning consequences. The G-Index and E-Index studies are the most commonly referenced evidence that the modern version of corporate governance "matters." Worse, a great deal of finance literature assumes these indices correspond in some relevant way with corporate governance, so the indices are used as dependent variables when examining other questions. The conclusions of all these other papers are thus rendered suspect.

The only response to criticisms of these indices came in 2010, when the authors of the E-Index published a paper admitting the abnormal returns to low E-Index companies they described as existing in the 1990s had disappeared in the subsequent decade.[45] They attribute this change to the market coming to fully price the value of good governance. Even if this is true (as opposed to the E-Index being simply mistaken), all it demonstrates is that a market using the E-Index (or similar schemes) to measure governance is giving a mistaken premium to companies that score well on the E-Index. It doesn't tell us anything about what we really care about: the impact of the E-Index on the performance of the underlying business.

It would be strange if the E-Index or G-Index actually did have any inherent predictive ability as they are mostly measuring nonsense. Professor Michael Klausner points out that all but one of the takeover defenses measured by the E-Index and the G-Index either have no actual real-world impact, have an impact only under limited circumstances, or are demonstrably positive for corporate governance.[46] For example, the presence or absence of a poison pill in the day-to-day life of US companies means little when a pill can be introduced at any time in the face of a hostile bid. Directors are aware of the availability of a pill when needed and so its absence at other times signifies nothing. It is hard to believe that indices made up of these red herrings are producing real-world effects.

There have been other academic attempts to assemble a collection of best practices and measure their outcomes, but as one academic survey of the literature observed, these studies "have not yielded much evidence that these 'usual suspects' have any meaningful connection to firm performance."[47] A meta-analysis of over 100 studies of CEO roles, board structure, board size, and director shareholdings failed to find any predictable relationship between these factors and investment outcomes.[48] A recent study using machine learning to evaluate 100 different corporate governance practices concluded that these practices had "a trivial causal effect relative to firm characteristics, if any."[49]

3.3 GOVERNANCE RANKINGS PRODUCED BY REGULATORY ACTION

Securities regulators have inadvertently joined academics and commercial firms in the enterprise of testing best practices. In the USA, these practices are often mandatory, whereas Canada and the UK have largely adopted a "comply or explain" regime.[50] Companies are not required to adopt a particular practice but must report annually to explain their decision. In reality, there are strong pressures, particularly from institutional shareholders and proxy advisory firms, to adopt the best practices.[51] Nevertheless, comply or explain regimes afford researchers an opportunity to compare the performance of firms fully compliant with best practices with those that only partially comply. This provides us with another rating system for governance that can be compared to corporate performance.

The UK regime has produced a number of studies, all of which suggest that fully compliant firms do not outperform partial adopters. One of the most commonly cited studies, published in 2005, found only weak evidence that compliance with the UK Combined Code is correlated with stock price performance and no evidence that compliance is correlated with operating performance.[52] Several other studies have failed to find positive outcomes associated with full compliance, looking specifically at asset-to-market value ratios (Tobin's Q).[53]

3.4 SUMMARY – EXPLAINING THE FAILURE OF GOVERNANCE RATINGS

There are three possible ways of understanding the failures of corporate governance ratings to predict real-world outcomes.

The first is that the best practices reflected in the ratings are correct, but errors exist in the collection and analysis of data. Companies that should be rated as poorly governed are mistakenly categorized as better than they are, not because the models are wrong, but because of human error. This is not a problem to be taken lightly. In order for a company's governance arrangements to be evaluated, the accurate identification of multiple board processes, compensation practices, and the terms of various legal agreements must be understood and recorded correctly. One set of scholars note "the commercial ratings contain a large amount of measurement error."[54] There is ample evidence from other sources that the often inadequately trained and temporary employees of proxy advisors such as ISS regularly make mistakes of this sort in related work streams.

The problem with attributing the failure of governance ratings to measurement error is the sheer number of ratings – commercial, academic, and "regulatory" – that fail to predict future corporate performance. While academic governance indices typically rely on limited numbers of databases, the commercial firms – ISS and MSCI – have access to vast, proprietary datasets they generate themselves. The data used in Canada and the UK to evaluate the merits of the comply or explain regime are created from yet other databases.

Finally, even when academics go back to the underlying data and correct the errors, the results generated by the ratings models still fail to provide statistically significant guidance.[55] It seems unlikely that the problem with governance rankings is primarily errors made in assembling the data.

The second possibility is that the indices of best practices we have been examining contain the wrong best practices. This incurably optimistic approach involves hoping that there are, in fact, corporate structures and compensation mechanisms that will produce superior results across disparate companies and industries, but they are not the ones contained in the commercial, academic, or regulatory indices of best practices we have discussed. Several academic studies proposing measurement schemes less prominent than the ones we have been evaluating make this claim. Again, the range of governance ratings we have examined, all of which contain slightly different best practices and use different schemes for weighting those practices, makes this possibility less likely. It seems unlikely that crucial best practices capable of explaining and predicting future corporate performance have been neglected or ignored by the many academics, regulators, and commercial firms attempting to measure corporate governance.

Finally, there is the third possibility: best practices don't tell you much of what you need to know about how a company is actually being governed. No indices of best practices will produce useful predictive information because there is a difference between actual good governance and "best practices," and the indices measure only the adoption of best practices. That is, the rating models fail statistically because they mostly measure noise. As we saw in Chapter 2, when various best practices are examined in isolation, they appear to fail to predict anything we care about. It shouldn't be surprising that when aggregated into rating models they continue to fail to predict anything useful.

NOTES

1 *Report on US Sustainable and Impact Investing Trends 2020*, US SIF Foundation (2020), online (pdf): www.ussif.org/files/Trends/2020_Trends_Highlights_OnePager.pdf at 1.
2 *Report on US Sustainable, Responsible and Impact Investing Trends 2014*, US SIF Foundation: The Forum for Sustainable and Responsible Investment (2014), online (pdf): www.ussif.org/Files/Publications/SIF_Trends_14.F.ES.pdf at 13–14.
3 Robert M. Daines, Ian D. Gow and David F. Larcker, "Rating the Ratings: How Good Are Commercial Governance Ratings?" (2010) 98:3 *Journal of Financial Economics* 439–461 at 440 [Daines, Gow and Larcker, "Rating the Ratings"]. See also, Sharon Muli, "Sustainability Rankings: Impacts on Corporate Sustainability," Masters of Environmental Studies Capstone Project, University of Pennsylvania (2013), online (pdf): http://repository.upenn.edu/cgi/viewcontent.cgi?article=1053&context=mes_capstones at 35–36.
4 Geoffrey Smith and Roger Parloff, "Hoaxwagon: How the Massive Diesel Fraud Incinerated VW's Reputation – and Will Hobble the Company for Years to Come," *Fortune*, March 7, 2016, online: http://fortune.com/inside-volkswagen-emissions-scandal/. See also, Mark Odell, "Volkswagen: A History of Scandals," *Financial Times*, September 23, 2015, online: www.ft.com/cms/s/0/22ca0e9a-6159-11e5-9846-de406ccb37f2.html [Odell, "Volkswagen"].
5 Odell, "Volkswagen," above at note 4. See also, Dina Medland, "Volkswagen: When 'Hubris' Leads to a Corporate Governance Disaster – and Shareholder Pain," *Forbes*, March 12, 2016, online: www.forbes.com/sites/dinamedland/2016/03/12/volkswagen-when-hubris-leads-to-a-corporate-governance-disaster-and-shareholder-pain/#6ebc1a5a163f; Charles M. Elson, Craig K. Ferrere and Nicholas J. Goossen, "The Bug at Volkswagen: Lessons in Co-determination, Ownership and Board Structure" (2015) 27:4 *Journal of Applied Corporate Finance* 36–43 at 36.
6 Volkswagen News Release, "Volkswagen is World's Most Sustainable Automotive Group" (September 11, 2015), online: *Automotive World*, www.automotiveworld.com/news-releases/volkswagen-worlds-sustainable-automotive-group/.
7 *Ibid.*
8 *FTSE4 Good Semi-Annual Review December 2015*, FTSE Russell (December 8, 2015), online: www.ftserussell.com/press/ftse4good-semi-annual-review-december-2015.
9 See John C. Coffee, *Gatekeepers: The Professions and Corporate Governance* (Oxford: Oxford University Press, 2006) (for six consecutive years, it resided on Fortune's annual list of America's "Most Admired" corporations and in 2001, it was ranked second in "quality of management" at p. 18), p. 25. See also, Bethany McLean and Peter Elkind, *The Smartest Guys in the Room: The Amazing Rise and Scandalous Fall of Enron* (New York: Penguin, 2013) at p. 239.
10 Bryce C. Tingle, "What is Corporate Governance? Can We Measure It? Can Investment Fiduciaries Rely on It?" (2018) 43:2 *Queen's Law Journal* 223–262 at 236 [Tingle, "Can We

Measure It"]; *Governance QualityScore*, Institutional Shareholder Services Inc., online: www.issgovernance.com/esg/ratings/governance-qualityscore/.

11	*ESG Ratings*, MSCI Inc., online: www.msci.com/our-solutions/esg-investing/esg-ratings.

12	Tingle, "Can We Measure It," above at note 10 at 236.

13	*Governance QualityScore: Methodology Fundamentals*, International Shareholder Services Inc. (November 9, 2022), available online: www.issgovernance.com/esg/ratings/governance-qualityscore/.

14	Tingle, "Can We Measure It," above at note 10 at 239.

15	*MSCI ESG Ratings Methodology: Accounting Key Issue*, MSCI ESG Research LLC (October 2022) (listing one key metric); *MSCI ESG Ratings Methodology: Board Key Issue*, MSCI ESG Research LLC (April 2023) (listing forty one key metrics); *MSCI ESG Ratings Methodology: Business Ethics Key Issue*, MSCI ESG Research LLC (October 2022) (listing nine key metrics); *MSCI ESG Ratings Methodology: Ownership & Control Key Issue*, MSCI ESG Research LLC (October 2022) (listing twenty six key metrics); *MSCI ESG Ratings Methodology: Pay Key Issue*, MSCI ESG Research LLC (October 2022) (listing twenty two key metrics); *MSCI ESG Ratings Methodology: Tax Transparency Key Issue*, MSCI ESG Research LLC (October 2022) (listing one key metric), all available online: www.msci.com/our-solutions/esg-investing/esg-ratings.

16	G. Kevin Spellman and Robert Watson, "Corporate Governance Ratings and Corporate Performance: An Analysis of Governance Metrics International (GMI) Ratings of US Firms 2003 to 2008" (2009), online: SSRN, https://ssrn.com/abstract=1392313.

17	David Larcker and Brian Tayan, *Corporate Governance Matters: A Closer Look at Organizational Choices and their Consequences* (Upper Saddle River, USA: FT Press, 2011) at pp. 445, 456 note 23 [Larcker and Tayan, *Corporate Governance Matters*].

18	The study is: Quantitative Services Group (QSG), "Finding Value in Corporate Governance: Does it Impact Equity Returns?" (March 2010) QSG Equity Research. See a discussion of its problems in Larcker and Tayan, *Corporate Governance Matters*, above at note 17 at p. 445.

19	Daines, Gow and Larcker, "Rating the Ratings", above at note 3 at 443–444.

20	*Ibid* at 460. See also, Rob Bauer, Nadja Guenster and Rogér Otten, "Empirical Evidence on Corporate Governance in Europe: The Effect on Stock Returns, Firm Value and Performance" (2004) 5:2 *Journal of Asset Management* 91–104 at 101.

21	See Mei Sun, Katsuya Nagata and Hiroshi Onoda, "The Investigation of the Current Status of Socially Responsible Investment Indices" (2011) 3:13 *Journal of Economics and International Finance* 676–684 at 678–683; Aaron Chatterji and David Levine "Breaking Down the Wall of Codes: Evaluating Non-Financial Performance Measurement" (2006) 48:2 *California Management Review* 29–51.

22	Marco Nicolosi, Stefano Grassi and Elena Stanghellini, "Item Response Models to Measure Corporate Social Responsibility" (2014) 24:22 *Applied Financial Economics* 1449–1464 at 1453 [Nicolosi, Grassi and Stanghellini, "Item Response Models"]; Stephen Brammer, Chris Brooks and Stephen Pavelin, "Corporate Social Performance and Stock Returns: UK Evidence from Disaggregate Measures" (2006) 35:3 *Financial Management* 97–116 at 101–102.

23	Nicolosi, Grassi and Stanghellini, "Item Response Models," above at note 22 at 1463. See also, Marc Orlitzky, Frank L. Schmidt and Sara L. Rynes, "Corporate Social and Financial Performance: A Meta-analysis" (2003) 24:3 *Organization Studies* 403–441; Philipp Schreck, "Reviewing the Business Case for Corporate Social Responsibility: New Evidence and Analysis" (2011) 103:2 *Journal of Business Ethics* 167–188 [Schreck, "Business Case"].

24 See Aaron K. Chatterji and Barak D. Richman, "Understanding the 'Corporate' in Corporate Social Responsibility" (2008) 2:1 *Harvard Law and Policy Review* 33–52 at 34; Masud Chand, "The Relationship Between Corporate Social Performance and Corporate Financial Performance: Industry Type as a Boundary Condition" (2006) 5:1 *The Business Review* 240–245 at 243; Philip L. Baird, Pinar Celikkol Geylani and Jeffrey A. Roberts, "Corporate Social and Financial Performance Re-Examined: Industry Effects in a Linear Mixed Model Analysis" (2012) 109:3 *Journal of Business Ethics* 367–388.

25 Meir Statman and Denys Glushkov, "The Wages of Social Responsibility" (2009) 65:4 *Financial Analysts Journal* 33–46 at 39 [Statman and Glushkov, "Social Responsibility"].

26 Nicolosi, Grassi and Stanghellini, "Item Response Models," above at note 22 at 1458.

27 *Ibid* at 1458.

28 Cristiana Manescu, "Stock Returns in Relation to Environmental, Social and Governance Performance: Mispricing or Compensation for Risk?" (2011) 19:2 *Sustainable Development* 95–118 at 111; Andrij Fetsun and Dirk Söhnholz, "A Quantitative Approach to Responsible Investment: Using a ESG-Multifactor Model to Improve Equity Portfolios" (2014), *Working Paper, Veritas Investment Research Corporation*, online (pdf): https://naaim .org/wp-content/uploads/2014/04/00P_Dr_Fetsun_Dr_Soehnholz_A_Quantitative_ Approach.pdf at 2, 5; Dolf Diemont, Kyle Moore and Aloy Soppe, "The Downside of Being Responsible: Corporate Social Responsibility and Tail Risk" (2016) 137:2 *Journal of Business Ethics* 213–239 at 224–225; Benjamin R. Auer and Frank Schuhmacher, "Do Socially (Ir)responsible Investments Pay? New Evidence from International Data" (2016) 59 *The Quarterly Review of Economics and Finance* 51–62 at 61; Statman and Glushkov, "Social Responsibility," above at note 25; Nicolosi, Grassi and Stanghellini, "Item Response Models," above at note 22. But see, Schreck, "Business Case," above at note 23 (the paper finds a positive association between corporate governance and equity-market measures of performance, but fails to find the expected evidence the former causes the latter, possibly as a result of limitations in the dataset).

29 Aaron K. Chatterji et al., "Do Ratings of Firms Converge? Implications for Managers, Investors and Strategy Researchers: Do Ratings of Firms Converge?" (2016) 37:8 *Strategic Management Journal* 1597–1614 at 1598.

30 *Ibid* at 1607.

31 *Ibid* at 1598.

32 Paul Gompers, Joy Ishii and Andrew Metrick, "Corporate Governance and Equity Prices" (2003) 118:1 *The Quarterly Journal of Economics* 107–156.

33 *Ibid* at 109.

34 K. J. Martijn Cremers and Vinay B. Nair, "Governance Mechanisms and Equity Prices" (2005) 60:6 *Journal of Finance (New York)* 2859–2894. See also, Sanjai Bhagat, Brian J. Bolton and Roberta Romano, "The Promise and Peril of Corporate Governance Indices" (2008) 108:8 *Columbia Law Review* 1803–1882 at 1846.

35 John E. Core, Wayne R. Guay and Tjomme Rusticus, "Does Weak Governance Cause Weak Stock Returns? An Examination of Firm Operating Performance and Investor Expectations" (2006) 61:2 *Journal of Finance (New York)* 655–687 at 683.

36 Kenneth Lehn, Sukesh Patro and Mengxin Zhao, "Governance Indices and Valuation Multiples: Which Causes Which?" (2007) 13:5 *Journal of Corporate Finance* 907–928.

37 Aaron K. Chatterji and David I. Levine, "Imitate or Differentiate? Evaluating the Validity of Corporate Social Responsibility Ratings" (2008), online: *UC Berkeley Center for Responsible Business*, http://escholarship.org/uc/item/3sz7k7jc#page-1.

38 Lucian A. Bebchuk, Alma Cohen and Allen Ferrell, "What Matters in Corporate Governance?" (2009) 22:2 *The Review of Financial Studies* 783–827 at 784–787.

39 Lucian Arye Bebchuk, *Links to 1002 Studies that Use the Entrenchment Index* (June 2023), online: *Harvard University Law*, www.law.harvard.edu/faculty/bebchuk/studies.shtml.

40 See for example, Dean Diavatopoulos and Andy Fodor, "Does Corporate Governance Matter for Equity Returns?" (2016) 16:5 *Journal of Accounting and Finance* 39–59; Lucien A. Bebchuk, Alma Cohen and Charles C. Y. Wang, "Learning and the Disappearing Association Between Governance and Returns" (2013) 108:2 *Journal of Financial Economics* 323–348 [Bebchuk, Cohen and Wang, "Learning"]; Larcker and Tayan, *Corporate Governance Matters,* above at note 17 at p. 453.

41 Shane A. Johnson, Theodore C. Moorman and Sorin Sorescu, "A Reexamination of Corporate Governance and Equity Prices" (2009) 22:11 *Review of Financial Studies* 4753–4786. But see, Xavier Giroud and Holger Mueller, "Corporate Governance, Product Market Competition, and Equity Prices" (2011) 66:2 *Journal of Finance (New York)* 563–600 at 578–579 (arguing that the E-Index is predictive of performance if a larger dataset is used, though only for companies in noncompetitive industries).

42 Sanjai Bhagat and Brian Bolton, "Corporate Governance and Firm Performance" (2008) 14:3 *Journal of Corporate Finance* 257–273.

43 *Ibid* at 271.

44 David F. Larcker, Peter C. Reiss and Youfei Xiao, "Corporate Governance Data and Measures Revisited" (2015), *Rock Center for Corporate Governance Working Paper Series No. 211,* online: *SSRN,* https://ssrn.com/abstract=2694803 [Larcker, Reiss and Xiao, "Corporate Governance Data"].

45 Bebchuk, Cohen and Wang, "Learning," above at note 40.

46 Michael Klausner, "Fact and Fiction in Corporate Law and Governance" (2013) 65:6 *Stanford Law Review* 1325–1370.

47 Yangmin Kim and Albert A. Cannella, Jr., "Toward a Social Capital Theory of Director Selection" (2008) 16:4 *Corporate Governance: An International Review* 282–293 at 282.

48 David Finegold, George S. Benson and David Hecht, "Corporate Boards and Company Performance: Review of Research in Light of Recent Reforms" (2007) 15:5 *Corporate Governance: An International Review* 865–878. See also, Sydney Finkelstein and Ann C. Mooney, "Not the Usual Suspects: How to Use Board Process to Make Boards Better" (2003) 17:2 *Academy of Management Perspectives* 101–113.

49 Ian D. Gow, David F. Larcker and Anastasia A. Zakolyukina, "How Important is Corporate Governance? Evidence from Machine Learning" (2023), *Chicago Booth Research Paper No. 22–16,* online: *SSRN,* https://ssrn.com/abstract=4231644 at 23.

50 *The UK Corporate Governance Code,* Financial Reporting Council (July 2018), online: www.frc.org.uk/directors/corporate-governance-and-stewardship/uk-corporate-governance-code; *Rules and Policies – National Policy 58-201: Corporate Governance Guidelines,* Ontario Securities Commission (June 17, 2005), online (pdf): www.osc.gov.on.ca/documents/en/Securities-Category5/rule_20050617_58-201_corp-gov-guidelines.pdf.

51 *Corporate Governance Review 2019,* Grant Thornton (2019), available online: www2 .grantthornton.co.uk/Corporate-governance-review-2019.html at 41.

52 Carol Padgett and Amama Shabbir, "The UK Code of Corporate Governance: Link Between Compliance and Firm Performance" (2005), *ICMA Centre Finance Discussion Paper No. DP2005-17,* online: *SSRN,* https://ssrn.com/abstract=934313. See also, Amama Shabbir, "To Comply or Not to Comply: Evidence on Changes and Factors Associated with the Changes in Compliance with the UK Code of Corporate Governance" (2008), online: *SSRN,* https://ssrn.com/abstract=1101412.

53 Nikos Vafeas and Elina Theodorou, "The Relationship Between Board Structure and Firm Performance in the UK" (1998) 30:4 *The British Accounting Review* 383–407;

Charlie Weir, David Laing and Phillip J. McKnight, "Internal and External Governance Mechanisms: Their Impact on the Performance of Large UK Companies" (2002) 29:5–6 *Journal of Business Finance and Accounting* 579–611 at 601, 604; Amama Shaukat and Grzegorz Trojanowski, "Board Governance and Corporate Performance" (2018) 45:1–2 *Journal of Business Finance and Accounting* 184–208 at 187, 204. See also, Fodil Adjaoud, Daniel Zeghal and Syed Andaleeb, "The Effect of Board's Quality on Performance: A Study of Canadian Firms" (2007) 15:4 *Corporate Governance: An International Review* 623–635; Lorne N. Switzer and Catherine Kelly, "Corporate Governance Mechanisms and the Performance of Small-cap Firms in Canada" (2006) 2:3–4 *International Journal of Business Governance and Ethics* 294–328.

54 Daines, Gow and Larcker, "Rating the Ratings," above at note 3 at 440. See also, Larcker, Reiss and Xiao, "Corporate Governance Data," above at note 44 at 5.

55 Larcker, Reiss and Xiao, "Corporate Governance Data," above at note 44.

4

Do We Understand Executive Compensation
Best Practices?

There are many ways of understanding executive compensation. An entirely logical approach is to consider supply and demand: how many good executives are there? How many firms need them? Fancier approaches look at the fundamental drivers of supply and demand by characterizing the market value of an individual as a function of their marginal contributions to firm productivity. The more productive an employee, the more valuable they become. (This is why, for example, most of America's inequality problems appear to be the result of differences between pay at productive and less productive firms, rather than a result of differences in pay within firms.[1]) There is also the classical economic approach, now only really found among Marxists and Twitter users, that believes pay is connected to the amount of effort put into making a product, less the amount extracted by the factory owner.

The most popular way of characterizing executive compensation in modern corporate governance discussions, however, is as an instantiation of agency costs. A good example is provided by Thomas Piketty in his nonfiction treatment of the *Hunger Games* trilogy. In *Capital in the Twenty-First Century*, Piketty argues that inequality-causing executive compensation is relatively arbitrary (because determining the marginal productivity of executives is nearly impossible) and driven primarily by corporate governance considerations, namely that executives essentially set their own salary.[2]

Piketty's identification of the morally suspect reasons for executive pay growth reflects the dominant consensus. Since the publication of Jensen and Meckling's *Theory of the Firm*, executive pay practices have been seen primarily as illustrating a particular version of agency cost theory. In its full sense, any pay at all given to executives is an agency cost, as it is part of the expense attached to employing an agent. But no corporate officer would work if they weren't being paid, so the focus of corporate governance is on what we might call "inefficient" pay: compensation in excess of what the agent would accept to do their job, or compensation that establishes perverse incentives. In the version of the agency cost story that we are considering in this book, inefficient pay practices are understood to be the result of conflicts of interest and negligence on the part of executives and boards.

4.1 THE RECENT HISTORY OF EXECUTIVE PAY

As we saw in the Introduction to this book, CEO pay was much lower for most of the twentieth century. Median CEO pay in the United States stayed constant, around $1 million a year, between the 1940s and 1970s.[3] But between 1978 and 2020, average CEO compensation in America's largest companies increased by 1,322 percent in real terms.[4] For perspective, the average wage of nonmanagement employees rose only 5.7 percent over approximately the same period.[5] The ratio of CEO pay to that of the median employee was 31:1 in 1978, 118:1 in 1995, and 351:1 in 2020.[6]

Even for those monsters who don't care about income inequality, there is still plenty of bad news. As we noted in the Introduction, the growth in CEO compensation has also outstripped the returns to shareholders: CEO pay growth has doubled the rise of the S&P Index over the past thirty years, and payments to the five highest-paid senior executives have doubled the percentage of profits they consume. In 1993 payments to the five highest-paid senior executives in a US company absorbed, on average, 5 percent of its profits; by 2003, this had increased to 10 percent.[7]

There is one obviously weird thing about this trend: the rise in executive pay appears to correspond almost perfectly with the rise of the modern corporate governance regime. Did the modern corporate governance regime arise in reaction to the increasing pay, or did it somehow cause the rise in pay? If the modern governance regime didn't cause the rise in pay, what did? Almost certainly, the automatic tendency of the governance industry to blame the greed of executives and the pusillanimity of boards is wrong. Cowardice and avarice existed in corporate boardrooms before the explosion in executive pay levels in the 1990s. As we shall see, it is suspicious, as well, that the leap in executive pay was largely driven by the use of the very pay strategies recommended by the governance industry.

4.2 EXECUTIVE PAY BEST PRACTICES

Modern corporate governance has two slightly contradictory philosophies about executive compensation. The first is that the main purpose of executive compensation is to align the interests of corporate managers with those of their principals, the shareholders. This follows quite naturally from agency cost theory and has historically taken the form of awarding managers stock options, granting them shares, requiring them to purchase shares (often with loans from the company), or using some form of cash bonus plan that tracks the economic performance of the corporation's equity.

The second philosophy is that executive compensation should, as precisely as possible, track the performance of the executive in question. In other words, compensation should not reflect returns to shareholders but rather the executives' contribution to value, measured in relation to some formal metric such as achieving a revenue target or outperforming competitors. This "pay-for-performance" philos-ophy obviously contradicts the "shareholder alignment" approach, as the former pays out even if the share price declines (so long as the CEO achieves their targets), while the latter pays out even if share prices increase because of something (like a change in commodity prices) unconnected to a CEO's actions.

Shareholder alignment was probably the dominant governance idea in the 1980s and 1990s, but since the beginning of this century, pay-for-performance has increas-ingly been seen as the most important compensation objective. (The giant equity-driven payouts by objectively badly run firms in the late 1990s, symbolized by Enron, had a great deal to do with this shift in sentiment.)

The change to performance-based pay best practices has resulted in a great deal of scorn being heaped by the governance industry on things like stock options and loans to purchase shares, but most companies still try to achieve shareholder align-ment as well as rewarding individual performance. The classic example of a reason to do this occurs in the context of a takeover. The governance industry assumes that management's natural incentives are to resist takeovers, no matter how accre-tive they are to the shareholders, as the usual consequence of being acquired is that executives are fired. Also, modern governance actors assume – without much investigation – that takeovers are about disciplining slack managers and therefore constitute a repudiation of the target company's executive team. (We will see in Chapter 6 that this is a poor explanation for takeovers, but the idea that tender offers are essentially about correcting managerial failures exercises almost hyp-notic power in academic discussions.) In any event, if corporate executives have exposure to the firm's equity, they will presumably be more willing to act in the interests of the shareholders and facilitate accretive transactions, even when this will result in the executives being turfed and returned to their mansions to cry into their gold pillows.

If we decompose the elements of executive pay, we find that most of the growth hasn't come in the form of salaries, but from increasing uses of equity and various pay-for-performance incentive schemes.[8] So, for example, during the period of the fastest growth in executive remuneration, 1992–2008, median salaries only grew from $0.8 million to $0.9 million and straight-forward cash bonuses from $0.6 million to $1 million.[9] Nearly all the growth in total pay came from increasing equity incentives such as share grants and stock options.[10] From the 1940s to the 1980s, plain-vanilla salary and bonuses accounted for 99 percent to 74 percent of CEO pay, but declined to approximately 40 percent by 2005.[11] By 2010, 62 percent of the compensation received by American large-company CEOs came from equity incentives alone.[12] Overall, by the beginning of the past decade, incentive pay of all types comprised almost 85 percent of CEO compensation.[13]

There is an easy way to summarize these statistics: over the period of time that executive pay has been increasing, nearly all the increase in pay has come from attempts by boards to introduce shareholder alignment and pay-for-performance. In other words, the compensation best practices recommended by the governance industry appear to be almost exclusively responsible for the growth in executive pay over the past forty years. This still doesn't tell us, though, whether these compensation best practices are worth it. Maybe we are getting much better outcomes thanks to the use of the governance industry's favorite remuneration devices.

4.3 SHAREHOLDER ALIGNMENT AS A BEST PRACTICE FOR EXECUTIVE COMPENSATION

Several prominent finance scholars in the 1990s describe the rationale for equity-based pay:

> [I]t is well known that a potential solution to the fundamental agency problem is to provide managers with equity stakes in their firms. Thus, managerial self-interest may be mitigated by aligning the interests of managers and shareholders, and it is presumed firm performance will improve as managers concurrently work for their own and shareholders' benefit.[14]

(Note the absence of any reference to equity in providing officers with individualized just desserts for their personal efforts.)

Prior to the rise of agency theory and modern corporate governance in the 1970s, the use of equity incentives was extremely rare.[15] It is now so ubiquitous that the default assumption of the governance industry is that equity grants are appropriate; proxy advisors and other governance industry members only concern themselves with identifying unacceptable types of equity grants.

At the time equity grants became a best practice, there was very little research supporting the idea. As we saw in the Introduction of this book, finance scholars beginning in 1980 and continuing through the next two decades repeatedly observed that the evidence in favor of equity grants was not visible in the published studies, which they characterized as "inconclusive," failing to provide "consensus," and lacking "consistency."

Finally, in 2003, scholars performed a meta-analysis of 229 empirical studies with a combined sample of 939,567 firms.[16] They found that, with the exception of earnings per share (EPS), management equity exposure had no effect on Tobin's Q, return on assets, return on equity, returns on investment, shareholder returns, the market-to-book ratio, and Jensen's Alpha, among other financial metrics. Even the impact on EPS was modest and, noted the researchers, might be attributed to management techniques designed to increase earnings without changing the performance of the firm, for example, through the use of increased leverage. The authors of the meta-study concluded, "the results of our meta-analyses do not support agency theory's proposed relationship between ownership and firm performance."[17]

Research since 2003 has tended to produce the same results.[18] A subsequent meta-analysis of thirty three studies in 2007, for example, found that market-based measures of performance (such as Tobin's Q) appeared to improve with increasing insider equity, but that actual corporate financial performance as measured by accounting metrics is unconnected to executive equity levels.[19] The conclusion of the authors of the study is that shareholders expect increasing executive equity ownership to improve corporate performance and so the stock price increases, but, "[t]his result is not confirmed by the real accounting returns."[20] In the period since 2003, stock options have come in for particular criticism. For example, several studies find that stock options are negatively associated with both firm value[21] and future operating performance.[22]

The lack of evidence about the benefits of equity contrasts with the abundant evidence of its adverse effects. Managers manipulate disclosure around CEO option awards, delaying the release of good news and accelerating the release of bad news.[23] There is a robust connection between CEO equity incentives and earnings manipulation[24] as well as fraud and indicia of fraud like shareholder litigation.[25] Equity compensation has been connected to larger restructurings and layoffs[26] and more voluntary corporate dissolutions.[27] The vesting of equity incentives in any given year is negatively correlated with corporate research and development (R&D) and capital expenditures.[28] Stock options produce a strong bias away from dividends (in which option holders do not participate) and towards stock repurchases,[29] creating the phenomena of predatory behavior as the corporation transacts with its own short-term shareholders.[30]

There is even debate around whether closely aligning managers' interests with the shareholders is a good idea at all, given the risk profile of shareholders (who can manage risk through appropriate portfolio strategies) is different from that of a company,[31] and that shareholders' investment horizon is frequently much shorter than that of a well-run business.[32]

4.4 PAY-FOR-PERFORMANCE AS A BEST PRACTICE FOR EXECUTIVE COMPENSATION

In the late 1980s and early 1990s, several important papers were written about the ways in which executive remuneration practices were insufficiently sensitive to executive performance.[33] In a popular phrase, Michael Jensen and Kevin Murphy commented in 1990 that corporate America paid "its most important leaders like bureaucrats."[34] The idea of instead paying executives like professional athletes or game show contestants gradually grew throughout the 1990s, and now performance is the central touchstone of most governance industry best practices for structuring executive pay. For example, ISS lists its "five global principles that most investors expect [from] corporations" as a way of introducing the more than seventy-five pages of compensation advice spread through four different documents. Two of those principles are maintaining "appropriate pay-for-performance alignment" and

"avoiding arrangements that risk 'pay for failure.'" Of course, paying for performance and avoiding paying for failure are, in fact, the same principle, but the fact
that it is repeated gives some clue to the principle's centrality to all the voting guidance that is going to follow.

Given the high level of consensus that exists throughout the governance industry on the merits of performance pay, it comes as a surprise how little empirical
evidence supports its use. Even in the 1990s, one of the leading scholars of executive remuneration, who helped coin the "paid like bureaucrats" phrase earlier in
the decade, observed: "there is surprisingly little direct evidence that higher pay-
performance sensitivities lead to higher stock-price performance."[35] A decade later,
several other finance scholars observed of this period,

> [M]ost of the normative contemporary CEO compensation schemes were devel-
> oped during the 1990s under a broad paradigm that the greater the financial incen-
> tives for CEOs the greater the financial returns to corporate operations. What we
> find disturbing by [*sic*] this paradigm is that it was developed as a theoretical prop-
> osition rather than a fact confirmed by empirical evidence. In short, little "heavy
> lifting" in empirical statistical research was undertaken.[36]

This lack of evidence about the benefits of pay-for-performance schemes continues
to the present.[37] In his book-length examination of incentive pay, Professor Michael
Dorff summarizes the state of the empirical research:

> Respected scholars who have carefully combed through the literature on this ques-
> tion – including some who favor performance pay – have concluded that there is
> no empirically demonstrable relationship between firms' use of performance pay
> and their success in the marketplace.[38]

In fact, several studies have found that performance pay schemes actually harm
corporate financial performance.[39] A recent study is worth noting in this regard as it
uses a very large dataset over a long time period (1994–2015) as well as sophisticated
statistical techniques to evaluate the impact of incentive pay on firm performance.[40]
(Earlier studies used small samples over more limited time horizons.) Relative to
corporate peers, the study finds that companies using high levels of incentive pay
underperform by surprisingly large amounts measured in both stock price and
return-on-asset calculations. The performance of these companies worsens significantly over time.[41] The researchers conclude:

> Our results imply that managerial compensation components such as restricted
> stock, options and long-term incentive payouts, that are meant to align managerial
> interests with shareholder value, do not translate into higher future returns, and
> quite in contrast, for firms with high paid CEOs, translate into lower future share-
> holder wealth.[42]

Laboratory studies only cast more doubt on the merits of incentive schemes for
executives. Professor Michael Dorff again summarizes the research:

When people are given dull, repetitive tasks like assembly line work, they perform faster and better when their rewards depend on productivity. The results are much different, though, when the tasks are interesting, especially if they involve creative or analytical thought. For these high-level tasks, performance pay actually *weakens* motivation and results in lower-quality work.[43]

One of the central issues seems to be that performance pay for a job displaces the intrinsic motivations to do the job such as the satisfaction of doing good work, helping an organization succeed, or the pleasure that arises from solving a problem.[44] Motivation declines along with creativity. Where tasks rely on lateral thinking or are cognitively demanding, incentive pay undermines performance, at least in a laboratory setting.[45] This results in groups that are not being paid, or are being paid very little, outperforming groups that stand to make lottery-sized gains for successfully completing cognitively challenging tasks.[46] One 2009 paper by several prominent behavioral finance scholars is titled, "Large Stakes and Big Mistakes."[47]

The problems with pay-for-performance schemes extend beyond the failure of empirical research to associate them with positive corporate or personal outcomes. Researchers have found that financial incentives have the effect of displacing what Professor Lynn Stout refers to as "pro-social" behavior.[48] Financial incentives make people more selfish, less concerned for others, and less trusting and loyal.[49] So, for example, starting to fine parents who are late picking their children up at day-care results in more late pickups.[50] Paying people to donate blood reduces blood donations,[51] and lawyers provide more legal work to indigent clients *pro bono* than they will if offered a modest fee.[52] Anyone who has worked in a large organization or is familiar with the radical incompleteness of executive and corporate contracting will appreciate the importance of cultivating generous and conscientious behavior amongst senior executives.[53] Pay-for-performance appears to weaken the social capital that is vital to modern economic enterprises.[54]

It is not surprising, therefore, to encounter a (very) large body of research finding that pay-for-performance is associated with financial fraud and accounting restatements.[55] Informed observers have blamed the Enron-era failures and the 2008 financial crisis on the use of high-powered incentives that had the effect of overwhelming executives' concern for risk or the long-term good of the organizations they stewarded.[56] The most common measure of performance tends to be one version or another of total shareholder return. The largest driver of this is share price performance, but since equity markets take into account future *expectations* of growth, Professor Roger Martin argues that the only way executives can materially increase share price is through improving the *rate* of growth. Obviously, this is impossible to do indefinitely, which leaves executives who are motivated to meet these types of performance targets with the alternatives of boosting the rate of growth through leverage, extreme risk taking, or financial fraud – all of which we have seen in the last two recessions.[57]

There are yet other bodies of research that call into question whether, even if we accepted all its questionable assumptions, we could create effective pay-for-performance contracts. For example, there is considerable evidence that outside of a few truly unusual executives, CEOs don't usually have much impact on corporate performance. One study found the difference in talent between the best CEO in the US and the 250th best CEO gave rise only to a 0.016 percent increase in market capitalization.[58] Another study of 167 large companies over a period of twenty years found that corporate performance, measured by sales, earnings, and profit margins, was largely determined by the company's industry and its position in that industry. Leadership changes explained only about 6.5 percent of the variance in sales performance, 7.5 percent of the variance in net income, and nearly 15 percent of the change in profit margin.[59] These sorts of conclusions are controversial, but they suggest that linking CEO pay to corporate performance may often connect rewards to factors outside the CEO's control.[60]

Even if CEOs were as powerful as pay-for-performance schemes seem to assume, attempting to find measures of the CEO's contribution is an impossible task. Thomas Piketty points out that unique jobs (like that of a CEO), the nature of which changes frequently to accommodate changes in the competitive environment, as well as the firm itself, don't lend themselves to measurement.[61] The environment the governance industry has created around executive remuneration exacerbates this problem. The fact that boards are increasingly accountable to shareholders and other governance monitors means that performance targets defensively chosen by boards tend to be objective, measurable, and connected to shareholder returns. This means many of the targets (like increases in a company's share price) lie largely outside of the CEO's power.[62] It also means that important nonfinancial metrics such as customer satisfaction, product innovation, and employee morale are ignored.[63] There is abundant evidence that executives focus excessively on the incentivized tasks and shirk on the tasks that are not measured, imposing further costs on the organization.[64]

4.5 WHY COMPENSATION BEST PRACTICES LEAD TO HIGHER PAY

Shareholder-alignment and pay-for-performance compensation practices seem to fall naturally out of the agency cost story, with the assumption that the main problem to be solved is insiders' tendency to act as economic self-maximizers at the expense of the organizations they manage. These compensation practices seem intuitive, and if the evidence suggests they are not effective (and possibly detrimental), it does not necessarily explain why these practices are automatically associated with higher executive pay levels.

Common sense, however, tells us that risky compensation structures will generally have the effect of increasing total pay levels. This is just another manifestation of the well known relationship between risk and reward. The risk premium actually tends to be higher than one would expect, because an executive already has significant undiversified investments in the firm (in the form of continuing employment,

personal reputation, salary, etc.) and so the marginal utility of increased exposure
to firm performance tends to be surprisingly low. In addition, most studies find that
executives place a very low value on things like equity incentives because so much
of their value is contingent on factors outside their control.[65] Scholars estimate
that one-third to one-half of fluctuations in share prices are attributable to market-
wide causes.[66] Executives tell investigators that they discount long-term incentives
by at least 50 percent from the already discounted value generated by accounting
metrics.[67] Some studies have found the discount applied by executives to be even
greater.[68]

Many firm-specific targets lie outside the control of the corporation or are due
entirely to the actions of others within the organization. Even bonuses predicated
entirely on achieving internal metrics, such as reducing the cost of sales, depend
on the work of other people and the actions of competitors. Simply remaining
employed in the company long enough to receive a long-term incentive pay-out can
seem risky. The average CEO tenure in America has fallen to less than six years.[69]
When in a CEO's tenure, then, does a five-year incentive plan start to feel chancy?
When a company's industry declines from the 90th percentile to the 10th percentile
within the economy, something totally outside of an executive's control, the CEO is
twice as likely to be fired, regardless of the firm's performance relative to its peers.[70]
Thus, to be effective as incentives, these structures must provide the promise of
payouts commensurate with their risk.

The best evidence that CEOs and boards actually believe this, themselves, is
that modern pay practices always produce large increases in total levels of executive
compensation. Companies would not need to offer lottery-sized paydays if they were
rewarding executives for achieving goals that lay well within their personal control.
The much decried but relatively common practice of boards making mid-stream
adjustments to performance targets also likely reflects this sense that executives are
often not to blame if the targets now appear out of reach.[71]

To summarize, the adoption of at-risk pay-for-performance schemes has probably
contributed significantly to the rise in executive compensation. The basic rule of
risk and reward operates in this area and so potential payouts increase to lottery-like
levels. Pay-for-performance even makes it easier for boards to justify higher remuneration levels to shareholders. This is particularly the case as total shareholder return
is often a prominent metric in these plans and thus appears to align the rewards
received by executives with increases in the wealth of shareholders, the group most
likely to complain about compensation decisions.

4.6 WHO IS TO BLAME FOR THE RISE IN EXECUTIVE PAY?

Directors set executive pay with input (as in any negotiation) from the executives
themselves. But they do not set pay in a vacuum. Since the time that pay practices
began changing, the corporate governance industry has grown into an increasingly

loud source of advice to boards. As we have seen in Chapters 2 and 3, boards have adopted the recommendations of the governance industry under some combination of external pressure and internal motivation to do what they are told is right. There is plenty of evidence that the failures in executive compensation are the result, not of over-powerful CEOs confronting supine boards, but of directors and management earnestly striving to follow bad "best practices" promulgated by the corporate governance industry.

This is a thesis that is entirely compatible with believing individual boards can, and occasionally have, failed to meet any reasonable construction of their duty in paying their executives. There is ample evidence that this happens. Rather, this chapter only argues that these types of board failures do not characterize executive compensation decisions in the English-speaking world; instead, boards generally attempt to follow the best advice available to them on the subject. This is advice, after all, that is backed up by the growing power of institutional shareholders, regulators, proxy advisors, and the media over corporate governance.

We have already encountered two pieces of evidence that it is the governance industry itself that has produced the explosion in executive pay. First, the rise in pay levels corresponds almost perfectly with the growing power of the governance industry. Second, the rise in pay levels is almost entirely due to the increasing use of equity incentives and pay-for-performance in executive compensation design. These are the very "best practices" recommended by the governance industry.

4.6.1 *The Direction of Causality Displayed in Stock Options*

The rise and fall of stock option popularity provides a useful case study in the direction of causality when it comes to executive compensation. It is difficult to remember now, but in the 1980s and early 1990s, the use of stock options was strongly encouraged by leading finance scholars. Even Congress used tax laws to signal the desirability of stock options.[72] Throughout the 1990s, institutional shareholders such as CalPERS and governance think-tanks such as the National Association of Corporate Directors advocated for greater use of options.[73] In 2000, the Harvard Business Review opined, "Options are the best compensation mechanism we have for getting managers to act in ways that ensure the long-term success of their companies and the well-being of their workers and stockholders."[74] Corporate behavior followed this consensus, with the 1990s being marked by the increasing use of options as a remuneration device.

Then, suddenly, stock options fell out of general favor with the corporate governance industry in the years after the dot-com collapse. The recommended alternative in the United States was restricted share grants. Boards dutifully abandoned stock options in favor of restricted share grants, which are now a much more important source of pay than options.[75] By 2012, restricted stock grants contributed 35 percent of the average CEO's pay, compared to the 14 percent from options.[76]

In the UK, in contrast, the corporate governance industry began to criticize options much earlier than in the US, at least in part because of their role in outsized compensation gains received by British executives when utilities were privatized in the early 1990s.[77] The 1995 Greenbury Committee Report recommended the use of "challenging performance criteria" as conditions for option exercise and this was embraced by other elements of the governance industry.[78] The Association of British Insurers, which sets influential governance best practices (and in this respect functions similarly to proxy advisory firms in America), issued guidelines in 1994 that suggested options should be constrained to a value no higher than four times cash compensation. The result was that stock option use declined sharply in the UK well before it did in the US, and that, also unlike the US, performance-vesting now predominates in that country.[79]

After considering and rejecting the limited possible agency cost explanations for the different patterns and levels of compensation between the US and the UK, one team of scholars concluded, "Overall, there are no compelling agency-theoretic explanations for the relative reliance on equity-based compensation in the United States."[80] Obviously, the differences are due to historical changes in the recommendations of influential members of the governance industry. The best evidence we have at our disposal on the question of causality suggests that boards follow, and do not lead, the consensus best practices developed by the corporate governance industry. Finance scholars, themselves, recognize (often ruefully) that boards are significantly influenced by academic theories about executive pay and the ways these theories are popularized.[81]

If you ask executives themselves about why they have adopted performance pay schemes, they will usually tell you it is in response to governance industry advice and pressure. Even as incentive pay dominates compensation schemes, surveys of executives find they do not actually believe that performance pay materially impacts their behavior.[82]

4.6.2 *The Direction of Causality Demonstrated by Declining CEO Power*

If the agency story's explanation for executive pay problems was accurate, we would expect to see that changes in governance structures which increase the independence and power of the directors relative to the CEO lead to better pay practices. Fortunately, the period we have been considering has been marked by significant changes to corporate governance regimes, which affords an opportunity to test the theory.

The most significant change has been the rise in independent directors.[83] When it comes to the impact of this trend on executive pay levels, even as far back as 1994 and 1999, scholars were reporting that firms with a higher fraction of outside directors were more likely to reward executives with higher remuneration.[84] The reason for this is suggested by studies that find independent directors are correlated with a greater use of equity compensation structures.[85]

Later studies confirmed these initial findings that greater board independence leads to higher executive pay.[86] A 2005 meta-analytic review of research in the area that included more than 30,000 observations found no evidence that independent boards did better at controlling executive pay.[87] The study concluded, "the results provide little support to agency theory's predictions on the impact of board composition on critical decisions that involve a potential conflict of interest between managers and shareholders."[88]

Compensation committees are another device designed to provide better independent oversight of executive compensation decisions. Over the past three decades, these committees have become ubiquitous and these days they are usually made up exclusively of independent directors.

As we saw in Chapter 2, the effects of compensation committees are similar to those we have seen with independent directors generally. Seven different studies have found that compensation committees with a higher proportion of outside directors have no significant impact on the level of CEO compensation, with several studies finding that a committee comprised entirely of independent directors actually leads to higher executive pay.

Yet another device that provides greater independence to boards is the increasingly common retention of compensation consultants. Third-party consultants provide directors with a source of information about the market for executive talent independent from the CEO or their subordinates in the company's human resources team. As well, compensation consultants present themselves as experts on optimal pay structures, shareholder and proxy advisor expectations, and evolving trends in good governance. Market checks conducted by third-party consultants provide directors with arguments to counter aggressive CEO proposals. Compensation consultants barely existed in 1980 and are now ubiquitous, partly as a result of the growing complexity of "best practices" when it comes to remuneration structures.

Research on the impact of compensation consultants finds their use is associated with higher executive pay, largely because of the greater use of equity and performance incentives.[89] Pay levels in a company increase immediately following the retention of a consulting firm.[90] Studies of foreign firms using US compensation consultants find their pay levels and structures more closely resemble those of the United States than their country of origin, "consistent with this practice [the use of consultants] being a transmission mechanism for pay practices."[91]

Several studies have debunked the claim that pay outcomes are driven by conflicts of interest on the part of the consultants.[92] The best reading of the evidence, therefore, is that compensation consultants produce higher pay because they recommend best practices that, as we have seen, are responsible for nearly all modern pay growth.

Over the past thirty years, boards have steadily grown more independent from management. This can be seen, for example, in the long-term rate increases in disciplinary terminations of underperforming CEOs.[93] Yet these increasingly independent boards are awarding increasing amounts of pay to CEOs and making increasing use of suboptimal compensation structures. Indeed, as we examine each corporate governance practice designed to increase board freedom from managerial power, we find evidence that these liberating practices, themselves, are associated with higher pay and greater use of equity and performance incentives. These are facts that are incompatible with the agency cost story about executive compensation.

A final inconvenient fact for those who rely on agency-cost explanations for executive pay arises from the secular trend of hiring external candidates for the top corporate positions (itself evidence of an erosion in the power of management teams). In the 1970s, fewer than 15 percent of CEOs were hired externally; this had risen to a third of hires by the beginning of the next century.[94] Researchers find that externally hired CEOs are paid more than internal candidates who assume the position.[95] Indeed, the median pay of external hires is higher than that of the CEOs they replace, notwithstanding external candidates have presumably little influence over the board of strangers hiring them.

4.6.3 *The Direction of Causality Demonstrated by Shareholder Involvement*

Shareholders comprise the constituency most directly harmed by executive pay practices. If the percentage of profits allocated to senior executives has more than doubled in America in the last thirty years, this money has come out of the pockets of investors as the residuary interest holders. If governance failures were the correct explanation for what has been going wrong with executive compensation, we should expect to see evidence that shareholder power is used to correct abuses.

Institutional shareholders are generally strong believers in the use of equity and pay-for-performance incentive schemes. This is visible in the proxy voting guidelines published by some of the larger investors, as well as the voting guidelines published by proxy advisory firms, whose business is catering to the prejudices of their institutional clientele. Think tanks and advocacy groups that receive their financial support from institutional investors also faithfully advocate the executive compensation best practices we have been considering.

Shareholder belief in these pay structures is sincere. Studies have repeatedly found that the market rewards companies that adopt equity and performance incentive schemes. We see evidence of shareholders' positive reaction to public announcements of these structures,[96] in the higher valuation of initial public offering (IPO) candidates making use of these structures,[97] and in the improvement in market-related performance measures for companies using these structures (even if actual corporate financial performance is unaffected).[98]

Private equity affords the best test case for the impact of shareholder power on executive remuneration, as private equity firms intensively manage their portfolio companies. The boards of these companies are almost entirely constituted by representatives of the shareholders, and directly or indirectly private equity shareholders tend to be deeply engaged in the day-to-day running of the business in a way alien to comparable public company boards. The scope for the kind of agency cost governance failures assumed by the governance industry would appear to be very circumscribed.

Yet, studies performed on private equity-backed companies find they compensate their executives in precisely the same way as widely-held companies.[99] The pay levels of CEOs in private equity-backed firms are "statistically indistinguishable" from those of public companies, as are the value of stock and stock options granted to these officers. In fact, executive remuneration actually goes up when companies go private,[100] and over the past three decades, pay in closely held firms has outpaced that of public companies.[101] Again, this phenomenon appears to be linked to the greater use of equity incentives.[102]

Given widespread shareholder commitments to suboptimal pay practices, we should not be surprised that various initiatives designed to increase shareholder influence over compensation in the public markets have had no real impact on existing practices. It is vanishingly rare for a company to lose a say-on-pay vote[103] (suggesting boards are largely doing what shareholders want to see done) and in neither the US nor the UK is there any evidence that say-on-pay proposals change the level or growth of CEO pay.[104] Indeed, executive compensation in the UK, which introduced mandatory say-on-pay votes in 2002, increased at greater rates than in the US over the following decade.[105] The only impact of say-on-pay (aside from rising pay levels) has been, in the words of Professor Jeffrey Gordon, to encourage firms to, "follow the guidelines, stay in the middle of the pack, and avoid change from a prior year, when the firm received a favorable vote."[106] In other words, he believes say-on-pay has brought "stasis rather than innovation" to companies.[107]

There is very little evidence in the social science literature to support the idea that directors as agents are deviating from what their principals, the shareholders, would like them to do in compensation decisions. "Shareholders are drinking from the same well as directors and executives," according to Professor Michael Dorff.[108]

4.7 SUMMARY – WHAT WE HAVE LOST IN MODERN COMPENSATION BEST PRACTICES

Throughout this discussion, we have been assuming the most important problem around our modern compensation practices is how badly they work, and to what degree they have led to the explosion in executive pay levels, but there are arguably bigger problems. The fixation of the agency cost story on the narrow question of incentivizing supposedly risk-adverse executives, combined with its crude models of human behavior, have combined to dramatically narrow the range of acceptable compensation practices.

As anyone who has served as a corporate director can tell you, the reality is that pay structures are designed to do much more than incentivize performance or align the executive's interests with the shareholders. Some pay structures, for example, are designed to compensate the executive for risk. This is the opposite of what pay-for-performance advocates would like to see, but the reality is that to induce an executive to leave a safe place of employment and to join a riskier venture – one whose possible failure could leave the executive without an income and with a tarnished reputation – requires some compensation arrangements that mitigate risk. Equity grants to the executive may vest on a time-passed, rather than a performance-metric-achieved basis, for example.

Fairness is another consideration in setting executive pay. This also runs counter to the focus on aligning the interests of agents and principals. Because increases in share price and improvements in corporate performance are not wholly under the control of the executive, boards have traditionally relied upon pay structures unconnected to these metrics. Occasionally, as well, unfairness that results from forces outside of the executive's control must be remedied. This occurs, for example, when options are re-priced, replacement equity granted, the terms of long-term incentive plans altered, and discretionary bonuses awarded. Again, anyone who has actually served as a director knows that the proper working of an institution depends (among other things) on employees feeling that the firm and the people who lead it are treating them fairly.

Sometimes pay structures are designed to respond to internal firm conditions. A growth company may not have sufficient free cash flow to pay a competitive salary, so it uses equity (including options) or large future bonuses to make up the difference. A company with a founding team serving in subordinate roles may need to use equity more generously with new senior hires, who otherwise will feel like second-class citizens, or who will feel it is unfair that they, now the star performers, are disproportionately making the founders rich.

There are many other perfectly valid considerations touching on compensation that are unrelated to agency theory's preoccupation with individual performance and shareholder alignment. In addition to the examples given, executive pay structures are used to: maintain employee morale (and sadly, it doesn't matter operationally that shareholder morale is also low); retain executives who have worked long and hard only to see their equity rendered worthless by a stock-market downturn; ease an executive out of the company, avoiding trouble through a generous severance payment; or control an overconfident CEO with a huge appetite for risk by loading her up with internal debt in the form of, say, a pension.[109] The lack of nuance in the best practices promulgated by the governance industry reflects a profound lack of sophistication about what happens in the real world inside companies.

To the extent the governance industry has stamped out these sorts of pay practices in favor of their narrow one-size-fits-all compensation structures, it has weakened America's companies.

NOTES

1 Erling Barth et al., "It's Where You Work: Increases in the Dispersion of Earnings across Establishments and Individuals in the United States" (2016) 34:S2 *Journal of Labor Economics* S67–S97; Giuseppe Berlingieri, Patrick Blachenay and Chiara Criscuolo, "The Great Divergence(s)" (2017), *OECD Science, Technology and Industry Policy Papers No. 39*, online: www.oecd-ilibrary.org/content/paper/953f3853-en.

2 Thomas Piketty, *Capital in the Twenty-First Century*, translated by Arthur Goldhammer (Massachusetts: Harvard University Press, 2014) at p. 302 [Piketty, *Capital*].

3 Carola Frydman and Dirk Jenter, "CEO Compensation" (2010) 2:1 *Annual Review of Financial Economics* 75–102 at 78–80 (Table 1 and Figures 2a and 2b) [Frydman and Jenter, "CEO Compensation"].

4 Lawrence Mishel and Jori Kandra, "CEO Pay has Skyrocketed 1,322% since 1978: CEOs Were Paid 351 Times as Much as a Typical Worker in 2020" (2021), available online: *Economic Policy Institute*, www.epi.org/publication/ceo-pay-in-2020/ [Mishel and Kandra, "Compensation Skyrocketed"]. See also, Lucian Bebchuk and Yaniv Grinstein, "The Growth of Executive Pay" (2005) 21:2 *Oxford Review of Economic Policy* 283–303 at 286–287 [Bebchuk and Grinstein, "Growth of Executive Pay"]; Harwell Wells, "US Executive Compensation in Historical Perspective" in Rendall S. Thomas and Jennifer G. Hill (eds.), *Research Handbook on Executive Pay* (Massachusetts: Edward Elgar Publishing, Inc., 2012), pp. 41–57 at p. 49; Martin J. Conyon, "Executive Compensation and Board Governance in US Firms" (2014) 124:574 *The Economic Journal* F60–F89 at F60 [Conyon, "Executive Compensation"].

5 Marc T. Moore, "Corporate Governance, Pay Equity, and the Limitations of Agency Theory" (2015) 68:1 *Current Legal Problems* 431–464 at 436.

6 Michael Doran, "Executive Compensation and Corporate Governance" (2022), online: SSRN, https://ssrn.com/abstract=4202403 at 4–5 citing Mishel and Kandra, "Compensation Skyrocketed," above at note 4.

7 Bebchuk and Grinstein, "Growth of Executive Pay," above at note 4 at 302.

8 Martin J. Conyon, "Executive Compensation and Incentives" (2006) 20:1 *Academy of Management Perspectives* 25–44 at 28–29; Carola Frydman and Raven E. Saks, "Executive Compensation: A New View from a Long-Term Perspective, 1936–2005" (2010) 23:5 *The Review of Financial Studies* 2099–2138 at 2106–2109 [Frydman and Saks, "Executive Compensation"].

9 Frydman and Jenter, "CEO Compensation," above at note 3 at 81. Lucian A. Bebchuk and Jesse M. Fried, "Pay Without Performance: Overview of the Issues" (2005) 17:4 *Journal of Applied Corporate Finance* 8–23 at 16–18. See also, Gian Luca Clementi and Thomas F. Cooley, "Executive Compensation: Facts" (2009), *National Bureau Economic Research Working Paper No. 15426*, online (pdf): NBER, www.nber.org/papers/w15426.pdf at 2.

10 Brian J. Hall and Jeffrey B. Liebman, "Are CEOs Really Paid Like Bureaucrats?" (1998) 113:3 *Quarterly Journal of Economics* 653–691 at 662–663; Frydman and Saks, "Executive Compensation," above at note 8 at 2106–2109.

11 Yvan Allaire, "Pay for Value: Cutting the Gordian Knot of Executive Compensation" (2012), *Institute for Governance of Private and Public Organizations – Working Group on Compensation of IGOPP Policy Paper*, online: SSRN, https://ssrn.com/abstract=2070766 at 19, Figure 4.

12 *Ibid* at 24, Figure 8. See also, Conyon, "Executive Compensation," above at note 4 at F74.

13   Tamara C. Belinfanti, "Beyond Economics in Pay for Performance" (2012) 41:1 *Hofstra Law Review* 91–153 at 103.

14   Dan R. Dalton et al., "Meta-Analyses of Financial Performance and Equity: Fusion or Confusion?" (2003) 46:1 *Academy of Management Journal* 13–26 at 13 [Dalton et al., "Fusion or Confusion"] summarizing. Charles P. Himmelberg, R. Glenn Hubbard and Darius Palia, "Understanding the Determinants of Managerial Ownership and the Link Between Ownership and Performance" (1999) 53:3 *Journal of Financial Economics* 353–384 at 354.

15   Frydman and Jenter, "CEO Compensation," above at note 3 at 80, Figure 2a; John Kay, *The Kay Review of UK Equity Markets and Long-Term Decision Making* (London: Business Innovation Skills, 2012), online (pdf): https://assets.publishing.service.gov.uk/government/uploads/system/uploads/attachment_data/file/253454/bis-12-917-kay-review-of-equity-markets-final-report.pdf at 77 [Kay, *The Kay Report*].

16   Dalton et al., "Fusion or Confusions," above note 14 at 16.

17   *Ibid* at 20.

18   See the discussion in Frydman and Jenter, "CEO Compensation," above at note 3 at 94–96; Brian L. Connelly et al., "Ownership as a Form of Corporate Governance" (2010) 47:8 *Journal of Management Studies* 1561–1589 at 1564–1566.

19   Juan P. Sánchez-Ballesta and Emma García-Meca, "A Meta-analytic Vision of the Effect of Ownership Structure on Firm Performance" (2007) 15:5 *Corporate Governance: An International Review* 879–892 at 887–888 [Sánchez-Ballesta and García-Meca, "Firm Performance"].

20   *Ibid* at 887.

21   Michel A. Habib and Alexander Ljungqvist, "Firm Value and Managerial Incentives: A Stochastic Frontier Approach" (2005) 78:6 *The Journal of Business* 2053–2094 at 2054–2055.

22   Michelle Hanlon, Shivaram Rajgopal and Terry J. Shevlin, "Large Sample Evidence on the Relation Between Stock Option Compensation and Risk Taking" (2004), online: SSRN, https://ssrn.com/abstract=427260 at 35.

23   David Aboody and Ron Kasznik, "CEO Stock Option Awards and the Timing of Corporate Voluntary Disclosures" (2000) 29:1 *Journal of Accounting and Economics* 73–100 at 75.

24   See, for example, Natasha Burns and Simi Kedia, "The Impact of Performance-based Compensation on Misreporting" (2006) 79:1 *Journal of Financial Economics* 35–67 at 37; Qiang Cheng and Terry D. Warfield, "Equity Incentives and Earnings Management" (2005) 80:2 *The Accounting Review* 441–476 at 443; Daniel Bergstresser and Thomas Philippon, "CEO Incentives and Earnings Management" (2006) 80:3 *Journal of Financial Economics* 511–529 at 514; Jap Efendi, Anup Srivastava and Edward P. Swanson, "Why Do Corporate Managers Misstate Financial Statements? The Role of Option Compensation and Other Factors" (2007) 85:3 *Journal of Financial Economics* 667–708 at 670; Julia Grant, Garen Markarian and Antonio Parbonetti, "CEO Risk-Related Incentives and Income Smoothing" (2009) 26:4 *Contemporary Accounting Research* 1029–1065 at 1030. But see, Christopher S. Armstrong, Alan D. Jagolinzer and David F. Larcker, "Chief Executive Officer Equity Incentives and Accounting Irregularities" (2010) 48:2 *Journal of Accounting Research* 225–271 (finding accounting irregularities less frequent at firms where CEOs have higher equity incentives).

25   Shane A. Johnson, Harley E. Ryan, Jr. and Yisong S. Tian, "Managerial Incentives and Corporate Fraud: The Sources of Incentives Matter" (2009) 13:1 *Review of Finance* 115–145 at 116–117; Lin Peng and Ailsa Röell, "Executive Pay and Shareholder Litigation" (2008) 12:1 *Review of Finance* 141–184 at 142; David J. Denis, Paul Hanouna and Atulya Sarin, "Is There a Dark Side to Incentive Compensation?" (2006) 12:3 *Journal of Corporate*

Finance 467–488 at 468 [Denis, Hanouna and Sarin, "Dark Side to Incentive Compensation"]; Joseph P. O'Connor, Jr. et al., "Do CEO Stock Options Prevent or Promote Fraudulent Financial Reporting" (2006) 49:3 *Academy of Management Journal* 483–500 at 492–493; Jared Harris and Philip Bromiley, "Incentives to Cheat: The Influence of Executive Compensation and Firm Performance on Financial Misrepresentation" (2007) 18:3 *Organization Science* 350–367 at 362 [Harris and Bromiley, "Incentives to Cheat"]; Nicolas Eugster, Oskar Kowalewski and Piotr Spiewanowski, "Internal Governance Mechanisms and Corporate Misconduct" (2022), IESEG *Working Paper Series 2022-ACF-05*, online: SSRN, https://ssrn.com/abstract=4211747 at 20.

26 Jay Dial and Kevin J. Murphy, "Incentives, Downsizing, and Value Creation at General Dynamics" (1995) 37:3 *Journal of Financial Economics* 261–314 at 305; Jeffrey T. Brookman, Saeyoung Chang and Craig G. Rennie, "CEO Equity Portfolio Incentives and Layoff Decisions" (2007) 30:2 *Journal of Financial Research* 259–281 at 260.

27 Hamid Mehran, George E. Nogler and Kenneth B. Schwartz, "CEO Incentive Plans and Corporate Liquidation Policy" (1998) 50:3 *Journal of Financial Economics* 319–349 at 320.

28 Alex Edmans, Vivian W. Fang and Katharina A. Lewellen, "Equity Vesting and Investment" (2017) 30:7 *The Review of Financial Studies* 2229–2271 at 2230.

29 George W. Fenn and Nellie Liang, "Corporate Payout Policy and Managerial Stock Incentives" (2001) 60:1 *Journal of Financial Economics* 45–72 at 47–48.

30 Jesse M. Fried, "The Uneasy Case for Favoring Long-Term Shareholders" (2015) 124:5 *Yale Law Journal* 1554–1627 at 1564. See also, Alex Edmans, Vivian W. Fang and Allen H. Huang, "The Long-Term Consequences of Short-Term Incentives" (2022) 60:3 *Journal of Accounting Research* 1007–1046.

31 Kenneth A. Kim, John R. Nofsinger and Derek J. Mohr, *Corporate Governance*, 3rd ed. (Toronto: Pearson Education Inc., 2010) at p. 107.

32 Kay, *The Kay Report*, above at note 15 at 33–34; Patrick Bolton, Jose Scheinkman and Wei Xiong, "Executive Compensation and Short-Termist Behaviour in Speculative Markets" (2006) 73:3 *The Review of Economic Studies* 577–610 at 579; Mahabaleswara Bhatta, "Kinetics of Individual Investors' Behaviour – A Conceptual View" (2012) 1:1 *International Journal of Applied Financial Management Perspectives* 39–42 at 39; John C. Bogle, *The Clash of the Cultures: Investment vs. Speculation* (Hoboken: John Wiley & Sons, Inc., 2012) at p. 1; Bryce C. Tingle, "Bad Company! The Assumptions Behind Proxy Advisors' Voting Recommendations" (2014) 37:2 *Dalhousie Law Journal* 709–748 at 735–738.

33 George P. Baker, Michael C. Jensen and Kevin J. Murphy, "Compensation and Incentives: Practice vs. Theory" (1988) 43:3 *The Journal of Finance* 593–616 at 594; Michael C. Jensen and Kevin J. Murphy, "CEO Incentives – It's Not How Much You Pay, But How" (1990) 68:3 *Harvard Business Review* 138–153 at 140–143 [Jensen and Murphy, "CEO Incentives"].

34 Jensen and Murphy, "CEO Incentives," above at note 33 at 138.

35 Kevin J. Murphy, "Executive Compensation" in Orley C. Ashenfelter and David Cards (eds.), *Handbook of Labor Economics* (Amsterdam: Elsevier Science B.V., 1999), vol. 3B, pp. 2485–2563 at p. 2539.

36 Dennis Wright Michaud and Yunwei Gai, "CEO Compensation and Firm Performance" (2009), online: SSRN, https://ssrn.com/abstract=1531673 at 6–7.

37 Frydman and Jenter, "CEO Compensation," above at note 3 at 96; Igor Filatotchev and Deborah Allcock, "Corporate Governance and Executive Remuneration: A Contingency Framework" (2010) 24:1 *Academy of Management Perspective* 20–33 at 21.

38 Michael Dorff, *Indispensable and Other Myths: Why the CEO Pay Experiment Failed and How to Fix it* (USA: University of California Press, 2014) at p. 128 [Dorff,

Indispensable]. See also, Andrew C. W. Lund and Gregg D. Polsky, "The Diminishing Returns of Incentive Pay in Executive Compensation Contracts" (2011) 87:2 *Notre Dame Law Review* 677–736 at 689–706 [Lund and Polsky, "Diminishing Returns"].

39   Matt Bloom and George T. Milkovich, "Relationships Among Risk, Incentive Pay, and Organizational Performance" (1998) 41:3 *Academy of Management Journal* 283–297 at 285; H. Young Baek and Jose A. Pagan, "Executive Compensation and Corporate Production Efficiency: A Stochastic Frontier Approach" (2003) 41:1/2 *Quarterly Journal of Business and Economics* 27–41 at 39; Michael J. Cooper, Huseyin Gulen and P. Raghavendra Rau, "Performance for Pay? The Relation Between CEO Incentive Compensation and Future Stock Price Performance" (2016), online: SSRN, https://ssrn.com/abstract=1572085 [Cooper, Gulen and Rau, "Performance for Pay?"].

40   Cooper, Gulen and Rau, "Performance for Pay?," above at note 39.

41   *Ibid* at 25–26.

42   *Ibid*.

43   Dorff, *Indispensable*, above at note 38 at p. 136.

44   Edward L. Deci, Richard Koestner and Richard M. Ryan, "A Meta-analytic Review of Experiments Examining the Effects of Extrinsic Rewards on Intrinsic Motivation" (1999) 125:6 *Psychological Bulletin* 627–668 at 628–629. See also, Roland Benabou and Jean Tirole, "Intrinsic and Extrinsic Motivation" (2003) 70:3 *The Review of Economic Studies* 489–520 at 492.

45   Colin F. Camerer and Robin M. Hogarth, "The Effects of Financial Incentives in Experiments: A Review and Capital-Labor-Production Framework" (1999) 19:1–3 *Journal of Risk and Uncertainty* 7–42 at 34; Dan Ariely et al., "Large Stakes and Big Mistakes" (2009) 76:2 *The Review of Economic Studies* 451–469 at 458–459 [Ariely et al., "Large Stakes"].

46   *Ibid*.

47   Ariely et al., "Large Stakes," above at note 45.

48   Lynn A. Stout, "Killing Conscience: The Unintended Behavioral Consequences of Pay for Performance" (2014) 39:3 *Journal of Corporation Law* 525–562 at 546–547.

49   *Ibid* at 554–555. See also, Ernst Fehr and Simon Gächter, "Do Incentive Contracts Undermine Voluntary Cooperation?" (2002), *Institute for Empirical Research in Economics University of Zurich Working Paper* No. 1424–0459, online: SSRN, https://ssrn.com/abstract=313028 at 1.

50   Uri Gneezy and Aldo Rustichini, "A Fine is a Price" (2000) 29:1 *The Journal of Legal Studies* 1–17 at 3.

51   Carl Mellström and Magnus Johannesson, "Crowding Out in Blood Donation: Was Titmuss Right?" (2008) 6:4 *Journal of the European Economic Association* 845–863 at 857.

52   Dan Ariely, *Predictably Irrational: The Hidden Forces that Shape Our Decisions* (New York: HarperCollins Publishers, 2008) at p. 71.

53   Stewart J. Schwab and Randall S. Thomas, "An Empirical Analysis of CEO Employment Contracts: What Do Top Executives Bargain For?" (2006) 63:1 *Washington and Lee Law Review* 231–270 at 240–241.

54   See, for example, Daniel H. Pink, *Drive: The Surprising Truth About What Motivates Us* (New York: Penguin Group (USA) Inc., 2009) at pp. 26–58; Bruno S. Frey and Felix Oberholzer-Gee, "The Cost of Price Incentives: An Empirical Analysis of Motivation Crowding-Out" (1997) 87:4 *The American Economic Review* 746–755 at 753–754; Alfie Kohn, "Why Incentive Plans Cannot Work" (1993) 71:5 *Harvard Business Review* 54–60 at 58–59; Canice Prendergast, "Intrinsic Motivation and Incentives" (2008) 98:2 *American Economic Review* 201–205 at 204; Martha Lagace, "Pay-for-Performance Doesn't Always

Pay Off" (April 14, 2003), *Harvard Business School Working Knowledge*, online: http://hbswk.hbs.edu/item/pay-for-performance-doesnt-always-pay-off.

55 Bruno S. Frey and Margit Osterloh, "Yes, Managers Should be Paid Like Bureaucrats" (2005) 14:1 *Journal of Management Inquiry* 96–111 at 97; Harris and Bromiley, "Incentives to Cheat," above at note 25 at 362; Denis, Hanouna and Sarin, "Dark Side to Incentive Compensation," above at note 25 at 470; David A. Becher, Terry L. Campbell II and Melissa B. Frye, "Incentive Compensation for Bank Directors: The Impact of Deregulation" (2005) 78:5 *The Journal of Business* 1753–1778 at 1759; Qiang Cheng and David B. Farber, "Earnings Restatements, Changes in CEO Compensation, and Firm Performance" (2008) 83:5 *The Accounting Review* 1217–1250 at 1246; James C. Spindler, "Endogenous Compensation in a Firm with Disclosure and Moral Hazard" (2009), *USC Center in Law, Economics and Organization Research Paper No. C09-20*, online (pdf): http://weblaw.usc.edu/assets/docs/contribute/C09_20_paper.pdf at 2.

56 Roger L. Martin, *Fixing the Game: Bubbles, Crashes, and What Capitalism Can Learn from the NFL* (Boston: Harvard Business Review Press, 2011) at pp. 5–6 [Martin, *Fixing the Game*]; Michael Faulkender et al., "Executive Compensation: An Overview of Research on Corporate Practices and Proposed Reforms" (2010) 22:1 *Journal of Applied Corporate Finance* 107–118 at 113–114, 117 [Faulkender et al., "Executive Compensation"].

57 Martin, *Fixing the Game*, above at note 56 at pp. 27–30.

58 Xavier Gabaix and Augustin Landier, "Why Has CEO Pay Increased So Much?" (2008) 123:1 *The Quarterly Journal of Economics* 49–100 at 50; Alex Edmans, Xavier Gabaix and Augustin Landier, "A Multiplicative Model of Optimal CEO Incentives in Market Equilibrium" (2009) 22:12 *The Review of Financial Studies* 4881–4917 at 4881–4886.

59 Stanley Lieberson and James F. O'Connor, "Leadership and Organizational Performance: A Study of Large Corporations" (1972) 37:2 *American Sociological Review* 117–130 at 123–124; See also, Marianne Bertrand and Antoinette Schoar, "Managing with Style: The Effect of Managers on Firm Policies" (2003) 118:4 *The Quarterly Journal of Economics* 1169–1208 at 1190–1191.

60 Alan Berkeley Thomas, "Does Leadership Make a Difference to Organizational Performance?" (1988) 33:3 *Administrative Science Quarterly* 388–400 at 397–398.

61 Piketty, *Capital*, above at note 2 at pp. 330–332.

62 Lucian A. Bebchuk and Jesse M. Fried, *Pay Without Performance: The Unfulfilled Promise of Executive Compensation* (Cambridge: Harvard University Press, 2004) at p. 139; Faulkender et al., "Executive Compensation," above at note 56 at 113–117.

63 Christopher D. Ittner and David F. Larcker, "Coming Up Short on Nonfinancial Performance Measurement" (2003) 81:11 *Harvard Business Review* 88–95 at 90–92.

64 Roland Bénabou and Jean Tirole, "Bonus Culture: Competitive Pay, Screening, and Multitasking" (2016) 124:2 *Journal of Political Economy* 305–370 at 311–314; Robert Gibbons, "Incentives Between Firms (And Within)" (2005) 51:1 *Management Science* 2–17 at 6.

65 Frydman and Jenter, "CEO Compensation," above at note 3 at 91. Also see, Gerald T. Garvey and Todd T. Milburn, "Asymmetric Benchmarking in Compensation: Executives are Rewarded for Good Luck but not Penalized for Bad" (2006) 82:1 *Journal of Financial Economics* 197–225 at 207–210; Kevin J. Murphy, "Explaining Executive Compensation: Managerial Power Versus the Perceived Cost of Stock Option" (2002) 69:3 *The University of Chicago Law Review* 847–869 at 862–863; Ingolf Dittmann and Ernst Maug, "Lower Salaries and No Options? On the Optimal Structure of Executive Pay" (2007) 62:1 *The Journal of Finance* 303–343 at 328.

66 Victor Brudney and Marvin A. Chirelstein, *Cases and Materials on Corporate Finance*, 2nd ed. (Mineola: The Foundation Press Inc., 1979) at p. 1153; Marianne Bertrand and Sendhil Mullainathan, "Are CEOs Rewarded for Luck? The Ones Without Principals Are" (2011) 116:3 *The Quarterly Journal of Economics* 901–932 at 929; Dirk Jenter and Fadi Kanaan, "CEO Turnover and Relative Performance Evaluation" (2015) 70:5 *The Journal of Finance* 2155–2184 at 2175–2177 [Jenter and Kanaan, "CEO Turnover"].

67 *Making Executive Pay Work: The Psychology of Incentive*, PricewaterhouseCoopers International Limited (2012), online (pdf): www.pwc.com/gx/en/hr-management-ser vices/publications/assets/making-executive-pay-work.pdf at 6; Brian J. Hall and Kevin J. Murphy, "Stock Options for Undiversified Executives" (2002) 33:1 *Journal of Accounting and Economics* 3–42 at 12–13 [Hall and Murphy, "Stock Options"].

68 Hall and Murphy, "Stock Options," above at note 67 at 11.

69 Steven N. Kaplan and Bernadette A. Minton, "How Has CEO Turnover Changed?" (2012) 12:1 *International Review of Finance* 57–87 at 81 [Kaplan and Minton, "CEO Turnover"].

70 Jenter and Kanaan, "CEO Turnover," above at note 66 at 2170.

71 Ruth Bender, "Onwards and Upwards: Why Companies Change their Executive Remuneration Schemes, and Why This Leads to Increases in Pay" (2007) 15:5 *Corporate Governance: An International Review* 709–723 at 712–713.

72 US Federal Tax Act, Internal Revenue Code, USC 1986, s. 162 (m) as it appeared on 17 February 1993.

73 Shamsud D. Chowdhury, "Director Compensation: The Growing Popularity of Deferred Stock Units" (2009) 73:1 *Ivey Business Journal* 11, online: http://iveybusinessjournal.com/ publication/director-compensation-the-growing-popularity-of-deferred-stock-units/.

74 Hall and Murphy, "Stock Options," above at note 67 at 122.

75 Conyon, "Executive Compensation," above at note 4 at F72, F74–F75.

76 *Ibid* at F75; Martin J. Conyon et al., "The Executive Compensation Controversy: A Transatlantic Analysis" (2011), *Cornell University ILR School Working Paper No. 2011–0002*, online: www.digitalcommons.ilr.cornell.edu/ics/5 at 26 [Conyon et al., "Compensation Controversy"].

77 Conyon et al., "Compensation Controversy," above at note 76 at 64.

78 *Directors' Remuneration: Report of a Study Group Chaired by Sir Richard Greenbury*, Study Group on Director's Remuneration (July 17, 1995), online: *ECGI*, www.ecgi .global/code/greenbury-report-study-group-directors-remuneration at 17.

79 Martin J. Conyon, John E. Core and Wayne R. Guay, "Are US CEOs Paid More Than UK CEOs? Inferences from Risk-adjusted Pay" (2011) 24:2 *The Review of Financial Studies* 402–438 at 404–409; Martin J. Conyon and Kevin J. Murphy, "The Prince and the Pauper: CEO Pay in the US and UK" (2000) 110:467 *Economic Journal* 640–671; Conyon et al., "Compensation Controversy," above at note 76 at 65–66.

80 Conyon et al., "Compensation Controversy," above at note 76 at 61.

81 *Ibid* ("[w]e believe there are three main factors that fueled the explosion in stock options: (1) increased shareholder activism and demands that pay be better linked to shareholder returns" at 15); Kevin J. Murphy, "Executive Compensation: Where We Are and How We Got There" in George M. Constantinides, Milton Harris and Rene M. Stulz (eds.), *Handbook of the Economics of Finance*, (Amsterdam: Elsevier, 2013), vol. 2A, pp. 211–356 at p. 284; Frank Dobbin and Jiwook Jung, "The Misapplication of Mr. Michael Jensen: How Agency Theory Brought Down the Economy and Why it Might Again" in Michael Lounsbury and Paul M. Hirsch (eds.), *Markets on Trial: The Economic Sociology of the US Financial Crisis: Part B* (Bingley: Emerald Group Limited, 2010), p. 29 at pp. 33–34.

82 Michael Beer and Nancy Katz, "Do Incentives Work? The Perceptions of a Worldwide Sample of Senior Executives" (2003) 26:3 *Human Resource Planning* 30–44 at 36.

83 Jeffrey N. Gordon, "The Rise of Independent Directors in the United States, 1950–2005: Of Shareholder Value and Stock Market Prices" (2007) 59:6 *Stanford Law Review* 1465–1568 at 1475.

84 Brian K. Boyd, "Board Control and CEO Compensation" (1994) 15:5 *Strategic Management Journal* 335–344 at 339; John E. Core, Robert W. Holthausen and David F. Larcker, "Corporate Governance, Chief Executive Officer Compensation, and Firm Performance" (1999) 51:3 *Journal of Financial Economics* 371–406 at 372.

85 Hamid Mehran, "Executive Compensation Structure, Ownership, and Firm Performance" (1995) 38:2 *Journal of Financial Economics* 163–184 at 173.

86 Martin J. Conyon and Lerong He, "Compensation Committees and CEO Compensation Incentives in U.S. Entrepreneurial Firms" (2004) 16:1 *Journal of Management Accounting Research* 35–56 at 47; Kam-Ming Wan, "Can Boards with a Majority of Independent Directors Lower CEO Compensation?" (2009), online: *SSRN*, https://ssrn.com/abstract=1421549 at 5; Joseph Gerakos, "CEO Pensions: Disclosure, Managerial Power and Optimal Contracting" (2010), online: *SSRN*, https://ssrn.com/abstract=982180 at 4; Conyon, "Executive Compensation," above at note 4 at F86.

87 Yuval Deutsch, "The Impact on Board Composition on Firms' Critical Decisions: A Meta-analytic Review" (2005) 31:3 *Journal of Management* 424–444 at 433.

88 *Ibid* at 424.

89 Martin J. Conyon, Simon I. Peck and Graham V. Sadler, "Compensation Consultants and Executive Pay: Evidence from the United States and the United Kingdom" (2009) 23:1 *Academy of Management Perspectives* 43–55 at 43 [Conyon, Peck and Sadler, "Consultants and Executive Pay"]; James B. Wade, Joseph F. Porac and Timothy G. Pollock, "Worth, Words, and the Justification of Executive Pay" (1997) 18:S1 *The International Journal of Industrial, Occupational and Organizational Psychology and Behavior* 641–664 at 644; Jenny Chu, Jonathan Faasse and P. Raghavendra Rau, "Do Compensation Consultants Enable Higher CEO Pay? New Evidence from Recent Disclosure Rule Changes" (2015), online: *SSRN*, https://ssrn.com/abstract=2500054 at 3 [Chu, Faasse and Rau, "Compensation Consultants"].

90 Chu, Faasse and Rau, "Compensation Consultants," above at note 89 at 24.

91 Joseph J. Gerakos, Joseph D. Puotroski and Suraj Srinivasan, "Which US Market Interactions Affect CEO Pay? Evidence from UK Companies" (2013) 59:11 *Management Science* 2413–2434 at 2414.

92 Brian Cadman, Mary Ellen Carter and Stephen Hillegeist, "The Incentives of Compensation Consultants and CEO Pay" (2010) 49:3 *Journal of Accounting and Economics* 263–280 at 264; Conyon, Peck and Sadler, "Consultants and Executive Pay," above at note 89 at 43; Kevin J. Murphy and Tatiana Sandino, "Executive Pay and 'Independent' Compensation Consultants" (2010) 49:3 *Journal of Accounting and Economics* 247–262 at 247. But see, Chu, Faasse and Rau, "Compensation Consultants," above at note 89 at 6 (finding that management-retained consultants do lead to higher pay than board-retained consultants).

93 Kaplan and Minton, "CEO Turnover," above at note 69 at 75; Mark R. Huson, Robert Parrino and Laura T. Starks, "Internal Monitoring Mechanisms and CEO Turnover: A Long-Term Perspective" (2001) 56:6 *The Journal of Finance* 2265–2297 at 2267–2268.

94 Kevin J. Murphy and Jan Zabojnik, "Managerial Capital and the Market for CEOs" (2007), online: *SSRN*, https://ssrn.com/abstract=984376 at 1–2.

95 *Ibid* at 27–28.

96   *Good Governance Is Good Business: Corporate Governance Principles and Proxy Voting Guidelines*, Ontario Teachers' Pension Plan (2019), online (pdf): www.otpp.com/content/dam/otpp/documents/news/teacherscorpgove.pdf at 34; Angela G. Morgan and Annette B. Poulsen, "Linking Pay to Performance – Compensation Proposals in the S&P 500" (2001) 62:3 *Journal of Financial Economics* 489–523 at 491.

97   S. Travis Certo et al., "Giving Money to Get Money: How CEO Stock Options and CEO Equity Enhance IPO Valuations" (2003) 46:5 *Academy of Management Journal* 643–653 at 644–645.

98   Sánchez-Ballesta and García-Meca, "Firm Performance," above at note 19 at 887–888.

99   Robert J. Jackson, Jr., "Private Equity and Executive Compensation" (2013) 60:3 *UCLA Law Review* 638–677 at 652.

100 Henrik Cronqvist and Rudiger Fahlenbrach, "CEO Contract Design: How Do Strong Principals Do It?" (2013) 108:3 *Journal of Financial Economics* 659–674 at 663 [Cronqvist and Fahlenbrach, "CEO Contract Design"].

101 Steven N. Kaplan, "Executive Compensation and Corporate Governance in the United States: Perceptions, Facts, and Challenges" (2012–2013) 2 *Cato Papers on Public Policy* 99–164 at 102.

102 Cronqvist and Fahlenbrach, "CEO Contract Design," above at note 100 at 660.

103 Jeffrey N. Gordon, "Say on Pay: Cautionary Notes on the UK Experience and the Case for Shareholder Opt-in" (2009) 46:2 *Harvard Journal on Legislation* 323–367 at 343 [Gordon, "Say on Pay"]; Conyon, "Executive Compensation," above at note 4 at F83; Brian V. Breheny et al., "Say-on Pay Votes and Compensation Disclosures" (January 6, 2021), *Harvard Law School Forum on Corporate Governance*, online: https://corpgov.law.harvard.edu/2021/01/06/say-on-pay-votes-and-compensation-disclosures/.

104 Fabrizio Ferri and David A. Maber, "Say on Pay Votes and CEO Compensation: Evidence From the UK" (2013) 17:2 *Review of Finance* 527–563 at 529; Martin Conyon and Graham Sadler, "Shareholder Voting and Directors' Remuneration Report Legislation: Say on Pay in the UK" (2010) 18:4 *Corporate Governance: An International Review* 296–312 at 297; David F. Larcker, "Ten Myths of 'Say on Pay'" (2012), *Rock Center for Corporate Governance at Stanford University Closer Look Series: Topics, Issues and Controversies in Corporate Governance* No.3 CGRP-26, online: SSRN, https://ssrn.com/abstract=2094704. But see, Martin J. Conyon, "Shareholder Dissent on Say-on-Pay Voting and CEO Compensation" (2016), online: SSRN, https://ssrn.com/abstract=2748645 (finding CEO pay at least increases at slower rates in the very few companies that have previously attracted high levels of dissent on say-on-pay votes).

105 Gordon, "Say on Pay," above at note 103 at 344.

106 *Ibid* at 347.

107 *Ibid* at 348. See also, Lund and Polsky, "Diminishing Returns," above at note 38 at 682; Felipe Cabezon, "Executive Compensation: The Trend Toward One Size Fits All" (2022), online: SSRN, https://ssrn.com/abstract=3727623.

108 Dorff, *Indispensable*, above at note 38 at p. 246.

109 Alex Edmans and Qi Liu, "Inside Debt" (2011) 15:1 *Review of Finance* 75–102 at 77; Chengyang Wei and David Yermack, "Investor Reactions to CEOs' Inside Debt Incentives" (2011) 24:11 *The Review of Financial Studies* 3813–3840 at 3831; Rangarajan K. Sundaram and David L. Yermack, "Pay Me Later: Inside Debt and Its Role in Managerial Compensation" (2007) 62:4 *The Journal of Finance* 1551–1588 at 1579.

5

What Explains Shareholder Voting?

At a time of unprecedented political polarization, there is one thing on which all Americans can agree: voters are idiots. This broadly shared opinion is about "voters," not "people." As it happens, "people" are generally rational in many areas of their lives. We know this from our day-to-day experiences with family members and friends. We may have a crazy uncle, but he is an outlier, and even he manages to generally accomplish the things he sets out to do. In fact, market economies are predicated in part on the idea that people know their business better than any remote group of experts, and if history has proven any proposition, surely it has proven that this is true. But when it comes to voting, we have an often-unvoiced suspicion that voters are not pulling the lever based on well-informed and coldly rational calculation. Instead, we tend to feel that they are often voting based on mood-affiliation, partisanship, and a toxic mix of half-truths, ignorance, and resentment.

Fortunately, political science has thoroughly investigated the question of voter rationality and empirically demonstrated that our intuitions are correct: voters *are* often idiots. Research on voting in civic elections shows that votes are often cast for expressive reasons unrelated to voters' self-interest or desired outcomes. The almost nonexistent marginal value of a single vote means that voters feel free to collect and process information in ways that make themselves feel good. The actual real-world impact of the vote is discounted to the point where time and energy are often not invested to gather the necessary information or to evaluate whether the politicians' proposed solutions are relevant to the claimed social, environmental, and economic problems. (In fact, quite often, even the problems that upset large segments of the voting population are either made-up or overblown.)

But is this political science research relevant to shareholder voting? After all, shareholders have money at stake, and many of them are among the most sophisticated actors in the economy. But, as we shall see, the empirical literature around shareholder voting shows the same thing we see in relation to civic elections: shareholders give their voting rights almost no value, vote in ways that do not reflect the economic performance of the company, do not vote for directors as if the individual in question matters, vote in ways that contradict their economic views (measured by looking at their trading decisions), and are driven by empirically questionable and often deliberately ineffective corporate governance practices. This is a big problem for the modern corporate governance project, which depends on assumptions of rational shareholder voting for many of its reforms.

5.1 THE GROWTH OF SHAREHOLDER VOTING POWER

The arrival of agency cost theory provided at one stroke both a rationale for the traditional privileging of shareholders by corporate law (they are the only corporate constituency that possesses the franchise) and a program for further reforms. If the central problem of corporate governance is managers acting in ways that run contrary to the best interests of their shareholder principals, then it makes sense to give shareholders authority over those managers.

When agency cost theory arrived in the late 1970s, shareholders had very limited voting power in America. Of course, they elected the directors, who in turn chose the executives, but in practice, managers were largely independent of shareholder influence owing to their control over the company's proxy process and the presence of collective action and free-riding problems that made it easier for shareholders to simply sell their shares rather than confront incompetent or venal managers. In 1988, an American court observed that shareholder voting was "a vestige or ritual of little practical importance."[1] Unless managerial failures or larceny became notorious, directors were generally re-elected without much difficulty.

Within a few years, however, the corporate governance revolution was underway, and shareholder voting became seen as an important device for improving America's biggest companies. One of the causes of this change was the absorption of the agency cost story into everyday understandings of corporate governance, but there were other causes as well. Institutional shareholders grew from nothing in the decades after the Second World War to the biggest participants in the market. Today, institutional shareholders own about 78 percent of the shares in the Russell 3000 and 80 percent of the S&P 500.[2] This increasing concentration of share ownership holds the promise of reducing the collective action and free-riding problems that had previously interfered with effective shareholder governance. As well, institutional shareholders are managed by experienced professional fund managers, often with advanced degrees in business or law, who seem well-equipped to both evaluate corporate performance and effectively confront underperforming managers.

The arrival of third-party proxy advisors (discussed in Chapter 7) only increased the governance industry's optimism about shareholder voting. These advisors could dedicate significant resources to analyzing the performance and governance of public companies, amortize the expense over all their clients, and thus reduce the costs of their institutional clients voting intelligently and effectively.

The idea that a renewed emphasis on shareholder voting was going to improve corporate governance was never fully accepted by academics. Scholars argued over whether the economic interests of shareholders were actually aligned with those of the corporation. Do some important corporate constituencies' interests (such as customers, debtholders, or employees) conflict with those of the shareholders? Are shareholders' economic incentives too short-term? Institutional investors typically build well-diversified portfolios, so do they have the same relationship to risk as other important parties to the corporate contract? Do public pension fund managers advance corporate governance agendas designed primarily to appeal to their political masters? Do union pension funds use their voting power tactically to advance their position at the bargaining table? Do mutual funds reflexively support management to avoid alienating the very people who decide what fund options will be offered to employees?

The debates also considered whether the replacement of retail investors (actual human beings with noninvestment day jobs) by professional fund managers was going to lead to better-quality voting. On the surface, this seems likely, but critics like Professor John Coffee pointed out that the "expected gains from most … governance issues are small, deferred, and received by investors, while the costs are potentially large, immediate, and borne by money managers."[3]

Institutional money managers worry primarily about their portfolio's relative performance against other funds or index benchmarks. Beating these benchmarks is how money managers build a reputation and attract more money to the funds they manage. As gains from shareholder voting are received by their competitors who often own shares in the same companies, as well as being reflected in the relevant benchmarks, some academics suggest professional managers choose to devote their resources instead on the activities that allow them to differentiate themselves and attract investment.[4] Certainly professional fund managers seem to hire, reward, and invest effort mostly in relation to stock picking and executing trading strategies. Blackrock indicates that while it submits votes at approximately 15,000 shareholder meetings per year in over ninety countries, it employs only twenty governance professionals.[5] That sure looks like voting decisions are being treated as relatively unimportant.

These academic debates were largely ignored by the governance industry. Shareholders liked the appealing image of themselves as the guardians of good governance; according to one survey, 80 percent of institutional investors "believe that proxy voting increases shareholder value."[6] Regulators also accepted that increasing shareholder voting power would contribute to improving corporate performance. In 1988, the US Department of Labor announced that ERISA pension fund managers had a duty to make informed decisions about how they voted the shares in their portfolios. In 2003, the SEC required mutual funds to ensure their voting power is exercised in the "best interests" of their beneficiaries. These two acts were largely responsible for creating the market for third-party proxy advisors, as the voting recommendations of these advisors could be relied upon by fund managers who might otherwise have either refrained from voting portfolio shares or reflexively voted them in favor of management's recommendations.

In 2010, Dodd-Frank introduced say-on-pay votes and "proxy access" (now "universal access") rules that reduce the costs associated with voting alternative directors onto a corporate board. Around the same time, widespread pressure by the governance industry led to the virtual elimination of staggered boards among the largest companies in America's public markets.[7] (The elimination of a staggered board means that shareholders have a chance to vote on a particular director every year, rather than only once every three years.) Shareholder proposals promoting the latest corporate governance practices flourished and achieved unprecedented electoral success.

It wasn't just that shareholders began voting more, they began to use the powers they were given by corporate law to vote on a much broader range of issues. One of the key elements of this transition was to leverage the vote for directors to drive changes to other kinds of corporate decisions. So, for example, a member of the compensation committee may be targeted for removal because of a pay plan that violates some best practice. A member of the governance committee can face an adverse voting recommendation if the company's constating documents restrict the shareholders' ability to amend the corporate bylaws. The entire board can be targeted if the company adopts takeover protections, such as a poison pill or staggered board.

The effect of this new approach to voting is that through their power over director elections, shareholders are able to push for changes throughout the organization, including on matters over which corporate law does not give shareholders a say. This constitutes a massive expansion of the shareholder franchise, and it is why proxy advisors' voting guidelines have expanded into hundreds of pages. In combination with an increasing use of shareholder proposals, boards face shareholder input on virtually every major strategic and policy decision they make. For example, the proxy advisors' guidelines now deal with whether pre-emptive rights should be given to shareholders, whether an increase in authorized share capital is acceptable, and whether greenhouse gas emissions should be reduced. We are a long way from the traditional role of the shareholder franchise as a device used to discipline only clearly incompetent or venal managers.

5.2 VOTING AND RATIONALITY

The empirical literature around political voting finds that the average voter, though rationally self-interested in their personal life, is irrational in the way they vote. This irrationality is actually a function of the self-interest that lies at the heart of economic explanations for human behavior. Political voters are, in the words of economist Bryan Caplan, "rationally irrational."[8]

Like a shareholder in a widely held company, the voters in a democracy individually have little chance of affecting the outcome of an election. As a result, they perform the same cost-benefit calculation around voting as shareholders. This calculation suggests the marginal value of their vote is insignificant, so they rationally choose not to expend the resources required to properly inform themselves prior to voting.[9] The empirical evidence of this ignorance is both vast and shocking to the uninitiated.[10] In the words of one author of a survey of the literature: "The reality that most voters are often ignorant of even very basic political information is one of the better-established findings of social science. Decades of accumulated evidence reinforce this conclusion."[11] It is hard choosing the most amazing illustrations of this ignorance. For example, fewer than 20 percent of Americans know who their senators are and less than half know their state has two of them.[12] Fewer than 40 percent of the electorate even know which party controls the Senate and which controls the House.[13]

This political ignorance should not come as a surprise. We are consistently ignorant on matters where our opinions will have little impact and, therefore, we have no incentive to inform ourselves. Over 20 percent of Americans do not know that the Earth revolves around the Sun rather than the reverse.[14] Less than 40 percent of Americans believe in the theory of evolution (the rest either disbelieve it or have no opinion).[15] Over one-third of Europeans and Americans believe genetically unmodified foods do not contain genes.[16] A quarter of Europeans believe that eating a genetically modified fruit can result in their bodies' genes being modified.[17]

Several aspects of this literature on rational ignorance must be made clear. The first is that this ignorance is a function of the individual's lack of influence over the outcome of an election; it is not a function of the importance of the ultimate outcome of the election. Obviously, it matters, even to the average citizen, what their government does, in the same way that it obviously matters to the average shareholder who occupies the seats in the boardroom. What drives voter ignorance is the insignificant marginal value of that individual's vote.

The second notable factor is that the motivation of the voter doesn't matter. It doesn't matter, for example, whether the voter is strongly self-interested or altruistic. The strongly self-interested will conclude that they have better things to do than invest a great deal of resources in gathering the information needed to vote wisely; the altruistic will conclude that resources spent informing themselves as a voter would be better devoted to activities with a much higher pay-off to the people they are trying to help.

An additional fact that emerges from the literature on political voting is that voter ignorance has not improved as levels of education and the availability of information have increased:

> [T]he level of political knowledge in the American electorate has increased only modestly, if at all, since the beginning of mass survey research in the late 1930s. A relatively stable level of ignorance has persisted even in the face of massive increases in educational attainment and an unprecedented expansion in the quantity and quality of information available to the general public at little cost.[18]

This is obviously discouraging news for proponents of the view that better shareholder voting only requires more, and less expensive to consume, information.

Thus far, the research into political voting resembles the usual collective action arguments found in academic discussions of shareholder voting. But it is here that the political science data goes in an unexpected direction. Given high and persistent levels of rational ignorance about political matters, how do citizens in a democracy decide to cast their vote? George Akerlof summarizes the choice facing individuals and the way that choice plays out:

> [I]nformation is interpreted in a biased way which weights [*sic*] two … goals: agents' desire to feel good about themselves, their activities and the society they live in, on the one hand, and the need for an accurate view of the world for correct decision making, on the other hand…. [B]ecause any individual's influence on the public choice outcome is close to zero, each individual has an incentive to choose a model of the world which maximizes his private happiness without any consideration of the consequences for social policy.[19]

This formulation goes beyond the "rational ignorance" of public choice theory. "[R]ational ignorance assumes that people tire of the search for truth, while rational irrationality says that people actively avoid the truth."[20] What do they pursue instead? They pursue self-expression. They vote in ways that make them feel better about themselves, that confirm and reflect their prejudices, and that help their political "team" score points. They will blame their troubles on harmless scapegoats, punish bearers of bad news for the sin of telling the truth, vote for policies that appear to make their country look "tough," vote for politicians who are like themselves or who tell them the solutions to problems are simple, refuse to believe news that casts a negative light on "their" politicians, choose news sources that confirm their prejudices, justify a politician's bad behavior by investing new importance to other aspects of their personality or actions, and adopt absurd conspiracy theories that make the other side look bad or explain away uncomfortable facts. In short, their political lives are a form of mood affiliation.

Professor Ilya Somin calls this behavior enjoying "the psychic benefits of being a political 'fan.'"[21] Sports fans invest time gathering information and following their team, not because of any expectation that by doing so they are affecting the outcome of the season, but rather because they find it interesting and enjoy rooting for "their" team. Political fans similarly derive enjoyment from supporting their preferred candidates, parties, or ideologies, and from denigrating the other side. They also benefit from the pleasure of having their pre-existing views validated and from associating with like-minded people with the same beliefs.

This view of voting explains why studies repeatedly find that the most knowledgeable voters tend to be the most biased in their interpretation of new information.[22] Bias in evaluating information increases with higher cognitive ability and stronger ideological views.[23] No matter where voters are on the spectrum, they prefer to talk politics with people who have similar opinions and receive news from sources that align with those views.[24] These are not the actions of people seeking truth, they are the actions of fans rationally pursuing their own peace of mind and sense of vindication. The entire dynamic is underwritten by the fact that "the market has a 'user fee' for irrationality, and democracy does not."[25]

This last statement may seem controversial because every voter obviously has a stake in the quality of government. Indeed, one of the most common assumptions about voting patterns is that voters often cast their votes to advance their own self-interest. "They vote their pocketbook" is a phrase at least as old as the time when pocketbooks existed – and were referred to as such. For example, there is a popular belief that rich people vote in favor of lower taxes while poor people vote in favor of more generous social programs.

Professor Bryan Caplan reviews extensive political science literature on this hypothesis that voting is characterized by self-interest and concludes: "[P]olitical scientists have subjected the SIVH [Self-Interested Voter Hypothesis] to extensive and diverse empirical tests. Their results are impressively uniform: The SIVH fails."[26] He provides numerous examples from the literature. For example, research has found there is only a slight connection between a person's income and their ideology or political party affiliation.[27] Elderly Americans are not more likely to be supporters of Medicare than the young.[28] Males vulnerable to the draft support it at the same rates as other segments of the population.[29]

One of the most famous books about this phenomenon of voting against your economic interests is the plaintively titled, *What's the Matter with Kansas?*[30] The answer, of course, is that nothing is uniquely wrong with Kansas. Voters don't automatically vote in their economic self-interest, and we already know why. The chance that their vote will actually have an impact on their economic interests is miniscule. However, they enjoy all the psychic benefits they will receive from voting in a way that flatters their self-image, reflects strongly held prejudices, advances their social standing, and causes the minimum intellectual discomfort. Their votes are entirely rational because the marginal impact of their vote is insignificant. There is literally nothing to be gained from sacrificing these private benefits.

It may be objected at this point that we are failing to give adequate weight to the rational self-interest of shareholders. Political voters become citizens mostly as a result of an accident of birth, and even if they immigrate consciously, they usually do so for considerations unrelated to their enthusiasm for the franchise. Shareholders, in contrast, choose to become shareholders in order to make money, and thus their relationship to a corporation is suffused with self-interest in a way not true for the average citizen of a democracy.

5.3 THE EMPIRICAL LITERATURE AROUND SHAREHOLDER VOTING

5.3.1 *The Value Placed by Investors on Their Votes*

Shareholders generally behave in ways that suggest they don't put a lot of value on the voting rights they are provided by corporate law. In fact, the central fact of corporate elections is that, "[i]ndividual shareholders routinely ignore requests to cast their proxy ballots in corporate elections."[31] As we have seen, institutional shareholders were also generally reluctant to spend time on their voting decisions, which is why, in 1988 and 2003, regulators had to step in to emphasize that voting conscientiously was a duty fund managers owed the beneficial owners of the fund. Even then, as we will see in Chapter 7, institutional investors delegated most of the work around voting to third-party proxy advisors.

When they do vote, shareholders are remarkably passive. They almost always leave managerial and board arrangements intact. In a typical year, for example, only eight out of 31,000 American directors failed to receive a majority of votes cast by shareholders.[32] Reviewing the data, one academic suggests, "while shareholders may be willing to withhold votes when such an action is merely symbolic, such willingness may wane when the action actually has an impact on a director's position."[33]

These preliminary observations are supported by the research on how voting rights are valued in the market. Looking at companies with dual-class shares, Luigi Zingales finds that the premiums for superior-voting shares in America are low and often indistinguishable from zero, except in cases where control of the company is up for grabs.[34] He notes that the "value of a vote is determined by the expected additional payments vote holders will receive if there is a control contest.... [T]he size of this differential payment is a function of the private benefits obtainable from controlling a company."[35] So, control over a company in circumstances where you can extract rents is valuable, but anything less than that is valued by the market as effectively worthless.

Another way of looking at the question of the value given to voting rights by public company investors is to examine the stock lending market. This market generally serves short sellers, but it also allows an investor to borrow shares for the purpose of utilizing the voting rights attached to them. A team of researchers found that the volume of lending activity in a company's shares increases to a level about 25 percent above normal on the record date for annual shareholder meetings, quickly returning to its usual levels afterwards.[36] There is no change in the costs associated with borrowing votes in this way. In fact, the costs of doing so are almost trivially low and do not increase on the record date when voting rights can be exercised.[37]

Recently, two different papers have attempted to determine the market value of voting rights by using bonds and options to replicate the cash flows associated with owning a share in a company.[38] This "contingent claims" approach is a method to separate out a share's economic value from its voting value. The two articles find that voting rights form very little of the value of a share. Their estimates range from 1.23 to 1.64 percent of a share's value.

These various lines of research suggest that shareholders value their vote about as much as citizens in a democracy: not much. This opens the possibility (but only the possibility at this point) that shareholders behave like ordinary political voters, remaining rationally ignorant and exclusively concerned with receiving certain private psychic and social benefits from their voting behavior. To evaluate whether we see the same kind of irrationality visible in popular elections, we will have to look at how shareholders actually exercise their franchise.

5.3.2 *Ordinary Uncontested Director Elections*

There is little support for the proposition (often assumed in discussions about shareholder voting) that voting decisions are driven by bottom-line corporate economic performance. The shareholder campaigns that generate abnormal numbers of "withhold" votes in an uncontested election only weakly reflect a corporation's economic performance.[39] Poor economic performance does predict fewer votes in favor of a director, but an entire standard deviation in EBITDA-to-Assets ratio relative to industry peers only results in an insignificant 0.37 percent decrease in support.[40] Several studies involving various accounting measures of performance find the same thing.[41] The evidence is even mixed about whether disappointing stock market returns produce withhold campaigns.[42] As one overview of the empirical literature concludes, "[c]ompany performance has only a limited impact on the outcome of a director election, with results ranging from a statistically but not economically significant relationship to no relationship at all."[43]

What drives voting behavior in uncontested director elections? To state it simply: corporate governance. This is not "corporate governance" in the older and everyday sense of effectively leading the company to commercial success; it is the modern conception of "corporate governance" we have been discussing in this book: adherence to a list of "best practices."

There is a strong correlation between an ISS "withhold" voting recommendation and the percentage of votes against a director.[44] The rationale given by ISS for a withhold recommendation therefore likely reflects the voting intentions of other institutional shareholders. Given the rarity of withhold votes, it seems unlikely that in a particular year, a body of shareholders engages in the exceptional process of dissenting from a management proxy for completely unrelated reasons. This allows us to explore the motivation behind institutional shareholder voting decisions.

The kind of corporate governance best practices that seem to predict voting behavior are familiar to anyone associated with corporate boardrooms over the past three decades.[45] One study looking at the votes received by S&P 500 companies over the period 2003–2010 found more than two-thirds of the withhold votes targeted against an individual director arose from concerns about their independence.[46] The remaining third reflected concerns over the director's "busyness" and meeting attendance record.[47] Where an entire board committee was targeted, it was usually a function of concerns with executive pay.[48] When the board as a whole received an abnormal number of withhold votes, it was due to a lack of responsiveness to shareholder proposals receiving a majority vote (such as declassifying the board) or the board's decision to adopt a poison pill.[49]

It is telling what does not appear to drive voting decisions in relation to directors: competence, experience, contributions to the board, and the underlying economic performance of the business. As one team of researchers observes, shareholders claim to vote for directors as if financial performance, director performance, and firm governance matter, but the impact of these factors on actual votes is trivial.[50]

Research suggests that boards are responsive to the underlying concerns of an abnormal withhold vote. For example, the chance that a board will declassify itself increases from 4.9 to 36.9 percent subsequent to a withhold recommendation from proxy advisors where this was a stated rationale.[51] In harmony with the vast literature about the irrelevance of these best practices for corporate performance, researchers looking at the S&P 500 companies between 2003 and 2010 concluded:

> [W]e compare the subsequent performance of responsive and unresponsive firms, but find no evidence of differences, even in the most severe cases. One explanation is that the items on which proxy advisors and voting shareholders focus have little effect on firm value, consistent with the claim that activists misdirect their efforts towards "symbolic" governance issues.[52]

In other words, shareholder voting in uncontested director elections is irrational.

This irrationality presents in other ways. For example, audit committee members are generally held responsible for accounting restatements, but not for weaknesses in the firm's internal controls.[53] In contrast, representatives of management on the board are held responsible for the latter but not the former. This demarcation of responsibility is mysterious, as audit committee charters usually contemplate responsibility for both matters. As we saw in Chapter 2, it is unlikely that the outsiders that now constitute audit committees could discover problems of either type given their dependence on management and auditors for information. It seems arbitrary to hold audit committee members accountable for one failure, but not the other. However, the arbitrary rule that management is responsible for control failures while the audit committee is responsible for restatements is useful in giving shareholders the impression that responsibility and punishment are discriminatorily allocated and administered. The truth about actual competence and failure is irrelevant.

Companies caught up in the last decade's option backdating scandals were significantly more likely to have their directors subjected to withhold votes, even though the actual backdating activities had occurred ten years before, and many of their directors joined the board after the backdating had occurred.[54] It is true that directors who had been on the board at the time of the backdating had higher withhold votes cast against them, but the difference was a relatively insignificant additional 3.8 percent of withheld votes. It is hard to see how penalizing individuals for something done years before they joined the board is rational. It does, however, allow a shareholder to express anger, demonstrate virtue, align themselves with a community, and, in short, behave exactly in the way researchers have come to expect of the average political voter. Indeed, the absence of real shareholder concern with the substance of the backdating scandal – the failure of directors to act with integrity – is clear given that directors who oversaw backdating at one firm did not receive statistically significant more withhold votes in relation to their board positions at other firms.

5.3.3 *Majority Voting*

"Majority voting" consists of the adoption by a company of a policy that requires directors to resign if they receive more "withhold" votes than "for" votes. Usually, the board is permitted to reject the resignation, but the expectation is that it would be extraordinary for the remaining directors to ignore the will of the shareholders. Majority voting is a device to increase the power of shareholder voting by simultaneously making the shareholder vote more powerful (as directors can more easily be voted out of office) and less expensive (as a rival slate of directors and accompanying arguments in their favor are no longer required).

Majority voting has been introduced in the United States by way of shareholder pressure. In 2005, less than 10 percent of the S&P 100 had majority voting policies; by 2014, almost 90 percent of the S&P 500 had some sort of majority voting.[55] (At the same time, less than 20 percent of small-cap companies had adopted majority voting.[56]) In keeping with the picture of shareholder disengagement on voting discussed thus far, labor union pension funds (which hold less than 0.01 percent of America's companies' shares) sponsored over 80 percent of the majority voting proposals.[57] Given what we know about the incentives of managers of labor union pension funds, it seems very possible the primary motive of the fund managers in this area was not to improve firms' economic outcomes. Indeed, the early adopters of majority voting policies cannot be distinguished from their peers in terms of economic performance.[58]

The most compelling evidence that activism around majority voting is more about self-expression than improving corporate performance is that directors of companies with majority voting are significantly less likely to be voted against. The difference is huge: the likelihood that a director of a company with plurality voting fails to receive a majority "for" vote is nineteen times higher than if they were subject to a majority voting policy.[59] So, at the very moment when voting against a director becomes more effective, the shareholders stop voting against directors. Even the percentage of shares cast in director elections declines slightly after the adoption of majority voting, a result that seems incompatible with assumptions that shareholders are motivated to substantively impact corporate performance.[60]

For their part, the people with the deepest knowledge about individual directors and the value those directors contribute to board activities, treat shareholder withhold votes with extreme skepticism. Because majority voting policies usually permit the board to refuse to accept a director's resignation when the director receives a majority of withhold votes, we can evaluate the board's view of the quality of these votes from its behavior. Where they have the power, boards tend to reject the director's resignation and, in many cases, the director is approved by the shareholders the next year.[61]

The failure of boards to respond to the shareholders' vote is usually seen by the governance industry as evidence of unaccountable self-interest and a scandal. It is just as likely that it reflects superior knowledge about the targeted director's contributions to board processes. As we have seen, directors are targeted largely because the board or a committee of the board has transgressed a governance "best practice." We have also seen that these governance practices generally do not improve corporate performance and that the allocation of responsibility for such decisions to a single director is usually absurd. To take an obvious example, executive compensation decisions receive considerable input from the board as a whole. Targeting a single compensation committee member for the result is not likely to be an accurate allocation of responsibility.

Almost the only area where directors are targeted for their own behavior is failing to attend a certain percentage of board meetings.[62] In an era of significant informal and year-round communication among directors and managers, formal meeting attendance is a very crude measurement of engagement and value creation. Thus, the most common reasons for a majority withhold vote are likely arbitrary, and the votes themselves cast in ignorance of the actual role played by the director in question. One group of scholars studying majority voting note that "rather than a channel to remove specific directors, director elections [under majority voting] are viewed by shareholders as a means to obtain specific governance changes."[63]

It seems unlikely that the same boards which voluntarily adopted majority voting policies in the first place, de-staggered themselves, created super-majorities of independent directors, and began to compensate their executives in the ways promoted by shareholder advocates suddenly decided to engage in dismissive self-dealing. It seems at least as likely that boards retaining directors who failed to obtain majority support are just trying to do their best to advance the interests of the company, notwithstanding a shareholder vote they regard as a mistake.

The economic effects following the adoption of majority voting are not well studied. There are three studies that look at the stock price reaction to the announcement that firms were adopting majority voting policies. One found a positive abnormal price return[64] and two found no statistically significant price movement.[65] Event studies of this type are not particularly helpful when evaluating corporate governance events. This is because news about most governance events is often anticipated by the market before it is officially announced. Moreover, it is rare that the adoption of some governance structure is announced at a time when no other announcements or conflating events occur (this is particularly the case when the announcement is about the results of a shareholder meeting).

The most useful empirical evidence examines the longer-term effects on corporate performance. There is only one study that looks at longer-term results and it finds that the adoption of majority voting is associated with worse firm performance relative to matched firms over the year following its adoption.[66] This underperformance can be seen in several areas, including return on assets and market adjusted stock returns.[67] It is hard to know what to make of these results, as one year seems too short to see the effects of a change in corporate governance structures. So, perhaps the only conclusion that can be drawn is that the empirical research on the subject (published in 2013) has not noticeably impacted shareholder enthusiasm for majority voting, and this feels telling.

5.3.4 *Voting in Contested Director Elections*

Contested director elections are usually fought on the basis of the quality of corporate governance at the targeted firm. The majority of communications in a proxy campaign explicitly reference the quality of corporate governance, even when there is also a clear disagreement on economic strategy at the heart of the campaign.

In a typical proxy campaign, most of the claims made by the insurgents concern allegations of poor corporate performance, bad governance practices, conflicts of interest, insider trading, overly-generous executive compensation, and problems with the quality and experience of individual directors. The arguments from the incumbents are similarly focused on repudiating the allegations, describing governance failures on the other side (such as "golden leash" payments), and criticizing the quality, track record, and independence of the candidates making up the dissident slate. It is this focus on corporate governance, the most visible aspect of proxy contests, that caused *The Economist* to famously refer to activist shareholders as "[c]apitalism's unlikely heroes."[68] Similarly, academics tend to have a favorable view toward activism because of its role in generating "superior corporate governance."[69] In a much-cited recent journal article, professors Ronald Gilson and Jeffrey Gordon argue, "[a]s governance intermediaries or governance arbitrageurs, activist shareholders can, in the right circumstances, serve to reduce the market's undervaluation of governance rights to the advantage of all shareholders."[70]

The surprising thing, then, about contested director elections is that when researchers study them, the elections do not appear to have anything at all to do with corporate governance. First, the companies that experience contested elections actually appear to be generally well-run. There are very few contested elections in the United States. Out of approximately 10,000 public companies, until 2013, there was only an average of thirty-five firms per year where the directors faced competition.[71] This total has increased in the years since to 187 companies in 2019.[72] Targeted companies tend to have "low market value relative to book value … with sound operating cash flows and return on assets."[73] Indeed, most studies have found that the targets of proxy fights are more profitable than control samples.[74] Stated simply, the common target of a contested election is an unusually profitable company, but with recent stock price performance lower than its peers.[75]

Second, if we take activist shareholders as the most significant source of contested elections, we know what drives their economic returns, and it is not changes to corporate governance. The real goal of activist shareholders is usually one of a limited range of measures designed to increase the short-term financial returns to the shareholders.[76] These include restructuring the company (spinning off a noncore asset or blocking an acquisition), changing a payout policy (increasing or implementing a share buyback program or increasing dividend payments), or selling the company.[77] Board or management changes are generally a prelude to enacting one of these strategies.[78] Virtually all the returns experienced from shareholder activism are attributable to those companies which are sold following their interventions.[79] This explains why unusually profitable companies are the most frequent targets: all of these financial maneuvers depend on fundamentally sound businesses with strong cash flows.[80]

Third, there is no evidence of measurable improvement in a firm's corporate governance following a successful proxy campaign. Operational metrics (such as growth in sales, asset size, profit margin, the spread in borrowing costs, return on assets, return on equity, and profitability) are all unaffected.[81] Indeed, for companies that experience a board change and that are not sold, the best reading of the available evidence is that they lag behind their peers over the long term.[82] Even when an activist only succeeds in placing a few of its directors on the incumbent board, the companies tend to experience significant underperformance in the following years.[83] All of this is problematic for proponents of the theory that shareholder activists improve corporate governance.

It is possible that corporate governance is, in a very weak sense, improved if we take its most narrow definition as referring solely to board independence. It is hard to imagine a more independent board than one imposed on the company by the victors in a contested election. Is there evidence that companies that experience a change of directors do a better job of constraining executive compensation and other illegitimate diversions of the firm's free cash flow? Unfortunately, this does not appear to be the case. As two scholars note, after surveying the empirical literature about what successful challengers actually do following an electoral victory, "the majority [of studies] do not report evidence of changes in real variables consistent with this free cash flow hypothesis."[84]

If the companies were not badly run before they were targeted for a contested election, and if it is clear that activist shareholders actually generate their returns in ways that have nothing to do with improving corporate governance, and if there is no improvement (or even a decline) in firm performance following the replacement of incumbent directors, then what is going on? Contested corporate elections appear to be fought on the basis of one thing – corporate governance – that doesn't actually seem to be the point. There are several possible explanations for what we see in contested elections.

One possible explanation is that the war of words around corporate governance has the effect of misleading shareholders in ways calculated to influence their voting. It is not that shareholders in a contested election vote against their economic interests, it is that they can be misinformed about where those interests lie. This is probably the most common explanation by critics of shareholder activism. It is probably not true, however. When we look at the actual economic decisions of shareholders, we find that they show a perfect understanding of the reality of contested board elections. In general, the announcement of a management victory in a contested election does not result in negative abnormal returns as we would expect if the market really believed a negligent or compromised board had succeeded in retaining its authority over the company.[85] Investment bank analysts do not expect post-activism improvements in corporate earnings as shown by their earnings per share forecasts.[86] As we have seen, they are not wrong.

Even more impressively, in a recent article, several scholars show that the market accurately prices the impact of the increase in information leakage that follows a settlement agreement placing hedge fund nominees on a corporate board.[87] The accuracy of the market's assessment extends to distinguishing between employees of the hedge fund and independent directors proposed by the hedge fund (information leakage only increases when the former goes on the board), as well as whether the settlement agreement contains confidentiality provisions (information leakage only increases in the absence of these provisions).[88] When it comes to buying and selling shares, it is clear that the market understands exactly what the effects of a change of directors are going to be and prices them surprisingly accurately.

This brings us to the second possible explanation for the prominence given to corporate governance claims in contested elections: the mistake is not on the part of the shareholders, but on the part of activist shareholders and incumbent boards. These latter two groups fight over corporate governance in the mistaken view that it matters, or in the cynical (but also mistaken) view that they can fool the shareholders.

This also seems an unlikely explanation. For one thing, it depends on a fairly fundamental mistake being made by quite sophisticated and well-informed parties, both with a deep knowledge of the market. If activists and boards hold the mistaken view that the corporate governance issues matter, then we have to believe that neither party understands the actual economic drivers of the business. If the mistake is that activists and incumbent boards incorrectly believe shareholders can be fooled, then we are again left with the question of how long can this mistake realistically last? There is near constant communication with shareholders in a contested election. Is it really plausible that a delusion of this sort could last through even a single contested election, much less the collective market experience of hundreds of such elections?

The argument being made in this chapter provides a third possible explanation: the corporate governance aspects of a contested election actually make a difference to how the shareholders vote, but this voting has nothing to do with the shareholders' clear-eyed assessment of the economic consequences of the corporate governance dispute. The merit of this explanation is that it does not require any of the three sophisticated parties in a proxy fight to labor under a persistent misapprehension. The activists and board are right to emphasize corporate governance matters because these, in fact, drive shareholder voting behavior. The shareholders are aware, in their buying and selling activities, that the corporate governance stuff won't make a difference, but, in their voting, they are taking a virtually costless opportunity to express their values, show solidarity with their tribe, and reaffirm strongly held beliefs about the necessity of shareholder oversight that reflect well on themselves.[89] The outcome may be irrational, but each party in the contest is behaving perfectly rationally.

5.3.5 *Voting on Corporate Governance Matters*

As we have seen, corporate governance best practices drive most shareholder voting in director elections, to the near exclusion of factors such as the firm's economic performance.[90] When we look at voting in other areas of the shareholder franchise, we find a similar focus on governance practices. In a recent representative year, for example, there were 315 shareholder proposals, of which 182 related to the adoption of corporate governance structures.[91] Of the thirty-three proposals that won majority support, all were related to corporate governance best practices.[92]

Corporate governance proposals are primarily made by a few public pension and labor funds.[93] The managers of these funds are hired by, and report to, constituencies that have a noneconomic interest in aggressively correcting corporate America. In contrast, for-profit investment managers are unlikely to initiate these types of proposals (in a particular year, less than one percent originate from this source) though they often vote in favor of corporate governance proposals.[94]

As we have seen thus far in this book, corporate governance best practices form an irrational basis for shareholder voting. The optimistic reading of the empirical literature is that corporate governance best practices make no difference on average; there is lots of evidence that those best practices lead to worse outcomes.

To truly appreciate the craziness of institutional investor corporate governance initiatives, it is helpful to learn that empirical studies exist which discredit the activities of specific shareholders – by name. Weirdly, these studies seem to make no difference to the institutions' governance activities. For example, CalPERS continues its activism around corporate governance even though a study published back in 1996 found that its interventions had only a very minor impact on share price and no impact at all on operating performance.[95] TIAA-CREF similarly continues its corporate governance activities notwithstanding a 1998 study that found these initiatives produced no significant changes in accounting measures of performance and even, in some cases, caused a decline in share prices.[96] More recent studies about specific funds active in corporate governance matters have found the same lack of effect, but this has not led to noticeable changes in those funds' behavior.[97] Carl Icahn still claims (and believes?) that he is waging the good fight against bad corporate governance despite the fact that a published study finds that any company he targets which is not fortunate enough to be rescued through an immediate sale suffers *very* negative returns.[98]

In contrast, the average institutional shareholder clearly understands that the corporate governance issues driving its voting decisions don't make much difference to the economic performance of its portfolios. As we have seen, most institutions – in particular those that compete for money on the basis of fund performance – don't actually engage in corporate governance activism, aside from casting votes. When scholars look at the companies acquired by institutional shareholders, they "find little evidence of an association between total institutional investor ownership and corporate governance."[99] In fact, only about 10 percent of institutional investors appear to invest in ways that are at all sensitive to firms' corporate governance arrangements.[100] Institutional investors usually separate the investing and voting decisions so they are done by completely different sets of people in completely different departments. This separation of economic decision-making from voting decision-making is suggestive of divergent objectives.[101]

A similar pattern exists around IPOs, where the decision to add a new company to an institution's portfolio appears to have little to do with the company's adherence to governance best practices.[102] This leads a team of researchers to draw the obvious conclusion: "the portfolio managers who buy shares in the IPO are less concerned with the hot-button governance issues … than are their colleagues who later have responsibility for voting those shares."[103] For example, approximately 90 percent of companies going public in America have plurality voting for uncontested director elections.[104]

Even when it comes to voting on the most straightforward issue imaginable – executive compensation – there is considerable evidence that shareholders are not paying attention. A recent study found, for example, that when shareholders reject an equity compensation plan, it has no long-term effect on the corporation's compensation practices or totals.[105] The company merely comes back later with a very similar proposal, which the shareholders approve, as if they had forgotten their earlier vote. The researchers dryly note, "the absence of an effect of a failed shareholder vote on future compensation is surprising."[106]

The clearest sign that shareholders want to avoid the economic consequences of their voting behavior can be seen in the kinds of governance initiatives they support. Professors Kahan and Rock describe their behavior as "symbolic corporate governance politics."[107] They observe repeated instances where shareholders choose to invest their energy in purely inconsequential reforms of corporate governance, staying away from changes that would actually impact operations. For example, shareholders invest considerable energy in pressuring companies to remove poison pills, but their efforts do nothing to prevent a board from introducing a poison pill unilaterally and instantly in the event of a hostile takeover bid. The shareholders could constrain the board's ability to adopt a pill through a charter amendment, but shareholder proposals do not ask for this. Instead, shareholders ask only for the purely symbolic removal of existing pills.

There are other circumstances which display similar patterns of shareholders denouncing certain governance structures but refraining from making proposals that would actually force a change on the company. These circumstances can be observed in relation to: proxy access (where shareholders choose not to force proxy access through bylaw amendments after Delaware made this possible), majority voting (under which, as we have seen, directors become less likely to be voted against), proposals to remove supermajority requirements in bylaws (which commonly apply only to matters that are either benign or practically irrelevant), and the scarcity of mandatory (as opposed to precatory) shareholder proposals.[108] Shareholders and their proxy advisors cannot be ignorant of the inconsequential aspects of their engagement with corporate governance, or of the stronger alternatives available to them. Yet, they often remain content with purely expressive activity in this field.

5.4 THE FUTURE LIES IN THE PAST

Political voting behavior in democracies is not, of course, always irrational. In circumstances where the cost of a miscast vote is very high, citizens behave rationally. The empirical literature about policy outcomes in democracies has some very good news. No mass famine has ever occurred in a modern democracy, no matter how poor the country.[109] Unlike dictatorships, democratic governments almost never engage in mass murder against their citizens.[110] Politicians accountable to the public do better at limiting the disruptions and harms caused by natural disasters.[111] In these sorts of cases, voters have enormous incentives to vote rationally. The actions of politicians in these areas have huge significance, are easily attributable, and are highly visible. In this context, the evidence is that voters invest the resources necessary to become informed and vote in their best interests. Politicians in democracies know this and conduct themselves accordingly; this is why democracies do better.

It is hard to avoid the fact that corporate law traditionally reserved the shareholder franchise precisely for the corporate equivalent of these major and highly public events: mergers, wind-ups, and amendments to the charter documents. Even voting for directors served mainly as a method of ensuring accountability that only really functioned when there was a major failure. But over the past several decades, we have attempted to drive shareholder voting into areas such as the adoption of corporate governance practices, executive compensation, business strategy, and even fine-grained assessments of the quality of individual directors. This goes well beyond the highly visible, hugely significant, and easily attributable matters that traditional corporate law reserved for shareholders. This chapter has described the slightly ridiculous results.

5.5 SUMMARY

An alternative title for this chapter might have been, "Shareholders – They're Just Like Us!" In making the argument that shareholders rationally vote in irrational ways, we are just arguing they make the exact same calculation about the marginal value of their vote as the rest of us. Like us they collect and process information in ways that flatter themselves and express solidarity with their tribe. If the governance reforms they force on American companies also reflect a bit badly on the executives who so often let them down, well, that is also a source of pleasure, as Nietzsche made clear. The agency cost story makes shareholders simultaneously into victims and heroes; it would take someone better than most of us to resist the invitation to vote accordingly.

NOTES

1 *Blasius Industries, Inc. v. Atlas Corp.*, 564 A (2d) 651 (Del. Ch. 1988) at 659.
2 *80% of Equity Market Cap Held by Institutions*, Pensions & Investments (April 25, 2017), online: www.pionline.com/article/20170425/INTERACTIVE/170429926/80-of-equity-market-cap-held-by-institutions.
3 John C. Coffee, Jr., "Liquidity Versus Control: The Institutional Investor As Corporate Monitor" (1991) 91:6 *Columbia Law Review* 1277–1368 at 1328.
4 Bryce C. Tingle, "Bad Company! The Assumptions Behind Proxy Advisors' Voting Recommendations" (2014) 37:2 *Dalhousie Law Journal* 709–748 at 715–716 [Tingle, "Bad Company"]; Bryce C. Tingle, "The Agency Cost Case for Regulating Proxy Advisory Firms" (2016) 49:2 *UBC Law Review* 725–787 at 738–739; Bryce C. Tingle, "Two Stories About Shareholders" (2021) 58:1 *Osgoode Hall Law Journal* 57–108 [Tingle, "Two Stories"]; Ronald J. Gilson and Jeffrey N. Gordon, "The Agency Costs of Agency Capitalism: Activist Investors and the Revaluation of Governance Rights" (2013) 113:4 *Columbia Law Review* 863–928 at 890 [Gilson and Gordon, "Agency Costs"].
5 Comment letter from Robert E. Zivnuska, Director, Head of Corporate Governance and Responsible Investment, BlackRock Americas, *Re: Canadian Securities Administrators Consultation Paper 25-401: Potential Regulation of Proxy Advisory Firms*, Ontario Securities Commission (September 20, 2012), online (pdf): www.osc.ca/sites/default/files/pdfs/irps/comments/SecuritiesLaw_com_20120920_25-401_zivnuskar.pdf at 1.
6 David F. Larcker et al., *2015 Investor Survey: Deconstructing Proxy Statements – What Matters to Investors*, Stanford Graduate School of Business (2015), online (pdf): www.gsb.stanford.edu [perma.cc/Z7QH-D2ZQ] at 2.
7 *2019 U.S. Spencer Stuart Board Index*, Spencer Stuart (2019), online (pdf): www.spencerstuart.com/-/media/2019/ssbi-2019/us_board_index_2019.pdf at 15.
8 Bryan Caplan, *The Myth of the Rational Voter: Why Democracies Choose Bad Policies* (Princeton: Princeton University Press, 2007) [Caplan, *Rational Voter Myth*].

9 See Anthony Downs, *An Economic Theory of Democracy* (New York: Harper and Row, 1957) at p. 259; Steve Rathje et al., "Accuracy and Social Motivations Shape Judgements of Mis(information)" (2023) 7:6 *Nature Human Behaviour* 892–903.

10 Summaries of this ignorance can be found in Caplan, *Rational Voter Myth*, above at note 8; Ilya Somin, *Democracy and Political Ignorance: Why Smaller Government is Smarter*, 2nd ed (Stanford: Stanford University Press, 2016) at p. 94 [Somin, *Democracy and Political Ignorance*]; Garett Jones, *10% Less Democracy: Why You Should Trust Elites a Little More and the Masses a Little Less* (Stanford: Stanford University Press, 2020) at pp. 95–117; Michael X. Delli Carpini and Scott Keeter, *What Americans Know About Politics and Why It Matters* (New Haven: Yale University Press, 1996) at pp. 135–177; Rick Shenkman, *Just How Stupid Are We? Facing the Truth About the American Voter* (New York: Basic Books, 2008) at pp. 13–36.

11 Somin, *Democracy and Political Ignorance*, above at note 10 at p. 17.

12 *2016 National Civics Survey Results*, Edward M. Kennedy Institute for the United States Senate, online (pdf): https://emki-production.s3.amazonaws.com/downloads/64/files/EMK_Institute_Nat._Civic_Survey_Results.pdf?1458221724.

13 Sean Sullivan, "Just 36 Percent of Americans Can Name Which Parties Control House, Senate," The Washington Post, September 22, 2014, online: www.washingtonpost.com/news/post-politics/wp/2014/09/22/just-36-percent-of-americans-can-name-which-parties-control-house-senate/.

14 See Jon D. Miller, "Public Understanding of, and Attitudes Toward, Scientific Research: What We Know and What We Need to Know" (2004) 13:3 *Public Understanding of Science* 273–294 at 280.

15 See Frank Newport, "On Darwin's Birthday, Only 4 in 10 Believe in Evolution," *Gallup*, February 11, 2009, online: news.gallup.com [perma.cc/88QR-L6JT].

16 See Robert Marchant, "From the Test Tube to the Table" (2001) 2:5 *EMBO Reports* 354–357 at 355 [Marchant, "Test Tube"]; Douglas Buhler and Sheril Kirshenbaum, "More than One-Third of Americans Do Not Know That Foods with Zero Genetically Modified Ingredients Contain Genes – and Why That Matters," Genetic Literacy Project, May 31, 2019, online: geneticliteracyproject.org [perma.cc/2SJC-V9AX].

17 Marchant, "Test Tube," above at note 16 at 355.

18 Somin, *Democracy and Political Ignorance*, above at note 10 at p. 21.

19 George A. Akerlof, "The Economics of Illusion" (1989) 1:1 *Economics & Politics* 1–15 at 1.

20 Caplan, *Rational Voter Myth*, above at note 8 at p. 123.

21 Somin, *Democracy and Political Ignorance*, above at note 10 at p. 94.

22 Charles S. Taber and Milton Lodge, "Motivated Skepticism in the Evaluation of Political Beliefs" (2006) 50:3 *American Journal of Political Science* 755–769 at 757, 767.

23 Dan M. Kahan, "Ideology, Motivated Reasoning, and Cognitive Reflection" (2013) 8:4 *Judgment and Decision Making* 407–424 at 416.

24 Alan S. Gerber et al., "Disagreement and the Avoidance of Political Discussion: Aggregate Relationships and Differences across Personality Traits" (2012) 56:4 *American Journal of Political Science* 849–874; Shanto Iyengar and Kyu S. Hahn, "Red Media, Blue Media: Evidence of Ideological Selectivity in Media Use" (2009) 59:1 *Journal of Communication* 19–39; Eric Lawrence, John Sides and Henry Farrell, "Self-Segregation or Deliberation? Blog Readership, Participation, and Polarization in American Politics" (2010) 8:1 *Perspectives on Politics* 141–157.

25 Caplan, *Rational Voter Myth*, above at note 8 at p. 134.

26 Caplan, *Rational Voter Myth*, above at note 8 at p. 149. See also, Somin, *Democracy and Political Ignorance*, above at note 10 at pp. 68–70, 104–112.

27 See Andrew Gelman, "Economic Divisions and Political Polarization in Red and Blue America" (2011) Summer 2011 *Pathways*, online (pdf): stat.columbia.edu [perma. cc/4NVE-M7U6] at 4; Terry Nichols Clark and Christopher Graziul, "Why Rich States Aren't Republican" (2008) 322:5902 *Science* 676–677; Jeff Manza and Clem Brooks, *Social Cleavages and Political Change: Voter Alignments and U.S. Party Coalitions* (Oxford: Oxford University Press, 1999) at pp. 49–84.

28 See, for example, Leonie Huddy, Jeffrey M. Jones and Richard E. Chard, "Compassionate Politics: Support for Old-Age Programs among the Non-Elderly" (2001) 22:3 *Political Psychology* 443–471 at 444; David O. Sears and Carolyn Funk, "Self-Interest in Americans' Political Opinions" in Jane J. Mansbridge (ed.), *Beyond Self-Interest* (Chicago: The University of Chicago Press, 1990), p. 147 [Sears and Funk, "Self-Interest"].

29 Sears and Funk, "Self-Interest," above at note 28. See generally, Richard R. Lau, Thad A. Brown and David O. Sears, "Self-Interest and Civilians' Attitudes Toward the Vietnam War" (1978) 42:4 *Public Opinion Quarterly* 464–482.

30 Thomas Frank, *What's the Matter with Kansas? How Conservatives Won the Heart of America* (New York: Henry Holt and Company, 2004). A similar attitude can be found in Paul Krugman, *The Conscience of a Liberal* (New York: WW Norton and Company, 2007).

31 Paul H. Edelman, Randall S. Thomas and Robert B. Thompson, "Shareholder Voting in an Age of Intermediary Capitalism" (2014) 87:6 *Southern California Law Review* 1359–1434 at 1384.

32 Lisa M. Fairfax, "The Future of Shareholder Democracy" (2009) 84:4 *Indiana Law Journal* 1259–1308 at 1294 [Fairfax, "Shareholder Democracy"]. See generally, Paul E. Fischer et al., "Investor Perceptions of Board Performance: Evidence from Uncontested Director Elections" (2009) 48:2–3 *Journal of Accounting and Economics* 172–189.

33 Fairfax, "Shareholder Democracy," above at note 32 at 1294.

34 Luigi Zingales, "What Determines the Value of Corporate Votes?" (1995) 110:4 *The Quarterly Journal of Economics* 1047–1073.

35 *Ibid* at 1071. See also, Luigi Zingales, "The Value of the Voting Right: A Study of the Milan Stock Exchange Experience" (1994) 7:1 *The Review of Financial Studies* 125–148.

36 Susan E. K. Christoffersen et al., "Vote Trading and Information Aggregation" (2007) 62:6 *The Journal of Finance* 2897–2929 at 2911 [Christoffersen, "Vote Trading"]. See also, Edwin Hu, Joshua Mitts and Haley Sylvester, "The Index-Fund Dilemma: An Empirical Study of the Lending-Voting Tradeoff" (2020), *Columbia Law and Economics Working Paper No. 647*, online: SSRN, https://ssrn.com/abstract=3673531.

37 Christoffersen, "Vote Trading," above at note 36 at 2912–2914.

38 Avner Kalay and Shagun Pant, "The Market Value of the Vote: A Contingent Claims Approach" (2010), online: SSRN, https://ssrn.com/abstract=1296269; Oğuzhan Karakaş, "Another Option for Determining the Value of Corporate Votes" (2009), online: SSRN, https://ssrn.com/abstract=1364052.

39 Jie Cai, Jacqueline L. Garner and Ralph A. Walkling, "Electing Directors" (2009) 64:5 *The Journal of Finance* 2389–2421 at 2416–2417 [Cai, Garner and Walking, "Electing Directors"].

40 *Ibid* at 2399.

41 See, for example, Diane Del Guercio, Laura Seery and Tracie Woidtke, "Do Boards Pay Attention When Institutional Investor Activists 'Just Vote No'?" (2008) 90:1 *Journal of Financial Economics* 84–103 [Del Guercio, Seery and Woidtke, "Pay Attention"]; Randall S. Thomas and Patrick C. Tricker, "Shareholder Voting in Proxy Contests for Corporate Control, Uncontested Director Elections and Management Proposals: A Review of the Empirical Literature" (2017) 70:1 *Oklahoma Law Review* 9–126 [Thomas and Tricker, "Proxy Contests"].

42 See Cai, Garner and Walking, "Electing Directors," above at note 39 at 2416. But see, Del Guercio, Seery and Woidtke, "Pay Attention," above at note 41 at 87 (finding negative market-adjusted returns in the prior year).

43 Thomas and Tricker, "Proxy Contests," above at note 41 at 70.

44 Stephen Choi, Jill Fisch and Marcel Kahan, "Who Calls the Shots: How Mutual Funds Vote on Director Elections" (2013) 3:1 *Harvard Business Law Review* 35–82. See also, Tingle, "Bad Company," above at note 4 at 718–719.

45 See, for example, Cai, Garner and Walking, "Electing Directors," above at note 39 at 2416–2417.

46 Yonca Ertimur, Fabrizio Ferri and David Oesch, "Understanding Uncontested Director Elections" (2018) 64:7 *Management Science* 3400–3420 at 3400–3401 [Ertimur, Ferri and Oesch, "Uncontested Director Elections"].

47 *Ibid* at 3401. See also, Marcel Kahan and Edward Rock, "The Insignificance of Proxy Access" (2011) 97:6 *Virginia Law Review* 1347–1434 at 1420 [Kahan and Rock, "Proxy Access"].

48 Ertimur, Ferri and Oesch, "Uncontested Director Elections," above at note 46 at 3401.

49 *Ibid*. See also, Cai, Garner and Walking, "Electing Directors," above at note 39 at 2417.

50 Cai, Garner and Walking, "Electing Directors," above at note 39 at 2391.

51 Ertimur, Ferri and Oesch, "Uncontested Director Elections," above at note 46 at 3401. See also, Kahan and Rock, "Proxy Access," above at note 47 at 1421.

52 Ertimur, Ferri and Oesch, "Uncontested Director Elections," above at note 46 at 3402.

53 Thomas and Tricker, "Proxy Contests," above at note 41 at 53.

54 Yonca Ertimur, Fabrizio Ferri and David A. Maber, "Reputation Penalties for Poor Monitoring of Executive Pay: Evidence from Option Backdating" (2012) 104:1 *Journal of Financial Economics* 118–144 at 123.

55 Stephen J. Choi et al., "Does Majority Voting Improve Board Accountability" (2016) 83:3 *University of Chicago Law Review* 1119–1180 at 1121 [Choi et al., "Majority Voting"].

56 *Ibid* at 1127.

57 Jay Cai, Jacqueline L. Garner and Ralph A. Walking, "A Paper Tiger? An Empirical Analysis of Majority Voting" (2013) 21 *Journal of Corporate Finance* 119–135 at 122–123 [Cai, Garner and Walking, "Paper Tiger"].

58 Choi et al., "Majority Voting," above at note 55 at 1146.

59 *Ibid* at 1136.

60 Cai, Garner and Walking, "Paper Tiger," above at note 57 at 131–132.

61 *Ibid* at 133; Choi et al., "Majority Voting," above at note 55 at 1122; Kimberly Gladman, Agnes Grunfeld and Michelle Lamb, *The Election of Corporate Directors: What Happens When Shareholders Withhold a Majority of Votes from Director Nominees?*, Investor Responsibility Research Center Institute (August 2012), online (pdf): https://perma.cc/R6AW-B8ZL at 2; Marcel Kahan and Edward Rock, "Symbolic Corporate Governance Politics" (2014) 94:6 *Boston University Law Review* 1997–2044 at 2012 [Kahan and Rock, "Symbolic Corporate Governance"].

62 Stephen J. Choi, Jill E. Fisch and Marcel Kahan, "Director Elections and the Role of Proxy Advisors" (2009) 82:4 *Southern California Law Review* 649–702 at 661–662, 671–673.

63 Yonca Ertimur, Fabrizio Ferri and David Oesch, "Does the Director Election System Matter? Evidence from Majority Voting" (2015) 20:1 *Review of Accounting Studies* 1–41 at 5.

64 *Ibid* at 6–16.

65 William K. Sjostrom, Jr. and Young Sang Kim, "Majority Voting for the Election Directors" (2007) 40:2 *Connecticut Law Review* 459–510 at 493–494; Cai, Garner and Walking, "Paper Tiger," above at note 57 at 129.

66 Cai, Garner and Walking, "Paper Tiger," above at note 57 at 132.

67 *Ibid.*

68 "Capitalism's Unlikely Heroes," *The Economist*, February 5, 2015, online: www.econo
mist.com [perma.cc/XC46-JPJ5].

69 Joel Slawotsky, "The Virtues of Shareholder Value Driven Activism: Avoiding
Governance Pitfalls" (2016) 12:3 *Hastings Business Law Journal* 521–569 at 527; See also,
John C. Coffee, Jr. et al., "Activist Directors and Agency Costs: What Happens When
an Activist Director Goes on the Board" (2019) 104:2 *Cornell Law Review* 381–466 at 387
[Coffee et al., "Activist Directors"].

70 Gilson and Gordon, "Agency Costs," above at note 4 at 877.

71 Lee Harris, "Corporate Elections and Tactical Settlements" (2014) 39:2 *Journal of
Corporation Law* 221–252 at 243.

72 Lindsay Fortado, "Companies Faced More Activist Investors than Ever in 2019," *Financial
Times*, January 15, 2020, online: www.ft.com [perma.cc/5Z66-R3H6].

73 Alon Brav et al., "Hedge Fund Activism, Corporate Governance, and Firm Performance"
(2008) 63:4 *The Journal of Finance* 1729–1775 at 1730 [Brav et al., "Hedge Fund Activism"].
See also, John C. Coffee, Jr. and Darius Palia, "The Wolf at the Door: The Impact of
Hedge Fund Activism on Corporate Governance" (2016) 41:3 *Journal of Corporation Law*
545–608 at 582 [Coffee and Palia, "Wolf at the Door"].

74 Coffee and Palia, "Wolf at the Door," above at note 73 at 582; April Klein and Emanuel
Zur, "Entrepreneurial Shareholder Activism: Hedge Funds and Other Private Investors"
(2009) 64:1 *The Journal of Finance* 187–229 at 189 [Klein and Zur, "Entrepreneurial
Shareholder"]; Brav et al., "Hedge Fund Activism," above at note 73 at 1753; Matthew
Denes, Jonathan M. Karpoff and Victoria B. McWilliams, "Thirty Years of Shareholder
Activism: A Survey of Empirical Research" (2017) 44:1 *Journal of Corporate Finance* 405–
424 at 415 [Denes, Karpoff and McWilliams, "Thirty Years"]. But see, C. N. V. Krishnan,
Frank Partnoy and Randall S. Thomas, "The Second Wave of Hedge Fund Activism:
The Importance of Reputation, Clout and Expertise" (2016) 40:1 *Journal of Corporate
Finance* 296–314 at 298–299.

75 Denes, Karpoff and McWilliams, "Thirty Years," above at note 74 at 413–415.

76 Marco Becht et al., "Returns to Hedge Fund Activism: An International Study" (2017) 30:9
The Review of Financial Studies 2933–2971 at 2953, Table 6 (source for data); Yvan Allaire,
The Case for and Against Activist Hedge Funds, Institute for Governance of Private and
Public Organizations (May 2015), online (pdf): SSRN, https://ssrn.com/abstract=2613154
at 9–10 (source for calculations) [Allaire, *For and Against*].

77 Allaire, *For and Against*, above at note 76 at 10.

78 Tingle, "Two Stories," above at note 4 at 87.

79 Robin Greenwood and Michael Schor, "Investor Activism and Takeovers" (2009) 92:3
Journal of Financial Economics 362–375 [Greenwood and Schor, "Investor Activism"];
Yvan Allaire and François Dauphin, "The Game of 'Activist' Hedge Funds: *Cui Bono?*"
(2016) 13:4 *International Journal of Disclosure and Governance* 279–308 at 296–299
[Allaire and Dauphin, "The Game"]; Coffee and Palia, "Wolf at the Door," above at note
73 at 588.

80 Thomas and Tricker, "Proxy Contests," above at note 41 at 36, citing Olubunmi Faleye,
"Cash and Corporate Control" (2004) 59:5 *The Journal of Finance* 2041–2060 at 2049–2050.

81 Coffee and Palia, "Wolf at the Door," above at note 73 at 591–592; Ed deHaan, David
Larcker and Charles McClure, "Long Term Economic Consequences of Hedge Fund
Activist Interventions" (2019) 24:2 *Review of Accounting Studies* 536–569 at 554 [deHaan,
Larcker and McClure, "Economic Consequences"]; Klein and Zur, "Entrepreneurial

Shareholder," above at note 74 at 223; David Ikenberry and Josef Lakonishok, "Corporate Governance Through the Proxy Contest: Evidence and Implications" (1993) 66:3 *The Journal of Business* 405–435 at 427–429 [Ikenberry and Lakonishok, "Proxy Contest"]; Tarun K. Mukherjee and Oscar Varela, "Corporate Operating Performance around the Proxy Contest" (1993) 20:3 *Journal of Business Finance & Accounting* 417–425 at 419–421.

82 For an evaluation of the various studies on the long-term outcomes of shareholder activism, see Tingle, "Two Stories," above at note 4; Coffee et al., "Activist Directors," above at note 69 at 384, note 1.

83 deHaan, Larcker and McClure, "Economic Consequences," above at note 81 at 564–565; Allaire and Dauphin, "The Game," above at note 79 at 303–304; Greenwood and Schor, "Investor Activism," above at note 79 at 368–370; William W. Bratton, "Hedge Funds and Governance Targets: Long-Term Results" (2010), *University of Pennsylvania Institute for Law & Economics Research Paper No. 10–17*, online SSRN, https://ssrn.com/abstract=1677517; Elaine Buckberg and Jonathan Macey, *Report on Effects of Proposed SEC Rule 14a-11 on Efficiency, Competitiveness and Capital Formation*, NERA Economic Consulting (August 17, 2009), online (pdf): www.nera.com [perma.cc/3JHM-M7RK] at 9. See also, Tarun K. Mukherjee, "Stock Price Behavior Surrounding Proxy Fights for Control: A Non-Parametric Approach" (1985) 21:1 *Review of Business and Economic Research* 85–104 at 100–101; Ikenberry and Lakonishok, "Proxy Contest," above at note 81 at 420–423.

84 Coffee and Palia, "Wolf at the Door," above at note 73 at 583.

85 Cindy R. Alexander et al., "Interim News and the Role of Proxy Voting Advice" (2010) 23:12 *The Review of Financial Studies* 4419–4454 at 4436.

86 deHaan, Larcker and McClure, "Economic Consequences," above at note 81 at 541–542, 561–563.

87 Coffee et al., "Activist Directors," above at note 69.

88 *Ibid.*

89 Thomas and Tricker, "Proxy Contests," above at note 41 at 31.

90 Suren Gomtsian, "Shareholder Engagement by Large Institutional Investors" (2020) 45:3 *Journal of Corporation Law* 659–711 at 659. See also, Dhruv Aggarwal, Lubomir P. Litov and Shivaram Rajgopal, "Big Three (Dis)Engagements" (2023), *Northwestern Law & Econ Research Paper No. 23-17*, online: SSRN, https://ssrn.com/abstract=4592727.

91 James R. Copland and Margaret M. O'Keefe, *A Report on Corporate Governance and Shareholder Activism*, Proxy Monitor (2015), online (pdf): www.proxymonitor.org [perma.cc/U6PD-5U3V] at 12–13 [Copland and O'Keefe, "Report on Corporate Governance"].

92 *Ibid.*

93 Ronald J. Gilson and Jeffrey N. Gordon, "Agency Capitalism: Further Implications of Equity Intermediation" in Jennifer G. Hill and Randall S. Thomas (eds.), *Research Handbook on Shareholder Power* (Cheltenham, UK: Edward Elgar, 2015), p. 32 at p. 38; Copland and O'Keefe, "Report on Corporate Governance," above at note 91 at 8.

94 Copland and O'Keefe, "Report on Corporate Governance," above at note 91.

95 Michael P. Smith, "Shareholder Activism by Institutional Investors: Evidence from CalPERS" (1996) 51:1 *The Journal of Finance* 227–252.

96 Willard T. Carleton, James M. Nelson and Michael S. Weisbach, "The Influence of Institutions on Corporate Governance through Private Negotiations: Evidence from TIAA-CREF" (1998) 53:4 *The Journal of Finance* 1335–1362 at 1351–1353.

97 Tracie Woidtke, "Public Pension Fund Activism and Firm Value: An Empirical Analysis," September 2015, online (pdf): *Manhattan Institute – Legal Policy Report*, https://media4.manhattan-institute.org/pdf/lpr_20.pdf at 5.

98 Vinod Venkiteshwaran, Subramanian R. Iyer and Ramesh P. Rao, "Is Carl Icahn Good for Long-Term Shareholders? A Case Study in Shareholder Activism" (2010) 22:4 *Journal of Applied Corporate Finance* 45–57 at 51.

99 Brian J. Bushee, Mary Ellen Carter and Joseph Gerakos, "Institutional Investor Preferences for Corporate Governance Mechanisms" (2014) 26:2 *Journal of Management Accounting Research* 123–149 at 125.

100 *Ibid.*

101 Charles M. Nathan, "The Parallel Universes of Institutional Investing and Institutional Voting" (April 6, 2010), *Harvard Law School Forum on Corporate Governance*, online: corpgov.law.harvard.edu [perma.cc/TNX5-4LMV].

102 Richard J. Sandler and Joseph A. Hall, *Corporate Governance Practices in US Initial Public Offerings*, The Conference Board (April 2014), online (pdf): www.davispolk.com/files/sandler.hall_.directors.notes_.article.apr14.PDF at 3 [Sandler and Hall, *US IPOs*].

103 Sandler and Hall, *US IPOs*, above at note 102 at 2.

104 *Ibid.*

105 Christopher S. Armstrong, Ian D. Gow and David F. Larcker, "The Efficacy of Shareholder Voting: Evidence from Equity Compensation Plans" (2013) 51:5 *Journal of Accounting Research* 909–950.

106 *Ibid* at 943.

107 Kahan and Rock, "Symbolic Corporate Governance," above at note 61.

108 *Ibid* at 2002–2021.

109 William Easterly, Roberta Gatti and Sergio Kurlat, "Development, Democracy, and Mass Killings" (2006) 11:2 *Journal of Economic Growth* 129–156 at 137; Amartya Sen, *Development as Freedom* (New York: Anchor Books, 1999) at p. 51.

110 Rudolph J. Rummel, *Power Kills: Democracy as A Method of Nonviolence* (Abingdon, UK: Routledge, 2017) at p. 91.

111 Alastair Smith and Alejandro Quiroz Flores, "Disaster Politics: Why Natural Disasters Rock Democracies Less," *Foreign Affairs*, July 15, 2010, online: www.foreignaffairs.com [perma.cc/4ZRR-89ZQ].

6

Shareholder Activism

In Chapter 5, we saw that shareholders don't reliably vote their shares in ways that meaningfully engage with firm-specific governance. Indeed, they don't reliably vote in ways that reflect either their past or anticipated economic returns. However, voting is a relatively costless exercise; we tend to treat things casually that come to us cheaply. What about the more expensive contributions shareholders make to corporate governance?

Corporate law provides shareholders with at least three additional ways of directly participating in corporate governance. They may make proposals that are voted on at meetings and which then can provide binding or nonbinding direction to the directors. They may propose an alternative slate of directors in a process called a "proxy fight" or even more generally referred to as "activism." Finally, shareholders have the power to remove directors and managers by selling their shares as a group to a single purchaser through a takeover. The modern corporate governance regime places a great deal of faith in these more consequential governance interventions by shareholders. Indeed, takeovers are characterized by legal and finance academics as making up "the market for corporate control," as if the main feature of takeovers isn't the transfer in ownership of productive assets, but a change in corporate governance.

Shareholder proposals, proxy contests, and takeovers require shareholders to back their opinions with money and time. Voting doesn't cost much but running a proxy campaign is expensive and time-consuming. In the case of takeovers and proxy contests, the shareholders also bear at least some of the costs of their interventions, since they will own meaningful amounts of stock following the intervention. At least that is the theory.

Just as we saw in relation to shareholder voting, there has always been a vigorous academic debate over whether various types of shareholder activism work in the ways we hope. Do shareholders have enough information to make informed decisions about firm strategy, opportunities, and governance? Do they have the appropriate incentives to make good long-term decisions in the best interests of companies? Do shareholders have incentives that conflict with what is in the best interests of other corporate constituencies? What is sacrificed as the traditional discretion afforded boards by American corporate law is eroded by increasing shareholder power?

Naturally, these scholarly debates have been ignored by everyone else. The governance industry's version of agency cost theory, with its strong moralizing story of corrupt managers and victimized shareholders, has generally been the exclusive driver of real-world reforms. As a well-known law professor notes, "[t]he hope of reducing agency costs through institutional activism has led to regulatory and structural changes to increase shareholder power."[1] We have already seen signs of this increasing shareholder power in the gradual disappearance of staggered boards and poison pills in America. This has left boards with so little power over the sale decision that boards now generally refer the decision to the shareholders.[2]

While we have seen that there is no evidence that independent directors improve corporate performance (and some evidence that they make it worse for certain types of companies), independent directors do give shareholders more power. Outside directors have less at stake when a disagreement about strategy arises with a powerful investor. Concerned primarily about their reputation – which in practice means the regard by which they are held by the institutional investor community – independent directors are less inclined to potentially offend shareholders than the insiders who once formed a large part of America's corporate boards.

Possibly the most consequential factor in increasing shareholder power is the rise of third-party proxy advisory firms like Glass Lewis and ISS. As we will see in Chapter 7, proxy advisors devote unprecedented resources to corporate governance questions, pressure companies to adopt shareholder-friendly policies, punish directors for taking certain actions without shareholder approval (even when this approval is not required by any regulator), and serve as a method of coordinating shareholder action by crystallizing significant voting blocks around their recommendations. Combined with the rise of activist institutional investors, proxy advisors have significantly increased the influence of shareholder sentiment in the boardroom. Studies have shown boards even take actions they believe will be value-destroying to avoid violating a proxy advisor's guidelines or to deflect an activist investor's attention.[3]

Shareholder power in corporate governance arrangements has also grown significantly through informal channels. Surveys suggest that over two-thirds of directors believe just the existence of shareholder activists has resulted in their companies altering operations and capital allocation.[4] Activist institutions also regularly persuade boards to take strategic steps or accept new directors without any public fight required. Professor Michael Klausner correctly observes that, "since the mid-2000s … management has responded to shareholder demands as never before."[5]

Academic attempts to score investor protection measures and track their changes over time find that, "without exception, all countries have increased the level of shareholder protection."[6] A European law professor and economist, Pavlos Masouros, has written the most extensive and rigorous attempt to measure the growth of shareholder power in the modern era.[7] He finds a sharp increase in shareholder power through every channel he examines. He writes that the "natural" trend of the major Western economies, "is persistently moving towards shareholder empowerment."[8]

In light of this growing power, Marcel Kahan and Ed Rock argue that CEOs are so hedged and second-guessed that they can only be described as "embattled."[9]

6.1 SHAREHOLDER PROPOSALS

Shareholder proposals are the least costly means of shareholder intervention, and though they are only advisory in nature, boards tend to implement proposals that win the support of a majority of the shareholders.[10] For this reason, the proposal mechanism has emerged in the last decade or so as a focus of corporate reformers who wish to expand its availability and scope.

6.1.1 *What Do We Know about Shareholder Proposals?*

The vast majority of proposals in the United States are made by individuals, and they are nearly always the same individuals making the same proposal to a wide spectrum of firms.[11] In one year, the New York Times reported that just three individual investors and their families accounted for over 70 percent of all proposals.[12] Among institutional investors, only public pension funds and union funds are significant sources of shareholder proposals.[13] Mutual funds are reflective of the for-profit investment industry generally; they initiated fewer than 1 percent of the proposals in a representative proxy season.[14] As Roberta Romano points out, the fact that the sponsors of most proposals are not private-sector funds competing for investor dollars and that they have political masters with noneconomic interests is suggestive of "private benefits" accruing to the sponsoring institutions.[15] Studies find, for example, that labor "unions use shareholder proposals as bargaining chips in contract negotiations."[16] Other studies find that public pension funds and labor funds disproportionately target Republican-leaning firms (measured by firms' campaign contributions).[17]

According to the Proxy Monitor in 2017, social or policy issues made up 56 percent of shareholder proposals.[18] Generally, these sorts of proposals tend to attract very little support from other shareholders.[19] In contrast, corporate governance-related proposals, in most years the largest category of proposal, attract an average of 35.9 percent support.[20] The vast majority of governance proposals are made by individuals unlikely to have the resources to analyze dozens of companies, so as one team of researchers notes, they "make one-size-fits-all proposals" about "corporate governance provisions that they have no experience in evaluating" and that, if adopted, "seem to be ill-conceived."[21] In fact, between 2003 and 2014, proposals submitted by active individual sponsors that appeared "generic" (67 percent) or "unfocused" (78 percent) made up the vast majority of proposals received by firms in the S&P's 1500 index. In most years, fewer than 20 percent of shareholder proposals put to the vote attract majority support.[22]

The targets of shareholder proposals tend to be significantly larger than comparable firms in their industry.[23] Shareholder proposals are thus not aimed at poorly performing firms – which makes sense since most proposals (whether relating to governance or social issues) are not firm-specific, but intended to effect a kind of political change (including to market norms).[24] Targeting the highest profile firms – usually the largest – provides maximum impact.

6.1.2 *What Do We Know about the Outcomes of Shareholder Proposals?*

While proposals tend to be effective at getting firms to change their governance arrangements, studies of the market reaction to proposals provide no evidence they are expected to create economic value.[25] One recent study using data from shareholder proposals uncertain to pass found "considerable heterogeneity in proposal returns, with some proposals experiencing significantly negative returns."[26]

The usefulness of these sorts of studies is questionable, however. Nearly all of them are "event" studies that look at the market reaction to the announcement of a shareholder proposal or the news that it has passed. Virtually all of these studies find no discernible evidence of value creation in these announcements. The problem is that shareholder proposals are frequently announced well before a company sends out its proxy materials and the results of the shareholder vote are usually anticipated before the meeting is held.[27] As well, both the proxy materials and the announcement of the meeting results contain a great deal of information besides that relating to the proposal, which likely contaminates any price reaction to the proposal.[28]

Attempts to solve these problems by looking only at "close-call" votes when the market could not reasonably have known whether the proposal would pass[29] suffer from significant problems with their internal validity for a variety of reasons, the most significant of which is that the studies of this type performed thus far use a dataset that does not measure voting support using the metric outlined in each firm's corporate charter.[30] They therefore mismeasure what constitutes a "close-call" vote. Studies looking at close-call votes also find themselves considering a tiny fraction of shareholder proposals, which makes it impossible to extract a general conclusion about the economic effects of this form of activism.

The problems with event studies (which predominate in the literature) mean that it is necessary to focus on the longer-term empirical studies. These either look at the long-run stock performance of the firms targeted by shareholder proposals or examine the actual business performance of the firms as measured by various accounting metrics. A recent review of the seventeen long-run share price studies on this topic concluded, "the available evidence is most consistent with the conclusion that shareholder proposals and negotiations are not associated with significant long-run stock returns."[31] A similar conclusion is drawn after looking at the shareholder proposal studies that use return on assets, return on equity, and return on sales as the key variables. "Most evidence … indicates that shareholder proposals and direct negotiations are not associated with increases in the target firms' operating performance."[32]

There are only a scattering of studies examining nonfinancial outcomes, but these tend to support the conclusion that shareholder proposals are not particularly valuable. For example, three different studies find that companies targeted by shareholder proposals and direct shareholder negotiations do not change their CEOs at a higher rate.[33]

6.1.3 *What Conclusions Can We Draw from Shareholder Proposals?*

The empirical evidence surrounding shareholder proposals can be easily summarized: they apparently provide no long-run benefits to the corporation, the vast majority appear to be generated for reasons that have little to do with improving the long-run financial performance of the company, and they have no impact on the most obvious target of the agency cost story – the CEO. As we saw in Chapter 5, there is also evidence that shareholders don't really want their proposals to have an impact, so they don't bring binding proposals and they don't ask for substantive changes to strategy or capital allocation.[34] Instead, they ask for window dressing, such as the production of reports that most shareholders will never read.

6.2 ACTIVIST CAMPAIGNS

Activist shareholder campaigns are costlier than launching a shareholder proposal, but obviously cheaper than a takeover. They therefore reflect a middle ground that might potentially be a fertile space for investor influence on corporate governance. Higher costs discourage uninformed activists while still permitting a wide range of institutions to participate.

It is hard to be certain about the scope of shareholder activism. Most years since 2006, there have been over 100 proxy fights launched by activists in the United States, but these represent only the last resort for an activist whose initial informal approaches have been repudiated by the board.[35] Probably the majority of activist campaigns don't normally get to the proxy fight stage, but rather result in a negotiated resolution.[36] If a proxy fight does occur, activists gain some measure of victory in over two-thirds of them.[37]

6.2.1 *What We Know about Activists and Their Targets*

Most, but not all, activist investors are hedge funds, and they share the same general characteristics as other hedge funds. The managers' compensation structures are strongly skewed to short-term payoffs. The most comprehensive attempt to model the economic incentives of hedge fund managers – direct and indirect – found they were strongly sensitive to the quarterly performance of the fund and that for young fund managers in particular, the incentives for making short-term results at the expense of the long term are "particularly large."[38] For "the manager of an average-size mutual fund," a 1 percent increase in the return to investors produces "$1,202,000 in expected future compensation."[39] In contrast to the typical lock-up in a private equity fund that restricts investors from getting their money back for five to ten years, hedge funds have lock-ups that only range from six months to two years.[40] This means that hedge funds compete for resources on a quarterly basis and that even small improvements in the near term produce enormous (one might say, "extraordinary") financial benefits for a manager.

As we would expect given these incentives, studies on activist hedge fund investment portfolios find that the median holding period for an investment is eighteen months by one measure and twenty two months by another.[41] Another study finds half of activist investments last slightly less than nine months.[42] The short-term horizon of activist investors does not, of course, tell us anything about the quality of their interventions into corporate governance, but it should put us on alert. As former Delaware Supreme Court Chief Justice, Leo Strine, notes, "[i]f out of this debate among those with short-term perspectives comes optimal policy for human investors with far longer time horizons, that happy coincidence would be remarkable."[43] The simple reality is that activist investors, with few exceptions, do not bear the risks associated with the long-term results of the strategies they impose on target companies.

As we saw in Chapter 5, one manifestation of this dynamic is that activist shareholders do not target companies whose businesses they like, but companies which offer the prospect of an intervention that will produce at least a short-term increase in share price. These are usually companies with "low market value relative to book value … with sound operating cash flows and return on assets."[44] These are not companies that are struggling. Indeed, most studies have found the targets of activists tend to be more profitable than control samples.[45]

The nature of the typical activist target is important because the activist playbook is limited. Looking at 1,358 activist engagements between 2000 and 2010, one team of researchers reported that 35.8 percent resulted in changes to the board (involving the replacement of the CEO, chair, or a nonexecutive director), 21.5 percent resulted in changes to pay-out policy (increasing or implementing a share buyback program, increasing dividend payments), 20 percent involved a restructuring (spinning off non-core assets or blocking a diversifying acquisition), and the remainder (22.7 percent) ended in a takeover of the target firm.[46] Most of these outcomes can broadly be described as "financial engineering." With the exception of board changes (which, themselves, are often precursors to a sale or cash distribution), these outcomes are all ways of delivering increased amounts of corporate cash to the shareholders.

There is little evidence that activist interventions involve questions of business strategy, operational efficiencies, improvements to top-line performance, the development of new products, or calls to increase investments in one aspect or another of the business. Even executive compensation, which commonly appears as a target of activist campaigns, is not usually impacted.[47]

Supporters of activist investors admit that hedge funds tend to focus on corporate finance initiatives as most hedge fund managers don't have much expertise in operational or managerial matters and they "are not experts in the specific business of their target firms."[48] There is little attempt to remedy these deficiencies. Directors nominated to boards by activists are more than three times more likely to be financial services professionals compared to the independent directors appointed by firms in the usual course.[49] Studies that have isolated activist campaigns in which the activist succeeds in placing directors on the board find the target companies experience significant underperformance afterwards, unless they are sold.[50] Companies targeted by activists have a significantly higher chance of filing for bankruptcy following the hedge fund's intervention.[51]

6.2.2 *What Do We Know about the Outcomes of Activist Campaigns?*

Ultimately, what matters is the actual impact of activist investors on target companies. Nearly all the research suggests that the principal effects of an activist intervention are a reduction in investment in capital assets and R&D spending, a decline or stagnation in employment levels and wages, a reduction in the amount of cash held by the corporation, and an increase in leverage.[52] The cash freed up from these changes is returned to shareholders in the form of increased dividend payouts or share buybacks.[53]

Some of these changes to corporate behavior result in straightforward expropriation of wealth from bondholders.[54] Some of the activists' proposals amount to basic financial maneuvers designed to improve return on assets and return on equity, which in turn drive share price improvements. Earlier studies in fact found that return on assets and return on equity did improve for targeted firms.[55] It is clear, however, that these improvements were not due to improved business results, but because of declines in the firms' assets and outstanding shares.[56] It may also be the case that even this improvement in metrics is illusory. The only study that has carefully matched targeted firms with control companies showing the same pre-intervention return on assets and financial trends as the targets found "no evidence of post-activism changes in ROA [return on assets] for target firms."[57] It also failed to find any evidence of improvements in return on equity.[58]

Similar results arise from looking at other operational metrics. After reviewing the evidence, Professors Coffee and Palia conclude, "[l]ittle evidence supports the thesis that hedge funds promote growth in sales or asset size."[59] A little later, they note more generally, it is "highly doubtful that operating performance improves as a result of activist interventions."[60] A more recent study on the topic looks at a broader set of accounting-performance measures, including things like profit margin, asset turnover, and spread over borrowing costs, but once again fails to find evidence of improvements following activist interventions.[61] This is broadly in line with earlier research that finds profitability either unaffected or negatively impacted by activist campaigns.[62] In all, four recent good-quality studies have all found that activism produces no significant improvement in business cash flows.[63] For their part, investment bank analysts apparently do not expect post-activism improvements in corporate earnings as shown by their earnings forecasts.[64]

If a target company's actual business performance doesn't improve from activist campaigns, does it at least become more valuable to the shareholders? In this regard, there are several difficulties with the empirical literature. Most of the studies focus on the short-term share price impact of 13D announcements by American activist investors that they have crossed the 5 percent share ownership threshold. There are several studies of this type, and they find positive abnormal returns between 3.39 percent and 6.97 percent in the month of the announcement.[65] The problem is that stock prices tend to appreciate in response to *all* 13D announcements, not just those filed by activist shareholders. The magnitude of share price appreciation in response to an activist hedge fund 13D filing is not materially different from the market response following 13D filings by insiders, buy-and-hold financial institutions, 10 percent holders, and others.[66] It appears that investors interpret a 13D filing as evidence that something new is happening with a company; they pile into the stock so they don't miss an opportunity. There is very little basis from these short-term studies to conclude that there is anything special about a corporate governance-inflected activist announcement.

Longer-term studies have their own problems. Many studies, especially the earliest, failed to use appropriate benchmarks or suitable control groups.[67] As a recent paper on this topic notes, "papers that find post-activism improvements in accounting-based operating performance either do not use a benchmark control group or identify a control group without accounting for pre-activism performance trends."[68] This is a particular problem given that the targets of hedge fund activists exhibit atypical market performance in the run-up to the intervention. (This is, after all, why they are undervalued relative to their peers.) Returns to activist campaigns tend to be almost exclusively generated by interventions at smaller firms (including a significant percentage not even listed on a national stock exchange[69]) where mispriced stocks are much more likely.[70] Firms with market values in excess of $40 million (a remarkably low cut-off for public companies) do not appear to experience any consistent increase in shareholder value from activist shareholder interventions.[71]

The short-term nature of much of the empirical research is also unhelpful. With only a couple exceptions, the studies measure the impact of hedge funds over a period of two years or less.[72] This is strange, given that the actual debate around activist shareholders is couched in terms of whether the financial engineering promoted by them is in the long-term interests of companies. Increasing dividends, share buybacks, and corporate sales are self-evidently in the short-term interests of the current shareholders, but what happens afterwards?[73] A surprisingly small body of research addresses itself to this – the real – debate.

Probably the best-known paper on the long-term consequences of hedge fund activism is by Professors Bebchuk, Brav, and Jiang, who look at companies for a suitably lengthy period of time (five years) and find value-weighted abnormal stock price returns of 5.81 percent over that period.[74] This is the headline result. Unfortunately, by another measure, the study found investors would have received a slightly negative abnormal return over the five years.[75] There are also serious methodological problems with the study, beginning with the fact that it starts with 1,584 companies and ends in year five with only 694 companies; there is no attempt to track the companies that are dropped.[76] Several different teams of scholars have written persuasively about other major flaws in the study.[77] But perhaps most interesting is that even if we accepted the paper uncritically, when the returns on assets experienced by the target companies are compared with the returns experienced by (inadequately) industry-matched control companies, "the positive impact of hedge funds, if that difference were really attributable to their intervention, would amount to going from a performance infinitesimally smaller than industry performance to a performance infinitesimally better than industry performance."[78]

Using the same dataset as Bebchuk, Brav, and Jiang, but more carefully matching control firms with the targets of hedge fund activism, a recent paper finds that "the firm value of the target firms tends to be 5.5 percent lower than the firm value of the control firms at the end of the fiscal year in which the activist hedge funds start their campaign, and about 9.8 percent lower three years thereafter."[79] The researchers note that this result is robust to several matching procedures and adding different fixed effects.[80]

This then raises the question: how do the activist hedge funds generate their returns if both corporate performance and share value lag? Some of it may be related to timing the sale of their shares, control premiums extracted from companies, and the use of leverage.[81] Given that the returns tend to be concentrated in the smallest target companies, some of the returns may be generated by identifying undervalued companies and bringing them to the attention of the market. However, what the evidence mostly suggests is that the vast majority of the returns generated from hedge fund activism arise from those cases when the activist intervention results in the sale of the company. As a recent study put it, "nearly all the positive long-term returns to activist interventions are concentrated among firms that are subsequently acquired."[82] Activist campaigns are followed by a significantly increased chance that the target firm will be acquired[83] and a large body of research suggests this phenomenon is the primary driver of hedge fund returns.[84]

6.3 WHAT CONCLUSIONS CAN WE DRAW FROM HEDGE FUND ACTIVISM?

There is very little support in the data we have reviewed for the idea that activist shareholders improve corporate governance. While activists replace CEOs at statistically significant rates,[85] there is little evidence the companies targeted by activists differ from their peers in the way managers were using free cash flows prior to the activists arriving on the scene,[86] and no evidence the returns generated by activist investors are connected with reducing these agency costs.[87]

The data contains considerable evidence that shareholders are a bad influence on firm performance, however. Activist interventions are short term, they bear little evidence that the activist firm understands the business of the target, they typically involve fairly routine financial engineering steps to boost share value while not improving the business and profits of the company, and while interventions increase share price in the short term, this is not likely due to the market anticipating improved corporate governance. Where the activist succeeds in placing nominees on the board, the companies significantly underperform their peers. Finally, the evidence suggests the target companies that survive do worse in the long term than carefully matched control firms.

6.4 TAKEOVERS

Of all the forms of shareholder activism, a takeover offer is the costliest. The offeror bears the entire burden of the intervention and its long-term consequences. The market for corporate control therefore provides the likeliest place to find support for the proposition that shareholders are an important part of corporate governance. Takeovers are popularly supposed to consist of a shareholder finding value through constraining agency costs by replacing negligent or self-serving corporate managers.

The merits of takeovers for the target company's shareholders seem obvious: acquisitions must always be conducted at a premium to the market. Nevertheless, some scholars express concern about two possible ways takeovers could hurt existing shareholders. First, value-decreasing takeovers are possible in circumstances where shareholder misinformation occurs.[88] This might be the case, for example, with companies characterized by nonlinear innovation, as the companies' current performance may not be a guide to its future performance. Some long-term investments will depress current earnings and the market price may not accurately reflect future cash flows.[89] Shareholders may also mistake the value of businesses that experience significant earnings volatility or whose market price is impacted by macro-economic or industry factors that don't reflect the companies' fundamentals.[90] Companies can be "caught" in a general market or industry sell-off. As two academics note about the frequently misunderstood Efficient Capital Markets Hypothesis, it "does not imply that the share price equals the pro rata value of the discounted free cash flows of the corporation.... To say that no investment strategy can outperform the market does not ... say anything about the stock price's accuracy in measuring the corporation's fundamental value."[91]

The second possible way takeovers could hurt the shareholders arises from what is referred to as the "Bonding Hypothesis." This is a theory that "takeover defenses increase the value of managers' commitments to maintain their promised operating strategy and not to opportunistically exploit their counterparties' investments in the ... firm."[92] The firm's counterparties – customers, lenders, employees, and suppliers – are encouraged to invest in the business, increasing its value, but this increase in value comes expressly from the assurance that these investments cannot be expropriated by the shareholders through a takeover. So, for example, the authors of one study find that takeover defenses are deployed by new firms joining the public markets precisely when those firms have large customers, dependent suppliers, or strategic partners.[93] The study finds that these relationships also last longer for firms with takeover defenses and these firms appear to get a higher price at the time of going public than firms without the defenses.

6.4.1 *What We Know about Takeovers*

Takeovers are generally very good for the shareholders of the target company. Between 1973 and 2002, the average acquisition premium was about 50 percent in the United States.[94] Takeovers are not, however, particularly good for the shareholders of the acquiring company.[95] A 2008 study found that the shares of the bidder experience no bump in price at the time the tender offer is announced; the returns on those shares are indistinguishable from those of the general market.[96] Hostile bids result in worse acquirer stock performance than friendly deals.[97] Possibly connected to this, hostile bids tend to present target company shareholders with a higher premium, doubtless in part because shareholders require an extra inducement to sell against the recommendation of the target firm's directors.[98]

Longer-term studies on the economics of M&A transactions are decidedly negative. For example, studies that measure operating performance over time (such as earnings or other measures of cash flows) largely find that acquirers tend to underperform their peers for the next several years.[99] Casting considerable doubt on one of the commonly given reasons for an acquisition, that there are synergies between the two companies that will lead to lower costs and higher profits, it appears that acquisitions of firms in the same industry as the bidder produce no financial performance advantages over acquisitions in an unrelated industry.[100]

Surveying the evidence, one team of authors observe, "[c]onsensus seems to have formed that the value of deals generally flows to shareholders of the target firm ... experience shows that the surviving firm often fails to realize economic value."[101] Where does the value received by target company shareholders come from? At least some of it appears to come from the expropriation of value from other corporate constituencies. For example, it can arise from increased leverage applied to the target business either from the addition of more debt, the sale of assets, or both. An American study looking at the impact of state takeover laws on corporate debt, found bonds in takeover-friendly states had significantly higher yields at the time of issue, and issuers had higher total levels of leverage.[102] Critics of takeovers argue that the premium received by target company shareholders also comes from redeploying target company cash from long-term projects, cutting capital expenditures, and reducing labor costs.[103] These are more contentious claims and sorting out the truth of them is not important for our purposes.

The question we are interested in is how much of the takeover premium is the result of reducing agency costs? This is the story commonly told about takeovers and it would provide powerful support for the story that shareholders are valuable contributors to firm governance.[104] The empirical literature suggests several problems with an uncritical acceptance of it. First, after studying over 2,000 corporations that were the targets of takeovers, Anup Agrawal and Jeffrey Jaffe concluded, "Overall, we do not find much support for the inefficient management hypothesis. Target firms as a group do not underperform over a decade-long pre-bid period, whether performance is measured by operating returns or stock returns."[105] Another study found that more than half of the companies targeted for acquisition in the 1980s outperformed the market in the two years prior and found no evidence of post-acquisition turnover of officers and directors.[106] Takeovers are not apparently a response to managerial misbehavior.

Indeed, the usual formula that takeovers discipline managers may be precisely backwards. Most senior executives have golden parachutes or severance clauses that produce major payouts on termination after a change of control. They have options and shares that market norms prevent them from selling while they are employed by the company, and the takeover premium will produce significant wealth for them in their capacity of equity holders as well. Possibly the most conclusive evidence that the agency cost explanation for takeovers is incorrect is seen in the impact of a takeover on executives' reputation. Far from being generally stigmatized as untrustworthy agents, displaced managers trumpet the fact they successfully sold the company at a significant premium for the shareholders. The vast majority of takeovers, after all, are not hostile, but friendly.[107] If we are looking for excessive agency costs in takeovers, they may at least be as likely manifested by managers selling the company for personal gain as by managers clinging to power to retain their perquisites.

Finally, while there are few good modern studies about companies that survive as independent firms following an unsolicited takeover offer, there is anecdotal evidence that many go on to outperform their peers.[108] The one study looking at the long-term outcomes of successful takeover defenses finds the companies outperform their peers by 40 percent over the five years following a successful defense, but only if the target companies increase their leverage.[109]

6.4.2 *What Do We Know about the Use of Takeover Defenses?*

Most of the research surrounding the market for corporate control has revolved around the use and effects of various takeover defenses. From 1980 to 2011, almost 2,000 articles on antitakeover provisions appeared in peer-reviewed academic journals.[110] Unfortunately, much of this research is deeply flawed. Some of the problems are of the garden-variety statistical nature, such as reverse causality.[111]

By far the biggest problem arises, however, from widely held misunderstandings about corporate law in the United States. A vast amount of the research on takeover defenses focuses on the poison pill, which, in the United States, acts as a complete bar to a takeover as long as the board keeps it in place. This research examines questions such as changes in firm value or business outcomes following the adoption or termination of a poison pill. It also looks at the relationship a pill has with executive compensation, CEO turnover, and other features of corporate governance. Unfortunately, as we have noted several times in this book, the presence or absence of a pill at any given time doesn't tell you anything about the company, as boards can introduce a pill at any time, even in the face of hostile bid, without seeking shareholder approval.[112] Corporate directors and their lawyers are very aware of this fact and so the presence or absence of a pill tells you nothing about how a company will react to a takeover, whether its directors feel vulnerable to a hostile bid, whether its management has too much influence over the board, whether the board holds shareholders in esteem or contempt, or whether the company is well governed or abused. It tells you nothing, in short, about the company or the degree of its exposure to the market for corporate control.[113]

This point about poison pills has been made repeatedly by several law professors since the turn of the century.[114] The failure of these warnings to impact the work of other members of the legal academy and finance scholars is surprising. We have already encountered the examples in Chapter 3 of the G-Index and E-Index, which both include the presence or absence of a poison pill as an important part of measuring the quality of companies' corporate governance.

The problems in the literature created by misunderstanding the role of poison pills are replicated in connection with other takeover defenses. Business combination statutes, fair price statutes or charter provisions, control share acquisition statutes, and cash-out statutes all have no impact on a firm's exposure to a hostile takeover.[115] Nevertheless, all of them are present as part of the G-Index. Other defenses examined in the literature, such as measures making it difficult or impossible for shareholders to call meetings, or restrictions on shareholder voting, don't have any impact on companies with a staggered board and while staggered boards are rare now, they were relatively common when much of the research on takeover defenses was conducted.[116] Provisions requiring supermajority shareholder votes to amend corporate charters or approve a merger also don't impact the outcome of hostile bids, as any charter amendment must also be approved by the board and a merger vote would only occur if the hostile bidder had been materially successful in his bid.[117] Golden parachutes, which are often assumed by researchers to inhibit takeovers, in fact likely encourage them.[118] This means, for example, that five of the six elements tracked by the E-Index are not useful measures of entrenchment or governance quality.

What in the takeover defense literature can be used to evaluate the agency cost governance story? The largest relevant body of research concerns staggered (or "classified") boards. Because poison pills form a complete barrier to a hostile takeover, the bidder must always gain control of the target board of directors to remove the pill. This takes two years for a US-incorporated firm with a staggered board. As a judge of the Delaware Court of Chancery observed in a 2011 case, "no bidder to my knowledge has ever successfully stuck around for two years and waged two successful proxy contests to gain control of a classified board in order to remove a pill."[119] It is the presence of a staggered board, therefore, not the presence of a poison pill, that says something meaningful about a company's exposure to the market for corporate control.

In relation to staggered boards, we see the same pattern in the research that we observed in relation to shareholder activism. Nearly all of the initial research found that staggered boards were associated with lower firm value as measured by Tobin's Q[120] and that introducing staggered boards was associated with negative abnormal returns.[121] These studies recognized that there could be problems with causality; since most governance arrangements are adopted in response to firm-specific circumstances, staggered boards could be produced by low firm values rather than (as was generally assumed) the other way around.

The early studies on staggered boards had another problem: they used a relatively limited time period (1995–2002) during which there were very few companies either adopting a staggered board or removing one.[122] In recent years, much larger studies have been performed, capturing the wave of staggered boards that arose in the 1980s and the opposite move to de-stagger boards in the years following 2005.[123] These studies also began looking at differences in firm value over several decades, as governance arrangements evolve, rather than simply comparing value across firms with different governance arrangements at a single point in time.[124]

These later, better studies find that the results of the earlier studies were the result of reverse causality. Low firm value appears to be a significant predictor of board staggering.[125] They also find that when the much larger data set of firms is examined, staggered boards are either positively associated with an increase in firm value[126] or that they produce no material change in firm value.[127] More interestingly, these studies find that while staggered boards apparently discourage hostile bids, when a hostile takeover is launched, the staggered board doesn't appear to affect the likelihood that the target is acquired, and it improves the premium paid to shareholders.[128] It is hard to see how this is compatible with the usual managerial entrenchment narrative surrounding takeover defenses. "These results are not consistent with the notion that classification, on average, facilitates self-dealing by incumbent managers at the expense of target shareholders."[129]

A possibly more helpful thread in the scholarly literature looks at board classification in several exogenous natural experiments in an attempt to disentangle the wealth effects of staggered boards from omitted variables and to reduce the risk of getting the direction of causality wrong. In this vein, the Harvard Shareholder Rights Project, which targeted companies for declassification between 2011 and 2014, without regard to other characteristics of the companies and without advanced notice to the market, has been found to have caused "economically and statistically significant reductions in firm value … both in absolute terms and relative to declassifications occurring [at other firms]."[130] These wealth effects appear to have largely arisen from affected firms with high R&D expenditures.[131]

Similarly, a law passed in Massachusetts that imposed a staggered board on all firms incorporated in that state produced significant and positive average increases in Tobin's Q.[132] (Affected companies also responded with more long-term investments reflected by increased capital expenditures, increased R&D expenditures, more patents, higher-quality patents, and greater profitability.[133]) Another study looked at the impact of various recent legislative and regulatory events in the United States potentially impacting staggered boards, finding that the market reaction in every case suggests staggered boards are value-enhancing.[134] Finally, "dead hand pills" serve as a kind of proxy for staggered boards since they are a poison pill that can only be removed by the same, "continuing" directors that imposed it. The research finds that dead-hand pills are associated with wealth gains to shareholders.[135]

Some studies have looked at the impact of staggered boards on things other than shareholder wealth. Several of these are relevant to evaluating the agency cost story. One study found that a staggered board was just as likely to terminate a CEO as a board elected annually.[136] Another study found that the presence of a staggered board had no impact on the amounts paid to executives or the pay structures used by the firm.[137] A study of American banks found that staggered boards were roughly 18 to 26 percent less likely to require state bailouts in the wake of the 2008 financial crisis.[138]

6.4.3 *What Conclusions Can We Draw from Takeovers?*

Once again, the empirical research around the market for corporate control provides little support for active shareholder participation in corporate governance. There does not appear to be managerial underperformance in the decade preceding a takeover bid; targets surviving as independent entities following a failed bid tend to outperform the market (notwithstanding management and boards remaining intact), and at least some, possibly all, of the gains to target company shareholders associated with a takeover are the result of the same kind of financial engineering we saw in activist campaigns. There is little evidence, in any event, that the premium paid on successful bids is generated by operating improvements under new management.

In contrast, there is a great deal of support for the proposition that shareholder governance interventions are problematic. The one effective takeover defense in the United States, the staggered board, is associated with: better firm performance; higher shareholder value (or no change to shareholder value); and immunity from the market for corporate control has no effect on CEO turnover or executive pay. To the extent there is variation among companies, there is evidence that companies pursuing long-term strategies (measured by R&D expenditures) and needing non-contractual investments from strategic partners (such as suppliers or customers) disproportionately benefit from protections against shareholder power.

6.5 SUMMARY

Shareholders have every right to take whatever steps the law permits to maximize the value of their shares. However, we have dramatically increased their power over the past several decades to intervene in the governance of corporations under the impression that this will improve the way corporations are run. This chapter suggests that it appears this assumption is mistaken.

NOTES

1 Jill E. Fisch, "Securities Intermediaries and the Separation of Ownership from Control" (2010) 33:4 *Seattle University Law Review* 877–888 at 884.
2 Leo E. Strine, "Can We Do Better by Ordinary Investors? A Pragmatic Reaction to the Dueling Ideological Mythologists of Corporate Law" (2014) 114:2 *Columbia Law Review* 449–502 at 470–471.
3 See for example, David F. Larcker, Allan L. McCall and Gaizka Ormazabal, "Proxy Advisory Firms and Stock Option Repricing" (2013) 56:2–3 *Journal of Accounting & Economics* 149–169; Rita D. Kosnik, "Greenmail: A Study of Board Performance in Corporate Governance" (1987) 32:2 *Administrative Science Quarterly* 163–185; See also, B. Espen Eckbo, "Valuation Effects of Greenmail Prohibitions" (1990) 25:4 *The Journal of Financial and Quantitative Analysis* 491–505.
4 *The Swinging Pendulum: Board Governance in the Age of Shareholder Empowerment – PwC's 2016 Annual Corporate Directors Survey*, PricewaterhouseCoopers International Limited (October 2016), online (pdf): www.pwc.com/us/en/corporate-governance/annual-corporate-directors-survey/assets/pwc-2016-annual-corporate-directors-survey.pdf at 14.
5 Michael Klausner, "Fact and Fiction in Corporate Law and Governance" (2013) 65:6 *Stanford Law Review* 1325–1370 at 1361 [Klausner, "Fact and Fiction"].
6 Simon Deakin, Prabirjit Sarkar and Mathias Siems, "Is There a Relationship Between Shareholder Protection and Stock Market Development?" (2018) 3:1 *Journal of Law, Finance and Accounting* 115–146 at 124.
7 Pavlos E. Masouros, *Corporate Law and Economic Stagnation: How Shareholder Value and Short-Termism Contribute to the Decline of the Western Economies* (The Netherlands: Eleven International Publishing, 2013).
8 *Ibid* at p. 301.
9 Marcel Kahan and Edward Rock, "Embattled CEOs" (2010) 88:5 *Texas Law Review* 987–1052.
10 Yonca Ertimur, Fabrizio Ferri and Stephen R. Stubben, "Board of Directors' Responsiveness to Shareholders: Evidence from Shareholder Proposals" (2010) 16:1 *Journal of Corporate Finance* 53–72.

11   Nickolay Gantchev and Mariassunta Giannetti, "The Costs and Benefits of Shareholder Democracy: Gadflies and Low-cost Activism" (2021) 34:12 *The Review of Financial Studies* 5629–5675 at 5630 [Gantchev and Giannetti, "Costs and Benefits"].

12   Steven Davidoff Soloman, "Grappling with the Cost of Corporate Gadflies," The New York Times, 19 August 2014, online: https://archive.nytimes.com/dealbook.nytimes .com/2014/08/19/grappling-with-the-cost-of-corporate-gadflies/.

13   Ronald J. Gilson and Jeffrey N. Gordon, "Agency Capitalism: Further Implication of Equity Intermediation" in Jennifer G. Hill and Randall S. Thomas (eds.), *Research Handbook on Shareholder Power* (Cheltenham: Edward Elgar, 2015), pp. 40–66 at p. 45.

14   Ronald J. Gilson and Jeffrey N. Gordon, "Agency Costs of Agency Capitalism: Activist Investors and the Revaluation of Governance Rights" (2013) 113:4 *Columbia Law Review* 863–928 at 887.

15   Roberta Romano, "Less Is More: Making Institutional Investor Activism a Valuable Mechanism of Corporate Governance" (2001) 18:2 *Yale Journal on Regulation* 174–251 at 231.

16   John G. Matsusaka, Oguzhan Ozbas and Irene Yi, "Opportunistic Proposals by Union Shareholders" (2019) 32:8 *The Review of Financial Studies* 3215–3265 at 3233.

17   Geeyoung Min and Hye Young You, "Active Firms and Active Shareholders: Corporate Political Activity and Shareholder Proposals" (2019) 48:1 *The Journal of Legal Studies* 81–116 [Min and You, "Active Firms"].

18   James R. Copland and Margaret M. O'Keefe, *Proxy Monitor 2017: Season Review*, Proxy Monitor (2017), online: www.proxymonitor.org/Forms/pmr_15.aspx.

19   Min and You, "Active Firms," above at note 17 at 92, 109. See also, Eugene F. Soltes, Suraj Srinivasan and Rajesh Vijayaraghavan, "What Else Do Shareholders Want? Shareholder Proposals Contested by Firm Management" (2017), *Harvard Business School Accounting & Management Unit Working Paper*, online: SSRN, https://ssrn .com/abstract=2771114 at 25.

20   Min and You, "Active Firms," above at note 17 at 109.

21   Gantchev and Giannetti, "Costs and Benefits," above at note 11 at 5630.

22   2022 *Proxy Season Review: Part 1*, Sullivan & Cromwell LLP (2 August 2022), online (pdf): www.sullcrom.com/SullivanCromwell/_Assets/PDFs/Memos/sc-publication-2022-Proxy-Season-Part-1-Rule-14a-8.pdf at 2; Matteo Tonello, "Shareholder Voting Trends (2018–2022)" (5 November 2022), *Harvard Law School Forum on Corporate Governance*, online: https://corpgov.law.harvard.edu/2022/11/05/shareholder-voting-trends-2018-2022/.

23   Gantchev and Giannetti, "Costs and Benefits," above at note 11 at 5639; Paul Washington and Merel Spierings, "2023 Proxy Season: More Proposals, Lower Support" (1 June 2023), Harvard Law School Forum on Corporate Governance, online: https://corpgov.law .harvard.edu/2023/06/01/2023-proxy-season-more-proposals-lower-support/; Yonca Ertimur, Fabrizio Ferri and David Oesch, "Does the Director Election System Matter? Evidence from Majority Voting" (2015) 20:1 Review of Accounting Studies 1–41 at 20; Jonathan M. Karpoff, "The Impact of Shareholder Activism on Target Companies: A Survey of Empirical Findings" (2006), online: SSRN, https://ssrn.com/abstract=885365 at 24; Johnathan M. Karpoff, Paul H. Malatesta and Ralph A. Walkling, "Corporate Governance and Shareholder Initiatives: Empirical Evidence" (1996) 42:3 Journal of Financial Economics 365–395 at 392 [Karpoff, Malatesta and Walking, "Shareholder Initiatives"].

24   See Fabrizio Ferri and Tatiana Sandino, "The Impact of Shareholder Activism on Financial Reporting and Compensation: The Case of Employee Stock Options Expensing" (2009) 84:2 *The Accounting Review* 433–466; Yonca Ertimur, Fabrizio Ferri and Stephen R. Stubben, "Board of Directors' Responsiveness to Shareholders: Evidence from Shareholder Proposals" (2010) 16:1 *Journal of Corporate Finance* 53–72.

25 Karpoff, Malatesta and Walking, "Shareholder Initiatives," above at note 23; Stuart L. Gillan and Laura T. Starks, "Corporate Governance Proposals and Shareholder Activism: The Role of Institutional Investors" (2000) 57:2 *Journal of Financial Economics* 275–305; Jie Cai and Ralph A. Walkling, "Shareholders' Say on Pay: Does it Create Value?" (2011) 46:2 *Journal of Financial and Quantitative Analysis* 299–339; Gantchev and Giannetti, "Costs and Benefits," above at note 11 at 5650, Table 6; Joao Dos Santos and Chen Song, "Analysis of the Wealth Effects of Shareholder Proposals – Volume II" (18 May 2009), US Chamber of Commerce, online (pdf): www.uschamber.com/sites/default/files/legacy/files/analysis_wealth_effects_volume2.pdf.
26 Gantchev and Giannetti, "Costs and Benefits," above at note 11 at 5632.
27 Gillan L. Stuart and Laura T. Starks, "The Evolution of Shareholder Activism in the United States" (2007) 19:1 *The Journal of Applied Corporate Finance* 55–73.
28 *Ibid*.
29 Vicente Cuñat, Mireia Gine and Maria Guadalupe, "The Vote is Cast: The Effect of Corporate Governance on Shareholder Value" (2012) 67:5 *The Journal of Finance*, 1943–1977.
30 Laurent Bach and Daniel Metzger, "How Close are Shareholder Votes?" (2019) 32:8 *The Review of Financial Studies* 3189–3214 at 3186.
31 Matthew Denes, Jonathan M. Karpoff and Victoria B. McWilliams, "Thirty Years of Shareholder Activism: A Survey of Empirical Research" (2017) 44:1 *Journal of Corporate Finance* 405–424 at 410 [Denes, Karpoff and McWilliams, "Thirty Years"].
32 *Ibid* at 411.
33 Diane Del Guercio and Jennifer Hawkins, "The Motivation and Impact of Hedge Fund Activism" (1999) 52:1 *Journal of Financial Economics* 293–340; Karpoff, Malatesta and Walking, "Shareholder Initiatives," above at note 23; Michael P. Smith, "Shareholder Activism by Institutional Investors: Evidence from CalPERS" (1996) 51:1 *The Journal of Finance* 227–252.
34 Marcel Kahan and Edward Rock, "Symbolic Corporate Governance Politics" (2014) 94:6 *Boston University Law Review* 1997–2044.
35 Michal Barzuza and Eric L. Talley, "Short-Termism and Long-Termism" (2016), *Columbia Law and Economics Working Paper No. 526*, online: SSRN, https://ssrn.com/abstract=2731814 at 4, Figure 1 [Barzuza and Talley, "Short-Termism"].
36 John C. Coffee, Jr., "The Agency Cost of Activism: Information Leakage, Thwarted Majorities, and the Public Morality" (2017), *European Corporate Governance Institute – Law Working Paper No. 373/2017*, online: SSRN, https://ssrn.com/abstract=3058319 at 2.
37 Barzuza and Talley, "Short-Termism," above at note 35 at 4.
38 Jongha Lim, Berk A. Sensoy and Michael S. Weisbach, "Indirect Incentives of Hedge Fund Managers" (2016) 71:2 *The Journal of Finance* 871–918 at 894.
39 *Ibid* at 897.
40 William W. Bratton, "Hedge Funds and Governance Targets" (2007) 95:5 *The Georgetown Law Journal* 1375–1433 at 1384; John C. Coffee, Jr. and Darius Palia, "The Wolf at the Door: The Impact of Hedge Fund Activism on Corporate Governance" (2016) 41:3 *Journal of Corporation Law* 545–608 at 573 [Coffee and Palia, "Wolf at the Door"].
41 Alon Brav et al., "Hedge Fund Activism, Corporate Governance, and Firm Performance" (2008) 63:4 *The Journal of Finance* 1729–1775 at 1749 [Brav et al., "Hedge Fund Activism"]. See also, Coffee and Palia, "Wolf at the Door," above at note 40 at 567, 572.
42 Yvan Allaire and François Dauphin, *"Activist" Hedge Funds: Creators of Lasting Wealth? What Do the Empirical Studies Really Say?*, Institute for Governance of Private and Public Organizations (17 July 2014), online (pdf): SSRN, https://ssrn.com/abstract=2460920 at 15 [Allaire and Dauphin, *Creators of Lasting Wealth?*].

43 Leo E. Strine, Jr., "Who Bleeds When the Wolves Bite? A Flesh-and-Blood Perspective on Hedge Fund Activism and Our Strange Corporate Governance System" (2017) 126:6 *The Yale Law Journal* 1870–1970 at 1874 [Strine, "Who Bleeds"].

44 Brav et al., "Hedge Fund Activism," above at note 41 at 1730; Coffee and Palia, "Wolf at the Door," above at note 40 at 582.

45 Coffee and Palia, "Wolf at the Door," above at note 40 at 582. See also, April Klein and Emanuel Zur, "Entrepreneurial Shareholder Activism: Hedge Funds and Other Private Investors" (2009) 64:1 *The Journal of Finance* 187–229 at 189 [Klein and Zur, "Entrepreneurial Shareholder"]; Brav et al., "Hedge Fund Activism," above at note 41 at 1754; Denes, Karpoff and McWilliams, "Thirty Years," above at note 31 at 415; C. N. V. Krishnan, Frank Partnoy and Randall S. Thomas, "The Second Wave of Hedge Fund Activism: The Importance of Reputation, Clout and Expertise" (2016) 40:1 *Journal of Corporate Finance* 296–314 at 298–299.

46 Marco Becht et al., "Returns to Hedge Fund Activism: An International Study" (2017) 30:9 *The Review of Financial Studies* 2933–2971 at 2953, Table 6 (source for data); Yvan Allaire, *The Case for and Against Activist Hedge Funds*, Institute for Governance of Private and Public Organizations (May 2015), online (pdf): *SSRN*, https://ssrn.com/abstract=2613154 at 9–10 (source for calculations). See also, Hadiye Aslan, "A Review of Hedge Fund Activism: Impact on Shareholders vs. Stakeholders" in Douglas Cumming, Sofia Johan and Geoffrey Wood (eds.), *The Oxford Handbook of Hedge Funds* (Oxford: Oxford University Press, 2021), pp. 283–317 at p. 291.

47 Coffee and Palia, "Wolf at the Door," above at note 40 at 583: Martin Cremers, Saura Masconale and Simone M. Sepe, "Activist Hedge Funds and the Corporation" (2016) 94:2 *Washington University Law Review* 261–340 [Cremers, Masconale and Sepe, "Activist Hedge Funds"].

48 Brav et al., "Hedge Fund Activism," above at note 41 at 1755.

49 Andrew Borek, Zachary Friesner and Patrick McGurn, "The Impact of Shareholder Activism on Board Refreshment Trends at S&P 1500 Firms" (August 2017), online: https://weinberg.udel.edu/the-impact-of-shareholder-activism-on-board-refreshment-trends-at-sp-1500-firms/ at 28.

50 Elaine Buckberg and Jonathon Macey, *Report on Effects of Proposed SEC Rule 14a-11 on Efficiency, Competitiveness and Capital Formation: In Support of Comments by Business Roundtable*, NERA Economic Consulting (17 August 2009), online (pdf): www.nera.com/upload/Buckberg_Macey_Report_FINAL.pdf at 9. See also, Zohar Goshen and Reilly Steel, "Barbarians Inside the Gates: Raiders, Activists, and the Risk of Mistargeting" (2023) 132:2 *Yale Law Journal* 411–486.

51 Cremers, Masconale and Sepe, "Activist Hedge Funds," above at note 47.

52 See Ian D. Gow, Sa-Pyung Sean Shin and Suraj Srinivasan, "Activist Directors: Determinants and Consequences" (2014), online: *SSRN*, https://ssrn.com/abstract=4321778; Caroline Heqing Zhu, "The Preventive Effect of Hedge Fund Activism: Investment, CEO Compensation and Payout Policies" (2013) 17:3 *International Journal of Managerial Finance* 401–415 [Zhu, "Preventive Effect"]; Alon Brav, Wei Jiang and Hyunseob Kim, "The Real Effects of Hedge Fund Activism: Productivity, Asset Allocation, and Labor Outcomes" (2015) 28:10 *The Review of Financial Studies* 2723–2769 at 2723; Anup Agrawal and Yuree Lim, "Where Do Shareholder Gains in Hedge Fund Activism Come From? Evidence From Employee Pension Plans" (2020) 57:6 *Journal of Financial and Quantitative Analysis* 2140–2176; Coffee and Palia, "Wolf at the Door," above at note 40 at 590–591, 592; Cremers, Masconale and Sepe, "Activist Hedge Funds," above at note 47 at 285; Yvan Allaire and François Dauphin, "The Game of 'Activist' Hedge Funds: Cui Bono?" (2016) 13:4 *International Journal of Disclosure*

and Governance 279–308 at 293–294 [Allaire and Dauphin, "The Game"]. See also, Denes, Karpoff and McWilliams, "Thirty Years," above at note 31 at 412, panel Table 2.

53 Brav et al., "Hedge Fund Activism," above at note 41 at 1771; Denes, Karpoff and McWilliams, "Thirty Years," above at note 31 at 412, panel B Table 2.

54 Hadiye Aslan and Hilda Maraachlian, "The New Kids on the Block: Wealth Effects of Hedge Fund Activism on Bondholders" (2009) [unpublished] *University of Houston Working Paper*; April Klein and Emanuel Zur, "The Impact of Hedge Fund Activism on the Target Firm's Existing Bondholders" (2011) 24:5 *The Review of Financial Studies* 1735–1771 at 1737. See also, Hadiye Aslan, "Shareholder Versus Stakeholders in Investor Activism: Value for Whom?" (2020) 60 *Journal of Corporate Finance* 101548.

55 Allaire and Dauphin, *Creators of Lasting Wealth?*, above at note 42 at 20–22; Alon Brav, Wei Jiang and Hyunseob Kim, "Hedge Fund Activism: A Review" (2009) 4:3 *Foundations and Trends in Finance* 1–66; Nicole M. Boyson and Robert M. Mooradian, "Corporate Governance and Hedge Fund Activism" (2011) 14:2 *Review of Derivatives Research* 169–204 [Boyson and Mooradian, "Corporate Governance"]; Christopher P. Clifford, "Value Creation or Value Destruction? Hedge Funds as Shareholder Activists" (2008) 14:4 *Journal of Corporate Finance* 323–336 [Clifford, "Creation or Destruction?"]; Nickolay Gantchev, Oleg R. Gredil and Chotibhak Jotikasthira, "Governance Under the Gun: Spillover Effects of Hedge Fund Activism" (2019) 23:6 *Review of Finance* 1031–1068; Zhu, "Preventive Effect," above at note 52. See also, Robin Greenwood and Michael Schor, "Investor Activism and Takeovers" (2009) 92:3 *Journal of Financial Economics* 362–375 [Greenwood and Schor, "Investor Activism"].

56 Clifford, "Creation or Destruction?," above at note 55 at 331.

57 Ed deHaan, David Larcker and Charles McClure, "Long Term Economic Consequences of Hedge Fund Activist Interventions" (2019) 24:2 *Review of Accounting Studies* 536–569 at 541 [deHaan, Larcker and McClure, "Long-Term Consequences"].

58 *Ibid*.

59 Coffee and Palia, "Wolf at the Door," above at note 40 at 591.

60 *Ibid* at 592.

61 deHaan, Larcker and McClure, "Long-Term Consequences," above at note 57 at 541.

62 Klein and Zur, "Entrepreneurial Shareholder," above at note 45 at 22; Victor Barros et al., "Shareholder Activism and Firms' Performance" (2023) 64 *Research in International Business and Finance* 101860 (decline in profitability following activist campaigns, though this study finds improvements in profitability connected to activist demands for board representation as opposed to a change of strategy or board control).

63 In the literature, "good quality" studies are ones that carefully match the control group with the targets of activist shareholders: Klein and Zur, "Entrepreneurial Shareholder," above at note 45 at 201; Clifford, "Creation or Destruction?," above at note 55 at 330–331; Boyson and Mooradian, "Corporate Governance," above at note 55 at 191; deHaan, Larcker and McClure, "Long-Term Consequences," above at note 57 at 541.

64 deHaan, Larcker and McClure, "Long-Term Consequences," above at note 57 at 565.

65 Brav et al., "Hedge Fund Activism," above at note 41 at 1729–1775; Klein and Zur, "Entrepreneurial Shareholder," above at note 45; Christopher P. Clifford and Laura Lindsey, "Blockholder Heterogeneity, CEO Compensation, and Firm Performance" (2016) 51:5 *The Journal of Financial and Quantitative Analysis* 1491–1520; Marco Becht et al., "Returns to Hedge Fund Activism: An International Study" (2017) 30:9 *The Review of Financial Studies* 2933–2971 at 2949.

66 Ulf von Lilienfeld-Toal and Jan Schnitzler, "What is Special about Hedge Fund Activism? Evidence from 13-D Filings" (2019), *Swedish House of Finance Research Paper No. 14–16*, online: SSRN, https://ssrn.com/abstract=2506704 at 38.

67 deHaan, Larcker and McClure, "Long-Term Consequences," above at note 57 at 538.

68 *Ibid*. See also, Cremers, Masconale and Sepe, "Activist Hedge Funds," above at note 47 at 282–284.

69 Allaire and Dauphin, "The Game," above at note 52 at 289.

70 deHaan, Larcker and McClure, "Long-Term Consequences," above at note 57 at 543, 564. See also, Dorothy S. Lund, "In Search of Good Corporate Governance" (2021) 131 *Yale Law Journal Forum* 854–872 at 868.

71 deHaan, Larcker and McClure, "Long-Term Consequences," above at note 57 at 564.

72 Allaire and Dauphin, *Creators of Lasting Wealth?*, above at note 42 at 3; Strine, "Who Bleeds," above at note 43 at 1966.

73 John Kay, *The Kay Review of UK Equity Markets and Long-Term Decision Making* (London: Business Innovation Skills, 2012), online (pdf): https://assets.publishing.service .gov.uk/government/uploads/system/uploads/attachment_data/file/253454/bis-12-917-kay-review-of-equity-markets-final-report.pdf.

74 Lucian A. Bebchuk, Alon Brav and Wei Jiang, "The Long-Term Effects of Hedge Fund Activism" (2015) 115:5 *Columbia Law Review* 1085–1156 at 1126–1127.

75 *Ibid*.

76 Allaire and Dauphin, *Creators of Lasting Wealth?*, above at note 42 at 9.

77 See Coffee and Palia, "Wolf at the Door," above at note 40 at 588; Allaire and Dauphin, *Creators of Lasting Wealth?*, above at note 42 at 9; deHaan, Larcker and McClure, "Long-Term Consequences," above at note 57.

78 Allaire and Dauphin, *Creators of Lasting Wealth?*, above at note 42 at 9.

79 K. J. Martijn Cremers et al., "Hedge Fund Activism and Long-Term Firm Value" (January 2016) *University of Notre Dame Working Paper*, online (pdf): https://ccl.yale.edu/ sites/default/files/files/le016_Sepe.pdf at 4–5.

80 *Ibid*. See also, Allaire and Dauphin, *Creators of Lasting Wealth?*, above at note 42.

81 Allaire and Dauphin, *Creators of Lasting Wealth?*, above at note 42 at 25.

82 deHaan, Larcker and McClure, "Long-Term Consequences," above at note 57 at 541.

83 Nicole M. Boyson, Nickolay Gantchev and Anil Shivdasani, "Activism Mergers" (2017) 126:1 *Journal of Financial Economics* 54–73.

84 deHaan, Larcker and McClure, "Long-Term Consequences," above at note 57; Greenwood and Schor, "Investor Activism," above at note 55; Allaire and Dauphin, *Creators of Lasting Wealth?*, above at note 42 at 25; Brav et al., "Hedge Fund Activism," above at note 41 at 1759; Coffee and Palia, "Wolf at the Door," above at note 40 at 588; J. B. Heaton, "The Unfulfilled Promise of Hedge Fund Activism" (2019) 13:2 *Virginia Law and Business Review* 317–334.

85 Bryce C. Tingle, "Two Stories About Shareholders" (2021) 58:1 *Osgood Hall Law Journal* 57–108 at 94, note 203 citing *Review of Shareholder Activism 3Q-2017 Report*, Lazard Shareholder Advisory Group (2017); Allaire and Dauphin, *Creators of Lasting Wealth?*, above at note 42 at 17–18; Zhu, "Preventive Effect," above at note 52 at 410–412.

86 Coffee and Palia, "Wolf at the Door," above at note 40 at 582–583.

87 *Ibid* at 589.

88 Jean-Jacques Laffont and Jean Tirole, "Repeated Auctions of Incentive Contracts, Investment, and Bidding Parity with an Application to Takeovers" (1988) 19:1 *The RAND Journal of Economics* 516–537.

89 Lynn A. Stout, "The Mechanisms of Market Inefficiency: An Introduction to the New Finance" (2003) 28:4 *Journal of Corporation Law* 653–669; Stephen F. LeRoy, "Efficient Capital Markets and Martingales" (1989) 27:4 *Journal of Economic Literature* 1583–1621; Louis Lowenstein, "Searching for Rational Investors in a Perfect Storm: A Behavioural Perspective" (2006) 7:2 *Journal of Behavioural Finance* 66–74.

90 Michael L. Wachter, "Takeover Defense When Financial Markets are (Only) Relatively Efficient" (2003) 151:3 *University of Pennsylvania Law Review* 787–824.

91 William W. Bratton and Michael L. Wachter, "The Case Against Shareholder Empowerment" (2010) 158:3 *University of Pennsylvania Law Review* 653–728 at 692.

92 William C. Johnson, Jonathan M. Karpoff and Sangho Yi, "The Bonding Hypothesis of Takeover Defenses: Evidence from IPO Firms" (2015) 117:2 *Journal of Financial Economics* 307–332 at 329.

93 *Ibid.*

94 B. Espen Eckbo, "Bidding Strategies and Takeover Premiums: A Review" (2009) 15:1 *Journal of Corporate Finance* 149–178. See also, Gregor Andrade, Mark Mitchell and Erik Strafford, "New Evidence and Perspectives on Mergers" (2001) 15:2 *Journal of Economic Perspectives* 103–120 [Andrade, Mitchell and Strafford, "New Evidence"]; Gregg Jarrell, James A. Brickley and Jeffry M. Netter, "The Market for Corporate Control: The Empirical Evidence Since 1980: The Efficiency Arguments" (1988) 2:1 *The Journal of Economic Perspectives* 49–68; Michael C. Jensen and Richard S. Ruback, "The Market for Corporate Control: The Scientific Evidence" (1983) 11:1–4 *Journal of Financial Economics* 5–50.

95 Bernard S. Black, "Bidder Overpayment in Takeovers" (1989) 41:3 *Stanford Law Review* 597–660.

96 Marina Martynova and Luc Renneboog, "A Century of Corporate Takeovers: What Have We Learned and Where Do We Stand?" (2008) 32:10 *Journal of Banking & Finance* 2148–2177 at 2159 [Martynova and Renneboog, "Century of Takeovers"].

97 Marc Goergen and Luc Renneboog, "Shareholder Wealth Effects of European Domestic and Cross-border Takeover Bids" (2004) 10:1 *European Financial Management* 9–45.

98 Andrade, Mitchell and Strafford, "New Evidence," above at note 94; Henri Servaes, "Tobin's Q and the Gains from Takeovers" (1991) 46:1 *The Journal of Finance* 409–419.

99 Martynova and Renneboog, "Century of Takeovers," above at note 96 at 2168.

100 *Ibid* at 2159.

101 David Larcker and Brian Tayan, *Corporate Governance Matters: A Closer Look at Organizational Choices and Their Consequences*, 2nd ed. (New York: Pearson Education, 2015) at p. 372.

102 Bill B. Francis et al., "The Effect of State Antitakeover Laws on the Firms' Bondholders" (2010) 96:1 *Journal of Financial Economics* 127–154.

103 Lynn A. Stout, "Takeovers in the Ivory Tower: How Academics Are Learning Martin Lipton May Be Right" (2005) 60:4 *The Business Lawyer* 1435–1454 at 1441; Ling Cen, Sudipto Dasgupta and Rik Sen, "Discipline or Disruption? Stakeholder Relationships and the Effect of Takeover Threat" (2016) 62:10 *Management Science* 2820–2841; R. Edward Freeman and John F. McVea, "A Stakeholder Approach to Strategic Management" in Michael A. Hitt, R. Edward Freeman and Jeffrey S. Harrison (eds.), *The Blackwell Handbook of Strategic Management* (Malden, USA: Blackwell Publishing Ltd., 2006), pp. 183–201; Hema A. Krishnan, Michael A. Hitt and Daewoo Park, "Acquisition Premiums, Subsequent Workforce Reductions and Post-Acquisition Performance" (2007) 44:5 *Journal of Management Studies* 709–732; Sara B. Moeller, Fredrik P. Schlingemann and René M. Stulz, "Wealth Destruction on a Massive Scale? A Study of Acquiring-Firm Returns in the Recent Merger Wave" (2005) 60:2 *The Journal of Finance* 757–782.

104 Henry G. Manne, "Mergers and the Market for Corporate Control" (1965) 73:2 *Journal of Political Economy* 110–120 at 117.

105 Anup Agrawal and Jeffrey F. Jaffe, "Do Takeover Targets Underperform? Evidence from Operating and Stock Returns" (2003) 38:4 *The Journal of Financial and Quantitative Analysis* 721–746 at 722.

106 James P. Walsh and Rita D. Kosnik, "Corporate Raiders and their Disciplinary Roles in the Market for Corporate Control" (1993) 36:4 *Academy of Management Journal* 671–700.

107 Lucian Bebchuk, John C. Coates and Guhan Subramanian, "The Powerful Antitakeover Force of Staggered Boards: Further Findings and a Reply to Symposium Participants" (2002) 55:2 *Stanford Law Review* 887–951 [Bebchuk, Coates and Subramanian, "Antitakeover Force"].

108 Yvan Allaire and François Dauphin, *The Value of "Just Say No": A Response to ISS*, Institute for Governance of Private and Public Organizations (November 2014), online: SSRN, https://ssrn.com/abstract=2531132 (examination of four companies: NRG Energy, AirGas, Casey's and Illumina); Sabastian V. Niles, "Shareholder Returns of Hostile Takeover Targets" (24 October 2014), *Harvard Law School Forum on Corporate Governance*, online: https://corpgov.law.harvard.edu/2014/10/24/shareholder-returns-of-hostile-takeover-targets (looking at Terra Industries); Martin Lipton, "Just Say No" (9 December 2014), *Harvard Law School Forum on Corporate Governance*, online: https://corpgov.law.harvard.edu/2014/12/09/just-say-no (looking at McGraw-Hill).

109 Assem Safieddine and Sheridan Titman, "Leverage and Corporate Performance: Evidence from Unsuccessful Takeovers" (1999) 54:2 *The Journal of Finance* 547–580.

110 Miroslava Straska and H. Gregory Waller, "Antitakeover Provisions and Shareholder Wealth: A Survey of the Literature" (2014) 49:4 *The Journal of Financial and Quantitative Analysis* 933–956.

111 Emiliano M. Catan, "The Insignificance of Clear-Day Poison Pills" (2018) 48:1 *The Journal of Legal Studies* 1–44.

112 John Coates, "Takeover Defenses in the Shadow of the Pill: A Critique of the Scientific Evidence" (2000) 79:2 *Texas Law Review* 271–382 at 286–287 [Coates, "Takeover Defenses"].

113 One study found, for example, that every company targeted by a hostile bid brought in a pill either in advance or after the bid was made: Bebchuk, Coates and Subramanian, "Antitakeover Force," above at note 107.

114 Coates, "Takeover Defenses," above at note 112 at 297–304; Klausner, "Fact and Fiction," above at note 5 at 1325–1367; Michael Klausner, "Empirical Studies of Corporate Law and Governance: Some Steps Forward and Some Steps Not" in Jeffrey N. Gordon and Wolf-Georg Ringe (eds.), *The Oxford Handbook of Corporate Law and Governance* (Oxford: Oxford University Press, 2018), pp. 184–213.

115 Klausner, "Fact and Fiction," above at note 5 at 1365; Emiliano M. Catan and Marcel Kahan, "The Law and Finance of Antitakeover Statutes" (2016) 68:3 *Stanford Law Review* 629–680 at 632.

116 See David F. Larcker, Gaizka Ormazabal and Daniel J. Taylor, "The Market Reaction to Corporate Governance Regulation" (2011) 101:2 *Journal of Financial Economics* 431–448 [Larcker, Ormazabal and Taylor, "Market Reaction"].

117 See also, Coates, "Takeover Defenses," above at note 112 at 320–323.

118 Richard A. Lambert and David F. Larcker, "Golden Parachutes, Executive Decision-Making and Shareholder Wealth" (1985) 7:1–3 *Journal of Accounting and Economics* 179–203.

119 *Air Products and Chemicals Inc. v. Airgas Inc.* (2011) 16A 3D 48 at 113.

120 Lucian A. Bebchuk and Alma Cohen, *The Costs of Entrenched Boards* (Cambridge, USA: National Bureau of Economic Research, 2004); Olubunmi Faleye, "Classified

Boards, Firm Value, and Managerial Entrenchment" (2007) 83:2 *Journal of Financial Economics* 501–529; Bebchuk, Coates and Subramanian, "Antitakeover Force," above at note 107; Alma Cohen and Chang-Yi Wang, "How Do Staggered Boards Affect Shareholder Value? Evidence from a Natural Experiment" (2013) 110:3 *Journal of Financial Economics* 627–641.

121 James M. Mahoney and Joseph T. Mahoney, "An Empirical Investigation of the Effect of Corporate Charter Antitakeover Amendments on Stockholder Wealth" (1993) 14:1 *Strategic Management Journal* 17–35; Bebchuk, Coates and Subramanian, "Antitakeover Force," above at note 107; Ronald W. Masulis, Cong Wei and Fei Xie, "Corporate Governance and Acquirer Returns" (2007) 62:4 *The Journal of Finance* 1851–1889.

122 K. J. Martijn Cremers, Lubomir P. Litov and Simone M. Sepe, "Staggered Boards and Long-Term Firm Value, Revisited" (2017) 126:2 *Journal of Financial Economics* 422–444 at 425 [Cremers, Litov and Sepe, "Staggered Boards"].

123 *Ibid*; K. J. Martijn Cremers and Simone M. Sepe, "The Shareholder Value of Empowered Boards" (2016) 68:1 *Stanford Law Review* 67–148 [Cremers and Sepe, "Empowered Boards"].

124 There are also problems in some of the earlier research arising from the incorporation of penny stocks traded over the counter or sample sizes that are too small; see a representative discussion in: Yakov Amihud, Markus Schmid and Steven Davidoff Soloman, "Do Staggered Boards Matter for Firm Value?" (2018) 30:4 *Journal of Applied Corporate Finance* 61–77 at 74 [Amihud, Schmid and Soloman, "Do Staggered Boards Matter"].

125 *Ibid* at 66.

126 Cremers, Litov and Sepe, "Staggered Boards," above at note 122 at 431, Table 4 and 441; Cremers and Sepe, "Empowered Boards," above at note 123 at 103–104. Two of the most prominent authors of the earlier research defended this in: Lucian A. Bebchuk and Alma Cohen, "Recent Board Declassifications: A Response to Cremers and Sepe" (2017), online: *SSRN*, https://ssrn.com/abstract=2970629. Cremers and Sepe, in more recent studies, responded convincingly (to this author anyways) in: K. J. Martijn Cremers and Simone M. Sepe, "Board Declassification Activism: Why Run Away from the Evidence?" (2017), online: *SSRN*, https://ssrn.com/abstract=2991854 at 3 [Cremers and Sepe, "Board Declassification Activism"]. See also, K. J. Martijn Cremers et al., "Poison Pills in the Shadow of the Law" (2023), *European Corporate Governance Institute – Finance Working Paper No. 595/2019*, online: *SSRN*, https://ssrn.com/abstract=3074658.

127 Amihud, Schmid and Soloman, "Do Staggered Boards Matter", above note 124; "New Law Reviews Study Findings Recently Were Reported by Y. Amihud and Co-Researchers (Settling the Staggered Board Debate)," Politics & Government Business, 7 March 2019, p. 98.

128 Thomas W. Bates, David Becher and Michael Lemmon, "Board Classification and Managerial Entrenchment: Evidence from the Market for Corporate Control" (2008) 87:3 *Journal of Financial Economics* 656–677.

129 *Ibid* at 669.

130 Cremers and Sepe, "Board Declassification Activism," above at note 126 at 2. See also, K. J. Martijn Cremers and Simone M. Sepe, "Board Declassification Activism: The Financial Value of the Shareholder Rights Project" (2017), online: *SSRN*, https://ssrn.com/abstract=2962162.

131 Cremers and Sepe, "Board Declassification Activism," above at note 126.

132 Robert Daines, Shelley Xin Li and Charles C. Y. Wang, "Can Staggered Boards Improve Value? Evidence from the Massachusetts Natural Experiment" (2021) 38:4 *Contemporary Accounting Research* 3053–3084.

133 *Ibid*. See also, I-Ju Chen, Po-Hsuan Hsu and Yanzhi Wang, "Staggered Boards and Product Innovations: Evidence from Massachusetts State Bill HB 5640" (2022) 51:4 *Research Policy* 104475.

134 Larcker, Ormazabal and Taylor, "Market Reaction," above at note 116.

135 Katharine I. Gleason and Mark S. Klock, "Is There Power Behind the Dead Hand? An Empirical Investigation of Dead Hand Poison Pills" (2008) 7:1 *Corporate Ownership and Control* 370–379.

136 Cremers, Litov and Sepe, "Staggered Boards," above at note 122 at 433.

137 Martijn Cremers, Saura Masconale and Simone M. Sepe, "CEO Pay Redux" (2017) 96:205 *Texas Law Review* 205–278.

138 Daniel Ferreira et al., "Shareholder Empowerment and Bank Bailouts" (2013), *European Corporate Governance Institute – Finance Working Paper No. 345/2013*, online: https://eprints.lse.ac.uk/56083/.

7

Proxy Advisors

In Chapters 5 and 6, we considered the evidence that institutional shareholders are not deeply engaged in corporate governance. This is what even a cursory consideration of the financial incentives of fund managers would predict. Yet, as we have seen, institutional investors seem to occupy a large space in modern corporate governance. Where do they get the time?

The answer is that institutional investors don't actually need the time. To a significant extent, they have handed off the time-consuming and detailed work of reading through corporate disclosure and formulating voting decisions to third-party proxy voting advisors. These advisory firms are some of the principal beneficiaries of our reforms to increase shareholder power.

Proxy advisory firms are intended to solve the problems surrounding institutional voting. They specialize in reviewing the proxy materials that accompany shareholder meetings and issuing recommendations on how shareholders should vote. The cost of these services is shared by their many clients, all of whom are institutional investors. On the face of it, proxy advisory firms have a business model that incentivizes them to provide accurate voting guidance to their clients, the professional money managers. Bad advice should, over time, lead to a decline in proxy firms' market share. Advisory firms can bring the dedicated resources needed to review and evaluate the tens of thousands of specific matters that come up for vote each year in American public markets. If investment funds organize themselves around research, selecting stocks, and trading, proxy advisory firms can focus on reviewing information circulars and evaluating corporate governance.

The position of proxy firms as the advisors to institutional shareholders gives their recommendations considerable influence. They publish "voting guidelines" each year, advising their institutional clients and the corporate issuers how they intend to vote on particular matters. As we have seen, the largest of the proxy advisory firms, ISS, now publishes well over 200 pages of material detailing their views on the corporate governance practices they expect firms to adopt.

The proxy advisory firms also do things like rank or rate firms' corporate governance for clients that want it, and provide assistance to companies in improving their corporate governance (as measured by the proxy advisors themselves). We discussed the failure of proxy advisors' governance ranking schemes in Chapter 3.

7.1 THE UNHELPFUL NATURE OF THE PROXY ADVISOR MARKET

The market for proxy advice is a market entirely made up of agents. The proxy advisory firms are agents for the institutional fund managers, and the institutional fund managers are agents for the beneficial owners of their funds. The actual human "owners" of a fund's portfolio of shares have little to no influence over fund activities and no realistic visibility into the fund's governance activities. Even if funds reported their governance activities each year, only the truly delusional would think a critical mass of their beneficiaries could read the disclosure and be able to evaluate the merits of the fund's interventions in each portfolio company.

While a fund's human principals have a real stake in the long-term governance quality of corporate America, the investment fund managers do not. As we have previously discovered, they are concerned about their fund's relative performance (usually over the short term), keeping their costs low, and engaging in activities that will be easily recognized as contributing value to their clients. Good corporate governance is, unfortunately for our purposes, a rising tide that lifts all boats. In other words, good governance is a public good that the structure of the market for institutional investment advice will underproduce.

As we would expect, therefore, the market for proxy voting advice bears all the hallmarks of a market in which no one really cares about the ultimate results of the advice, but everyone really cares about keeping the costs of that advice as low as possible. While ISS began providing proxy advice to clients in 1986, the market's growth was not exactly driven by shareholder enthusiasm. Well-intentioned regulatory interventions were needed. It took the 1988 US Department of Labor notice to pension funds and the 2003 SEC regulations directed at mutual funds to create the proxy advice market in its current form.

To satisfy the requirements imposed by the new rules, investment managers began turning to proxy advisory firms. By 2006, ISS could boast that its advice affected the "governance decisions of professional investors controlling ... half the value of the world's common stock."[1] Several new entrants came into the growing market, including Glass Lewis, Egan-Jones, and Proxy Governance Inc.[2] There were a series of mergers and acquisitions that left ISS the single largest player in the market and Glass Lewis the second largest firm.

The history of the market for proxy advice can thus be easily stated. Most shareholders didn't care about their voting decisions until the regulators told them they were legally obliged to care. The institutional shareholders then immediately turned to third parties to discharge their obligations in an act that can only be described as continuing not to care.

Glass Lewis and ISS collectively own 97 percent of the US market; ISS' market share is approximately twice that of Glass Lewis.[3] The market for proxy advice has none of the indicia of competition. Two firms control 97 percent of the market; there has been little change over a decade in their relative market share, and no new firms of any size have entered the market during that time.[4] "It's almost impossible to set up a proxy advisory (firm) today," was the conclusion of the president of Proxy Governance, a firm that left the market in 2010.[5] This suggests the market for proxy advice has a classic oligopolistic structure: large barriers to entry and strong network effects.[6] Since institutional investors hold shares in thousands of companies, a new entrant into the market must immediately have the scale that will enable it to provide voting recommendations for the proposals affecting all of these companies. An SEC Commissioner put it this way: "As an economist, my concern is heightened by the lack of competition in the proxy advisory market, which appears to be a stable duopoly preserved by near-impenetrable barriers for new entrants."[7]

There is absolutely no evidence that the proxy advisors compete meaningfully on the quality of their proxy advice. They don't report on the outcomes of their governance decisions, and such reporting would be impossible anyway, given the very long-term over which governance decisions play out and the hundreds of potentially conflating influences on corporate outcomes. Possibly the best evidence that the quality of proxy advice is not being evaluated and regulated by the market is that, as we will see, most of the proxy firms' voting advice is driven by the ineffective and occasionally counterproductive "best practices" we have already examined.

7.2 THE INFLUENCE OF PROXY ADVISORS

Academic attempts to measure the direct influence of proxy advisory firms on shareholder voting have generated results on the low end of 6 to 13 percent of the vote and on the high end of 13.6 to 25 percent.[8] For widely-held companies, even the low end of these ranges makes proxy firms the most influential constituency at shareholder meetings. Public companies tend to provide higher estimates of the direct control of proxy advisors: they control one-third or more of the vote (the Society of Corporate Secretaries and Governance Professionals),[9] or up to one-half of the vote (the Chairman of 3M and other business leaders.)[10] The variation between these estimates is largely a function of businesses looking at the number of shareholders who cast votes in accordance with a voting recommendation immediately following a proxy firm issuing the recommendation. Scholars, on the other hand, attempt to determine who is just "automatically" voting in accordance with the advice of the proxy firms, as opposed to coming to their own determination, with the proxy advice as just one input out of many.

Critics of proxy advisory firms point out that direct one-to-one causation is a limited way of looking at the industry's power in any event. Attempts to measure the influence of proxy advisory firms must include the ways their policies influence boardroom behavior generally. The influence of these firms in the boardroom is considerable, as anyone who has stepped foot in one over the past decade can testify. For example, a survey found that over 70 percent of directors reported that their boards' remuneration decisions were influenced by the proxy firms' guidelines.[11] Boards adopt corporate governance practices simply to satisfy proxy firms even in circumstances where they do not see the value of doing so.[12] In fact, at least one study has shown that boards will adopt practices recommended by proxy advisors that they *know* will be value-destroying, as measured by insiders' sale of shares before the practice is adopted.[13]

No one familiar with the modern boardroom seriously argues with the assessment of a commission struck by the NYSE that boards and their legal advisors routinely ask, "What are the proxy advisory firms' policies on this action?"[14]

7.3 THE DYSFUNCTIONAL WORLD OF PROXY ADVICE

If there is a moustache-twirling villain in the modern corporate governance landscape, it is most likely the proxy advisory firms. They come in for a great deal of criticism, particularly from the securities lawyers who must track their recommendations and apply them to companies the lawyers know pretty well. It doesn't help that proxy advisors have become the de facto regulators of corporate governance in America, with incredibly comprehensive and detailed governance preferences that no government regulator would ever attempt to enact. The SEC must apply cost-benefit analysis to its rules, a burden notably absent from the prescriptions of the advisory firms. The SEC also has oversight from various parties, including Congress, whereas proxy advisors are subject only to the oversight of their customers, and as we have seen fund managers have better things to do with their time.

7.3.1 *The Haphazard Development of Voting Guidelines*

Glass Lewis "provides little information to the general public on the development of their voting policies."[15] They also fail to "provide clarifying detail on how general corporate governance concepts and standards are translated into codified policy."[16] ISS is more forthcoming. They rely on an annual policy survey of institutional investors about corporate governance, combined in (unspecified ways) with industry roundtables, and feedback from market participants during proxy season.

Examining ISS's more transparent process, however, caused David Larcker, Allan McCall, and Brian Tayan to write a paper amusingly entitled "And Then a Miracle Happens!: How Do Proxy Advisory Firms Develop Their Voting Recommendations?"[17] Their conclusions are elegantly summarized by their title. They point to the extremely small (and declining) number of participants responding to the ISS survey. The apparent lack of interest in corporate governance among the thousands of institutional investors who received the survey – only 97 responded in 2012 – is not surprising given the many incentives money managers have to ignore corporate governance matters. The composition of respondents is not disclosed by ISS, so it is difficult to see if it is representative of the mainstream or if it reflects the opinions of a narrower set of activists.

Professor Larcker and his co-authors identify numerous instances of confusing or biased questions in the survey. (These include the use of words like "excessive" and "problematic" which nicely combine both bias and ambiguity.) They then point out that there is no information about how survey responses (which are quite general) are turned into concrete voting policies (which must be quite specific). At what precise point, for example, does the number of shares pledged by an executive director for a loan trigger a vote against that executive?

7.3.2 *The Dubious Assumptions behind Proxy Advisors' Voting Recommendations*

One of the most notable features of the way proxy advisors generate their policies is a steadfast refusal to engage deeply with the empirical literature around corporate governance. In general, advisors' voting guidelines reflect the conventional wisdom about corporate governance assumed by academics, regulators, and activists – but this is the same conventional wisdom that we have found is unsupported, or even contradicted, by empirical research.

An amusing example of ignoring of empirical research consists of the willingness of proxy advisors to support efforts by shareholder activists to install short-slate nominees as directors. If successful, this creates a "hybrid" board, consisting of management nominees as well as some directors nominated by an activist shareholder (often after an acrimonious proxy contest). As we saw in Chapter 5, the empirical literature generally finds these kinds of boards are bad news for shareholders. The amusing part is that one of the studies on this point was actually written by an individual working for ISS who, in that capacity, nevertheless recommended votes in favor of hybrid boards.[18] His study found that while the targets of short-slate contests increased in value through the contest period, if a hybrid board was actually installed, performance for those companies over the following three years lagged their peers by 6.6 percent.[19]

This curious blindness to even one's own research can only be explained by examining the basic assumptions made by proxy advisors in their voting recommendations. Without exceptions, these assumptions exist to facilitate the business model of proxy advisors, not to improve American corporate governance.

7.3.2.1 First Assumption: Director Independence

Probably the concept that drives the largest number of voting outcomes for proxy advisors is the idea of director independence. Just determining who counts as "independent" currently depends on evaluating twenty or so different types of relationships, plus a general catch-all excluding anyone with a relationship that a "*reasonable* person *might* conclude *could potentially* influence one's *objectivity* in the board-room in a manner that would have a *meaningful* impact."[20] Pity the poor lawyer who must navigate each of the vague words I have italicized in the quote above. Just determining how "might" impacts "could" would take a once-in-a-generation philo-sophical genius. "Objectivity" and "reasonable" are also challenging words to define. "Meaningful," which has presumably been deliberately used as an alternative from the much more common legal term "material," is also very, very vague. Taken all together, the sentence is what lawyers and nonlawyers refer to as "word salad."

This sort of rhetorical nonsense abounds in the voting guides, which are less use-ful as guidelines to companies than as an extended marketing document directed to proxy advisors' clients. Why would these clients care about the independence of directors? Because if you don't believe that managers are venal and boards are always at risk of capture, then there is no reason to believe that shareholder voting, and thus proxy advisors, are essential.

The constant reinforcement of the agency cost story is the single most effective marketing device proxy advisors possess. So, they really must lean into the impor-tance of independence at the board level, notwithstanding the overwhelming evi-dence (canvassed in Chapter 2) that it doesn't, on average, produce useful outcomes.

The consequence of this marketing imperative is that the role of board members in advising the CEO, serving as a sounding board, providing input on strategy, and making introductions is generally ignored by proxy advisors. Certainly, these activ-ities do not generate proxy advisors' voting outcomes. How could they, since these important board activities occur outside the view of third parties? Proxy advisors can, however, count independent directors, and so, because the only tool they have is a hammer, they ignore everything that isn't a nail.

7.3.2.2 Second Assumption: Shareholders Know Best

American corporate law has traditionally reposed authority in boards of directors. But, as we have seen, modern corporate governance consists of providing sharehold-ers with increasing power over boards and their decisions. Proxy advisors have been central to this process by linking voting recommendations to corporate strategy, gov-ernance, disclosure, and pay. Where corporate law or stock exchange regulations don't contemplate shareholder input on a decision, proxy advisors use the elections of individual directors to influence it.

The belief that shareholders know best is deeply engrained in the proxy advisors' work. For example, in relation to its policy that shareholder proposals passed at a meeting should be enacted, or the board removed, ISS received submissions from many of the largest corporations in the US, as well as the Business Roundtable and the National Association of Corporate Directors, all making the argument that, "[b]oards would be coerced to abdicate their fiduciary duties, which do not disap-pear or become less significant when a majority of votes cast at a meeting support a particular proposal. Boards should not feel compelled to act where they believe such action is not in the best interests of the company."[21] ISS nevertheless adopted the rule – a decision that can only be explained by their abiding belief that shareholders (and by extension ISS) are, in some sense, better qualified to manage wide aspects of a company's business.

There are only three possible rationales for the approach taken to shareholder empowerment by the proxy advisors. The first is that the proxy advisors genuinely believe that the shareholders simply know more about the business – are reliably smarter – than the directors. This seems unlikely, and as we have seen the empirical evidence suggests this is not true. The second reason for this approach could be that shareholders are better aligned with the interests of the corporation than the directors. On its face, this is a nonsensical position: (1) institutional shareholders can diversify away firm-specific risk in their portfolios; (2) the interests of the beneficial holders of a fund can diverge from the interests of the fund's managers; (3) long-term shareholders' interests diverge from those of shorter-term shareholders; and (4) shareholder interests come into direct conflict with those of many other important constituencies in a firm, such as employees or creditors.

The third rationale might be (and we are speculating here) that the proxy advisors simply don't care about the actual impact of shareholder power on the long-term performance of corporations. In some sense, the shareholders are the "owners" of the corporation (though "renters" might be a better metaphor) and they should be able to see it run however they like.

There are many problems with this last position, exhaustively canvassed by academics over the past forty years. For our purposes, it is simply enough to ask why we should accept the "it's my party and I'll cry if I want to" approach to shareholder power? Corporations affect the lives of many other constituencies – their employees, creditors, customers, suppliers, communities, and so on – why should we privilege shareholders in corporate governance matters if those shareholders are, in fact, doing a very bad job? Indeed, as we have seen in Chapters 5 and 6, institutional shareholders don't even appear to want the job of making hard decisions around corporate governance. They have better things to do.

Of course, there is another reason why proxy advisors might consistently build their voting recommendations on the assumption that shareholders know best: shareholders are their clients. Perhaps some of the catering to shareholders is just good salesmanship, flattering the customer. It doesn't hurt to imply that corporate executives and boards are always making mistakes or trying to get away with something, and only the proxy advisors' clients have the insight and integrity to set things right. Shareholder activists regularly cloak themselves in this sort of flattering guise and some of them appear to believe it. How else can we explain the sanctimony of their messaging?

It seems unlikely, however, that fund managers spend much time thinking about how power ought ideally to be allocated between corporate constituents.

I suspect most of them know they don't understand much about what is going on inside a company and that they don't really care about corporate governance issues that don't generate obvious changes to the financial statements. Instead, the benefit to the proxy advisors of the shareholders-know-best assumption is that it makes proxy advisors indispensable to their clients. The more things that are affected by shareholder votes, the more the institutional shareholders will need proxy advisors. Back when executive pay was uncomplicated and, in any event, not the subject of shareholder voting, an institutional investor didn't need to hire a third party to scour dozens of pages of disclosure around each portfolio company's pay practices.

7.3.2.3 Third Assumption: Good Governance Consists of Generalizable Best Practices

If there is one thing that everyone involved in the governance of America's public companies deprecates, it is "check-the-box" governance. Even proxy advisors criticize a one-size-fits-all approach.[22] Unfortunately, as should be abundantly clear at this point, corporate governance has largely become a matter of unthinking compliance with a variety of best practices, all of which are applied to all companies in more or less the same way. For example, one study found that to the extent independent directors influence executive compensation, various governance structures such as shareholder activism, a CEO/chair split, an independent board, and an independent compensation committee, all tend to substitute for one another.[23] It is not necessarily the case that good corporate governance requires all of these structures simultaneously (although proxy advisors' rules make this assumption). A strongly independent board can offset a compensation committee with a non-independent member, for example.

Even this sort of nuance, though, is missing from proxy advisor voting guidelines, because their business model depends on there being practices which can be applied across heterogeneous firms and which do not require much detailed firm-specific knowledge to apply. Proxy advisors know more about most firms' governance than their clients, but they don't know that much more. They don't know anything about the firm's strategic plans, the personalities inside and outside the company that are important to those plans, and the strategic initiatives of a firm's competitors, suppliers, creditors, and largest customers. In fact, they know nothing of the matters that, in practice, take up most of the directors' time. Like Peter Pan's method of flying, proxy advisors must refuse to doubt one-size-fits-all best practices, or their entire enterprise will come crashing down.

Unfortunately, as detailed in Chapters 2 and 3, there is no evidence for the existence of these "best practices" either taken individually or in aggregate. That doesn't stop proxy advisors from believing, though, and imposing those beliefs on the rest of the market. (Which is a thing, we can all agree, Peter Pan would never do.)

7.3.2.4 Fourth Assumption: Compliance Matters More Than Fairness or Business Objectives

Corporate law affords shareholders relatively little formal power over the corporation's decisions. This means that violations of some proxy advisor's best practice often produce very crudely applied consequences.

Even though very complex matters are sometimes placed before shareholders, their formal input on those matters is limited to a simplistic yes or no vote. This leads to strange results throughout proxy advisors' voting guidelines. For example, a violation of recommended compensation practices may result in recommendations against the re-election of members of the compensation committee.[24] But while the compensation committee investigates the details of compensation and negotiates with senior management, the board as a whole generally makes the ultimate decision on compensation. Indeed, under Delaware corporate law, the board retains extensive influence over any equity awards (and almost always this is the largest component of remuneration paid to a CEO).

Why have proxy firms decided to focus this penalty on the members of the compensation committee? First, there is no alternative penalty available to the advisors – only a "withhold" recommendation with its attendant reputational and professional consequences. This can be experienced as unfairness by a targeted director, but there is no other way for proxy firms to engage with the company. It might make more sense for the shareholders to reorganize the compensation committee, retain a third party to study the issuer's compensation practices, terminate an offending officer, or get rid of a particular unknown director who advocated for the offending pay practice. But shareholders, and therefore proxy advisors, don't have these alternatives available to them.

Another problem is that outside of the most egregious violations of remuneration best practices, it does not make sense to replace the entire board. Many, maybe even most, violations of the remuneration rules in the voting guidelines are technical or otherwise nonmaterial. Focusing the penalties on the members of the compensation committee actually reflects the most proportionate approach to the problem, given proxy advisors' limited tools. The policy's unfairness and logical inconsistencies are unavoidable side effects.

To take another example, proxy advisors' voting guidelines prescribe a number of rules for certain types of transactions. Failure to adhere to one of the rules often results in a vote against the transaction, regardless of its overall merits. For example, a failure to satisfy any one of the more than twenty requirements of a private placement, including some remarkably general ones (e.g., consider the alternatives to a placement), can result in a recommendation to vote against the entire transaction.[25]

Interviews with issuers and legal counsel turn up story after story of major, complex transactions imperiled by proxy advisors because of immaterial violations of the voting guidelines. I have the personal experience of seeing a stock option plan rejected because it did not contain a provision forbidding an action already banned by stock exchange rules. The company in question was in financial distress and the board was desperately restructuring its senior management team. The loss of the ability of the corporation to grant stock options would have been catastrophic. (Fortunately, we were able to convince the firm's largest shareholders that it was dumb to reject the option plan because it didn't ban something already banned.)

The disproportionate response of the proxy advisory firms to minor deviations from their rules might seem like the work of an unreasonable analyst, but it is built into the voting guidelines. The only way a proxy advisor can enforce the house rules is by being willing to burn down the house. The crude penalties found in the voting guidelines (and there are no others available) thus generate perverse outcomes: the advisors as tribune for the shareholders routinely recommend actions that run directly contrary to those shareholders' best interests.

7.3.2.5 Assumption Five: *Homo Economicus*

Economics is capable of considerable nuance in its description of human motivation. Indeed, the most sustained attack on economic models of rational human behavior, mounted by researchers in the area of behavioral economics, has now run into major problems. The underlying research in areas like loss aversion and priming turns out to have been flawed.[26] The headline results in behavioral economics suffer from the same replication difficulties visible in other fields of social science. Even more damaging, it turns out that behavioral economics interventions in practice turn out to be very weak.[27] "Nudges" and other paternalistic interference designed to correct assumed irrational individual decision-making don't turn out to have much effect.[28]

The difficulties encountered by behavioral economics suggest that it is hard to generalize about how people will behave in different circumstances. Human motivation, and what counts as "rational" in their decision-making, is highly nuanced and highly specific. Some people, in some circumstances, are exclusively motivated by money. Those same people, in other contexts, will be motivated by ends as varied as reputation, respect, security, love, altruism, morality, community, pride, and social norms. This is not a scandal; it is just human beings. Economics deliberately tends not to focus on ends but on the nebulous concept of "utility," which embraces many different possible goals.

Proxy advisors tend to focus exclusively on money. Their goal is to manipulate managers into making better decisions, and to do that, they need a universal theory about what motivates managers. The tool they need must be crude, as it must be generalized across hundreds of thousands of individuals in a near infinite number of personal circumstances. If they can't find a tool that applies to everyone, then the proxy advisors are out of business and corporate governance decisions go back to the directors who are best situated to understand the individuals they are trying to motivate, and who can deploy structures that address a variety of needs and desires and adjust those incentive structures to changing circumstances.

The motivational tool chosen by proxy advisors, money, is just one motive among others, and often not the most socially useful. Corporations are inherently social institutions. In Chapter 4, we saw how a crude economic model of human behavior embodied in certain pay practices not only fails to generate anticipated corporate performance outcomes but actually leads to underperformance and socially adverse behaviors. There is plenty of empirical evidence that other capital market actors, such as shareholders and directors, have considerably more nuanced views of human behavior.

For instance, a study looked at 2,008 firms in the Russell 3000 Index that held their shareholder meetings in 2011 and were required by the Dodd-Frank Act to have a shareholder say-on-pay vote on executive compensation, many of them for the first time.[29] A large number of these companies announced alterations to their executive compensation schemes in the eight months preceding their shareholder meeting, and many of these changes sought to better align the firms' executive compensation with published proxy advisor guidelines. The researchers found that the stock market reaction to these compensation changes was statistically negative. The "outsourcing to proxy advisory firms induce boards of directors to make compensation decisions that decrease shareholder value."[30] They decreased shareholder value, because shareholders understood that these changes, narrowly focused on controlling executives through greed, would backfire.

Of course, the proxy advisors' intervention would not be necessary if directors were exclusively using high-risk/high-return financial carrots and sticks to generate desired executive behavior. But directors in fact tend to use more nuanced tools, and thus proxy advisors find a raison d'être. We alluded earlier to research finding that boards knew proxy advisors' recommendations were a mistake when they published rules around stock option exchanges and re-pricing.[31] The pattern of insider trading demonstrated that directors and senior officers expected the new rules to be value-destroying. They were right. The proxy advisors relied on their crude model of human behavior to introduce high-powered incentives into a new area of executive compensation, and as a result, "future operating performance is lower and executive turnover is higher when the exchange program is constrained in the manner recommended by ISS."[32] The key point is that the directors already knew this.

7.3.2.6 The Consequences of the Assumptions

It is at this point that we can see the irony of the failure of proxy advisors' governance rankings to predict outcomes we care about. (This failure was discussed in Chapter 3.) These rankings measure corporate adherence to more than ninety different governance practices recommended by a proxy advisor like ISS, and nearly all these factors are based on at least one or more of the assumptions discussed in this section.[33] The irony arises from the fact that the rankings turn out not to be a referendum on the quality of the companies whose governance structures are being evaluated, but on the quality of the proxy advisors' assumptions about governance. The failure of the rankings to predict positive outcomes is conclusive evidence that the proxy advisors' assumptions about corporate governance are wrong. As we have seen, they aren't just wrong; they are always wrong in whatever way best promotes the proxy advisors' business model.

7.3.3　*Generating Voting Recommendations from General Rules*

Even when an issuer and its lawyers are armed with the latest proxy guidelines of an advisory firm, it is often difficult to predict a proxy advisor's recommendations in specific situations. The US Chamber of Commerce described ISS's process for making voting recommendations as a "black box."[34] The SEC's request for submissions about whether it should regulate proxy advisory firms was met with an enormous number of submissions from issuers. Summarizing these responses, one study reported: "The single most significant concern on the part of issuers is for the Commission to increase transparency on the part of proxy advisory firms."[35]

This lack of transparency comes in a number of different forms. As we saw with the absurd stacking of vague conditions measuring director independence, sometimes the ambiguity is built into the language of the guidelines. A "withhold" vote can be recommended against a director, for example, for adopting "egregious provisions" in corporate charter documents prior to a new listing, failing to "replace management as appropriate," or allowing "material failures of governance" and "stewardship."[36] There is nothing inherently incorrect about these guidelines, but they are obviously subject to a great deal of interpretation.

Another source of uncertainty for an issuer is that some voting recommendations depend on information that is not publicly available to the proxy advisory firm. So, for example, the ISS Guidelines indicate that while a director will be targeted if they attended fewer than 75 percent of the board and committee meetings, an exception will be made if the reasons for nonattendance include "illness" or "family emergencies."[37] The difficulty is that this sort of information is not normally disclosed anywhere in the public record. As a result, ISS must threaten to punish a director who misses the 75 percent threshold unless that director is prepared to publicly disclose, say, their child's drug overdose or their sister's miscarriage.

Sometimes the information is not available, and the proxy advisory firm has no leverage to obtain the information, because its very existence is unknowable to outsiders. For example, a director is not "independent" according to ISS if they have a family member (including in-laws) that is employed by a nonprofit that receives "material grants" from the company.[38] There is no explanation how the existence of this sort of relationship is going to be discovered by the ISS.

Generally, the core concept of "independence" used by proxy advisory firms depends on information that is usually available to the board but unavailable to outside parties. Indeed, the list of disqualifying relationships used by proxy advisory firms is obviously too narrow to capture the full range of incentives and relationships that might cause an outside director to favor management. Most scholars who have looked closely at the governance failures at Disney surrounding the shambolic hiring and termination of Michael Ovitz, for example, concluded that the relationships that existed between Disney CEO Michael Eisner and the nominally independent directors rendered "the bulk of the Disney board … not independent in any common sense of the term."[39]

On the other hand, many individuals identified by the proxy guidelines as "non-independent" are extremely effective directors, even at the monitoring aspects of the job. Former CEOs, for example, are caught in the ISS definition of "Affiliated Outside Director," an ISS non-independent category.[40] But anyone with a range of boardroom experience knows that, in many cases, few independent directors can match the searching skepticism of a previous CEO evaluating the decisions of their successor. In fact, the dynamic is often such that it is often felt to be unfair to the incoming CEO to retain their predecessor on the board.

Company founders also fail the ISS test for independent directors, but they bring the same incentives and familiarity with the company that make ex-CEOs such effective monitors.[41] In fairness, ISS does recognize this and advises in a footnote that, "[t]he operating involvement of the founder with the company will be considered" and may cause ISS to deem the founder as an independent outsider.[42] However, a lot of uncertainty for corporate counsel hangs on that "may." Plus, how does ISS measure the degree of a founder's "operating involvement"? They have no information on this subject.

Finally, some of the lack of transparency arises from proxy firms' inability or unwillingness to provide detail about their methodologies and procedures for generating proxy voting advice. In 2020, the Business Roundtable wrote to the SEC detailing many areas, particularly in executive compensation, where issuers were unable to determine or predict how proxy advisors would act.[43] In some cases, this was because the proxy advisors kept their method of performing certain key calculations secret; in others, it was because companies couldn't predict how advisors would pick the peer group companies used for comparison purposes.

Variation between the proxy advisory firms in what they consider to be "good governance" is surprisingly common. One set of researchers reported,

> [W]hile all of the proxy advisors considered a few specific factors important – such as poor director attendance – on most issues there was substantial variation. For example, ISS was significantly more likely to issue a withhold recommendation when the company board had refused to implement a shareholder resolution that had received majority shareholder support. Glass Lewis was significantly more likely to issue a withhold recommendation if the nominee was an inside director (other than the CEO). Egan Jones was significantly more likely to issue a withhold recommendation if the nominee was a board member at three or more other

companies. Proxy Governance was significantly more likely to issue a withhold recommendation if the company CEO received abnormally high compensation.[44]

The lawyers and corporate officers responsible for shareholder meetings regularly encounter proxy advisor voting recommendations that run contrary to every intuition they have about the reality of a director's engagement with the company, their independence, or the merits of a board action. The combination of ambiguous, broad general statements with proxy advisors' almost total ignorance of personalities and dynamics inside the corporation inevitably produces perverse voting recommendations.

7.3.4 *Complexity and Staffing*

According to ISS, it annually provides advice in relation to approximately 50,000 meetings in 115 markets.[45] "It does this with a research staff of fewer than 200 persons."[46] Glass Lewis handles more than 30,000 meetings each year with a total of 380 employees, more than half of whom are involved in research.[47] As well, over half of the shareholder meetings covered by these firms occur between April and June, so both firms are forced to hire temporary workers to manage the volume.[48] ISS advises it more than doubles its staff with temporary employees during proxy season.[49]

The sheer volume of material that must be analyzed for proxy firms to make a recommendation on each of the hundreds of thousands of resolutions a year alone accounts for the one-size-fits-all or check-the-box nature of their proxy advice. What we are interested in here, however, is the mismatch between the volume of work to be done in a very short period of time and the number of employees available. We are also interested in the mismatch between the complexities of that work and the relatively junior (and temporary) analysts employed by the proxy firms.

Out of several studies looking at whether ISS' voting recommendations on executive compensation are positively correlated with firm value, only one found this positive association but noted that it only existed for firms with non-December fiscal year-ends.[50] This "best case" result suggests that ISS analysts are making mistakes in relation to the more than half of American companies that have meetings during proxy season (April to June).

A common feature of responses to the SEC's request for comment on proxy firms over the past decade are concerns about the competence of proxy firm analysts to understand and correctly evaluate meeting proposals. There is a divergence in training and experience between the (usually) senior legal teams employed by issuers and the staff at proxy advisory firms. Corporate legal agreements and transaction structures can be among the most complex in existence. Many of the anecdotes related in SEC response letters involve proxy firm employees misunderstanding an agreement, getting hung up on irrelevancies, or failing to understand the alternatives to a transaction.

For example, Pfizer commented in a letter to the SEC, "one [proxy] firm issued a number of reports indicating that Pfizer requires a 'super-majority' shareholder vote on certain matters. The super-majority voting requirements were deleted from our Restated Certificate of Incorporation in 2006. However, it appears that the analysts reviewing our filings did not understand the various documents filed."[51]

In a letter to Canadian regulators, CI Financial described an analyst's failure to understand a provision in a proposed stock option plan, mistaking it as granting the directors the power to unilaterally revise the plan when its effect was, in fact, the opposite.[52] A relatively untrained analyst can misunderstand even very basic legal language. One corporation had the author of a proxy recommendation object to the phrase "to transact such other business as may properly come before the Meeting or any adjournment," apparently not understanding that this language is both benign and virtually standard in meeting materials.[53]

Because it is difficult to get visibility on the rationale for voting recommendations from the proxy advisory side of ISS, the most illuminating interactions occur with the side of ISS that provides consulting services to issuers hoping to design structures that will pass ISS review. Lawyers report experiences that range from being told by the consulting side of ISS that their analysts are not capable of understanding a shareholder rights plan (admittedly a very complex document) to obtaining approval for a transaction from the consulting side of ISS, only to have the transaction rejected by the proxy advisory side.[54] Legal structures are rejected because of possible contingencies that, when pressed, ISS analysts admit they cannot explain how they could occur.[55] Legal terms that have previously been acceptable are rejected without explanation or notice.[56]

7.3.5 *Mistakes*

Because advisory firms do not directly bear the costs of poor or mistaken proxy recommendations, there is a significant chance these firms will respond to other incentives. The most obvious of these is the way the profitability of the advisory firm can be increased by keeping research and analyst costs as low as possible.

In theory, the proxy advisory firm that underinvests in research and analysis might be subject to market discipline as client investment funds see the value of their portfolios compromised by mistakes made by the firm, but it seems likely this does not occur. Even apart from the rational apathy of fund managers towards governance, the damage effected by suboptimal voting is rarely visible to those outside the company and can always be attributed to other causes. The evidence we do have suggests that institutional investors are never held accountable for the way the shares held in their portfolios are voted, so it is very likely that proxy advisory firms are not held accountable either. (As we will see in Chapter 13, even when institutional investors *market* their funds as engaging in certain types of corporate governance activities, their real-world failure to do so apparently doesn't matter.) Additional time and effort spent by advisory firms to prevent mistakes will have no impact on their ability to attract new clients for their recommendations but will decrease their profitability. What all this means is that in a situation where there are no penalties for mistakes, along with big incentives to run the risk of mistakes, we should expect to see mistakes.

The work of proxy advisors operating with very similar best governance practices can be compared. The results of this empirical exercise suggest the presence of errors in the analysis. A research team that investigated the four largest proxy firms' evaluations of the corporate governance of various companies found little agreement between the proxy firms. "Since the commercial firms use the same basic governance data, examine similar governance dimensions (e.g., anti-takeover provisions, board structure, and executive compensation), and all claim to measure overall 'corporate governance,' we would expect their ratings to be highly correlated. However, one key finding is that ... these four ratings are close to being uncorrelated."[57] As we have seen generally with proxy advisor recommendations, "many large firms with substantial investor followings and long track records receive wildly disparate grades from the various services: AT&T, General Electric, General Motors, and Safeway received near perfect scores from one rating firm (a 99 or 100 from ISS) and near-failing grades from another."[58] The researchers conclude, "Our view is that a more plausible interpretation of the weak and mixed results we find is that the commercial [governance] ratings contain a large amount of measurement error."[59]

Surveys of corporate issuers about their experiences with third-party proxy recommendations tell a similar story. A study conducted by the American Society of Corporate Secretaries & Governance Professionals found that "65% of respondents experience – at least once – a vote recommendation based on materially inaccurate or incomplete information, or where the proxy advisory firm reported as a fact information that was incorrect or incomplete. One quarter of those respondents experienced inaccurate or incomplete information on several occasions."[60] Another survey found that in a two-year period, 53 percent of respondents had encountered factual mistakes just on the compensation analysis performed by proxy analysts.[61]

The American Council for Capital Formation conducts regular reviews of proxy advisors' work and finds that in a typical year, more than forty companies file supplementary proxy materials with the SEC alleging that proxy advisors have committed material errors such as basing voting recommendations on a peer group that includes none of the company's actual competitors.[62] In another example, for the second time in a row and after advising the proxy advisory firm of the error after the first year, a company faced a pay-for-performance calculation using a net income figure that was off by a rather material $1.7 billion. The number of these supplementary filings each year is very low compared to the total number of public companies in American markets, but the Council correctly points out that most issuers likely don't have the time or resources to bother with the extraordinary step of formally filing complaints with the SEC.

7.3.6 *Corrections*

When proxy advisors make mistakes, they don't have much interest in correcting those mistakes. In the United States, a survey of corporate officers indicates that in their experience only 43 percent of the mistakes are corrected when brought to the proxy advisors' attention, with a significant percentage of survey respondents indicating a blanket refusal on the part of proxy analysts to revisit their work.[63]

A moment's consideration is enough to tell anyone without a financial incentive to believe otherwise, that there are few if any incentives acting on proxy advisors to revisit their advice.[64] Such a move would be expensive and embarrassing. In 2020, the SEC adopted certain rules designed to require proxy advisors to increase their engagement with companies. SEC Commissioner Hester Pierce noted that, "since the adoption of the 2020 Rules, one of the largest proxy advisors has trended toward engaging *less* often with issuers."[65]

In a display of admirable candor, ISS advised Canadian securities regulators a few years ago that, "ISS believes that regulation prescribing increased activity or specific timing with respect to issuer engagement and/or draft reviews would require significant additional resources to manage at a cost that would ultimately have to be borne by our institutional clients."[66] In other words, the economics of the proxy advisory industry would be adversely impacted if proxy advisors were required to engage with companies in proxy season. This looks a lot like a classic agency cost: the economic interests of the parties in the proxy advice market would be damaged if they adopted a process designed to correct errors currently harming the ultimate principals.

7.4 PROXY ADVISORS ARE BAD FOR INVESTMENT FUNDS AS WELL

So far in this chapter, we have been acting as if the only thing that matters is the success of the American businesses that supply us with jobs, make the things we need and want, and generate the wealth we use to tackle social problems.[67] There may be a reader with the very reasonable attitude of "but what have they done for us *recently?*" Instead, this reader's principal concern might be for the wealthy finance professionals who run investment funds. Shouldn't we care about their social, political, and governance opinions?

Unfortunately, the news for supporters of Wall Street influence over companies is also quite bad when it comes to proxy advisors. A recent study looked at the votes cast by 155 mutual fund families in over 6 million corporate votes between 2004 and 2017.[68] The researchers looked at ten issues that were repeatedly voted upon during this period, such as proxy access, removing a staggered board, and requiring companies to disclose their political contributions. The researchers were able to figure out which investment funds failed to access the corporation's proxy materials in the lead-up to the vote. They were also able to figure out which of these funds (the "uninformed" funds) relied on the services of a proxy advisor. They discovered that the funds that actually accessed the company's proxy materials (the "informed" funds) had very different voting behavior than the uninformed funds that depended only on the advice of ISS and Glass Lewis. "Funds that acquired information (but not proxy advice) were less likely than uninformed funds to vote in favor on nine out of 10 issues."[69]

ISS was particularly bad: "One key finding is that … ISS advice shifted their votes in the opposite direction as self-information."[70] This appears to mean "that ISS's advice was inferior to funds' self-information and distorted their voting from their preferred/optimal choices."[71] In other words, the advice of proxy advisors causes funds to vote in very different ways than they would if they were collecting and processing the information on their own. Could there be better evidence of dysfunction in the market for proxy advice than it induces shareholders to exercise their franchise in ways that apparently contradict the shareholders' own opinions and judgment?

7.5 SUMMARY

The market for proxy advice presents a weird intellectual Mobius loop. The market supposedly exists because of the risk of agency costs presented by managers ignoring their principals. But the proxy advice market is actually a market made up only of agents, excluding the beneficial owners of shares entirely. It is *much worse* than the governance market it is expected to correct. Companies' shares go up and down as, among other things, their corporate governance succeeds or fails, but the proxy advice market is static, providing neither competitive penalties nor rewards. It is like a market made up of quasi-monopolistic utilities that, instead of water and power, produce ridiculous governance ideas and mistakes. Surely all we need to know about the past thirty years of corporate governance reforms is that business has been very good for the firms producing the product we have been evaluating so far in this book.

NOTES

1 Robert D. Hershey, Jr., "A Little Industry with a Lot of Sway on Proxy Votes," *The New York Times*, June 18, 2006, online: www.nytimes.com/2006/06/18/business/yourmoney/18proxy.html?pagewanted=all&_r=0.
2 Stephen J. Choi, Jill E. Fisch and Marcel Kahan, "Director Elections and the Role of Proxy Advisors" (2009) 82:4 *Southern California Law Review* 649–702.
3 Tamara C. Belinfanti, "The Proxy Advisory and Corporate Governance Industry: The Case for Increased Oversight and Control" (2009) 14:2 *Stanford Journal of Law, Business and Finance* 384–439 at 395–397 [Belinfanti, "Proxy Advisory"].
4 *Corporate Shareholder Meetings: Issues Relating to Firms that Advise Institutional Investors on Proxy Voting (GAO-07-765)*, US Government Accountability Office (June 29, 2007), online: www.gao.gov/products/gao-07-765 [GAO, *Corporate Shareholder Meetings*].

5 Barry B. Burr, "SEC Round Table Discusses Shift in Who Pays for Proxy Voting Services," *Pensions & Investments*, December 5, 2013, online: www.pionline.com/article/20131205/ONLINE/131209921/sec-round-table-discusses-shift-in-who-pays-for-proxy-voting-services.

6 David F. Larcker, Allan L. McCall and Gaizka Ormazabal, "Stock Option Repricing" (2013) 56:2–3 *Journal of Accounting and Economics*, 149–169; Jodi Slaght, "Whatever Happened to the Prudent Man? The Case for Limiting the Influence of Proxy Advisors through Fiduciary Duty Law" (2012) 9:1 *Rutgers Business Law Review* 1 at 12–13; Belinfanti, "Proxy Advisory," above at note 3 at 428–435.

7 Michael S. Piwowar, Commissioner of US Securities and Exchange Commission, *Opening Statement at the Proxy Advisory Services Roundtable*, US Securities and Exchange Commission (December 5, 2013), online: www.sec.gov/news/statement/2013-12-05-opening-statement-roundtable-msp.

8 See the discussion in Bryce C. Tingle, "Bad Company! The Assumptions behind Proxy Advisors' Voting Recommendations" (2014) 37:2 *Dalhousie Law Journal* 709–748 at 719; See also, the discussion in John G. Matsusaka and Chong Shu, "Does Proxy Advice Allow Funds to Cast Informed Votes?" (2022), *USC Law Legal Studies Paper No. 21-37*, online: SSRN, https://ssrn.com/abstract=3866041 at 4 [Matsusaka and Shu, "Informed Votes"]; Stephen J. Choi, Jill E. Fisch and Marcel Kahan, "The Power of Proxy Advisors: Myth or Reality?" (2010) 59:4 *Emory Law Journal* 869–918 at 906 [Choi, Fisch and Kahan, "Power of Proxy Advisors"]. In the context of some votes, such as those relating to mergers and acquisitions, academic research suggests the influence of proxy advisors increases: Cindy R. Alexander et al., "Interim News and the Role of Proxy Voting Advice" (2010) 23:12 *The Review of Financial Studies* 4419–4454 at 4422.

9 *A Call for Change in the Proxy Advisory Industry Status Quo: The Case for Greater Accountability and Oversight*, Center on Executive Compensation (January 2011), online (pdf): www.wsj.com/public/resources/documents/ProxyAdvisoryWhitePaper02072011.pdf at 20 [CEC, *Call for Change*].

10 Comment letter from W. James McNerney, Jr., Chairman of the Board and Chief Executive Officer of 3M, *Re: File No. S7-19-03 Security Holder Director Nominations*, US Securities and Exchange Commission (December 5, 2003), online: www.sec.gov/rules/proposed/s71903/3m120503.htm.

11 David F. Larcker, Allan L. McCall and Brian Tayan, *The Influence of Proxy Advisory Firm Voting Recommendations on Say-on-Pay Votes and Executive Compensation Decisions*, The Conference Board (March 2012), online (pdf): www.shareholderforum.com/e-mtg/Library/20120300_ConferenceBoard.pdf.

12 GAO, *Corporate Shareholder Meetings*, above at note 4 at 10.

13 David F. Larcker, Allan L. McCall and Gaizka Ormazabal. "Proxy Advisory Firms and Stock Option Repricing" (2013) 56:2–3 *Journal of Accounting & Economics* 149–169 at 151 [Larcker, McCall and Ormazabal, "Stock Option Repricing"].

14 *Report of the New York Stock Exchange Commission on Corporate Governance*, New York Stock Exchange (September 23, 2010), online: www.ecgi.global/code/report-new-york-stock-exchange-commission-corporate-governance at 15.

15 David F. Larcker, Allan L. McCall and Brian Tayan, "And Then a Miracle Happens!: How Do Proxy Advisory Firms Develop Their Voting Recommendations?" (2013), *Rock Center for Corporate Governance at Stanford University Closer Look Series: Topics, Issues and Controversies in Corporate Governance and Leadership No. CGRP-31*, online: SSRN, https://ssrn.com/abstract=2224329 at 2 [Larcker, McCall and Tayan, "Miracle Happens!"].

16 *Ibid.*

17 *Ibid.*

18   Bryce C. Tingle, "The Agency Cost Case for Regulating Proxy Advisory Firms" (2016) 49:2 *UBC Law Review* 725–788 at 751–752 [Tingle, "Agency Cost Case"].

19   Chris Cernich et al., "Effectiveness of Hybrid Boards" (2009), *Proxy Governance Working Paper*, online: SSRN, https://ssrn.com/abstract=1410205 at 39.

20   *United States Proxy Voting Guidelines: Benchmark Policy Recommendations*, Institutional Shareholder Services Inc. (December 13, 2022), online (pdf): www.issgovernance.com/file/policy/active/americas/US-Voting-Guidelines.pdf at 12 [ISS, *Proxy Voting Guidelines*].

21   Comment letter from Matthew Lepore, Vice President and Corporate Secretary, Chief Counsel – Corporate Governance, Pfizer Inc., *Re: 2013 Proxy Voting Policies*, Institutional Shareholder Services Inc. (November 7, 2012), online (pdf): www.issgovernance.com/file/files/PfizerInc..pdf at 1; See also, Larcker, McCall and Tayan, "Miracle Happens!," above at note 15 at 3.

22   See, for example, Comment letter from Debra L. Sisti, Vice President Canadian Research ISS, and Martha Carter, Managing Director Global Research ISS, *Re: Consultation Paper 25-401: Potential Regulation of Proxy Advisory Firms*, Ontario Securities Commission (August 10, 2012), online (pdf): www.osc.ca/sites/default/files/pdfs/irps/comments/com_20120810_25-401_sistid_carterm.pdf at 15 [Sisti and Carter, *ISS letter to CSA*].

23   Shamsud D. Chowdhury and Eric Z. Wang, "Institutional Activism Types and CEO Compensation: A Time-Series Analysis of Large Canadian Corporations" (2009) 35:1 *Journal of Management* 5–36 at 30.

24   ISS, *Proxy Voting Guidelines*, above at note 20 at 16–17.

25   ISS, *Proxy Voting Guidelines*, above at note 20 at 42–43.

26   See for example, Ulrich Schimmack, Moritz Heene and Kamini Kesavan, "Reconstruction of a Train Wreck: How Priming Research Went off the Rails," *Replicability-Index Blog*, 2 February 2017, online: https://replicationindex.com/2017/02/02/reconstruction-of-a-train-wreck-how-priming-research-went-of-the-rails/; Eldad Yechian, "Acceptable Losses: The Debatable Origins of Loss Aversion" (2019) 83:7 *Psychological Research* 1327–1339; David Gal and Derek D. Rucker, "The Loss of Loss Aversion: Will It Loom Larger Than Its Gain?" (2018) 28:3 *Journal of Consumer Psychology* 497–516.

27   Stefano DellaVigna and Elizabeth Linos, "RCTs to Scale: Comprehensive Evidence from Two Nudge Units" (2022) 90:1 *Econometrica* 81–116.

28   *Ibid*; Stephanie Mertens et al., "The Effectiveness of Nudging: A Meta-analysis of Choice Architecture Interventions across Behavioral Domains" (2022) 119:1 *Proceedings of the National Academy of Sciences* e2107346118; Harriet Rosanne Etheredge, "Assessing Global Organ Donation Policies: Opt-In vs Opt-Out" (2021) 2021:14 *Risk Management and Healthcare Policy* 1985–1998.

29   David F. Larcker, Allan McCall and Gaizka Ormazabal, "Outsourcing Shareholder Voting to Proxy Advisory Firms" (2015) 58:1 *The Journal of Law and Economics* 173–204 [Larcker, McCall and Ormazabal, "Outsourcing to Proxy Firms"].

30   *Ibid* at 203.

31   Larcker, McCall and Ormazabal, "Stock Option Repricing," above at note 13.

32   David F. Larcker and Brian Tayan, "Do ISS Voting Recommendations Create Shareholder Value?" (2011), *Rock Center for Corporate Governance at Stanford University Closer Look Series: Topics, Issues and Controversies in Corporate Governance No. CGRP-13*, online: SSRN, https://ssrn.com/abstract=1816543 at 2.

33   *ISS Governance QuickScore 2.0: Overviews and Updates*, Institutional Shareholder Service Inc. (January 2014), online (pdf): www.issgovernance.com/file/files/ISSGovernanceQuickScore2.0.pdf; Guhan Subramanian, "Corporate Governance 2.0" (March 2015), *Harvard Business Review*, online: https://hbr.org/2015/03/corporate-governance-2-0.

34 Rachel McTague, "Chamber Approaches Risk Metrics with Proposed Changes to Policy Setting" (2008) 40 *Securities Regulation and Law Report* 569 at 589.

35 Tingle, "Agency Cost Case," above at note 18 at 756, note 108, citing Kenneth L. Altman and James F. Burke, *Proxy Advisory Firms: The Debate Over Changing the Regulatory Framework, An Analysis of Comments Submitted to the SEC in Response to the Concept Release on the US Proxy System*, Special Report by The Altman Group (1 March 2011) at 18.

36 ISS, *Proxy Voting Guidelines*, above at note 20 at 14, 17.

37 *Ibid* at 12.

38 *Ibid* at 10.

39 Claire A. Hill and Brett McDonnell, "Disney, Good Faith, and Structural Bias" (2007) 32:4 *Journal of Corporation Law* 833–864 at 845–846.

40 ISS, *Proxy Voting Guidelines*, above at note 20 at 10.

41 *Ibid* at 10.

42 *Ibid* at 11.

43 Tami Groswald Ozery, "Business Roundtable Comment Letter to SEC on Proposed Proxy Rules for Proxy Voting Advice" (February 28, 2020), *Harvard Law School Forum on Corporate Governance*, online: https://corpgov.law.harvard.edu/2020/02/28/business-roundtable-comment-letter-to-sec-on-proposed-proxy-rules-for-proxy-voting-advice/.

44 Choi, Fisch and Kahan, "Power of Proxy Advisors," above at note 8 at 880–881.

45 ISS makes reference to these statistics, under the subsection "Global Meeting Results," Institutional Shareholder Services Inc. online: www.issgovernance.com/solutions/proxy-voting-services/global-meeting-results.

46 Tingle, "Agency Cost Case," above at note 18 at 763, note 135 citing *A Dialogue with Institutional Shareholder Services*, Audit Committee Leadership Network in North America ViewPoints (November 7, 2012) at 6 [ViewPoints, *Dialogue with ISS*].

47 *Company Overview*, Glass Lewis, online: www.glasslewis.com/company-overview/.

48 ViewPoints, *Dialogue with ISS*, above at note 46 at 3.

49 RiskMetrics, *Annual Report* (Form 10-K) (2009), *US Securities and Exchange Commission*, online: www.sec.gov/Archives/edgar/data/1295172/000104746910001246/a2196648z10-k.htm at 18.

50 Ana Albuquerque, Mary Ellen Carter and Susanna Gallani, "Are ISS Recommendations Informative? Evidence from Assessments of Compensation Practices" (2020), online: SSRN, https://ssrn.com/abstract=3590216 [Albuquerque, Carter and Gallani, "ISS Recommendations"]. See also, Larcker, McCall and Ormazabal, "Outsourcing to Proxy Firms," above at note 29.

51 Comment letter from Matthew Lepore, Vice President and Chief Counsel Corporate Governance of Pfizer, *Re: File No. S7-14-10 Release Nos. 34-62495/IA-3052/ IC-29340 Concept Release on the US Proxy System*, US Securities and Exchange Commission (November 23, 2010), online (pdf): www.sec.gov/comments/s7-14-10/s71410-277.pdf at 6.

52 Comment letter from Sheila A. Murray, Executive Vice President, General Counsel and Secretary of CI Financial, *RE: CSA Consultation Paper 25-401: Potential Regulation of Proxy Advisory Firms*, Ontario Securities Commission (September 21, 2012), online (pdf): www.osc.ca/sites/default/files/pdfs/irps/comments/SecuritiesLaw_com_20120921_25-401_murrays.pdf at 3.

53 Comment letter from Tom Enright, President and Chief Executive Officer of Canadian Investor Relations Institute, *Re: CSA Consultation Paper 25-401: Potential Regulation of Proxy Advisory Firms*, Ontario Securities Commission (September 12, 2012), online

(pdf): www.osc.ca/sites/default/files/pdfs/irps/comments/com_20120912_25-401_enrightt.pdf at 21.

54 Tingle, "Agency Cost Case," above at note 18 at 766, notes 146–147 citing Interview of Trudy Curran, Senior Vice President, General Counsel and Corporate Secretary of Canadian Oil Sands (May 17, 2013).

55 *Ibid.*

56 *Ibid.*

57 Robert M. Daines, Ian D. Gow and David F. Larcker, "Rating the Ratings: How Good are Commercial Governance Ratings?" (2012) 98:3 *Journal of Financial Economics* 439–461 at 444.

58 *Ibid* at 444.

59 *Ibid* at 460.

60 Comment letter from Neila B. Radin, Chair of Securities Law Committee of The Society of Corporate Secretaries & Governance Professionals, *Re: Concept Release on the US Proxy System, File No. S7-14-10 Proxy Advisory Firms (Section V)*, US Securities and Exchange Commission (December 27, 2010), online (pdf): www.sec.gov/comments/s7-14-10/s71410-289.pdf at 6 [Radin, *Concept Release Letter*].

61 CEC, *Call for Change*, above at note 9 at 10.

62 Kyle Isakower, "Analysis of Proxy Advisors' Recommendations During the 2020 Proxy Season" (August 5, 2020), *Harvard Law School Forum on Corporate Governance*, online: https://corpgov.law.harvard.edu/2020/08/05/analysis-of-proxy-advisors-recommendations-during-the-2020-proxy-season/.

63 Radin, *Concept Release Letter*, above at note 60 at 6.

64 See, for example, Comment letter from Carlo Passeri, Senior Director of Capital Markets and Financial Services Policy, Biotechnology Innovation Organization, *Re: Request for Comment on Proposed Amendments to Rules Governing Proxy voting Advice (File Number S7-17-21)*, US Securities and Exchange Commission (December 23, 2021), online (pdf): *US Securities and Exchange Commission*, www.sec.gov/comments/s7-17-21/s71721-20110739-264606.pdf at 1–2; Comment letter from Benjamin Zycher, Senior Fellow, American Enterprise Institute, *Comment Submitted on Rule Proposed by the Securities and Exchange Commission: Amendments to Federal Proxy Rules Governing Proxy Voting Advice October 14, 2021*, US Securities and Exchange Commission (December 27, 2021), online (pdf): www.sec.gov/comments/s7-17-21/s71721-20110748-264612.pdf at 3; Comment letter from Tom Quaadman, Executive Vice President, Center for Capital Markets Competitiveness, US Chamber of Commerce, *Re: File Number S7-17-21 Proxy Voting Advice*, US Securities and Exchange Commission (December 23, 2021), online (pdf): www.sec.gov/comments/s7-17-21/s71721-20110258-264516.pdf at 4.

65 Hester M. Pierce, *U-Turn: Comments on Proxy Voting Advice*, US Securities and Exchange Commission (July 13, 2022), online: www.sec.gov/news/statement/peirce-statement-proxy-voting-advice-071322#:~:text=Proxy%20advisors%20play%20a%20very,companies%20in%20which%20they%20invest (emphasis in original).

66 Sisti and Carter, *ISS letter to CSA*, above at note 22 at 15.

67 Most studies find proxy advice reduce firm value: Larcker, McCall and Ormazabal, "Stock Option Repricing," above at note 13; Larcker, McCall and Ormazabal, "Outsourcing to Proxy Firms," above at note 29; Peter Iliev and Michelle Lowry, "Are Mutual Funds Active Voters?" (2015) 28:2 *The Review of Financial Studies* 446–485. But at least one unpublished study finds that for firms with non-December fiscal year-ends, ISS' assessment of compensation packages appears accurate: Albuquerque, Carter and Gallani, "ISS Recommendations," above at note 50.

68 Matsusaka and Shu, "Informed Votes," above at note 8.
69 John G. Matsusaka and Chong Shu, "Does Proxy Advice Allow Funds to Cast Informed Votes?," The Columbia Law School's Blog on Corporations and the Capital Markets, July 22, 2021, online: https://clsbluesky.law.columbia.edu/2021/07/22/does-proxy-advice-allow-funds-to-cast-informed-votes/.
70 Matsusaka and Shu, "Informed Votes," above at note 8 at 2.
71 *Ibid* at 23.

PART II

What Can We Conclude about Our Theories of Corporate Governance?

Wherein:

- We examine the key theoretical underpinnings of the modern corporate governance project, considering the empirical research we reviewed in Division I. (Unkindly, we consider the possibility that "theoretical underpinnings" might be giving too much credit to the intellectual rigor of the modern corporate governance project.)
- We evaluate whether, considering the empirical evidence, agency cost theory is useful in predicting corporate outcomes.
- We consider the unthinkable: maybe corporate managers are generally loyal to the firms they lead?
- We discuss the market dynamics that generated corporate governance arrangements before the modern governance regime arose.
- We look at the transition of corporate law from enforcing bargains to attempting to secure outcomes like economic efficiency. We examine the harm done to our public markets, where this transition occurred.

8

Taking Stock of the Argument So Far

We Need a Better Theory of the Firm

If there is one thing modern practitioners of corporate governance seem to believe, it is that business executives are a slippery bunch. They are generally lazy and incompetent, except when it comes to enriching themselves at the expense of the corporation, when they display a Satanic energy and preternatural guile.

This is obviously an absurd thing to believe, and of course, every modern corporate governance participant would disavow such a crude caricature, but something like this assumption lies behind the modern governance regime's relentless and exclusive focus on monitoring and controlling executives. What else can account for the fact that the only concern of reformers has been reducing managerial shirking and self-enrichment, and that this concern has underlain three decades of constant reforms? It must be a serious problem!

In Chapter 1, we reviewed the history of corporate governance and saw that its modern form arose out of agency cost theory. Credited with originating agency theory, Jensen and Meckling were initially only interested in describing firms rather than advocating for dramatic changes to the ways they were governed.[1] They were admirers of the evident success of the large public company as a business form, and careful readers of their initial paper came away with the impression that they regarded the governance arrangements produced by the market as optimal. However, this attitude did not last. Agency cost theory very quickly went from being a description of what occurred within the black box of the firm to being normative. It seemed obvious to most observers and, eventually, even to Jensen, that firms should make use of an array of devices to eliminate the hazard of run-amok managers. We have examined most of the devices historically proposed for this task in the first part of this book.

The strangest aspect of the reception history of *Theory of the Firm*, however, is that over time everyone forgot that it had originally been a partial equilibrium model that "assume[d] that management moral hazard is the firm's only unsolved problem."[2] In other words, Jensen and Meckling quite consciously and clearly ignored every other kind of corporate problem: competing successfully in product, supplier, and labor markets, conducting R&D, raising capital, managing a workforce, and so on. Now, obviously, these kinds of problems, which we can call "making-a-profit problems," are very hard to solve. Anyone who has been employed by a business corporation will intuitively understand that most of the employees' time and effort is devoted to solving these making-a-profit problems. Yet, corporate governance specialists quickly came to ignore them, focusing instead on the much less important task of reducing agency costs.

We can speculate on the reasons agency cost theory led to the eclipse of other considerations, such as making profits. Much of the most important work establishing the worldview of the modern corporate governance project was done by academics who, in fact, had not usually spent much time working in business corporations. There were a large number of outsiders, like shareholders, proxy firms, think tanks, regulators, and media reporters, that wanted to talk about the governance of corporations, but lacked the knowledge and expertise to talk about firms' latest product strategies or R&D milestones. Finally, of course, humans instinctively respond to authority, and by the late 1980s and early 1990s, most authorities, including regulators, high-profile investors, politicians, and captains of industry, were all talking about corporate governance through the lens of agency cost theory.

As the prominent corporate law scholar, Ronald Gilson, observed, "the intellectual mission of American corporate governance took the form of a search for the organizational Holy Grail, a technique that bridged the separation of ownership and control by aligning the interests of shareholders and managers."[3] In this way, agency theory became the dominant theory of the public corporation.

8.1 FIGURING OUT IF AGENCY COST THEORY IS TRUE

Agency cost theory is axiomatically true. There are always costs to employing an agent; at the very least, shareholders must reconcile themselves to the need to pay corporate executives, who won't work for free. Agency cost theory is certainly true in another way: it tells us to expect some self-interested behavior from corporate actors and this is obviously likely.

We can also say, with the benefit of four decades of empirical work, that agency cost theory is after-the-fact descriptively true, though this is not a particularly interesting piece of information as there is no method of actually proving or disproving it on this basis. As various costs are hidden or incalculable, and as there are many corporate agents possessing a wide variety of interests, agency theory can retrospectively explain or justify any arrangement. Stephen Ross noted as far back as 1987,

> The agency approach has pointed in some intriguing directions, but it fares poorly if judged by asking what it is that would be a counter observation or count as evidence against it. To the contrary, no phenomenon seems beyond the reach of 'agency costs' and at times the phrase takes on more of the trappings of an incantation than an analytical tool.[4]

To see why this is so, imagine that the corporate world is swept by a trend of adding members of various monastic orders to boards of directors. No matter what the measured outcome of this trend turned out to be, agency cost theory would provide an explanation. If corporate performance improved, agency cost theory would explain this by referencing the monks' greater independence from the CEO, or their moral influence on self-interested managers. On the other hand, if corporate performance declined, the monks' lack of business expertise, their dependence on managers for information, and the existence of whatever social and economic ties brought them to the board in the first place could all be deployed to explain the results. In this way, agency cost theory explains any outcome. "When all these [agency cost] arguments hinge on asserted costs that are unobservable, the resulting explanations may be no more than 'just so stories.'"[5] This chapter is not about whether agency cost theory is *descriptively* true. Rather, it is about whether agency cost theory is *normatively* true. Does it tell us anything useful about how corporations *should* be run?

In answering this question, I will refrain from the usual "theoretical" arguments about agency cost theory that litter the academic literature. It doesn't matter to me, or really any likely reader of this book, whether the agency relationship is an accurate characterization of the roles of shareholders, officers, and directors. Shareholders may only poorly meet the criteria for a "principal," and there may be many other constituencies that also deserve that title. Managers may also not stand in something very much like an actual agency relationship to *any* particular constituency. Firms may be more than a nexus of contracts. We would not care about these abstract failures if agency cost theory were normatively true. If it generated hypotheses that turned out to improve real-world economic outcomes, it would not matter very much that, as a metaphor, agency costs applied only awkwardly to a body of corporate law and theory that developed for centuries before agency cost theory arose in the 1970s.

For similar reasons, this book is not concerned with the limitations of Jensen and Meckling's work as a model. Models are simplifications of a more complex reality, and we would not care about this kind of failing if the agency cost model nevertheless generated hypotheses that proved useful.

This chapter is interested in only one question: does the theory work? Agency cost theory was quickly understood to suggest certain things about the real world and to imply a way to make the real world better. This was, as far as the record shows, the nearly universal assumption among lawyers, regulators, and finance academics. It is impossible to read any part of the vast literature that has grown out of agency cost theory without encountering the (usually implied) assumption that the theory is a guide to how the real world works and how it might be made to work better.

Well, agency cost theory almost immediately generated numerous testable hypotheses. Over the past forty years, we have duly tested all of them. Let's step back and review the results.

8.2 TESTING THE HYPOTHESES

From the outset, there were broadly accepted implications of agency theory that could have been otherwise, but for whatever reasons, they were positions understood to fall out of the theory. For example, it is possible to conclude from agency theory that a major problem in corporate governance is the role of shareholders when they are empowered by corporate law to act as agents of the corporation. This occurs when they vote, make proposals, wage proxy fights, or collectively decide to sell the business. They have interests that may diverge from the corporation as a whole, as well as each other. (This is not merely hypothetical; this sort of agency-cost argument has been made.[6]) However, this is not how agency theory was generally understood.

To the contrary, almost from the beginning, it was anticipated that increasing shareholder power relative to managers was an important part of reducing agency costs. As this was the generally accepted implication of agency cost theory, and as it reflects the clear trend in corporate governance regulation over the past thirty years, one hypothesis we will test in this paper is whether increasing shareholder power leads to improved governance, not the reverse. We will follow the same rule in relation to the generation of the other hypotheses.

Much of what follows is a quick summary of matters discussed at greater length in earlier chapters. The only justification for reviewing these matters again is to draw the empirical literature into a whole and organize it in thematic ways to see what conclusions we can draw from it. Details on most of the following topics must be sought in the relevant chapter.

8.2.1 *Testing Hypothesis 1: Increasing Shareholder Power Over Managers Will Lead to Better Corporate Outcomes*

Any parent in possession of a cookie jar is well aware that the best way to reduce pilfering is to assert greater control and oversight over the jar. Similarly, the idea that managerial malfeasance will be reduced if shareholders are given more power over, and visibility into, the workings of the corporation was one of the earliest conclusions drawn from agency cost theory. Stock exchanges, securities regulators, corporate governance codes, and the various third parties that make up the governance industry all duly threw their support behind initiatives that increased shareholder power relative to management. This in turn generated a great deal of activity that can be used to evaluate the hypothesis.

8.2.1.1 Institutional Shareholders

The early 1990s were a time of considerable enthusiasm about the rise of institutional shareholdings in public markets. Law review articles were published with titles like "The Value of Institutional Investor Monitoring," "Agents Watching Agents: The

Promise of Institutional Investor Voice," and "The Case for Increasing Shareholder Power."[7] For those looking at the growth of investment funds from the perspective of agency cost theory, it seemed obvious that highly educated and experienced fund managers would prove superior corporate monitors compared to the retail investors they were replacing. The much larger shareholdings managed by these professionals would provide them with greater incentives to actively engage with firms to reduce agency costs while, at the same time, providing them with greater power over corporate boards.

While there were a couple initial papers that seemed to suggest institutional share ownership was connected with superior corporate outcomes,[8] contrary evidence eventually accumulated to the point where most observers have concluded this is not true. Two meta-studies of the research published in this century have found that there is no positive relationship between institutional ownership of a firm's securities and that firm's financial performance, measured either by looking at market returns or accounting measures of performance.[9]

This is not to say, of course, that different kinds of institutional shareholders don't have differing impacts on firm governance. (For example, several studies have found long-term investors with low portfolio turnover are associated with longer-term corporate strategies in their portfolio companies, measured by R&D expenditures and capital investments.[10]) Rather, the point is that agency cost theory's straightforward prediction that stronger shareholders would lead to better outcomes proved to be false. A recent literature review on this point concludes, "the extensive literature examining relationships between equity ownership and firm financial performance yields little support for the mitigation of the fundamental agency problem."[11]

8.2.1.2 Shareholder Voting

Shareholders' supervision of their agents starts with their voting power. Indeed, former Delaware Supreme Court Chief Justice Leo Strine argues that no changes made to the character of corporate law will be sufficient to displace shareholders from their preferred position in corporate decision-making, so long as shareholders retain the franchise.[12] (We have at least three different types of empirical studies vindicating Strine's view.[13]) Unsurprisingly, therefore, agency cost theory has historically been understood to support extensions of shareholder voting power.

As we saw in Chapter 5, though, there isn't much evidence that shareholders either value their voting power or use it particularly wisely. Just by way of reminder, in a typical year, out of the 31,000 American directors, only eight failed to receive a majority of votes. Various attempts at measuring the cash value given voting rights by investors find they are judged as either worthless or nearly worthless by the market.

Several studies have found that the shareholder voting patterns they examine do not have much to do with the relative financial performance of the corporation. Instead, withhold votes against directors primarily arise as a consequence of that director or company failing to adopt certain corporate governance best practices. As we have seen, there is no evidence that these sorts of best practices are correlated with positive financial firm outcomes. Unsurprisingly, when the firm responds to an abnormally high withhold vote by fixing the offensive corporate governance practice, researchers find no difference in their subsequent operating and stock performance.

In Chapter 5, we discovered that directors of companies with majority voting policies are *less* likely to be the subjects of withhold votes. The difference is huge: a director of a company without majority voting is nineteen times more likely to lose a vote. At the very moment shareholders gain power over corporate managers, they become less likely to use it. Similarly, companies with majority voting policies see a slight decline in the total number of shares voted in director elections.

In summary, the empirical results appear to suggest that shareholder voting power is not regarded as valuable by the shareholders and not deployed in the way we would expect when looking at it from the perspective of agency cost theory. Voting outcomes do not generally appear to be driven by financial performance or, in other words, by agency costs.

8.2.1.3 Shareholder Proposals

One step beyond shareholder voting is the power given to shareholders under corporate legislation to make proposals that can have the effect of changing the way a firm operates. Analysis of shareholder proposals through the lens of agency cost theory has resulted in a widespread assumption that proposals are a valuable method of constraining corporate agents' discretion.

As we saw in Chapters 5 and 6, the reality is that shareholder proposals have little impact on the operation of companies, and there is evidence that this is what shareholders want. Professors Kahan and Rock note that proposals tend to be merely symbolic.[14]

The investment funds most focused on the financial performance of companies generate virtually none of the shareholder proposals in a given year. Proposals tend to reflect the latest governance or ESG fad and rarely show any evidence that the proposal reflects the peculiarities of the targeted company. In most years, fewer than 20 percent of proposals put to the vote attract majority support from other investors.

Far from being a useful tool for reducing agency costs, shareholder proposals are not aimed at obviously poorly performing companies. The targeted firms tend to be larger than their peers, showing better operational performance but worse stock performance. The research on the outcomes produced by proposals finds that they either generate no returns or negative returns around the meeting date. A review of the seventeen long-run share price studies in the area concluded that shareholder proposals are not associated with positive long-run returns. A similar conclusion can be drawn from studies looking at operational metrics. "Most evidence ... indicates that shareholder proposals and direct negotiations are not associated with increases in the target firms' operating performance."[15]

In terms of noneconomic outcomes, there have been three different studies that each found that companies targeted by proposals do not change their CEOs at higher rates.

8.2.1.4 Proxy Contests (Shareholder Activism)

Activist campaigns result in shareholders being presented with both a real choice for the election of directors and considerably more information about the relative merits of the various candidates. It is widely assumed that these proxy contests are an important disciplinary mechanism for controlling agency costs.

In Chapter 6, we saw that scholars who look at whether shareholder activists target companies misallocating their free cash flow (including diverting some of that cash flow to insiders) found that "the majority [of the empirical studies] do not report evidence of changes in real variables consistent with this free cash flow hypothesis."[16]

When activists succeed in placing their own nominees on corporate boards, we saw in Chapter 6 that the target companies tend to experience significant subsequent underperformance unless they are sold. The best study looking at carefully matched firms that activists actually take control of, finds no evidence that the activists improved return on assets, return on equity, or any other accounting performance measure it examined. This comes as no surprise to investment bank analysts, who do not predict post-activism improvements in their earnings forecasts.

There is thus no evidence that shareholder activism results in better corporate performance or meaningful changes to the internal cash flows that are the particular focus of agency cost theory. When we look at the long-term performance of market price, the best and most recent research finds that "targets tend to decrease in value over time relative to the control firms."[17]

When positive long-term shareholder returns follow an activist intervention in corporate management, it appears from multiple studies that this is nearly entirely a function of the companies being sold to another company. As we have seen in Chapter 6, this takeover-generated return has nothing to do with agency costs either.

8.2.1.5 Dual-Class Shares

Dual-class shares have generally been understood as giving rise to significant agency costs. "[T]he agency costs associated with [controlling minority structure] firms increase very rapidly as the fraction of equity cash-flow rights held by controllers declines."[18] As well, Daniel Fischel observed that "[t]he cost of dual class common stock is that the effectiveness of the market for corporate control as a monitoring device is reduced."[19]

Contrary to the assumptions of agency cost theory, however, the motivation behind adopting dual-class structures is not agents trying to escape oversight from their principals. One study found that the greatest determinant of dual-class structures at the time of IPO was the relative importance of the founders' idiosyncratic vision, measured by media coverage.[20] Other studies have found dual-class structures to be predicted by the importance of R&D activities for adopting companies and their exposure to longer-term growth opportunities.[21] These sorts of findings explain why dual-class structures are currently most associated with rapidly growing technology firms.[22]

The evidence about what occurs inside firms with dual-class structures is mixed. Firms with dual-class shares pay their executives more, make more acquisitions that the market regards as value-destroying, and make capital expenditures that have lower impacts on shareholder value.[23] These results are usually understood as examples of agents exploiting the power provided by unequal voting rights, but they are compatible with another explanation. We have already seen that dual-class share structures tend to predominate in innovative companies pursuing idiosyncratic long-term strategies. We would expect they would pay the authors of their idiosyncratic strategies more and make investments the market doesn't regard as accretive until later.[24] As it happens, it appears that the increase in executive pay does not come in the form of simple cash payouts, which we might expect from the agency cost story, but from heavier use of equity incentives with contingent payouts, which have the effect of aligning managerial interests with the shareholders.[25] More importantly, companies with dual-class structures pay more cash out to shareholders than matched firms.[26]

In terms of economic returns, Professor Bobby Reddy finds that the studies on this subject fall into three categories. The first is a group of studies that find investors discount dual-class share companies relative to their peers.[27] However, a second group of studies looks at the relative performance of a portfolio of dual-class companies compared to a matched portfolio of nondual-class firms and finds the dual-class portfolio generates higher returns.[28] If the market valuation of dual-class firms was correct, the two portfolios should generate identical returns, so this group of studies suggests investors are, in fact, systematically undervaluing companies with dual-class shares. The third group of studies looks at measures of actual operating performance: several find dual-class firms display superior operating performance results, none find underperformance.[29]

The picture that thus emerges is that the market believes the agency cost story, but the market is wrong.[30] Managers entrenched by dual-class shares are not measurably worse agents, and they may even be superior. Professor Reddy summarizes his analysis, "[t]he better operating performance of dual-class firms is so stark that investors can earn greater returns from portfolios of such stock ... even though the market perpetually undervalues the stock."[31] Along this line, a study published since Professor Reddy's analysis finds that dual-class share structures *increase* the market valuation of high-growth firms.[32]

In terms of nonfinancial outcomes, the empirical literature contains findings that dual-class firms provide the market with "higher-quality" financial disclosure as well as experiencing fewer restatements than their peers.[33] Dual-class shares are also negatively associated with corporate misconduct.[34] These sorts of findings suggest that, contrary to the predictions of the agency cost story, managerial behavior improves with greater freedom from shareholder monitoring.

8.2.1.6 Voting on Executive Compensation

Right from the beginning, agency cost theory was suspicious of managerial power over compensation decisions. Eugene Fama noted in 1980, that "[h]aving gained control of the board, top management may decide that collusion and expropriation of security holder wealth are better than competition among themselves."[35] It has generally been assumed that increasing shareholder oversight of executive compensation will lead to lower pay packages as the opportunities for self-dealing are reduced. This has been the clear direction of regulation over the past thirty years.

On the face of things, the increasing power of shareholders over compensation decisions appears – if it had any effect at all – to have led to significant increases in executive compensation, which has exploded over the period we are considering, as described in Chapter 4. In other words, the most readily apparent measure of agency costs has increased at precisely the same time shareholders were getting more information and authority in this area.

The usual agency cost assumption that the growth of executive compensation levels is due to managers running amok turns out to not be a very good explanation for what has occurred over the past three decades. As we saw in Chapter 4, to the extent there is evidence on causality, it suggests shareholders and the tribunes of good governance are to blame for nearly the entire rise in executive compensation. This rise has come from trying to align managers' economic interests with those of the shareholders (as entailed by agency cost theory). Managers have simply been following the best practices (using equity incentives and pay-for-performance structures) recommended to them.

Whatever the merits of this argument, attempts to empower shareholders have not had the effect of holding down compensation levels. An examination of institutional investors' proxy voting guidelines (which includes the guidelines published by proxy advisors whose work is designed to appeal to their institutional clients) shows that the pay practices most associated with the increase in total compensation levels are the very ones enjoined on companies. Studies detailed in Chapter 4 show that companies which adopt these pay practices are rewarded by the market, despite the fact that they have led to much higher amounts being diverted to managers. This improvement in market value occurs even where there is no discernible improvement in corporate financial performance.

If we look at private equity compensation practices, where the shareholders have complete control over remuneration decisions, we find their pay practices indistinguishable from those of public companies. In fact, executive compensation actually goes up when a company goes private and shareholder authority over managers becomes absolute. Over the past several decades, the pay at closely held firms has outpaced that of public companies.

Turning to say-on-pay votes, we saw in Chapter 4 that companies almost never lose them. Neither the US nor the UK provide evidence that say-on-pay has changed the overall level or growth of executive compensation. Managerial pay in the UK, which introduced say-on-pay in 2002, actually increased faster than in the US over the following decade.

8.2.1.7 Summary

There is virtually no evidence that shareholder power reduces agency costs. Shareholder behaviors do not appear motivated to accomplish anything along this line, and the ways shareholders do use their power have little impact on the financial performance, behavior, or cash flows of their firms. Where we can see any impact of shareholder influence at all, the effects seem to be negative. Strangely for agency theory, this means agents do a better job without the oversight of their principals.

8.2.2 *Hypothesis 2: A More Independent Board Will Better Monitor Managers, Improving Outcomes*

As we have already seen, one of the earliest conclusions drawn from agency cost theory was the important role directors could play in monitoring managers. Over time, inside directors, aside from the CEO, have almost disappeared in American public companies. This triumph of the monitoring conception of the board occurred even while actual sitting directors continue to believe the monitoring role is less important than a board's role in succession planning, strategy, and developing talent within the organization.[36] It has also occurred during a time that the advantages of inside directors, with their superior knowledge, have increased as a result of companies becoming larger, more complex, and more focused on technical innovation. The move towards independence was even oddly accelerated as a result of the Enron-era scandals, which clearly demonstrated that independent directors were too reliant on CEOs for their information about what was transpiring within the company to provide effective monitoring.[37]

8.2.2.1 Independent Directors

As we saw in Chapter 2, no aspect of corporate governance has been more exhaustively empirically tested than the impact of board independence. The results have been well-known for decades with embarrassingly little impact on the behavior of institutional shareholders, regulators, proxy advisors, or governance experts. As evidenced by the multitude of studies discussed in Chapter 2, there is no connection between board independence and company performance. Almost the only exception to this are the studies in Chapter 2 pointing to the negative impact of independent directors, particularly for companies with complex operations.

We have also seen that if we use executive remuneration as the most easily measured manifestation of agency costs, it appears independent directors do not have any impact on this either. A meta-analytic review of research on the question found no evidence independent directors do better at controlling executive pay and correctly concluded that its findings provide "little support to agency theory predictions."[38] In fact, a number of studies have found that executive pay increases under independent directors, likely as a result of the increased use of equity compensation structures. Relatedly, independent boards also do not do any better at identifying and terminating underperforming CEOs than insider-dominated boards.

8.2.2.2 Independent Committees

Chapter 2 noted that there is no evidence that the current imperative to create board committees comprised of independent directors improves anything we care about. The most prominent of these board committees is the audit committee, precisely for the reason that it is the most intimately connected to the monitoring conception of the board advanced by the agency cost story. Of seven studies looking at earnings accruals as a measure of audit integrity, which were discussed in Chapter 2, five failed to find any benefits of having a majority of independent directors on the audit committee and none found any benefit from the current practice of requiring all members of the committee to be independent. Chapter 2 also detailed studies that use third-party evaluations of financial reporting or the content of earnings announcements to measure audit committee quality, which also failed to turn up any evidence that independent committees do better. When researchers examined the companies that fraudulently manipulated their financial statements between 1982 and 2000, they found that the bad actors had the same percentage of independent directors on their audit committees as the control sample.

It is also worth considering the performance of independent directors on compensation committees because these committees are also closely tied to the core activity of monitoring and constraining agency costs. Chapter 2 discussed many studies on CEO compensation, including seven different studies which have found that compensation committees with a higher proportion of independent directors have no significant impact on the level of CEO compensation. The remaining studies on the subject find that compensation committees comprised entirely of independent directors lead to higher executive pay.

8.2.2.3 Separation of the CEO and Chair Roles

At the beginning of agency cost theory's rise to prominence, the common American practice of combining the CEO and board chair roles was sharply criticized in two articles by Eugene Fama and Michael Jensen.[39] If the board is to serve as an effective monitor of management, it cannot be the case that it is "run" by the very person it is ostensibly monitoring. The trend since then has been increasing numbers of firms splitting the two positions.

As we saw in Chapter 2, there have been many empirical studies of the question of whether separating the CEO and chair positions leads to better outcomes. They make it clear that there are, on average, no benefits to having an independent chair. My favorite quote on the subject bears repeating: "we are not aware of a body of literature in corporate governance – or elsewhere – where null results present with such consistency."[40] When we do see the combined roles making a difference, it is often positive. For example, CEOs who are also board chairs do better at negotiating takeovers.

8.2.2.4 Summary

The hypothesis that increasing the independence of boards would lead to better outcomes – a logical result of the monitoring conception of the board in agency cost theory – is contradicted by the available evidence. This is true whether we are defining better outcomes in terms of firm performance, increasing the accuracy of firm reporting, terminating underperforming executives, or controlling the direct expropriation of value from the corporation through executive pay.

As we saw in Chapter 2, the failure of the monitoring conception of the board suggests both that independent directors are poorly equipped for the task of monitoring the managers who are their only source of information about the business, and that whatever benefits independent directors bring as monitors, those benefits are matched or exceeded by independent directors' lack of experience in the firm's day-to-day operations and their greater exposure to conventional wisdom and shareholder pressure. All of this is perfectly compatible with independent directors doing their level best – no libels about "shirking" or "conflicts of interest" required.

8.2.3 *Hypothesis 3: Aligning Managers' Interests with Those of the Shareholders Will Produce Better Outcomes*

At the heart of agency cost theory is the observation that agency costs increase as managers' equity interests decline, widening the divide between ownership and control. The conclusion drawn early in the agency cost era was that better aligning managers' interests with those of their principals, the shareholders, would therefore reduce agency costs. This led to an emphasis on managers' owning shares and being compensated through equity incentives or performance programs tied to shareholder outcomes.

8.2.3.1 Equity Ownership

Jensen and Meckling referred to agency theory as "a theory of ownership," and so some of the earliest studies on reducing agency costs looked at the impact of managers' shareholdings on firm value.[41] The earliest studies appeared to find that firm value did, in fact, vary according to changes in executives' shareholdings.[42] However, "[w]hen... these studies are corrected for missing controls and other problems, the relationship between the division of cash flows and firm performance tends to disappear."[43] All of the most recent studies, including several making use of the same earlier data for meta-analysis, consistently find no relationship between insider equity holdings and corporate performance.[44] As a recent literature review concludes, "[w]ith regards to equity holdings, the empirical evidence is … enervated…. [T]his literature does not provide linkages to corporate financial performance."[45]

8.2.3.2 Equity Incentives

Equity incentives (principally stock options and conditional share grants) were a logical extension of agency theory's expectation that placing managers on the same footing as their principals would lead to superior outcomes. With encouragement from academics and the governance industry, equity incentives became the main contributor to the modern rise in executive compensation. This is an irony worth savoring: a device intended to reduce agency costs actually had the effect of doing more than any other practice to double the portion of corporate profits diverted from shareholders to managers.

What did shareholders get for their investment? As we saw in Chapter 4, a 2003 meta-analysis on the question found that management equity exposure had no effect on all other financial metrics, except for earnings per share, where a modest impact was found, which could have been attributed to managerial techniques to increase per share earnings without improvements to operating results. The authors of the study concluded, "the results of our meta-analyses do not support agency theory's proposed relationship between ownership and firm performance."[46]

Similar results were found by the authors of a 2007 meta-analysis. This study did find evidence that the market had an expectation that equity incentives would improve performance, but "[t]his result is not confirmed by real accounting returns."[47] Stock options have particularly come in for opprobrium; several studies find they are negatively associated with both firm value and future operating results.

Chapter 4 of this book also detailed a large and growing body of research on the negative impact of equity incentive schemes on executive behavior, including manipulating disclosure at the time of equity awards, delaying or accelerating the release of news, manipulating earnings, and the occurrence of fraud or the indicia of fraud like shareholder litigation. Equity compensation is linked to larger restructurings and layoffs, voluntary corporate dissolutions, and declines in corporate R&D and capital expenditures in the years when executives' equity vests.

8.2.3.3 Pay-for-Performance

In a popular phrase already discussed in Chapter 4, Jensen and Murphy noted that corporate America paid "its most important leaders like bureaucrats."[48] Their point was that managers ought to be incentivized to take risks (the risk aversion of managers is another frequent assumption of agency theory) and to deliver value to shareholders. This is a suggestion that goes beyond merely aligning the interests of agents with their principals through the use of equity incentives. Pay-for-performance has become a popular touchstone in discussions about executive compensation. What counts as "performance" varies according to the scheme, but it tends to be tied closely to total shareholder return. As a result, for the past two decades, CEO pay has closely tracked the returns received by individual firms' shareholders.[49]

As we saw in Chapter 4, there is very little evidence that performance pay schemes (whether they consist of cash or equity awards) improve corporate performance. Several studies find that performance pay schemes actually harm corporate financial performance. The most recent of these finds that incentive pay not only does not result in better performance but "translate[s] into lower future shareholder wealth."[50] If these results seem counterintuitive, it may be helpful to recall that there were a number of behavioral experiments detailed in Chapter 4 that demonstrated that the presence of large incentives actually causes subjects to perform worse at high-level tasks that require creative or analytical thought.

We also saw in Chapter 4 a considerable body of research indicating that, as with equity incentives, pay-for-performance schemes appear to be associated with financial fraud and accounting restatements. One of the possible reasons for this is that it turns out CEOs probably do not, in most cases, have much control over the market value of their firms. Tying life-changing financial rewards to something most CEOs can only indirectly affect creates perverse incentives.

8.2.3.4 Summary

The normative program drawn from agency cost theory is relatively crude, and nowhere is that more obvious than in relation to the hypothesis about using equity holdings or compensation to align managers' interests with those of the shareholders. In focusing on one thing – the possibility that managers might ignore shareholder value – agency cost theory ignored many other important things: the fact that managers are motivated by things like a concern for their reputation, a desire to succeed at something challenging, satisfaction at solving problems, a desire to feel useful, loyalty to their subordinates, as well as a desire not to let down the employees and other corporate constituencies. It paid no attention to the way supercharged incentives could crowd out these pro-social motivations, as detailed in Chapter 4. It paid no attention to how a focus on financial metrics could crowd out the important nonfinancial objectives that can only be poorly measured, such as customer satisfaction, product innovation, and employee morale. (Unsurprisingly, research finds executives tend to work on incentivized tasks rather than those that are not measured.) Finally, the normative agency cost project also ignored the ways in which the interests of shareholders could deviate from those of the firm in ways that made managerial alignment harmful to the corporation itself.

8.2.4 *Hypothesis 4: The Market for Corporate Control Is an Important Mechanism for Controlling Agency Costs*

From the outset, agency cost theory was understood to strongly support a robust market for corporate control. Some of the earliest law review articles making use of agency theory emphasized the role of takeovers "in monitoring the performance of corporate managers."[51] Takeovers have several aspects that make them congenial to agency cost analysis: a premium is paid, which suggests the change in management increases firm value by reducing agency costs, and the shareholders of the target must tender their shares, which suggests they have independently come to the conclusion that the existing managers will not reduce the relevant agency costs if left in charge. Best of all, a hostile takeover does not require the cooperation of self-interested managers.

8.2.4.1 Hostile Takeovers and Agency Costs

The agency cost explanation for takeovers finds little support in the empirical literature. After studying 2,000 companies targeted for acquisition, Anup Agrawal and Jeffrey Jaffe concluded that there was no evidence that target firms were underperforming their peers in the decade before the takeover. Another study of the companies targeted for acquisition in the takeover frenzy of the 1980s found that more than half of them had outperformed the market over the previous two years.

As we saw in Chapter 6, there are almost no modern studies about firms that survive as independent concerns following an unsolicited bid, though there is anecdotal evidence that some of them, at least, outperform their peers. One of the only statistical studies on this topic found that companies that successfully resisted a takeover outperformed their peers by 40 percent over the following five years, but only if they increased their leverage.

When we look at what occurs following a successful takeover bid, there is again little evidence for the agency cost story. The fact that bidders overpay for acquisitions is, at this point, proverbial. Long-term studies that measure operating performance over time (such as earnings or other accounting measures) largely find that acquirors underperform their peers for the next several years. Hostile bids, the ideal mechanism for circumventing expensive managers, result in worse acquiror stock performance than friendly deals. Another study found there was no evidence of the post-acquisition turnover of officers and directors that we would expect if we accepted the disciplining effect assumed by agency cost theory. There is thus little in the literature to suggest that takeovers arise from agency costs remedied by a successful bidder.

8.2.4.2 Takeover Defenses

Because takeover defenses inoculate managers against the discipline of the market for corporate control, agency cost theory assumes they permit managers to increase their waste or diversion of the shareholders' property. As Ronald Gilson noted in 1981, takeover defenses were particularly inappropriate because of the way they frustrated the market for corporate control's ability to reduce agency costs.[52]

Unfortunately, as we saw in Chapter 6, a great deal of the research on takeover defenses relies, in whole, or in part, on treating the presence of poison pills, antitakeover statutes, and certain charter provisions as meaningful indicia of firms' ability to stand off a hostile bid. As various legal academics have pointed out, these "defenses" either have no relevance to resisting a hostile bidder or, like the pill, they can be adopted at a moment's notice. Only staggered boards are the real indicia of "entrenched" managers.

Chapter 6 noted that the early research around staggered boards had significant problems and that more recent research, with larger and longer-term data sets, found that staggered boards either have no material effect on firm value or they increase it. Studies that have looked at exogenous events that impact corporations' use of staggered boards reinforce this picture. These studies consistently find staggered boards are value-enhancing. "Dead hand pills," which serve as a kind of proxy for staggered boards since they can only be lifted by the directors that imposed them, apparently are also associated with wealth gains for shareholders.

There are comparatively fewer studies that look at the impacts of staggered boards on matters other than firm value. What studies exist also contradict the expectations of agency cost theory. Staggered boards are just as likely to terminate a CEO as a board elected annually. The existence of a staggered board has no impact on the amounts paid to executives or the pay structures used by the firm. Banks with staggered boards were much less likely to require state bailouts following the 2008 financial crisis. None of this suggests "entrenchment" has the effects predicted by agency cost theory.

8.2.4.3 Summary

The market for corporate control cannot be explained by agency cost theory. On average, takeovers apparently have little to do with replacing underperforming managers, and takeover defenses do not lead to an increase in managerial self-dealing or underperformance. Agency theory's failures in this area likely result from its myopic focus on only one aspect of the firm. Doubtless, there are agency cost-driven takeovers, but these are swamped in the statistics by takeovers where agency costs are not relevant and the premium paid by shareholders is extracted from employees, debtholders, or the acquiring firm's own shareholders. More positively, some premiums might arise from business synergies, including a reduction in product market competition following the acquisition. They do not mainly appear to arise, however, from reducing agency costs.

The failure of agency cost theory to predict the ways managers protected by takeover defenses will behave should, at this point, not seem extraordinary. It is worth noting, however, that the agency cost assumption that managers' self-interest automatically lies in resisting exposure to the market for corporate control is absurd to anyone with actual experience in that market. Managers have golden parachutes, severance clauses, and retention bonuses that pay out fortunes after a change of control. (This is in addition to the money executives make on their equity.) As nearly all takeovers occur at a substantial premium to the market, managers who sell their firms gain the reputational credit of providing investors with a lucrative exit. Most takeovers are, in fact, friendly. If there is an agency cost risk, it might be that managers are too willing to see their businesses sold, regardless of their firms' prospects or the impact sales will have on non-shareholder constituencies.

8.2.5 *Hypothesis 5: Because the Principal–Agent Relationship Exists in all Firms, There Are Best Practices Generalizable across Firms*

Agency cost theory, like any theory, claims to transcend the particular and arrive at the universal. It doesn't merely describe what happens at a few firms; it explains the outcomes experienced by all, or at least most, firms. This has certainly been how agency cost theory has been understood by the people that make use of it. Not long after the theory developed, academics and regulators were arguing that certain corporate structures and practices were superior.

8.2.5.1 Individual Best Practices

In considering the hypotheses around shareholder influence, monitoring boards, the market for corporate control, and executive compensation, we have seen that every recommended practice fails to find much support in the empirical literature. That is, the normative version of agency cost theory fails to produce successful general predictions about corporate governance.

One possible objection to this skeptical take on best practices is that the practices we have examined are too crude. A critic could argue, for example, that scholars' market-wide evaluations of the best practices making up monitoring boards have failed to take account of various personal and corporate factors that do produce better outcomes from independent directors. Research described in Chapter 2 suggests, for instance, that independent directors do, in fact, have a beneficial influence on CEO pay if they make less money or are a very different age from the CEO. Similarly, splitting the CEO and board chair role is not especially bad in companies that do not have significant knowledge assets (measured as patent citations and R&D spending) or that are relatively straightforward. The impacts of the CEO also serving as chair also appear to vary according to the stage the CEO is at in their own career, where the firm is at in the CEO succession process, the size of the board, the size of the CEO's shareholdings, and the degree of the CEO's reputation risk.

The problem with findings like these is that they are not generalizable. Far from agency cost theory generating predictions that prove to be true as a function of the corporate form (the compelling initial promise of agency theory), it turns out that positive corporate outcomes depend on a host of idiosyncratic variables. This permits agency cost theory to provide retrospective explanations but not useful prospective suggestions for corporate practice. In other words, if too many variables are required, agency theory ceases to be a useful theory and instead becomes a series of "Just-So Stories" explaining how a highly contingent outcome came to be.

In fact, the research about corporate governance is full of interesting, fine-grained distinctions about the way various practices produce different outcomes, and while the results are often explained with reference to agency cost theory, it is not clear what the theory is contributing. If we asked an informed observer whether greater board independence would benefit a particular company, they would be required to engage in a particularized analysis of the firm's circumstances, personalities, markets, suppliers, strategy, and assets before providing an answer. Where is the theory in this process?

8.2.5.2 Broad Measures of Good Governance

Another test of agency theory's ability to produce useful generalizations about corporate governance outcomes is to look at the various attempts to create an overall index that measures multiple best practices suggested by the theory. We reviewed the empirical evidence around these attempts to measure or rank governance in Chapter 3.

Looking first at commercial services, we saw that the largest and most recent study corrected for methodological failures in earlier studies and found that the rating schemes of the most prominent firms failed to correlate with accounting restatements, class action lawsuits, return on assets, market-to-book ratio, and stock price performance. The study concluded, "these governance ratings have either limited or no success in predicting firm performance or other outcomes of interest to shareholders."[53] In relation to various commercial ESG indices, there are at least six peer-reviewed academic studies that decompose the indices to examine the "governance" aspects; all find "governance" to be unrelated to various measures of corporate performance.

In Chapter 3, we saw that the most prominent of the academic efforts to create governance indices of best practices (the "G-Index" and the "E-Index") all failed to yield predictive results. Lesser-known attempts by academics to rank firms on the basis of a wide range of governance best practices have also failed to provide meaningful connections to firm performance. How could they? After the failures reported by all the studies we have reviewed in this book, it would be surprising if some combination of them suddenly proved a success. A meta-analysis of over 100 studies of CEO roles, board structure, board size, and director shareholdings failed to find any predictable relationship between best practices in these areas and investment outcomes.

Turning now to the best practices selected by regulators, Canada and the United Kingdom have adopted "comply or explain" regimes that allow us to evaluate the relative performance of high-complying firms with those that adopt fewer of the recommended practices. Six studies described in Chapter 3 all fail to find meaningful differences between the two types of companies.

8.2.5.3 Summary

There is little evidence that corporate best practices generalized from agency cost theory, either individually or collectively, produce the expected corporate outcomes. Even if we use a firm's broad-based adherence to a range of best practices as a general measure of its' dedication to managing agency costs, we do not see the outcomes the theory predicts. Surveying the research, one scholar observes "agency theory, which underlies the entire intellectual edifice ..., has little explanatory or predictive power."[54]

8.3 SUMMARY

It is very hard to give agency theory much credit for being useful. It can explain almost anything but appears to predict nothing. It is not a surprise that studies find that when new governance rules come into force, they are viewed skeptically by corporate insiders and even shareholders. In their paper, "The Market Reaction to Corporate Governance Regulation," Professors Larcker, Ormazabal, and Taylor note that, "[c]ollectively, we find robust evidence of a negative stock price reaction for firms whose governance practices would be most altered by the proposed regulations."[55] Annoyingly, this suggests the market knows right from the beginning that our modern, agency-inflected governance innovations are a mistake.

NOTES

1 Brian R. Cheffins, "What Jensen and Meckling Really Said About the Public Company" in Elizabeth Pollman and Robert B. Thompson (eds.), *Research Handbook on Corporate Purpose and Personhood* (Cheltenham, UK: Edward Elgar Publishing Limited, 2021), pp. 2–26 at p. 3.
2 William W. Bratton and Simone M. Sepe, "Corporate Law and the Myth of Efficient Market Control" (2020) 105:3 *Cornell Law Review* 675–740 at 678 [Bratton and Sepe, "Myth of Efficient"].
3 Ronald J. Gilson, "Corporate Governance and Economic Efficiency: When Do Institutions Matter" (1996) 74:2 *Washington University Law Quarterly* 327–346 at 331.
4 Stephen A. Ross, "Finance" in John Eatwell, Murray Milgate and Peter Newman (eds.), *The New Palgrave: A Dictionary of Economics* (New York: Norton, 1987) at p. 29. See also, J. B. Heaton, "Corporate Governance and the Cult of Agency" (2019) 64:2 *Villanova Law Review* 201–222 at 211–212 [Heaton, "Cult of Agency"].
5 Heaton, "Cult of Agency," above at note 4 at 212. See also, Ian D. Gow, David F. Larcker and Anastasia A. Zakolyukina, "How Important is Corporate Governance? Evidence from Machine Learning" (2023), *Chicago Booth Research Paper No. 22-16*, online: SSRN, https://ssrn.com/abstract=4231644 at 8.

6   For example, Zohar Goshen and Richard Squire, "Principal Costs: A New Theory of Corporate Law and Governance" (2017) 117:3 *Columbia Law Review* 767–830 at 777 [Goshen and Squire, "Principal Costs"]. See also, Bratton and Sepe, "Myth of Efficient," above at note 2; Heaton, "Cult of Agency," above at note 4.

7   Bernard S. Black, "The Value of Institutional Investor Monitoring: The Empirical Evidence" (1992) 39:4 *UCLA Law Review* 895–940 [Black, "Institutional Monitoring"]; Bernard S. Black, "Agents Watching Agents: The Promise of Institutional Investor Voice" (1992) 39:4 *UCLA Law Review* 811–894 [Black, "Agents Watching Agents"]; Lucian A. Bebchuk, "The Case for Increasing Shareholder Power" (2005) 118:3 *Harvard Law Review* 833–914 [Bebchuk, "Increasing Shareholder Power"].

8   See, for example, Jeffrey G. MacIntosh, "Institutional Shareholders and Corporate Governance in Canada" (1992) 26:2 *Canadian Business Law Journal* 145–188 at 146. See also, Black, "Institutional Monitoring," above at note 7; Black, "Agents Watching Agents," above at note 7; Bebchuk, "Increasing Shareholder Power," above at note 7; Bernard S. Black, "Institutional Investors and Corporate Governance: The Case for Institutional Voice" (1992) 5:3 *Journal of Applied Corporate Finance* 19–32; Mark J. Roe, "A Political Theory of American Corporate Finance" (1991) 91:1 *Columbia Law Review* 10–67; Paul A. Gompers and Andrew Metrick, "Institutional Investors and Equity Prices" (2001) 116:1 *The Quarterly Journal of Economics* 229–259.

9   Dan R. Dalton et al., "Meta-Analyses of Financial Performance and Equity: Fusion or Confusion?" (2003) 46:1 *Academy of Management Journal* 13–26 [Dalton et al., "Fusion or Confusion"]; Chamu Sundaramurthy, Dawna L. Rhoades and Paula L. Rechner, "A Meta-Analysis of the Effects of Executive and Institutional Ownership on Firm Performance" (2005) 17:4 *Journal of Managerial Issues* 494–510 [Sundaramurthy, Rhoades and Rechner, "Effects of Ownership"].

10 Brian J. Bushee, "The Influence of Institutional Investors on Myopic R&D Investment Behavior" (1998) 73:3 *Accounting Review* 305–333; Robert E. Hoskisson et al., "Conflicting Voices: The Effects of Ownership Heterogeneity and Internal Governance on Corporate Innovation Strategies" (2002) 45:4 *Academy of Management Journal* 697–716; Yueting Li, Jianling Wang and Xuan Wu, "Distracted Institutional Shareholders and Managerial Myopia: Evidence from R&D Expenses" (2019) 29 *Finance Research Letters* 30–40.

11 Dan R. Dalton et al., "The Fundamental Agency Problem and Its Mitigation: Independence, Equity, and the Market for Corporate Control" in James P. Walsh and Arthur P. Brief (eds.), *The Academy of Management Annals* (New York: Lawrence Erlbaum Associates, 2007), vol. 1, pp. 1–64 at p. 23 [Dalton et al., "Fundamental Agency Problem"].

12 Leo E. Strine, Jr., "Corporate Power is Corporate Purpose I: Evidence from My Hometown" (2017) 33:2 *Oxford Review of Economic Policy* 176–186.

13 Bryce C. Tingle and Eldon Spackman, "Do Corporate Fiduciary Duties Matter?" (2014) 4:4 *Annals of Corporate Governance* 272–326.

14 Marcel Kahan and Edward Rock, "Symbolic Corporate Governance Politics" (2014) 94:6 *Boston University Law Review* 1997–2044 at 1999–2001.

15 Matthew Denes, Jonathan M. Karpoff and Victoria B. McWilliams, "Thirty Years of Shareholder Activism: A Survey of Empirical Research" (2017) 44:1 *Journal of Corporate Finance* 405–424 at 411.

16 John C. Coffee, Jr. and Darius Palia, "Wolf at the Door: The Impact of Hedge Fund Activism on Corporate Governance" (2016) 41:3 *Journal of Corporation Law* 545–608 at 583.

17 K. J. Martijn Cremers et al., "Hedge Fund Activism and Long-Term Firm Value" (2020), online: *SSRN*, https://ssrn.com/abstract=2693231 at 24. See Bryce C. Tingle, "Two Stories About Shareholders" (2021) 58:1 *Osgoode Hall Law Journal* 57–108 at 93–94.

18 Lucian A. Bebchuk, Reinier Kraakman and George Triantis, "Stock Pyramids, Cross-Ownership, and Dual Class Equity: The Mechanisms and Agency Costs of Separating Control from Cash-Flow Rights" in Randal K. Morck (ed.), *Concentrated Corporate Ownership* (Chicago: The University of Chicago Press, 2000), pp. 295–318 at pp. 310–311. See also, Lucian A. Bebchuk and Kobi Kastiel, "The Untenable Case for Perpetual Dual-Class Stock" (2017) 103:4 *Virginia Law Review* 585–630; Ronald W. Masulis, Cong Wang and Fei Xie, "Agency Problems at Dual-Class Companies" (2009) 64:4 *The Journal of Finance* 1697–1727 [Masulis, Wang and Xie, "Agency Problems"].

19 Daniel R. Fischel, "Organized Exchanges and the Regulation of Dual Class Common Stock" (1987) 54:1 *University of Chicago Law Review* 119–152 at 140.

20 Adi Grinapell, "Dual-Stock Structure and Firm Innovation" (2020) 25:1 *Stanford Journal of Law, Business & Finance* 40–85; Adi Grinapell, "What Drives the Use of Dual-Class Structures in Technology IPOs?" (2022) 17:1 *Journal of Law, Economics & Policy* 28–53.

21 Jordan D. Bradford, Soohyung Kim and Mark H. Liu, "Growth Opportunities, Short-term Market Pressure, and Dual-Class Share Structure" (2016) 41 *Journal of Corporate Finance* 304–328 [Bradford, Kim and Liu, "Growth Opportunities"]; Kenneth Lehan, Jeffry Netter and Annette Poulsen, "Consolidating Corporate Control: Dual-Class Recapitalizations Versus Leveraged Buyouts" (1990) 27:2 *Journal of Financial Economics* 557–580 [Lehan, Netter and Poulsen, "Consolidating Control"]; Hyunseob Kim and Roni Michaely, "Sticking Around Too Long? Dynamics of the Benefits of Dual Class Structures" (2019), *European Corporate Governance Institute – Finance Working Paper No. 590/2019*, online: SSRN, https://ssrn.com/abstract=3145209 [Kim and Michaely, "Sticking Around"].

22 Jay R. Ritter, "Initial Public Offerings: Dual Class Structures of IPOs Through 2022" (24 April 2023), online (pdf): https://site.warrington.ufl.edu/ritter/files/IPOs-Dual-Class.pdf. See generally, *Dual-Class IPO Snapshot: 2017–2019 Statistics*, Council for Institutional Investors (January 2020), online (pdf): www.cii.org/files/issues_and_advocacy/DualClassStock/Jan%202020%20Dual%20Class%20Update%20for%20Website.pdf; Bobby V. Reddy, "More Than Meets the Eye: Reassessing the Empirical Evidence on US Dual-Class Stock" (2021) 23:4 *University of Pennsylvania Journal of Business Law* 955–1017 [Reddy, "More Than Meets"].

23 Masulis, Wang and Xie, "Agency Problems," above at note 18.

24 One of the authors of the study finding possible agency cost problems makes this argument in a subsequent paper: Suman Banerjee and Ronald W. Masulis, "Ownership, Investment and Governance: The Costs and Benefits of Dual Class Shares" (2018), *European Corporate Governance Institute – Finance Working Paper No. 352/2013*, online: SSRN, https://ssrn.com/abstract=2182849.

25 Ben Amoako-Adu, Vishaal Baulkaran and Brian F. Smith, "Executive Compensation in Firms with Concentrated Control: The Impact of Dual Class Structure and Family Management" (2011) 17:5 *Journal of Corporate Finance* 1580–1594.

26 Bradford D. Jordan, Mark H. Liu and Qun Wu, "Corporate Payout Policy in Dual-Class Firms" (2014) 26 *Journal of Corporate Finance* 1–19.

27 Reddy, "More Than Meets," above at note 22.

28 Ekkehart Böhmer, Gary C. Sanger and Sanjay B. Varshney, "The Effect of Consolidated Control on Firm Performance: The Case of Dual Class IPOs" in Mario Levis (ed.), *Empirical Issues in Raising Equity Capital* (Amsterdam: Elsevier, 1996), p. 95 at p. 109 [Böhmer, Sanger and Varshney, "Consolidated Control"]; Ronald C. Anderson, Ezgi Ottolenghi and David M. Reeb, "The Dual Class Premium: A Family Affair" (2017), *Fox School of Business Research Paper No. 17-021*, online: SSRN, https://ssrn.com/abstract=3006669 at 23; Valentin Dimitrov and Prem C. Jain, "Recapitalization of One Class of Common Stock

into Dual-Class: Growth and Long-run Stock Returns" (2006) 12:2 *Journal of Corporate Finance* 342–366 at 347 [Dimitrov and Jain, "Recapitalization"]; Scott Bauguess, Myron B. Slovin and Marie E. Sushka, "Large Shareholder Diversification, Corporate Risk Taking, and the Benefits of Changing to Differential Voting Rights" (2012) 36:4 *Journal of Banking & Finance* 1244–1253 at 1251 [Bauguess, Slovin and Sushka, "Diversification"]; Thomas J. Chemmanur, Imants Paeglis and Karen Simonyan, "Management Quality and Antitakeover Provisions" (2011) 54:3 *The Journal of Law and Economics* 651–692 at 681 [Chemmanur, Paeglis and Simonyan, "Management Quality"]; Wayne H. Mikkelson and M. Megan Partch, "The Consequences of Unbundling Managers' Voting Rights and Equity Claims" (1994) 1:2 *Journal of Corporate Finance* 175–199 at 191 (finding lower returns in the first year and positive returns thereafter) [Mikkelson and Partch, "Unbundling Managers"]; Martijn Cremers, Beni Lauterbach and Anete Pajuste, "The Life-Cycle of Dual Class Firm Evaluation" (2018), *European Corporate Governance Institute – Finance Working Paper No. 550/2018*, online: SSRN, https://ssrn.com/abstract=3062895 at 24 [Cremers, Lauterbach and Pajuste, "Life-Cycle"]; Scott B. Smart, Ramabhadran S. Thirumalai and Chad J. Zutter, "What's in a Vote? The Short- and Long-run Impact of Dual-Class Equity on IPO Firm Values" (2008) 45:1 *Journal of Accounting and Economics* 94–115 at 106 [Smart, Thirumalai and Zutter, "What's in a Vote"].

29 Onur Arugaslan, Douglas O. Cook and Robert Kierschnick, "On the Decision to Go Public with Dual Class Stock" (2010) 16:2 *Journal of Corporate Finance* 170–181; Cremers, Lauterbach and Pajuste, "Life-Cycle," above at note 28; Böhmer, Sanger and Varshney, "Consolidated Control," above at note 28; Lehan, Netter and Poulsen, "Consolidating Control," above at note 21; Chemmanur, Paeglis and Simonyan, "Management Quality," above at note 28; Gabriel Morey, *Multi-Class Stock and Firm Value*, Council of Institutional Investors (May 2017), online (pdf): www.cii.org/files/publications/misc/05_10_17_dual-class_value_study.pdf; Mikkelson and Partch, "Unbundling Managers," above at note 28; Smart, Thirumalai and Zutter, "What's in a Vote," above at note 28; Kim and Michaely, "Sticking Around," above at note 21; Bauguess, Slovin and Sushka, "Diversification," above at note 28; Dimitrov and Jain, "Recapitalization," above at note 28.

30 Reddy, "More Than Meets," above at note 22.

31 *Ibid* at 962.

32 Bradford, Kim and Liu, "Growth Opportunities," above at note 21.

33 Rimona Palas and Dov Solomon, "The Quality of Earnings Information in Dual-Class Firms: Persistence and Predictability" (2022) 7:1 *Journal of Law, Finance, and Accounting* 127–164.

34 Nicolas Eugster, Oskar Kowalewski and Piotr Spiewanowski, "Internal Governance Mechanisms and Corporate Misconduct" (2022), *IESEG Working Paper Series 2022-ACF-05*, online: SSRN, https://ssrn.com/abstract=4211747 at 22.

35 Eugene F. Fama, "Agency Problems and the Theory of the Firm" (1980) 88:2 *Journal of Political Economy* 288–307 at 293.

36 Robert C. Clark, "Harmony or Dissonance? The Good Governance Ideas of Academics and Worldly Players" (2015) 70:2 *The Business Lawyer* 321–346 at 331–332.

37 Roberta Romano, "Quack Corporate Governance" (2005) 28:4 *Regulation* 36–44; Bethany McLean and Peter Elkind, *The Smartest Guys in the Room: The Amazing Rise and Scandalous Fall of Enron* (New York: Penguin, 2013).

38 Yuval Deutsch, "The Impact on Board Composition on Firms' Critical Decisions: A Meta-analytic Review" (2005) 31:3 *Journal of Management* 424–444 at 438.

39 Duality was criticized right from the beginning of agency cost theory: Eugene F. Fama and Michael C. Jensen, "Agency Problems and Residual Claims" (1983) 26:2 *The Journal of*

Law and Economics 327–349 at 331; Eugene F. Fama and Michael C. Jensen, "Separation of Ownership and Control" (1983) 26:2 *The Journal of Law and Economics* 301–325 at 314–315. See also, Mark S. Mizruchi, "Who Controls Whom? An Examination of the Relation Between Management and Boards of Directors in Large American Corporations" (1983) 8:3 *Academy of Management Review* 426–435.

40 Dan R. Dalton and Catherine M. Dalton, "Integration of Micro and Macro Studies in Governance Research: CEO Duality, Board Composition, and Financial Performance" (2011) 37:2 *Journal of Management* 404–411 at 408. See also, Ryan Krause, Matthew Semadeni and Albert A. Cannella, "CEO Duality: A Review and Research Agenda" (2014) 40:1 *Journal of Management* 256–286 at 282.

41 Jensen and Meckling, "Theory of the Firm," above at note 9 at 309. See also, Harold Demsetz and Kenneth Lehn, "The Structure of Corporate Ownership: Causes and Consequences" (1985) 93:6 *Journal of Political Economy* 1155–1177 at 1156 [Demsetz and Lehn, "Causes and Consequences"]; Michael C. Jensen, "Agency Costs of Free Cash Flow, Corporate Finance and Takeovers" (1986) 76:2 *The American Economic Review* 323–329.

42 Demsetz and Lehn, "Causes and Consequences," above at note 41. See, for example, Benjamin E. Hermalin and Michael S. Weisbach, "The Effects of Board Composition and Direct Incentives on Firm Performance" (1991) 20:4 *Financial Management* 101–112 at 111; Clifford G. Holderness, Randall S. Kroszner and Dennis P. Sheehan, "Were the Good Old Days that Good? Changes in Managerial Stock Ownership Since the Great Depression" (1999) 54:2 *The Journal of Finance* 435–469 at 466; John J. McConnell and Henri Servaes, "Additional Evidence on Equity Ownership and Corporate Value" (1990) 27:2 *Journal of Financial Economics* 595–612 at 604; Randall Morck, Andrei Shleifer and Robert W. Vishny, "Management Ownership and Market Valuation" (1988) 20 *Journal of Financial Economics* 293–315 at 311.

43 Goshen and Squire, "Principal Costs," above at note 6 at 815. See also, Dalton et al., "Fundamental Agency Problem," above at note 11 at p. 16.

44 Dalton et al., "Fusion or Confusion?," above at note 9; Sundaramurthy, Rhoades and Rechner, "Effects of Ownership," above at note 9; Charles P. Himmelberg, R. Glenn Hubbard and Darius Palia, "Understanding the Determinants of Managerial Ownership and the Link Between Ownership and Performance" (1999) 53:3 *Journal of Financial Economics* 353–384; Harold Demsetz and Belen Villalonga, "Ownership Structure and Corporate Performance" (2001) 7:3 *Journal of Corporate Finance* 209–233. See also, Sanjai Bhagat, Bernard Black and Margaret Blair, "Relational Investing and Firm Performance" (2004) 27:1 *Journal of Financial Research* 1–30.

45 Dalton et al., "Fundamental Agency Problem," above at note 11 at p. 33.

46 Dalton et al., "Fusion or Confusion?," above at note 9 at 20.

47 Juan P. Sánchez-Ballesta and Emma García-Meca, "A Meta-Analytic Vision of the Effect of Ownership Structure on Firm Performance" (2007) 15:5 *Corporate Governance: An International Review* 879–892 at 887.

48 Michael C. Jensen and Kevin J. Murphy, "CEO Incentives – It's Not How Much You Pay, But How" (1990) 68:3 *Harvard Business Review* 138–153 at 138.

49 Martin J. Conyon, "Executive Compensation and Board Governance in US Firms" (2014) 124:574 *The Economic Journal* F60–F89 at F62, F79; Ron Schmidt, "The Relationship Between Shareholder Return and CEO Pay Over a CEO's Full Period of Service" (2021) 33:1 *Journal of Applied Corporate Finance* 68–84; Michael Faulkender et al., "Executive Compensation: An Overview of Research on Corporate Practices and Proposed Reforms" (2010) 22:1 *Journal of Applied Corporate Finance* 107–118 at 109.

50 Michael J. Cooper, Huseyin Gulen and P. Raghavendra Rau, "Performance for Pay? The Relation Between CEO Incentive Compensation and Future Stock Price Performance" (2016), online: *SSRN*, https://ssrn.com/abstract=1572085 at 26.

51 Frank H. Easterbrook and Daniel R. Fischel, "The Proper Role of a Target's Management in Responding to a Tender Offer" (1981) 94:6 *Harvard Law Review* 1161–1204 at 1169; Frank H. Easterbrook and Daniel R. Fischel, "Corporate Control Transactions" (1982) 91:4 *Yale Law Journal* 698–738.

52 Ronald J. Gilson, "A Structural Approach to Corporations: The Case Against Defensive Tactics in Tender Offers" (1981) 33:5 *Stanford Law Review* 819–892.

53 Robert M. Daines, Ian D. Gow and David F. Larcker, "Rating the Ratings: How Good are Commercial Governance Ratings?" (2012) 98:3 *Journal of Financial Economics* 439–461 at 460. See also, Rob Bauer, Nadja Guenster and Rogér Otten, "Empirical Evidence on Corporate Governance in Europe: The Effect on Stock Returns, Firm Value and Performance" (2004) 5:2 *Journal of Asset Management* 91–104 at 101.

54 Sumantra Ghoshal, "Bad Management Theories are Destroying Good Management Practices" (2005) 4:1 *Management Learning & Education* 75–91 at 80.

55 David F. Larcker, Gaizka Ormazabal and Daniel J. Taylor, "The Market Reaction to Corporate Governance Regulation" (2011) 101:2 *Journal of Financial Economics* 431–448 at 433. Interestingly, some of the most robust negative market reactions came in relation to actions that would have increased shareholder power such as providing enhanced proxy access or reducing the power of staggered boards.

9

How Crooked Is the Timber?

For a book written by a legal academic, there has been very little reference to Immanuel Kant. By way of addressing this deficiency, we will be considering his famous aphorism that "out of the crooked timber of humanity, no straight thing was ever made."[1] So far, we have seen that our corporate governance initiatives to reform the shape of human lumber have generally not been successful. This could be because we aren't applying enough force, or perhaps because we are missing some important tool or technique, or it could be because executives aren't quite as bent as we expected.

As far back as Adam Smith, it has been understood that when the corporate form results in some persons managing the wealth of others, there is a risk of inefficiency. In his famous work, *An Inquiry into the Nature and Causes of the Wealth of Nations*, Smith wrote that managers would not watch over others' resources "with the same anxious vigilance" one would expect of owners, and that "negligence and profusion, therefore, must always prevail, more or less, in the management of the affairs of such a company."[2] The well-known debates among Adolph Berle, Merrick Dodd, and Gardiner Means in the first decades of the twentieth century also drew attention to the separation of ownership and control, along with the possibility that managers might have interests that diverged from those of the shareholders.

It is interesting to consider why, notwithstanding these very prominent warnings, corporate governance as a field of intellectual activity arose only decades later. The idea that managers could act in self-interested ways is not, after all, a very novel idea. We've all read Kant, or barring that, we all have a friend or relative to whom we try very hard not to lend our stuff. It isn't rocket science to extend that distrust to the people flying around in the corporate jet. As well, outside of the novels of Ayn Rand, our society generally casts business executives as villains in popular culture. (The only group to more uniformly be cast as villains are Nazis, which tells you all you need to know about the popularity of corporate managers.)

Yet, as we have seen, it wasn't until the 1970s that the key ideas behind corporate governance gained widespread traction. What can explain the failure of earlier generations to adopt the idea that controlling managerial misbehavior should be the focus of extensive reform efforts? The most likely explanation is that prior generations didn't believe managerial malfeasance was a widespread and systemic problem.

As we saw in Chapter 1, until the mid-1970s, finance scholars remained confident that managers were faithful stewards of corporate resources and generally acted to maximize corporate cash flows. This included Nobel laureates like Eugene Fama and Merton Miller, who were very well-informed about the state of the empirical research.[3]

Similarly, discussions of boards of directors prior to the 1970s generally came from the perspective that they were doing what they were expected to do: supervising their firm's business activities. Boards were usually conceptualized as partners with the corporation's senior management in driving corporate performance. As law professor John Hetherington wrote in 1979, "apart from occasional management frauds, which probably cannot be prevented at acceptable cost under any scheme of corporate governance, the behavior of corporate management generally conforms with investor expectations."[4] The failure of previous generations of corporate law scholars to focus attention on the independence of directors from managers makes no sense if there was a widely-held belief that managers are always and everywhere about to misbehave and directors exist to stop them.

It wasn't until Melvin Eisenberg's influential 1976 book, *The Structure of the Corporation* (published the same year as Jensen and Meckling's *Theory of the Firm*) that the view became widespread that the essential function of directors was to monitor senior executives.[5] He argued that all other functions of the board – advising the CEO, generating strategy, making introductions, and authorizing major corporate decisions – were of minor importance or would seldom produce real value. Directors went from the managers of some of America's most important institutions to security guards watching the loading docks – never the most prestigious position in any business.

From a distance, the history of corporate governance thus seems relatively straightforward: executives and directors were generally believed to be faithful and competent stewards of corporate resources, then this belief changed, giving rise to modern corporate governance. This change did reflect some high-profile failures of American corporate managers in the 1970s. In his excellent history of corporate governance, *The Public Company Transformed*, Professor Brian Cheffins describes the business failures and scandals that supported the change in belief about managers.[6]

The position this book takes is that the governance reformers of the 1970s and subsequent decades are generally wrong. The realities of running a corporation operating in competitive markets provide very few opportunities for the slack and diversion assumed by modern corporate governance. Succeeding in business is difficult, profit margins tend to be low, capital is expensive, and most people promoted to the highest levels of a company are extremely focused on making profits (otherwise known as "remaining solvent") and work very, very hard. There are exceptions, of course, possibly many of them, but the question that must be answered before making legal reforms to corporate governance is which of the two views of executives is correct in the most instances. No one could object to the proposition that in companies like Enron and WorldCom, there were major managerial failures to act in the best interests of shareholders and other constituencies. The question is whether these sorts of governance failures are so widespread as to be systemic, justifying our systematic overhaul of corporate governance. In attempting to answer that question, this chapter will evaluate several bodies of research.

9.1 THE FAILURES OF PREVIOUS HYPOTHESES

In Chapter 8, we surveyed all of the devices we assumed would control the "negligence and profusion" of corporate managers. Curiously, none of them appear to make much of a difference. The failure of the hypotheses in Chapter 8 serves as strong evidence that agency cost theory's foundational assumption of unfaithful agents is wrong. Every effort we have made over the past forty years to monitor, control, and properly incentivize corporate executives has made little to no difference in the ways they manage their businesses.

The simplest explanation for these results is that managers do not engage in much slack and diversion, even when they are not subject to the various governance structures designed to make them faithful stewards of the shareholders. Looking at where we would most expect opportunistic behavior: (1) managers of companies with dual-class shares distribute more cash to shareholders, financially outperform their peers, and generally behave better; (2) staggered boards protected from takeovers perform just as well or better than peers, as well as paying and firing their CEOs in precisely the same ways as unprotected boards; and (3) "entrenched" managers who are prepared to violate the cannons of good governance as measured by governance rating schemes generate superior returns and those managers are disciplined by their boards in exactly the same ways as other firms. There is nothing in the empirical literature we have considered in this book that would surprise Fama and Miller in 1972 or Hetherington in 1979.

9.2 THE APPARENT IRRELEVANCE OF LEGAL DUTIES

The most important duty imposed by law on corporate actors is the fiduciary duty. This encompasses both a duty to exercise care and diligence (thus avoiding "negligence" or "slack") and a duty to put the interests of the firm before their own (thus avoiding "profusion," "diversion," and worse). In other words, the fiduciary duty is the legal instantiation of the agency cost story.

Natural experiments arising over the past several decades allow us to explore whether the fiduciary duty makes any difference to managers' behavior. Given the sheer amount of ink legal academics have spilled on debating the nature, contours, and proper objects of the fiduciary duty, even professors with little interest in max-imizing shareholder wealth have a stake in the outcome of these experiments. If major alterations in the fiduciary duty have no impact whatsoever on managerial behavior, then it is not just the assumptions of agency theory that are called into question, but possibly the whole notion that we can use corporate governance chan-nels to achieve nonfinancial outcomes.

9.2.1 *Constituency Statutes*

The first body of empirical research about the corporate fiduciary duty arose in connection with the adoption of constituency statutes by various state legislatures in the 1980s and 1990s. These statutes gave the managers of companies incorpo-rated in those states permission, or in a few cases, a duty, to consider a range of stakeholders when making corporate decisions.[7] This was widely expected to increase agency costs as corporate fiduciaries were no longer legally obliged to maximize shareholder returns.[8] In particular, by increasing the number of objects of the fiduciary duty, academics making use of agency cost theory predicted major increases in managerial self-dealing and shirking, as virtually any corporate action could be defended as advancing the interest of some constituency. A duty to every-body is, in fact, a duty to nobody, so the effect of constituency statutes was essen-tially to remove a major aspect of the fiduciary duty from the lives of corporate executives.

However, the empirical literature on constituency statutes has pretty clearly found that when provided with the freedom to engage in the behaviors agency cost theory assumes are probable, managers remain faithful stewards of the firm – in particu-lar, the shareholders. First, managers don't take advantage of constituency statutes by transferring into more management-friendly jurisdictions.[9] Second, constituency statutes don't impact the rate of hostile takeovers in a jurisdiction.[10] Third, share-holders show little sign in their portfolio decisions that they expect management behavior to change when the fiduciary duty is altered to remove shareholders from their privileged position.[11] Finally, event studies found the adoption of constituency statutes either produced no effect on shareholder wealth or a very small impact (0.33 percent) that quickly dissipated.[12]

When the constituency statutes began being passed by various states, prominent corporate law professors, operating through an agency cost lens, predicted they would be "the most significant change in United States corporate law since the New Deal federal securities laws or even the enabling corporate codes of the [nineteenth] century" and they were "potentially revolutionary."[13] But by 2010, it was probably right to conclude that "it would seem that these statutes have not had a huge impact on commercial life in the US thus far, in fact they may be said to have no direct impact."[14] Academics who have studied the role constituency statutes play in the lit-igation that almost inevitably arises in connection with every merger and acquisition transaction in the United States have found "constituency statutes appear to have had minimal impact on the advice furnished to corporate boards."[15]

Freed from the most powerful legal restriction on their ability to act contrary to investors' interests, managers appear to consistently decline the invitation. However gratifying this must be to the owners of America's capital, it should generate sober reflection on the part of corporate governance reformers, particularly those who wish to displace investors as the exclusive object of managerial effort.

9.2.2 *Corporate Opportunity Waivers*

Another major change to fiduciary duties arose in 2000, when Delaware granted companies the right to waive the corporate opportunity doctrine – a central aspect of the traditional duty of loyalty to the corporation. These waivers facilitated overlapping directorships as well as resolving issues relating to allocating corporate opportunities between connected firms. Waivers did this by essentially relieving directors of their duty of undivided loyalty to the company in question. Other states followed Delaware's lead, and within fifteen years, more than 1,500 public companies had granted waivers.[16] That is a lot of companies choosing to contract out of a central element of the traditional fiduciary duty.

In a familiar pattern, a review of case law since Delaware's reforms shows that, "[t]he footprint of Delaware's statutory reform in case law and commentary has been surprisingly faint."[17] In fact, only one case has turned on the use of a corporate opportunity waiver.

The researchers found that the new laws were not disproportionately used by under-achieving firms using waivers as a pretext to divert value away from investors, but that waivers tended to be used by "relatively healthy companies with robust cash-flow potential and an established record of delivering attractive returns to their capital investors."[18] When they examined the impact on shareholder wealth at the time a corporate opportunity waiver was announced, they found a consistent positive abnormal return between 0.5 percent and 1.3 percent.[19] In other words, equity holders responded positively to the news that directors and officers were being granted the right to divide their loyalty to the shareholders, so they might instead privilege the interests of an entirely different firm. It is worth considering: why aren't shareholders worrying?

9.2.3 *Replacing a Duty to Shareholders with a Duty to Stakeholders*

The Supreme Court of Canada only rarely involves itself in corporate law. Corporate law is not really the Supreme Court of Canada's area of expertise, so these rare interventions often have the hold-your-breath tension that normally only accompanies the moment a ball is bouncing into place on a roulette wheel. Of course, Canada is not the United States (much to the mutual relief of both countries), but its corporate law and markets are broadly similar to those here. That makes the largest natural experiment in altering fiduciary duties relevant to American observers.

In 2008, a decision of the Supreme Court of Canada unilaterally and instantly changed the fiduciary duty in Canada from one that, like Delaware, was ultimately focused on maximizing shareholder wealth outcomes, to holding the duty applied to a wide range of corporate stakeholders, including the environment and taxing authority.[20] (The last elicits gasps of shock when communicated to certain American lawyers.) Securities regulation, legal transactional practice, and previous corporate law decisions had all made shareholders the principal recipients of the Canadian fiduciary duty. Then, suddenly, they weren't.

Canadian legal academics, viewing the 2008 Supreme Court of Canada decision through the same agency cost lenses that we saw in relation to the adoption of constituency statutes, predicted more or less the same things would occur: freed from a duty to a single group (shareholders), executives could be expected to engage in less disciplined and more self-interested behavior, safely confident that the legal fiduciary duty had been drained of nearly all its power.[21] Almost any corporate decision can be justified as advancing the interest of some constituency, so almost anything goes.

However, all those Canadian legal academics were wrong. The behavior of market actors didn't change.[22] Takeover premiums, which should have gone down as executives focused on things other than maximizing shareholder returns, instead increased significantly. The price-earnings ratio also increased. It should have gone down as shareholders priced the risk that managers would sacrifice shareholder interests for their own interests or that of some other constituency. The discount for new equity declined. For all intents and purposes, it appears that Canadian managers continued to run their companies in more or less the same way they had run those companies prior to the Supreme Court of Canada's decision to liberate corporate managers from shareholder primacy.

9.3 DIRECT EVIDENCE OF MANAGERIAL MOTIVATION

Studies that have as their direct object the investigation of whether managers are, in fact, motivated to be bad agents are surprisingly rare. As a recent paper noted, "the primacy of self-interest is also an empirical claim…. Direct testing of this assumption is notably absent in our literature, even though existing literature in accounting and elsewhere indirectly raises significant questions about the validity of the assumption of strictly self-interested behavior."[23] The authors of this paper go on to cite several studies that found managerial self-interest was constrained by ethical considerations[24] and considerations of fairness to others.[25] There is evidence visible throughout the vast literature on corporate governance that managers care about shareholder value and sacrifice to achieve it.[26] (Indeed, the revolution in corporate governance – restructuring boards and increasing the power of shareholders – has often been implemented with the cooperation of corporate managers themselves.)

When we look at the ways managers use cash, we find, in relation to windfalls such as those provided by recent American corporate tax reforms, that managers return that money to shareholders rather than wasting or diverting it.[27] As well, when directors obtain some measure of freedom from shareholder oversight, investments in things like R&D go up instead of compensation.[28] As J. B. Heaton, a prolific finance scholar and hedge fund manager, recently observes, "[d]espite its influence, more than forty years of active research have yet to uncover any good evidence that managers are systematically disloyal."[29] He goes on to point out something that is familiar to everyone who actually works with corporate managers: "[t]he notion of corporate directors and managers looking for every self-serving opportunity to shirk their duties … strikes directors, officers, and their professional advisors, like bankers and lawyers, as flatly untrue."[30]

When boards, themselves, are asked about their firms' dedication to maximizing value, they clearly believe they are faithful agents.[31] This is why support for various agency theory-inflected "best practices" is generally dismissed by corporate directors as unimportant.[32] As we have seen, this cannot be dismissed as a manifestation of self-interest; the preponderance of evidence is that directors are correct in their assessment of the merits of these practices. Could they also be correct in their assessment that the directors and managers they work with closely over many years are faithful agents?

9.4 WHAT EXPLAINS THE FAILURES OF CORPORATE GOVERNANCE'S ASSUMPTIONS ABOUT MANAGERS?

Most professionals genuinely like the corporate managers with whom they work. These managers seem honest and sincerely motivated to do their best for the corporations they manage. This is obviously not true of every corporate manager, but the exceptions tend to stick out simply because they are exceptions. If you want proof of this, invite any professional familiar with business executives, perhaps a corporate lawyer or accountant, to watch any movie that purports to deal with real-life boardroom behavior. Does the professional scoff at Hollywood's depiction of dastardly business executives? Yes. Yes, they do.

9.4.1 *Explanation #1: Managers and Directors Are Basically Trustworthy*

Corporate governance's cartoonish version of corporate managers is wrong for some obvious reasons. Behavioral scientists have repeatedly found prosocial behavior in the participants of their various experiments.[33] These experiments have uncovered large, consistent deviations from the self-interest predicted by narrow economic models of human behavior.[34]

Hundreds of experiments in dozens of countries, using a variety of game structures and experimental protocols, have suggested that in addition to their own material payoffs, [participants] care about fairness and reciprocity and will sacrifice their own gains to change the distribution of material outcomes among others, sometimes rewarding those who act prosocially and punishing those who do not.[35]

Indeed, there are many scientists who conclude, along with the famous social science scholar James Q. Wilson, "on balance, I think other-regarding features of human nature outweigh the self-regarding ones."[36]

Business involves working cooperatively with other people to accomplish shared aims. This is an environment that over the length of a professional career tends to reward prosocial behavior. Most people who are not fundamentally trustworthy eventually get that reputation, and then are either not promoted or find it difficult to attract high-quality people (the kind of people with employment options) to join them in various projects. (Bad actors also usually do not get invited onto boards of directors, an institution that works by consensus and cooperation.) Max Weber noted that "along with clarity of vision and ability to act, it is only by virtue of very definite and highly developed ethical qualities that it has been possible for [a modern entrepreneur] to command the absolutely indispensable confidence of his customers and workmen."[37]

Historians observe changes in moral behavior that occurred around the time modern large-scale businesses began to be formed. The historian Thomas Haskell notes,

Conscience and promise keeping emerged in human history, of course, long before capitalism ... it was not until the eighteenth century, in Western Europe, England, and North America, that societies first appeared whose economic systems depended on the expectation that most people, most of the time, were sufficiently conscience-ridden (and certain of retribution) that they could be trusted to keep their promises.[38]

In his impressive book, *The Moral Foundation of Economic Behavior*, David Rose convincingly argues that large-scale economic activity (of the sort performed by widely-held corporations, for example) can only exist in places where economic actors can be trusted not to act in self-interested ways when the opportunity arises.[39] Rose points out that modern businesses depend on discretion being delegated and exercised by employees with highly specialized, local knowledge.[40] Other interested parties, including managers, customers, and shareholders, have a limited ability to observe these business actors' behavior or even to second-guess those decisions that come to their attention. The law is useless to prevent opportunistic behavior in these circumstances, as most potential violations of trust are invisible, incalculable, and unprovable.[41] Unless market actors consistently reject the ubiquitous opportunities to engage in small and invisible acts of shirking or self-enrichment, large-scale commerce will collapse. Only widely practiced moral integrity of a particular kind can generate the levels of social trust needed for economic activity on a large scale among strangers.

Of course, there are exceptions to this rosy picture of business managers, but they are exceptions, not the rule. Indeed, when social scientists actually test the relative prosocial orientation of business executives against other populations, they find, for example, that executives show more trust (and are more trustworthy) than undergraduate students.[42] (I am the proud father of several undergraduate students, and this experiment may admittedly be setting the bar too low.)

It is not necessary, however, to accept the prevalence of integrity and trustworthiness among businesspersons. You can retain the view that, contrary to all evidence and common sense, business executives are, in the immortal words of Matt Taibbi (describing Goldman Sachs), "a great vampire squid wrapped around the face of humanity, relentlessly jamming its blood funnel into anything that smells like money."[43] Even if you believe this, however, you still must account for the seas in which those vampire squids swim.

9.4.2 *Explanation #2: Behavioral Constraints Imposed by Markets*

Business corporations compete in markets. We have already observed that modern corporate governance generally doesn't concern itself with this fact, but this doesn't mean that markets don't exist. Indeed, the reason the corporate governance world seems a little inessential to business actors is that it has very little to do with their central preoccupations. ("Preoccupations" in this case is just a fancy word for "what they spend *all* their time on when at work.") Obviously, most corporate actors' attention and anxiety are focused on the firm's competitive activities in various markets.[44] This is why responsibility for "corporate governance" disclosure and verifying-the-boxes-have-been-checked is usually delegated to someone sitting off in a corner of the organization chart with very few direct reports.

It seems likely that markets impose pressures that constrain managerial behavior in ways that seldom permit the "negligence and profusion" expected by the agency cost story. Said another way, markets prevent the sort of "slack" that would permit executives – even if they were so-minded – to deviate from working hard to maximize firm profits. In fact, there are studies that find that even when slack resources exist, and are used for stakeholder-focused investments, the accounting returns are positive, suggesting managers are nearly always focused on the bottom line, even when they are ostensibly free to do something else.[45]

In a perfectly competitive market, no corporation can voluntarily increase its costs and remain in business if its competitors do not act similarly. In such a market, the price of goods sold is identical to their cost (which includes, of course, the cost of executive compensation). In this sort of market, we would not expect managers to be able to pay themselves materially more for any length of time.

Of course, markets are not perfectly competitive. How closely do our largest American firms approach the ideal of perfect competition? According to one poll, a random selection of American adults thought corporations made an average

36 percent profit as a percentage of sales after taxes.[46] If that number were true, it would mean most companies do not confront particularly competitive product markets and, as a result, there is ample room for managers to engage in making dumb or unprofitable decisions. Unfortunately, the reality is that public companies make much less. In 2019 (the last full year without Covid), US nonfinancial companies averaged a 6.35 percent pre-tax net margin on sales.[47] Out of this profit margin must come taxes and the cost of capital.[48]

How much of the average American firm's profit margin was left after all costs (including capital and taxes) were paid? This is a surprisingly difficult question to answer because we don't have good *ex ante* evidence for the cost of capital.[49] Professors Fama and French, looking at the period between 1950 and 1996, believe that American businesses realized an average 1.43 percent "profit" over all firm costs.[50] Using the same methodology, another set of researchers found that between 1996 and 2005, nontechnology companies generated returns over their costs of 1.39 percent.[51] (Technology firms generated 3.44 percent returns, but these were driven by the fact that for three years during the dot-com boom, technology firms' cost of capital was actually negative.[52]) Using a different methodology, another scholar has estimated that for the first seven years of the 1990s, average corporate returns fell below their marginal costs and barely broke even for the next seven years.[53]

The difficulty of achieving profits over costs is most visible in research that looks at the equity risk premium generated by US stocks over the twentieth century. The equity risk premium is the amount a share returns to its holder over the amount that holder would have received if they had simply invested their money in US government bonds, generally regarded as the safest investment possible. A recent study finds that the entire equity premium generated by companies in US stock markets since 1926 has been produced by only 4 percent of those companies.[54] Every other company – 96 percent of them – failed to generate returns over the risk-free rate and thus failed to meet the cost of their equity.

The problems in estimating the cost of capital raise questions about the precision of these sorts of studies, but they clearly suggest the average American company is not earning significant returns over its costs. Along with the low net margin on sales, this suggests, in turn, that American firms find themselves embedded in competitive markets that generally resemble the ones assumed by economic theory. We would, therefore, expect little scope for negligent or diversionary behavior on the part of the average firm.

The scope for these "bad" expenditures appears even narrower if we consider that a firm earning only a couple of percentage points above its costs is not going to feel like it has the freedom to introduce significant inefficiencies into its business. Business markets are volatile as a result of innovation, new entrants, shifts in consumer sentiment, or changes to the macroeconomic environment. A prudent regard for the future will therefore encourage corporate managers to operate as efficiently as they are able. There is no point in introducing long-term deviations from maximizing market efficiency if, in so doing, the firm itself will fail because of a slight change in its markets over the coming years. The repeated bailouts required by the US auto industry provide notable examples of the way generous behavior towards employee pay made under one set of market conditions can threaten a firm's continuing existence when those conditions change.

If the average American firm is embedded in competitive markets, what about those corporations (like Facebook, Alphabet [the parent of Google], and Apple) that have significantly above-average net profit margins?

Even though these sorts of companies seem like they will occupy a permanent commanding position in our economy, few individuals in boardrooms think this way. Back in 1964, the average tenure of companies on the S&P 500 was thirty-three years. That narrowed to twenty-four years by 2016, and according to one study, is expected to shrink to twelve years before the end of this decade.[55] An astonishing 76 percent of the companies that formed part of the UK FTSE 100 have disappeared in the last thirty years.[56] Another study looking at all 29,688 companies that listed on US public markets between 1960 and 2009 found that companies that listed before 1970 had a 92 percent chance of surviving the next five years, whereas companies that listed after 2000 had only a 63 percent chance of surviving that long, even when the authors controlled for the financial crisis and dot-com recession.[57] This trend is particularly driven by tech companies since they don't have the barriers to disruptive competition provided by extensive physical assets.[58] (Note that these papers look only at the most successful companies, the ones that make it to an IPO. The US Bureau of Labor Statistics finds 75 percent of all businesses fail in less than fifteen years.[59]) Directors are well aware that successful companies can be left behind; there is thus an always well-founded paranoia that will work against deliberately inefficient investments of the sort that worries modern governance reformers.

The second obstacle to even an unusually successful company spending money recklessly or self-interestedly arises from its embeddedness in financial markets. To the extent a firm's income is reduced by negligent or self-interested expenditures, the share price will decline until the shares provide the market rate of return on investments with a similar risk profile.[60] This means: (1) as the shares decline, some shareholders may object to the misuse of corporate resources and vote against the board accordingly; (2) the close tie between corporate managers' remuneration and equity prices will lead to declines in executive pay, possibly leading to departures of the most valuable employees; (3) activist shareholders and potential acquirors will note that the shares are undervalued relative to the profit-making potential of the business, taking action to displace the board; and (4) the company's cost of capital will increase to take into account that corporate revenues are being used in nonremunerative ways. It is not likely that boards will find these consequences appealing.

Of course, there are transaction costs associated with things like finding another job, proxy fights, and takeovers. Provided a company keeps its negligent and self-interested expenditures below these transaction costs, it may not suffer adverse consequences. There are a couple of problems, however. The first is that the transaction costs we are talking about are actually quite low – almost nonexistent in the case of shareholder voting – and currently around $11 million for activist campaigns and takeovers.[61] The second problem is that these transaction costs are paid only once, while the monies lost to a business boondoggle, such as hiring too many staff, usually recur every year, so the transaction costs will have to be further discounted. The third problem is that the profits to be made by share-holders, activists, and acquirors who eliminate this nonsense can be very high, particularly when leverage is applied. What all this means is that the size of dumb expenditures even a very successful company can get away with is minimal, at least theoretically.

The most obvious objection that can be made to this picture of executives virtu-ously constrained by market pressures to pursue wealth maximization is that some of the things governance reformers worry about are too small to significantly impair a firm's competitive position. The best example of such a "bad" expenditure would be excessively high CEO compensation. You can't get away with overpaying your senior managers in a small company, in which cash flows and investor sentiment are a matter of life or death, but in the biggest companies in America's public markets, probably the difference between "reasonable" and "excessive" pay packages is not going to be particularly affected by the kinds of product market pressures we have been discussing.

There are markets, though, that we have not discussed that might, in theory any-way, operate to constrain executive compensation. There is a labor market for senior executives that should generally tie an executive's pay to their marginal value to a company. As well, there is, for want of a better term, a "governance" market made up of investors, employees, and other parties that can withhold support from com-panies with a CEO abusing their position.

It would be reasonable to ask why these labor and governance markets failed to constrain the enormous rise in executive compensation over the past three decades. This is where the discussion in Chapter 4 about the origin of the recent explosion in executive compensation becomes relevant. In Chapter 4, we discovered that the best evidence we have is that the vast pay increases were the natural result of firms adopting the pay practices forced on them by the united voices of the governance industry, including the largest institutional investors in the country. In other words, something intruded into the market that had historically generated executive com-pensation outcomes.

This intrusion affected all companies at more or less the same time and displaced the usual market processes of bargaining, innovation, and individualized firm- and person-specific deals. These were replaced by a one-size-fits-all solution to executive compensation. The result was, as we saw in Chapter 4, that companies all changed how they compensated their executives in ways that led to a rise in executive pay. The labor market for senior managers didn't disappear, but it was rendered much less relevant as companies added share grants, stock options, and performance incentives to often already existing (and more modest) pay arrangements.

At the same time, the most obvious counterparties in the market for executive compensation – boards and investors – were the very ones urging the adoption of these new compensation strategies. Executives weren't going to suddenly start negotiating against themselves. As the book will discuss at greater length in Chapter 10, the activities that we associate with markets, such as bargaining and innovation, must often be cultivated. It is very easy for private and public actors to discourage them.

9.5 SUMMARY

Whatever explanation we choose, the empirical evidence is that managers tend not to shirk their responsibilities to maximize corporate profits. They simply don't consistently behave like the narrowly self-interested utility maximizers assumed by popular versions of the agency cost story. It doesn't ultimately matter for our purposes whether the data is best explained by executives being motivated by prosocial considerations, or reputational considerations, or whether executives are constrained by various market pressures. The assumption that executives are always and everywhere badly warped timber doesn't seem true enough to serve as the base of the governance edifice we have constructed.

Looking for evidence of systemic executive malfeasance in the empirical literature on corporate governance is disorienting. At first, one feels, like Charlie Brown, that there is a chance a governance best practice will succeed in kicking the football through the uprights. As one gets deeper, one begins to feel a certain inevitability that the ball will be pulled away at the last minute. Eventually, one begins to doubt the existence of football. The final stage is when one realizes that what is actually going on is a game of soccer. That is the stage described in this chapter.

NOTES

1 Immanuel Kant, "Idee zu einer allgemeinen Geschichte in weltbürgerlicher Absicht" (1784) [Idea for a Universal History with a Cosmopolitan Purpose] in *Schriften zur Anthropologie, Geschichtsphilosophie, Politik und Pädagogik* (Darmstadt, Germany: Wissenschaftliche Buchgesellschaft, 1964), pp. 33–50.
2 Adam Smith, *An Inquiry into the Nature and Causes of the Wealth of Nations* (London: W. Strahan and T. Cadell, 1776) at p. 324.
3 Eugene F. Fama and Merton H. Miller, *The Theory of Finance* (New York: Holt Rhinehart & Winston, 1972) at p. 75.
4 J. A. C. Hetherington, "When the Sleeper Awakes: Reflections on Corporate Governance and Shareholder Rights" (1979) 8:1 *Hofstra Law Review* 183–255 at 187.
5 Melvin Aron Eisenberg, *The Structure of the Corporation: A Legal Analysis* (Washington, DC: Beard Books, 1976) at p. 162.
6 See for example, Brian R. Cheffins, *The Public Company Transformed* (New York: Oxford University Press, 2018) at pp. 101–154.

7   Andrew Keay, "Moving Towards Stakeholderism? Constituency Statutes, Enlightened Shareholder Value, and all that: Much Ado About Little" (2011) 22:1 *European Business Law Review* 1–50 at 8 [Keay, "Towards Stakeholderism"].

8   Roberta Romano, "A Guide to Takeovers: Theory, Evidence, and Regulation" (1992) 9:1 *Yale Journal on Regulation* 119–180 at 172.

9   Christopher Geczy et al., "Institutional Investing When Shareholders Are Not Supreme" (2015) 5:1 *Harvard Business Law Review* 73–139 at 119 [Geczy et al., "Shareholders Not Supreme"].

10 Matthew D. Cain, Stephen B. McKeon and Steven Davidoff Solomon, "Do Takeover Laws Matter? Evidence from Five Decades of Hostile Takeovers" (2017) 124:3 *Journal of Financial Economics* 464–485 at 476.

11 Geczy et al., "Shareholders Not Supreme," above at note 9.

12 Roberta Romano, "Comment: What is the Value of Other Constituency Statutes to Shareholders?" (1993) 43:3 *The University of Toronto Law Journal* 533–542 at 542; John C. Alexander, Michael F. Spivey and M. Wayne Marr, "Nonshareholder Constituency Statutes and Shareholder Wealth: A Note" (1997) 21:3 *Journal of Banking and Finance* 417–432 at 426.

13 Stephen M. Bainbridge, "Interpreting Nonshareholder Constituency Statutes" (1992) 19:3 *Pepperdine Law Review* 971–1026 at 973; Jonathan R. Macey, "An Economic Analysis of The Various Rationales for Making Shareholders the Exclusive Beneficiaries of Corporate Fiduciary Duties" (1991) 21:1 *Stetson Law Review* 23–44 at 32; Frank H. Easterbrook and Daniel R. Fischel, *The Economic Structure of Corporate Law* (Cambridge: Harvard University Press, 1991); Oliver Hart, "An Economist's View of Fiduciary Duty" (1993) 43:3 *University of Toronto Law Journal* 299–314 at 303. See also, ABA Committee on Corporate Laws, "Other Constituencies Statutes: Potential for Confusion" (1989) 45:4 *Business Lawyer (ABA)* 2253–2272 at 2269; Bryce C. Tingle and Eldon Spackman, "Do Corporate Fiduciary Duties Matter?" (2019) 4:4 *Annals of Corporate Governance* 272–326 at 296–297 [Tingle and Spackman, "Fiduciary Duties"].

14 Keay, "Towards Stakeholderism," above at note 7 at 18 citing Thomas W. Dunfee, "Corporate Governance in a Market with Morality" (1999) 62:3 *Law and Contemporary Problems* 129–157 at 136. See also, Julian Velasco, "The Fundamental Rights of the Shareholder" (2006–2007) 40:2 *UC Davis Law Review* 407–468 at 463.

15 Robb S. Davids, "Constituency Statutes: An Appropriate Vehicle for Addressing Transition Costs?" (1994) 28:1 *Columbia Law Journal* 145–202 at 148.

16 Gabriel Rauterberg and Eric Talley, "Contracting Out of the Fiduciary Duty of Loyalty: An Empirical Analysis of Corporate Opportunity Waivers" (2017) 117:5 *Columbia Law Review* 1075–1152.

17 *Ibid* at 1098.

18 *Ibid* at 1132.

19 *Ibid* at 1134.

20 *BCE Inc. v. 1976 Debentureholders*, 2008 SCC 69.

21 Tingle and Spackman, "Fiduciary Duties," above at note 13 at 296.

22 *Ibid*.

23 Jeffrey R. Cohen and Lori L. Holder-Webb, "Rethinking the Influence of Agency Theory in the Accounting Academy" (2006) 21:1 *Issues in Accounting Education* 17–30 at 23.

24 Douglas Stevens, "The Effect of Reputation and Ethics on Budgetary Slack" (2002) 14:1 *Journal of Management Accounting Research* 153–171; John H. Evans et al., "Honesty in Managerial Reporting" (2001) 76:4 *The Accounting Review* 537–559; Robert W. Rutledge and Khondkar E. Karim, "The Influence of Self-interest and Ethical Considerations on

Managers' Evaluation Judgments" (1999) 24:2 *Accounting, Organizations and Society* 173–184 at 181–182. See also, Patrice Gélinas and Lisa Baillargeon, "CEO Perquisites in Canada, 1971–2008: Certainly Not 'Pure' Managerial Excess" (2018) 13:5 *International Journal of Business and Management* 105–122.

25 Lori Holder-Webb et al., "The Effect of Perceived Fairness on the Agency Problem" (2004) (Presented at the American Accounting Association Annual Meeting, Orlando, FL); Theresa Libby, "Referent Cognitions and Budgetary Fairness: A Research Note" (2001) 13:1 *Journal of Management of Accounting Research* 91–105.

26 See for example, Vincente Cuñat, Yiqing Lü and Hong Wu, "Managerial Response to Shareholder Empowerment: Evidence from Majority Voting Legislation Changes" (2019), *European Corporate Governance Institute – Finance Working Paper No. 622/2019*, online: SSRN, https://ssrn.com/abstract=3219188 at 5; Douglas Cummings, Bryce C. Tingle and Feng Zhan, "For Whom (and For When) is the Firm Governed? The Effect of Changes in Corporate Fiduciary Duties on Tax Strategies and Earnings Management" (2021) 27:5 *European Financial Management* 755–813.

27 Dhammika Dharmapala, C. Fritz Foley and Kristin J. Forbes, "Watch What I Do, Not What I Say: The Unintended Consequences of the Homeland Investment Act" (2011) 66:3 *The Journal of Finance* 753–787.

28 Caroline Flammer and Aleksandra J. Kacperczyk, "The Impact of Stakeholder Orientation on Innovation: Evidence from a Natural Experiment" (2016) 62:7 *Management Science* 1982–2001; Robert Daines, Shelley Xin Li and Charles C. Y. Wang, "Can Staggered Boards Improve Value? Causal Evidence from Massachusetts" (2021) 38:4 *Contemporary Accounting Research* 3053–3084 at 3053.

29 J. B. Heaton, "Corporate Governance and the Cult of Agency" (2019) 64:2 *Villanova Law Review* 201–222 at 214.

30 *Ibid* at 216–217.

31 *Ibid* at 206; Steven Boivie et al., "Corporate Directors' Implicit Theories of the Roles and Duties of Boards" (2021) 42:9 *Strategic Management Journal* 1662–1695.

32 See, for example, *What Matters in The Boardroom? Director and Investor Views on Trends Shaping Governance and the Board of the Future*, PricewaterhouseCoopers International Limited (2014), online (pdf): www.pwc.pl/pl/pdf/forum-rad-nadzorczych/pwc-what-matters-in-the-boardroom-director-investor-views.pdf; *The Swinging Pendulum: Board Governance in the Age of Shareholder Empowerment – PwC's 2016 Annual Corporate Directors Survey*, PricewaterhouseCoopers International Limited (October 2016), online (pdf): www.pwc.com/us/en/corporate-governance/annual-corporate-directors-survey/assets/pwc-2016-annual-corporate-directors-survey.pdf; Silvia Ascarelli, "Corporate Europe Is Skeptical About Tougher Governance Codes," The Wall Street Journal, October 7, 2004, online: www.wsj.com/articles/SB109710683845238701; Beckey Bright, "Investors Are Skeptical of Success of Sarbanes-Oxley, Poll Finds," *The Wall Street Journal*, October 14, 2005, online: www.wsj.com/articles/SB112912865268466716.

33 See, for example, Colin F. Camerer and Richard H. Thaler, "Anomalies: Ultimatums, Dictators and Manners" (1995) 9:2 *Journal of Economic Perspectives* 209–219; Lynn Stout, *Cultivating Conscience: How Good Laws Make Good People* (Princeton: Princeton University Press, 2010) [Stout, *Cultivating Conscience*].

34 Deirdre Nansen McCloskey, *The Bourgeois Virtues: Ethics for an Age of Commerce* (Chicago: The University of Chicago Press, 2006) (quoting Vernon Smith, "laboratory experiments also support reciprocity in two person extensive form games under very unfavorable conditions in which we give the self-interest its best shot: *complete anonymity*" at 128 [emphasis in original]); Colin F. Camerer, *Behavioral Game Theory: Experiments in*

Strategic Interaction (Princeton, USA: Princeton University Press, 2003); Ernst Fehr and
Simon Gächter, "Altruistic Punishment in Humans" (2007) 415:6868 *Nature* 137–140;
Elizabeth Hoffman, Kevin A. McCabe and Vernon L. Smith, "Behavioral Foundations
of Reciprocity: Experimental Economics and Evolutionary Psychology" (1998) 36:3
Economic Inquiry 335–352.

35 Joesph Henrich et al., "Economic Man in Cross-Cultural Perspective: Behavioral
Experiments in 15 Small-Scale Societies" (2005) 28:6 *Behavioral and Brain Sciences*
795–815 at 797; See also, Robert B. Chaldini, Carl A. Kallgren and Raymond R. Reno,
"A Focus Theory of Normative Conduct: A Theoretical Refinement and Reevaluation
of the Role of Norms in Human Behavior" (1991) 24 *Advances in Experimental Social
Psychology* 201–234; Vernon L. Smith and Bart J. Wilson, *Humanomics: Moral Sentiments
and the Wealth of Nations for the Twenty-First Century* (Cambridge, UK: Cambridge
University Press, 2019).

36 Quoted in Robert H. Nelson, *Economics as Religion: From Samuelson to Chicago and
Beyond* (University Park: Pennsylvania State University Press, 2001) at p. 8. See also, James
Q. Wilson, *The Moral Sense* (New York: Free Press, 1993); Amartya Sen, "Foreword"
in Avner Ben-Her and Louis Putterman (eds.), *Economics, Values, and Organization*
(Cambridge, UK: Cambridge University Press, 1998) at viii; C. Daniel Batson, *Altruism
in Humans* (New York: Oxford University Press, Inc., 2011); Avney Ben-Ner and Louis
Putterman, "Values and Institutions in Economic Analysis" in Avner Ben-Her and Louis
Putterman (eds.), *Economics, Values, and Organization* (Cambridge, UK: Cambridge
University Press, 1998) at p. 7. See also, Stout, *Cultivating Conscience* above at note 33.

37 Max Weber, translated by Talcott Parsons, *The Protestant Ethic and the Spirit of
Capitalism* (New York: Charles Scribner's Sons, 1958) at p. 69; See also, Charles Taylor,
The Explanation of Behaviour (New York: Routledge & Kegan Paul, 1964); Charles
Taylor, "The Politics of Recognition" in Amy Gutmann (ed.), *Multiculturalism and the
Politics of Recognition* (Princeton: Princeton University Press, 1994).

38 Thomas L. Haskell, "Capitalism and the Origins of the Humanitarian Sensibility, Part 2"
(1985) 90:3 *The American Historical Review* 547–566 at 553.

39 David C. Rose, *The Moral Foundation of Economic Behavior* (New York: Oxford
University Press, 2011). See also, the research discussed in Quentin Dupont and Jonathan
M. Karpoff, "The Trust Triangle: Laws, Reputation, and Culture in Empirical Finance
Research" (2020) 163:2 *Journal of Business Ethics* 217–238.

40 See also, Frederick A. Hayek, "The Use of Knowledge in Society" in Paul S. Myers (ed.),
Knowledge Management and Organizational Design (London: Routledge, 1996) at pp.
7–15.

41 Stewart Macauley, "Non-contractual Relations in Business: A Preliminary Study" (1963)
28:1 *American Sociological Review* 55–67 at 65.

42 Ernst Fehr and John A. List, "The Hidden Costs and Returns of Incentives – Trust and
Trustworthiness among CEOs" (2004) 2:5 *Journal of the European Economic Association*
743–771.

43 Matt Taibbi, "The Great American Bubble Machine," *Rolling Stone*, April 5, 2010,
online: www.rollingstone.com/politics/politics-news/the-great-american-bubble-
machine-195229/.

44 See Bryce C. Tingle, "Returning Markets to the Center of Corporate Law" (2023) 48:4
Journal of Corporation Law 663–718.

45 James E. Mattingly and Lori Olsen, "Performance Outcomes of Investing Slack Resources
in Corporate Social Responsibility" (2018) 25:4 *Journal of Leadership and Organizational
Studies* 481–498. See also, Bryce C. Tingle, "The Limits of Corporate Governance in
Contributing Solutions to Social and Environmental Problems" (forthcoming).

46 Reason-Rupe Public Opinion Survey, *May 2013 Topline Results*, Scribd (May 17, 2013), online: www.scribd.com/document/166175880/Reason-Rupe-Poll-May-2013-Toplines.

47 *Data: Archives*, Damodaran, online: http://pages.stern.nyu.edu/~adamodar/New_Home_Page/dataarchived.html ("operating and net margins by industry 1/20").

48 *Ibid* ("cost of capital by industry 1/20" estimating the cost of capital in 2019 to be 6.90 percent with the cost of equity 8.21 percent).

49 See, for example, Edwin J. Elton, "Presidential Address: Expected Return, Realized Return, and Asset Pricing Tests" (1999) 54:4 *The Journal of Finance* 1199–1220.

50 Eugene F. Fama and Kenneth R. French, "The Corporate Cost of Capital and the Return on Corporate Investment" (1999) 54:6 *The Journal of Finance* 1939–1967 at 1940.

51 Michael J. Alderson and Brian L. Betker, "Additional Evidence on the Corporate Cost of Capital and the Return to Corporate Investment" (2009) 19:1/2 *Journal of Applied Finance* 91–102 at 97.

52 *Ibid.*

53 Gerard T. Olson and Michael S. Pagano, "The Empirical Average Cost of Capital" (2020), *Villanova School of Business Working Paper*, online: SSRN, https://ssrn.com/abstract=348800 at 4.

54 Hendrik Bessembinder, "Do Stocks Outperform Treasury Bills?" (2018) 129:3 *Journal of Financial Economics* 440–457.

55 Scott D. Anthony et al., *2018 Corporate Longevity Forecast: Creative Destruction is Accelerating*, Innosight (February 2018), online (pdf): www.innosight.com/wp-content/uploads/2017/11/Innosight-Corporate-Longevity-2018.pdf at 2.

56 Alex Hill, Liz Mellon and Jules Goddard, "How Winning Organizations Last 100 Years" (September 27, 2018), *Harvard Business Review*, online: https://hbr.org/2018/09/how-winning-organizations-last-100-years.

57 Vijay Govindarajan and Anup Srivastava, "Strategy When Creative Destruction Accelerates" (2016), *Tuck School of Business Working Paper No. 2836135*, online: SSRN, https://ssrn.com/abstract=2836135. See also, Dane Stangler and Sam Arbesman, *What Does Fortune 500 Turnover Mean?*, Ewing Marion Kauffman Foundation (June 2012), online (pdf): www.kauffman.org/wp-content/uploads/2012/06/fortune_500_turnover.pdf.

58 Patrick George, "The Scary Trust about Corporate Survival" (December 2016), *Harvard Business Review*, online: https://hbr.org/2016/12/the-scary-truth-about-corporate-survival.

59 Table 7, *Survival of Private Sector Establishments by Opening Year*, US Bureau of Labor Statistics, online: www.bls.gov/bdm/us_age_naics_00_table7.txt.

60 Eugene F. Fama, "Efficient Capital Markets: A Review of Theory and Empirical Work" (1970) 25:2 *The Journal of Finance* 383–417.

61 Nickolay M. Gantchev, "The Cost of Shareholder Activism: Evidence from a Sequential Decision Model," PhD thesis, University of Pennsylvania (Fall 2011) 442 *Publicly Accessible Penn Dissertations*; online: https://repository.upenn.edu/edissertations/442 at 2.

10

Markets and Corporate Governance

Chapter 9 considered several explanations for the evidence that managers are not systemically disloyal. It discussed a controversial claim: markets constrain agency costs even in the absence of things like majority-independent boards and increased shareholder power. In Chapter 4, we also saw how a market that had imposed a certain amount of discipline on executive compensation for forty years suddenly seemed to stop working once the corporate governance movement got started in the late 1980s and 1990s.

This argument will have struck many readers as "under-theorized" to quote my personal criticism of most superhero movies. What is "the market for corporate governance"? How can it be said to have been damaged, given the government still leaves most issues up to the private actors? What separates this book's analysis from the bromides about "free enterprise" familiar to anyone who has attended a local Chamber of Commerce event? All excellent questions.

10.1 WHAT DO WE MEAN BY MARKETS?

The term "markets," like most important words in our dystopian politics, can stand in as code for something else: "no government." For example, I cannot say I favor restoring small children with their nimble fingers to our proud nation's factories, but if I say I favor "markets," lots of people will know what I am talking about, while preserving plausible deniability when confronted by angry parents. I am not using the term "markets" in this way.

One of the reasons I am not using "markets" as a code word for "no government" is that I am a parent myself, and my experience with my children leads me to believe they don't have the work ethic to improve industrial output. The second reason is that no one who actually pays attention to how markets function thinks that large-scale modern markets work well without some measure of centralized authority, usually supplied by the government. If this were not the case, we would expect modern, large-scale, impersonal markets to flourish in places where the writ of government was unknown. But, instead, we generally see that the weaker the state and its regulatory apparatus, the weaker the markets in that country.[1] Somalia, which lacked a central government for fifteen years, and the tribal regions of Pakistan are not noted for the quality of their markets.

Large-scale impersonal markets are complex and sometimes delicate. They must attract a critical mass of those persons interested in buying or selling a commodity, they must be free of violent expropriation and other forms of predatory behavior, possess a means of efficiently settling disputes, provide disclosure incentives (and penalties) that permit price discovery, allow for experimentation and innovation, enforce bargains, and they must operate in predictable ways as most transactions reflect expectations about the future.[2]

Regardless of what a person might think about the role of government in large-scale modern markets, there can be no doubt that government is essential in the markets that involve corporations, and that is because corporations are artificial creations of statute. Without government, there would be no corporations.

It is more useful to look at market *activity* as a measure of market quality and health rather than the presence or absence of government regulation. Markets can be wrecked by private actors as well as by bad government regulation. Why else would we traditionally be concerned about monopolistic firms or predatory behavior by private actors? Markets, at least as I will be using the term in this book, aren't defined by the presence or absence of either government or private parties; they are defined by the presence of certain kinds of activities. The most important of these activities are experimentation, cooperation, competition, and firm-specific bargaining.[3] As we will see later in this chapter, these are the qualities of markets that corporate law in America traditionally attempted to foster.

10.2 WHAT IS THE GOVERNANCE MARKET?

The "governance market," as I intend to use the term, refers to the market activities that regulate the affairs of a business corporation. It forms the heart of corporate law and much of securities regulation. It exists because of the legal structure and competitive circumstances of business corporations.

The corporation is one of the most important things we have ever invented. Economic historians believe the invention of the corporation was one of the factors leading to the economic rise of Europe in the modern period; even now, the ease and cheapness of incorporating a business are used to predict the development path of countries.[4] Corporations are incredibly useful because they facilitate – even create – markets. That is what the "business" in "business corporations" means.

The modern corporation has several advantages when it comes to participating in markets: it is an entity that survives the death of a founder (unlike a traditional partnership); it permits the capital of many people to be pooled together; it allows risk to be shared rather than born by a few; it separates ownership and control in ways that permit investors unfamiliar with a business to entrust their money to experienced managers; it provides a sort of platform that can be used to assemble the talent and experience needed to conduct business; and it provides checks on managerial opportunism.

The separation of ownership and control, the transferability of shares, limited shareholder liability, and the development of disclosure mechanisms such as audits and a financial press, created markets for the ownership interest in businesses themselves. By serving as the locus of many different bargains, the corporation also created a unique market that produces governance outcomes.

The governance market allocates control over the business, sometimes in very fine-tuned ways, among the various constituencies that form around corporations. Economists often refer to these constituencies as the "productive coalition" that is necessary for a corporation to carry out its functions. This coalition includes employees, executives, directors, shareholders, creditors, customers, suppliers, business partners, and even more remote third parties like the communities in which a business operates and on whose goodwill a business might depend. Corporate governance is the way the company organizes itself, sets priorities, establishes culture, makes decisions, and allocates financial claims.

Many corporate governance discussions focus on just the three constituencies that possess formal power under corporate statutes: shareholders, directors, and officers. More adventurously, they might also include certain types of creditors, who derive their governance powers from the contracts governing the debt and from various insolvency regimes. But it is important to note that all of a corporation's constituencies can influence its governance. Their power over governance is a function of their power in the various markets in which they participate. The employees of some technology companies have demonstrated they have considerable power over whether, for example, a company like Alphabet pursues military contracts, operates in certain countries, or adopts diversity objectives in their hiring.[5] Tech workers are difficult to replace and tend to have more power in labor markets (signaled by the wages they are able to earn) than other types of employees, who find themselves with comparatively less influence over the direction of their employers.

The influence of corporate constituencies on the firm's norms, practices, structures, strategies, and personalities often occurs in informal ways. Creditors may not lend money if the corporation appears too willing to take on risk. Shareholders may sell their shares if the company loses the interest or ability to generate profits. Employees may choose to work elsewhere if the corporation seems like it will abandon them quickly whenever the occasion arises. Business partners and suppliers may not make informal firm-specific investments if they feel they can't trust the corporation to treat them fairly over the life of those investments. Customers abandon companies whose actions manifest contempt for their values. Senior executives won't join a corporation unless the governance environment allows them to pursue their vision or approach to business. Not just directors, but shareholders, employees, business partners, and even customers, get a say in whether a CEO keeps their job.

A CEO who creates problems with employees, or who can't close deals with important customers, is a CEO whose job is in jeopardy.

Who rises to the top, what they do there, how they are monitored and regulated, and their strategic options are all determined to a significant degree by the bargaining and decisions that make up the governance market. The market sets the terms on which various corporate constituencies will cooperate, whether they will enter the market, and how they will behave once there.[6] It is where new kinds of bargains for the firm – experiments – are tried out and either succeed or fail. It is the most important market in which corporations participate because it affects the corporation's behavior and success in all the other markets it joins.

Professor Gordon Smith is correct that "[p]ared to its core, 'corporate law' is the set of rules that defines the decision-making structure of corporations."[7] The "governance market" as I am defining it is the central preoccupation of corporate law.

10.3 A BRIEF HISTORY OF THE GOVERNANCE MARKET

During its nineteenth-century evolution, corporate law developed one of its dominant characteristics: protecting bargains. Bargains are the key element in market transactions. The bargains enforced by corporate law can be found embedded in the bylaws or articles of the corporation, they may appear in the disclosure issued by corporations, they may be found in various contracts, or they may merely exist in the unwritten "expectations" of counterparties. For example, before there were formal legislative rules governing the treatment of some constituencies, American courts created legal rules that protected the implied bargains found in their reasonable expectations. Creditors were protected by the "trust fund doctrine" originally formulated by a court in 1824, preventing shareholders from withdrawing capital unless the company was able to discharge its debts.[8] Employees' expectation of being paid was protected by creating an exception to corporate limited liability by imposing enforceable obligations on shareholders, personally, for unpaid wages.[9]

The making and keeping of bargains was facilitated by the increasing freedom awarded to directors to make decisions with very little interference from other constituencies.[10] Referring to the changes that began around 1880 to create the modern American corporation, Professor Vasudev notes the "shift of corporate powers from the shareholders to the directors."[11] This was accomplished by significantly reducing the matters shareholders were permitted to vote on, replacing a requirement for shareholder unanimity with a majority rule, permitting the creation of nonvoting shares and dual-class voting structures, removing fetters on issuing new shares, and providing directors with new areas over which they had complete discretion.

The independence of directors from other constituencies was important because it permitted corporations to make credible long-term bargains. Many commercial arrangements involving corporations are not reduced to formal written documents, either for reasons of cost, time, or to preserve flexibility.[12] One large manufacturing

company audited its records and found that 60–75 percent of the time it failed to enter
into formal contracts with its customers.[13] Each party apparently trusted the other to act
reasonably. The chief economist of Ford Motor Company noted that he "was surprised
to learn that Ford made billions of dollars of purchases a year through regular suppliers
over the telephone with only the skeleton of a contract and with few contract disputes."[14]
There is a vast literature on "incomplete" contracts (such as employment agreements)
where the relevant markets depend on the trustworthiness of counterparties rather than
the law or formalized covenants.[15] (Incidentally, this is all further evidence agency cost
theory's fears about corporate managers are considerably exaggerated.)

The trustworthiness found in markets is important because, as the Nobel prize-
winning economist Douglass North reminds us, "[e]ven in the modern western
world the costs of contract enforcement in a world characterized by the assumptions
of economic theory (where all the players maximize at every margin) would be
prohibitive."[16]

This network of bargains, social trust, and innovation is what the corporate governance market looked like for most of the twentieth century. For example, it took
innovation and creativity for the governance market to manage the rise of the large
modern public company, with its novel separation of ownership and control, in the
first decades of the century. The governance market also found itself required to
facilitate corporate adaptation to the unusual regulatory conditions of the Second
World War, the growth of international business in the post-war period, the brutal
conditions created by oil shocks and stagflation in the 1970s, the rise and then break-
up of conglomerates, the leveraged buy-out activity of the 1980s, the rise of foreign
challengers to American manufacturing in the final decades of the century, and
the growth to market dominance of professionally managed institutional shareholders. In fact, the twentieth century demanded considerable flexibility and innovation
from the governance market.

10.4 THE GOVERNANCE MARKET ON THE BRINK OF
THE CORPORATE GOVERNANCE REVOLUTION

One of the most famous textbooks ever written about corporate law is *The Economic
Structure of Corporate Law* by Professors Easterbrook and Fischel, published in
1991.[17] It is particularly useful to anyone interested in how the governance market
operated just as the governance industry was beginning to get traction on its favored
reforms. The textbook emphasizes the sheer range of alternatives then open to market actors in how they organized and ran widely held corporations. After noting that
the governance structures of different types of companies ought to be different, they
wrote, "[t]he best structure cannot be derived from theory; it must be developed
by experience."[18] They repeat this point several times: "[j]ust as there is no right
amount of paint in a car, there is no right relation among managers, investors, and
other corporate participants. The relation must be worked out one firm at a time."[19]

Markets can and should produce corporate governance: "[c]osts of knowing about a firm's governance are low. Firms and teams of managers can compete with each other over the decades to design governance structures and to build in penalties for malfeasance. There is no substantial impediment to the operation of the competitive process at the level of structure."[20]

Easterbrook and Fischel were engaged in a project, of course, so they were not merely reporting facts on the ground. But to persuade readers, their text had to describe a world that plausibly resembled the one those readers inhabited. In the era before the 1990s, there really was considerable heterogeneity in the way widely held firms were structured and run.[21] The governance market was a prominent fact. The lists of governance best practices proposed in 1992 by the UK's influential Cadbury Committee and eventually adopted throughout the English-speaking world over the next decade would not have been necessary if this heterogeneity hadn't existed.

10.5 THE INTELLECTUAL SHIFT FROM BARGAINS TO OUTCOMES

If modern science has taught us anything at all, it is that the Earth is supported on the back of an elephant, which in turn stands upon the back of the first of at least several stacked turtles. In much the same way, this book has focused on agency cost theory as a way of understanding the intellectual shift that led to the modern corporate governance system, but there was a deeper shift that was responsible for making the agency cost story more plausible in the first place. The elephant of agency cost theory rests firmly on the turtle of economic efficiency.

Ironically, the project of Easterbrook and Fischel was very much part of this deeper intellectual transition towards importing economic considerations into corporate law. However natural it might seem to us to focus on achieving certain outcomes, at the time it was occurring, economic approaches to law were highly controversial.[22] As we have seen, historically corporate law focused mostly on protecting the deals made by various corporate constituencies rather than attempting to generate particular outcomes like wealth maximization. The fancy Latin way of saying this is that the law cared about *ex ante* bargains, not the *ex post* results of those bargains.

Traditional corporate law is deeply concerned about fairness, expectations, and enforcing deals, which conflicts with the idea that the law ought to just maximize shareholder wealth. The goal of the dominant economics-inflected approach to corporate law is to arrive at rules that generate a state of "Pareto optimality," which means a state of wealth distribution in which you cannot make a change to any one person's wealth without making another person worse off. Pareto optimality is the only realistic thing we can hope for in the legal allocation of resources and rights, but it says nothing about how it is achieved.[23] It could be achieved by edict, expropriation, or fraud. It does not necessarily entail market activities.

The interminable corporate law debate around insider trading illustrates this point. On one side of the debate, economics-inflected scholars have pointed out the way permitting and incentivizing insiders to trade on information they alone possess would lead to more efficient price discovery.[24] It seems safe to say, however, that the law has criminalized insider trading because it seems unfair to other market actors.[25] In fact, to the extent policy outcomes drive legal decision-making in this area, it is a concern that market participation would decline if the law permitted some participants to take advantage of others.[26]

While market facilitation sits at the very center of corporate law, economic efficiency is a late arrival, often ignored in real-world legal arguments. Reviewing the origin and development of modern American corporate law, Professor Vasudev notes that "efficiency was not the starting point of the changes that occurred in corporate law beginning from the 1880s. Rather the efficiency argument was developed, ex post, to rationalize the libertarian state that corporate law attained."[27]

A good example of the point I am trying to make is provided by *Salomon v. Salomon*, arguably the most important English corporate law decision, because it upheld the idea that the corporation was a separate entity from its shareholders and managers, and that creditors of the corporation could look only to the corporation for redress in the event of a default on its debts. One obvious fact about the decision was that none of the judges in that case appeared to have believed that the result in that case was efficient.[28] In fact, they noted that it would create transaction costs, as now creditors must do the work of making inquiries about the solvency of a corporation rather than relying on the law to place their interests ahead of insiders.[29] The main point of the court was that bargains should be upheld and not subjected to *ex post* revision, whatever we might think of the result.[30] This kept the market activity of *ex ante* bargaining at the moral center of corporate law.

Interestingly, recent empirical research supports the traditional focus of corporate law on *ex ante* market conditions. Numerous behavioral economics experiments involving the interaction between individuals find that manipulating intentions or the context of participants' interactions (all market-related *ex ante* conditions) has a greater impact on their choices than varying payoffs.[31] The fact is that the conditions of the market appear to be more important than the *ex post* wealth incentives in generating behavioral outcomes.

10.6 PURSUING ECONOMIC OUTCOMES DISPLACES MARKETS

The central normative concept in economics is efficiency, in the sense of productive and allocative efficiency.[32] Efficient outcomes are wealth-maximizing outcomes, so when economics encountered corporate law, the focus of corporate law quickly became shareholder wealth maximization, to be achieved by driving out (to the extent possible) the inefficiencies that arise from the corporate form, particularly the separation of ownership and control.[33] This of course accounts for why agency cost theory arose when it did and why it became so universally popular.[34]

Markets obviously have something to do with efficiency, so naïve observers of corporate law could be forgiven for believing no conflicts exist between the two. Indeed, there is a generally held assumption among legal actors that economics-inflected approaches to corporate law "cumulatively tend to produce market institutions."[35] But whereas markets tend to produce efficient outcomes, a focus on efficiency often fails to produce markets.

As a normative ideal, economic efficiency provides ample reason for the law to intervene in markets. Inefficiencies in market processes can be produced by externalities, informational asymmetries, strategic behavior, laziness, irrationality, and the risk that market actors will bring competing moral priorities such as distributional equity to their decisions. Obviously, any market comprised of human beings will be characterized by some or all of these behaviors.

A particular problem for markets is the ubiquity of transaction costs. The economic approach to law often justifies legal interventions to eliminate transaction costs in order to advance the ideal of frictionless bargaining. This ideal was, and is, absurd. One study found that roughly 40 percent of the entire US economy consists of transaction costs.[36] The economist Stanley Fischer observes, "[t]ransaction costs have a well-deserved bad name as a theoretical device … [partly] because there is a suspicion that almost anything can be rationalized by invoking suitably specified transaction costs."[37] For example, defenders of proxy advisors often justify their activities by pointing out how advisory firms reduce the transaction costs that would otherwise result from individual shareholders addressing governance practices on a firm-by-firm basis. By now, it should be clear that this is like drinking poison to save a few dollars on your grocery bill.

The most famous law and economics theoretician, Richard Posner, argued that wherever low transaction costs and cooperative behavior were not met, the law could step in by "mimicking" the outcomes of a more frictionless market.[38] This is a recipe for much more law and much less market, regardless of how confident you are in our ability to "mimic" an institution whose principal value is its ability to produce outcomes reflecting vastly more information than any central authority could possess, and that also produces important social goods over and above its contributions to efficient outcomes.[39]

The great law and economics scholar Ronald Coase himself observed that "[a]lthough economists claim to study the working of the market, in modern economic theory the market itself has an even more shadowy role than the firm."[40] He also made the point this chapter is making: "In an economic theory which assumes that transaction costs are nonexistent, markets have no function to perform…. [W]hen economists do speak of market structure, it has nothing to do with the market as an institution."[41]

The Nobel Prize-winning economist Douglass North agreed, pointing out that notwithstanding the centrality of markets to economists' models, the actual institutional arrangements and incentives of the markets themselves are usually ignored:

"[T]he neo-classical paradigm is devoid of institutions, and pareto efficiency is meaningless when it comes to exploring different institutional structures and their implications for economic performance through time."[42]

The truth is that market behavior – with its messiness, mistakes, experimentation, disparate objectives and priorities, time- and resource-consuming bargaining, and many failures – does not appear efficient. It is here that the neoclassical economics blind spot about market activities creates problems because it lacks a theoretical framework for understanding what types of inefficiencies are important, even essential, to maintaining a market. When, in other words, should the law intervene?

The practice in much of corporate law scholarship and policy-making over the past forty years has been to indiscriminately propose interventions everywhere the author discovers inefficiencies (or "transaction costs" or "failures") in the market. As Ronald Gilson notes, the modern innovations in corporate law were motivated by "the hypothesis [that] better governance yields more efficient production."[43] Efficiency alone was a justification for reform.

This book has barely scraped the surface of the many governance reforms enacted over the past thirty years, but it should be clear at this point that we have experienced changes to the governance market that, as an observer noted, constitute "something like a hundred year flood of reform."[44] Corporate law's encounter with economics did not have to go this way. A concern for maximizing societal wealth could have manifested itself in skepticism about interfering with market processes. After all, it is widely accepted (especially by economists) that markets are an important part of generating the modern era's unprecedented level of wealth.[45] For whatever reason, however, the influence of wealth maximization norms on academics and regulators in corporate law was instead largely directed into debates around the various sorts of market interventions we have been discussing in this book.

10.7 BREAKING THE CORPORATE GOVERNANCE MARKET

These extensive interventions in the governance market could possibly be justified if the efficiency gains were sufficiently large to offset the social costs of curtailing the bargaining, experimentation, and compromise that would otherwise characterize corporate governance-related market behavior. However, as we have seen in this book, there is very little evidence of much efficiency gain from our governance practices. In every area, the results are so disappointing as to call into question the entire project. This result should not be slightly surprising to anyone familiar with the literature comparing market outcomes to centrally directed planning. In many cases, governance practices have been imposed on corporations even in the face of abundant prior empirical evidence that they were ineffective or harmful.[46]

Unlike mistakes arising out of market experiments, the flawed market interventions we are discussing affect all public firms and have persisted for a very long time. A highly regarded corporate law professor, Lynn Stout described the problem:

Rather than evolving naturally from the collective needs of those who have a long-term stake in the business world – entrepreneurs, executives, employees, creditors, and the majority of investors deciding whether or not to buy shares – the philosophy of shareholder primacy [and I would add every other aspect of the current governance regime] was an attempt at top-down "intelligent design" by a small cadre of academics and policy entrepreneurs.[47]

The inefficiencies or "market failures" targeted by these third-party reformers were, of course, the result of earlier market activity producing other sorts of bargains. For example, as we have seen in Chapter 2, beginning in the late 1970s, scholars began arguing that the presence of inside directors on boards was the result of failures in the market activity that produced corporate governance. They theorized that financial claim holders had (for various plausible reasons) failed to either recognize the advantages or advance the use of independent directors in firms. Managers had somehow broken the market for corporate governance as described by Easterbrook and Fischel, and the result was insufficiently independent boards doing a suboptimal job of monitoring management.

To remedy this market failure, stock exchanges, regulators, proxy advisors, and other members of the "governance industry" all worked over the next several decades to create boards dominated by independent directors. What happened following this revolution in the boardroom? As we have seen, nothing. Maybe worse than nothing.

So, it turns out the reformers were wrong. The market as it existed in the 1970s, producing significant numbers of inside directors, does not appear to have been the result of an obvious failure. Inside directors know the business better than other directors. They aren't solely reliant on the CEO for information about what is going on in the company. They are better able to evaluate the merits of the firm's technical R&D initiatives, they are more likely to spot problems with corporate strategy, and they are better connected to other actors in the firm's markets. Insiders are less likely to evaluate corporate performance solely on the basis of share price and they are less concerned with their reputation with the investor community. There are many reasons, therefore, why financial claim holders and the other important constituencies that form around a corporation might have preferred (or at least not objected to) large numbers of insiders on corporate boards.

Looking back, we see in the case of independent directors that academics and policymakers assumed, without much introspection, that they could improve upon the outcomes generated by the market. They ignored the fact that even imperfect markets tend to perform better than various academic models predict.[48]

10.8 EVIDENCE THAT THE GOVERNANCE MARKET IS BROKEN

So far, the conversation in this chapter has been mostly theoretical: market activities around corporate governance decisions used to exist to a greater degree than they do now, corporate law was about encouraging and facilitating the bargains that made up this market, and then under the influence of economic theory, we became much more interested in improving wealth outcomes. This in turn seemingly made interventions in the governance market irresistible. But how bad were these interventions really? Most governance practices were imposed by private actors, such as institutional asset managers and proxy advisors, and companies clearly retain considerable control over their businesses, even if their board processes and pay practices are effectively set elsewhere.

Modern markets are more fragile than most people think. For example, by the early eighteenth century, the British had created a well-functioning stock market that seems to have been roughly as efficient at pricing shares as its modern equivalents.[49] By the end of the century, however, this market had "devolved" and capital was once again sourced through local, ad hoc, personal channels.[50] Weirdly, as we shall see, we seem to be facing a very similar public market trend today. There are several lines of argument that demonstrate the governance market for public companies is broken. Though the evidence is necessarily indirect, it is visible almost everywhere.

First, market actors regularly tell us that they hold aspects of the new market for governance in low regard. In a typical recent survey of directors, more than half of them expressed skepticism about various trending governance practices.[51] Almost every time a new governance practice is introduced by regulation or through the agency of powerful third parties, directors and other market actors express skepticism about the change.[52] Even companies' professional advisors, who are paid to assist boards deal with evolving governance practices, express skepticism about the trajectory of governance changes.[53] The best evidence we have suggests that boards of directors are dragged into new governance arrangements they do not regard as in the company's best interests.[54] They may be biased or wrong, but the people most familiar with the company are generally unconvinced. As we have seen, one striking finding is that governance practices are now adopted by companies even when the managers, directors, and shareholders are aware (as demonstrated by their stock-selling decisions) that the practices will be value-destroying.[55]

A second sign the market for governance has been adversely affected is that the governance arrangements of very different firms, with very different issues and challenges, have come to resemble one another in almost every particular. According to Spencer Stuart, even those governance structures not imposed by regulations of some sort are now replicated in virtually every widely held company. In the United States, 98 percent of the S&P 500 firms had annual board performance evaluations,[56] 85 percent of the directors are independent (essentially all companies have super-majority independent boards), and 62 percent of these companies have eliminated *all* inside directors except the CEO[57]; 90 percent of boards are not staggered[58]; 89 percent have some form of majority voting[59]; 72 percent have deferred compensation plans; 91 percent don't provide meeting fees and 89 percent of boards now reject the once ubiquitous stock options[60]; 94 percent have director share ownership requirements; and 98.4 percent of the Russell 1000 don't use poison pills.[61]

They all tend to have the same board committees (including committees that are not made mandatory by regulation), the same policies on things like director service on other boards, and they appear to generally hire people with the same educational and professional backgrounds. This monoculture is even more prevalent in other English-speaking countries.[62]

The process described by Easterbrook and Fischel in which the governance arrangements of a corporation evolved through market bargaining is nowhere in evidence. We currently live in a world of one-size-fits-all corporate governance. This might be unproblematic if the monoculture imposed by regulators and proxy advisors was, in fact, best for every company, but by now in this book, we can say the empirical research (and common sense) suggests this is not true.

The first two lines of evidence about the broken governance market can be summarized as follows: directors do not generally regard new governance practices as valuable to their firms, they nevertheless feel compelled to adopt them regardless of their idiosyncratic circumstances, and subsequent empirical research strongly suggests the directors' original skepticism is usually correct.

The third piece of evidence is that the market for governance is not working as it once did is the absence of experimentation in governance arrangements.[63] Of course, this is implicit in the development of a homogeneous governance system across firms, but it is visible in other ways. The most dramatic American experiments in corporate governance currently underway involve firms legally organized as "benefit corporations" or "social enterprise corporations."[64] Almost none of these companies have entered the public stock markets where the governance monoculture exists.[65] There have been a couple of public companies certified as "B Corps" (Etsy and Laureate Education) but this is out of nearly 2,000 privately held B Corps that choose to remain private, including prominent names like Patagonia, Method, and New Belgium Brewing.[66] In the case of Etsy, originally organized as a benefit corporation, an encounter with hedge fund activists after it went public resulted in the immediate loss of its CEO, then the abandonment of its B Corp certification, and finally any claim to possessing a distinctive corporate governance structure.[67] This is how monocultures are created.

The most popular form of new business entity in the United States is the limited liability corporation (LLC).[68] One reason for its popularity (though less important than its tax advantages) is the freedom it provides to experiment with new corporate governance arrangements, even permitting the elimination of the fiduciary duty.[69] In one representative year, more than three times as many Delaware LLCs were formed than corporations.[70] Only a handful of these firms have chosen to enter the public markets, however.[71] Of those that have entered the public markets, all but a tiny minority have brought their arrangements into something roughly resembling the governance industry's consensus.[72]

The fourth piece of evidence that the governance market for widely held corporations is broken is the conspicuous unwillingness on the part of corporations to enter it.[73] American public markets have lost approximately half of the companies they possessed in 2000.[74] Canada's TSX and the United Kingdom's LSE have experienced similar declines over the same period.[75] In both cases, the evidence strongly suggests that the problem is caused mainly by the reluctance of new firms to go public. In the United States, new listings for the past two decades have averaged less than one-third of the total number of companies that went public in an average year between 1980 and 2000.[76]

A reluctance on the part of potential participants to enter a market is the most direct evidence possible that the market is damaged.[77] I have argued elsewhere that the prominent alternative explanations for the collapse in the IPO market have difficulty accounting for the facts in a single country and completely fail to explain why the collapse is occurring across many different countries.[78] The United Kingdom and Canada avoided the worst of the Sarbanes-Oxley era regulation; they have very different market structures than the United States, and different industries dominate their listings, but they have virtually identical governance markets to the United States, and they are experiencing identical declines.

Corporate managers are quite clear that one of the main reasons they try not to go public is to avoid the governance market we have created over the past thirty years.[79] They prefer private markets. This isn't because managers have less oversight in the private markets; the reverse is generally the case. Private equity funds, venture capitalists, and angel investors all tend to sit on private company boards and usually possess extensive contractual control rights. It is unlikely that executives prefer private markets because it allows them to avoid exposing matters to shareholder scrutiny. Rather, it is the *quality*, not the quantity, of shareholder oversight that distinguishes a venture capitalist appointing a sizable minority of the board from its public market-facing institutional investor counterpart that, in contrast, knows little about the company and bases its governance decisions on proxy advisor recommendations or the arguments of short-term activists.

The quality of governance is higher for private firms because the governance market for these firms largely continues to exist intact. Private companies are generally free to select the aims, board composition, legal structures, and voting arrangements that they want. Academics who study the private governance market emphasize that "a corporate governance framework for nonlisted companies is highly contractual in nature."[80] Constituencies that form around private firms can still bargain *ex ante* "to improve their governance structure and maximize the value of their investment."[81] Researchers find, for example, that going private leads to significant increases in long-term innovation.[82] They also find evidence that, to the extent they can be isolated statistically, the corporate governance arrangements of private firms lead to superior operating performance compared to their public peers.[83]

Say what you want about such notable exemplars of stupidity as FTX, WeWork, and Theranos, but they did reflect genuinely idiosyncratic experiments in corporate governance. Their governance arrangements were very, very bad, but they were unique. Thousands of private companies have similarly experimental governance cultures; most are more successful.

When US companies do go public, they often have nonconforming governance arrangements. For example, they are much more likely to have interlocking directorships[84] and much more likely to have "busy" or "overboarded" directors.[85] These heterogeneous corporate governance arrangements persist even in the context of the going public transaction in which companies have "every incentive to adopt governance structures that appeal to outside investors."[86] For their part, the companies that choose to leave the public markets are often the ones apparently resisting the imposition of some new governance practice, such as splitting the CEO and chair roles.[87]

The really noteworthy thing, however, is the ways new entrants into the public markets try to adopt structures that will permit them to full-on escape the governance aspects of those markets. The most dramatic method is to list with dual-class shares.[88] More than a quarter of new firms now list multiple classes of stock possessing unequal voting rights.[89] The percentage of companies using this approach to stave off the governance market has more than doubled in the last decade.[90] Companies with dual-class share structures have included Google, Facebook, LinkedIn, Yelp, and Zillow.

Dual-class share structures aren't the only way for new market entrants to try to escape the governance market. Most of the other structures designed to preserve board independence from outside pressure are deployed by companies going public. For example, contracts are regularly created at the time of IPO to give managers control over matters shareholders might otherwise influence.[91] In 2018, only 8 percent of the S&P 500 had a staggered board,[92] but 90 percent of IPO companies had one.[93] Eighty-nine percent of large public companies had adopted majority voting policies,[94] but only 6 percent of IPO firms followed suit.[95] Roughly 40 percent of large public companies prohibit shareholders from calling a special meeting,[96] but 84 percent of IPO companies go public with this prohibition.[97] Doesn't this look like new companies in our public markets trying to escape the governance industry's assistance?

Even if they stay in the public markets, boards try hard to retain their historic discretion over corporate decisions.[98] Whatever they might say, the actual opinions of managers must be discerned by their behavior, and whenever possible, they have a clear tendency to structure the corporation's affairs so as to avoid the cost, uncertainty, and delay of, for example, a shareholder vote.[99] Research in Australia and the United States finds companies structure their private placements to avoid crossing a threshold that would lead to a special shareholder meeting.[100] When the stock exchange rules in Australia changed the threshold from 10 percent to 15 percent of outstanding shares, private placements changed in size from new issuances falling just below the 10 percent threshold to new issuances falling just below 15 percent. Among other things, this suggests that companies under the earlier regime were deliberately raising less capital than they required just to avoid a shareholder vote. Corporate managers in America similarly try to avoid shareholder votes in the merger context, even though in practice these votes are overwhelmingly supportive.[101]

It is important to keep in mind when evaluating why boards no longer take their companies public, that outside of the dysfunction in the governance market, the economic incentives provided by the public markets remain intact. Listed companies have generally been awarded higher valuations than they ever received in the last century. Public companies are also now paying directors and executives more than ever before. Executive pay as a percentage of corporate profits is now twice as high as it was in 1990. It is only the governance aspects of the public markets that have grown less appealing.

10.9 SUMMARY

For many decades, American public companies got along without anything like the corporate governance industry. The implicit assumption of the agency cost story that unconstrained executives would go crazy isn't borne out by the relatively staid ways in which executives paid themselves and pursued corporate success in the decades prior to the 1980s. Chapter 9 argued that part of what kept managerial opportunism and self-interest in check was robust markets of all types, including the governance market. Once the governance market was replaced by top-down, inorganic, one-size-fits-all corporate governance practices, various types of dysfunctions occurred.

It shouldn't be surprising, therefore, that managers began trying to avoid the modern governance world altogether. Sure, some companies go public with dual-class shares, staggered boards, and various types of protection from shareholder pressure to adopt trendy governance practices, but increasing numbers of companies apparently decide not to go public at all. This is evidence, visible to anyone without a vested interest in the modern governance regime, of a market failing in its core task: drawing in the relevant parties.

NOTES

1 Stephan R. Epstein, *Freedom and Growth: The Rise of States and Markets in Europe, 1300–1750* (London: Routledge, 2000), vol. 7. See also, Avner Greif, "Political Organizations, Social Structure, and Institutional Success: Reflections from Genoa and Venice During the Commercial Revolution" (1995) 151:4 *Journal of Institutional and Theoretical Economics (JITE)/Zeitschrift für die gesamte Staatswissenschaft* 734–740; Tilman Altenburg and Wilfried Lütkenhorst, *Industrial Policy in Developing Countries: Failing Markets, Weak States* (Cheltenham, UK: Edward Elgar Publishing Limited, 2015).

2 See, for example, Guillaume Haeringer, *Market Design: Auctions and Matching* (Cambridge: The MIT Press, 2017) at pp. 4–5 [Haeringer, *Market Design*]; Nathan B. Oman, *The Dignity of Commerce: Markets and the Moral Foundations of Contract Law* (Chicago: The University of Chicago Press, 2017) at pp. 23–29.

3 Rebecca E. Hollander-Blumoff and Matthew T. Bodie, "The Market as Negotiation" (2020–2021) 96:3 *Notre Dame Law Review* 1257–1318 at 1259.

4 Robert A. G. Monks and Nell Minow, *Corporate Governance*, 5th ed. (West Sussex: John Wiley & Sons, 2011) at p. 110; Timur Kuran, "Why the Middle East is Economically Underdeveloped: Historical Mechanisms of Institutional Stagnation" (2004) 18:3 *Journal of Economic Perspectives* 71–90 at 71; Avner Greif, "The Fundamental Problem of Exchange: A Research Agenda in Historical Institutional Analysis" (2000) 4:3 *European Review of Economic History* 251–284; Avner Greif, "Commitment, Coercion, and Markets: The Nature and Dynamics of Institutions Supporting Exchange" in Claude Ménard and Mary M. Shirley (eds.), *Handbook of New Institutional Economics* (Amsterdam: Springer, 2005), pp. 727–786; John Micklethwait and Adrian Wooldridge, *The Company: A Short History of a Revolutionary Idea* (New York: Modern Library, 2003).

5 Shane Scott and Daisuke Wakabayaski, "'The Business of War': Google Employees Protest Work for the Pentagon," *The New York Times*, April 4, 2018, online: www.nytimes .com/2018/04/04/technology/google-letter-ceo-pentagon-project.html; Alexia Fernández Campbell, "How Tech Employees are Pushing Silicon Valley to Put Ethics Before Profit," October 18, 2018, online: www.vox.com/technology/2018/10/18/17989482/google-amazon-employee-ethics-contracts; Julie Creswell and Kevin Draper, "Adidas Pledges to Increase Diversity. Some Employees Want More," *The New York Times*, June 10, 2020, online: www.nytimes.com/2020/06/10/business/adidas-black-employees-discrimination .html.

6 Gary B. Gorton and Alexander K. Zentefis, "Corporate Cultures as a Theory of the Firm" (2020), *National Bureau of Economic Research, Working Paper No. 27353*, online: *NBER*, www.nber.org/papers/w27353.

7 D. Gordon Smith, "The Dystopian Potential of Corporate Law" (2008) 57:4 *Emory Law Journal* 985–1010 at 990 [Smith, "Dystopian Potential"].

8 *Wood v. Dummer*, 3 Mason 308 (1824); *Railroad Company v. Howard*, 74 U.S. 392 (1868).

9 James Willard Hurst, *The Legitimacy of the Business Corporation in the Law of the United States, 1780–1970* (Virginia: University Press of Virginia, 1970) at p. 27.

10 Stephen M. Bainbridge, "Director v. Shareholder Primacy in the Convergence Debate" (2002) 16:1 *Transnational Lawyer* 45–62 at 48; Jeffrey M. Lipshaw, "The False Dichotomy of Corporate Governance Platitudes" (2021) 46:2 *Journal of Corporation Law* 345–384.

11 P. M. Vasudev, "Corporate Law and its Efficiency: A Review of History" (2008) 50:3 *The American Journal of Legal History* 237–283 at 268 [Vasudev, "Corporate Law Efficiency"]. See also, Smith, "Dystopian Potential," above at note 7 at 992.

12 Stewart Macauley, "Non-Contractual Relations in Business: A Preliminary Study" (1963) 28:1 *American Sociological Review* 55–67 [Macauley, "Non-Contractual Relations"]; George Baker, Robert Gibbons and Kevin J. Murphy, "Relational Contracts and the Theory of the Firm" (2002) 117:1 *The Quarterly Journal of Economics* 39–84 [Baker, Gibbons and Murphy, "Relational Contracts"].

13 Macauley, "Non-Contractual Relations," above at note 12 at 60.

14 William A. Niskanen, "The Soft Infrastructure of a Market Economy" (1991) 11:2 *Cato Journal* 233–238 at 236.

15 Oliver E. Williamson, "The New Institutional Economics: Taking Stock, Looking Ahead" (2000) 38:3 *Journal of Economic Literature* 595–613; Baker, Gibbons and Murphy, "Relational Contracts," above at note 12; Benjamin E. Hermalin and Michael L. Katz, "Judicial Modification of Contracts Between Sophisticated Parties: A More Complete View of Incomplete Contracts and their Breach" (1993) 9:2 *The Journal of*

Law, Economics, and Organization 230–255; Rebecca Stone and Alexander Stremitzer, "Promises, Reliance, and Psychological Lock-In" (2020) 49:1 *The Journal of Legal Studies* 33–72.

16 Douglass C. North, "The Evolution of Efficient Markets in History" (1994), *Economic History, Working Paper No.* 9411005, online: *Indiana University Digital Library of the Commons:* https://dlc.dlib.indiana.edu/dlc/bitstream/handle/10535/4429/9411005.pdf at 2 [North, "Evolution of Markets"].

17 Frank H. Easterbrook and Daniel R. Fischel, *The Economic Structure of Corporate Law* (Cambridge: Harvard University Press, 1991).

18 *Ibid* at p. 5.

19 *Ibid* at p. 14.

20 *Ibid* at p. 7.

21 Brian R. Cheffins, "Corporate Governance Since the Managerial Capitalism Era" (2015) 89:4 *Business History Review* 717–744 [Cheffins, "Corporate Governance"]; Brian R. Cheffins, "The History of Corporate Governance" in Mike Wright et al. (eds.), *The Oxford Handbook of Corporate Governance* (Oxford: Oxford University Press, 2013); Eric Hilt, "History of American Corporate Governance: Law, Institutions, and Politics" (2014) 6:1 *Annual Review of Financial Economics* 1–21.

22 See, for example, Stephen A. Smith, *Contract Theory* (New York: Oxford University Press, Inc., 2004) at p. 132; Jules Coleman, "The Normative Basis of Economic Analysis: A Critical Review of Richard Posner's 'The Economics of Justice'" (1982) 34:5 *Stanford Law Review* 1105–1131; Stephen E. Ellis and Grant M. Hayden, "The Cult of Efficiency in Corporate Law" (2010) 5:2 *Virginia Law and Business Review* 239–266 at 250–262.

23 Jules L. Coleman, "Efficiency, Exchange, and Auction: Philosophic Aspects of the Economics Approach to Law" (1980) 68:2 *California Law Review* 221–249.

24 Henry G. Manne, "Insider Trading and Property Rights in New Information" (1985) 4:3 *Cato Journal* 933–944; Zvi Bodie et al. (eds.), *Investments*, 9th Canadian ed. (Canada: McGraw-Hill Education, 2019) at p. 108. See also, Kevin S. Haeberle and M. Todd Henderson, "Making a Market for Corporate Disclosure" (2018) 35:2 *Yale Journal on Regulation* 383–436.

25 Patricia H. Werhane, "The Indefensibility of Insider Trading" (1991) 10 *Journal of Business Ethics* 729–731; Jennifer Moore, "What is Really Unethical about Insider Trading?" (1990) 9:3 *Journal of Business Ethics* 171–182; Hayne E. Leland, "Insider Trading: Should It Be Prohibited" (1992) 100:4 *Journal of Political Economy* 859–887 at 860.

26 See, for example, *S.E.C. v. Texas Gulf Sulphur Co.*, 401 F.2d 833 (2nd Cir., 1968), cert. denied, 394 U.S. 976 (1969) at para 37.

27 Vasudev, "Corporate Law Efficiency," above at note 11 at 237–238.

28 *Salomon v. A Salomon & Co., Ltd.*, [1896] UKHL 1, [1897] AC 22.

29 *Ibid* (Lord Halsbury referred to this process as "taking the trouble" to investigate at 40).

30 *Ibid* ("[n]o one need trust a limited liability company unless he so please, and that before he does so he can ascertain, if he so please, what is the capital of the company and how it is held" at 46. See also, Lord MacNaghten referring approvingly to a decision that reversed an attempt to impose *ex post* considerations in similar circumstances at 52).

31 See the discussion in Vernon L. Smith and Bart J. Wilson, *Humanomics: Moral Sentiments and the Wealth of Nations for the Twenty-First Century* (Cambridge, UK: Cambridge University Press, 2019) at p. 87. See also, Kevin A. McCabe, Vernon L. Smith and Michael LePore, "Intentionality Detection and 'Mindreading': Why Does Game Form Matter" (2000) 97:8 *Proceedings of the National Academy of Sciences* 4404–4409.

32 Russell Hardin, "Magic on the Frontier: The Norm of Efficiency" (1996) 144:5 *University of Pennsylvania Law Review* 1987–2020 [Hardin, "Magic Frontier"]; Jules L. Coleman, "Economics and the Law: A Critical Review of the Foundations of the Economic Approach to Law" (1984) 94:4 *Ethics* 649–679 at 672 [Coleman, "A Critical Review"]. See also, Thomas Sowell, *Basic Economics*, 3rd ed. (New York: Basic Books, 2007) at p. 5.

33 Richard A. Posner, *Economic Analysis of Law*, 9th ed. (Boston: Aspen Publishing, 2014) at pp. 12–16 [Posner, *Economic Analysis*]; Alexander Styhre, "The Making of the Shareholder Primacy Governance Model: Price Theory, the Law and Economics School, and Corporate Law Retrenchment Advocacy" (2017) 8:3 *Accounting, Economics, and Law: A Convivium* 20160021 [Styhre, "Making of the Model"].

34 Styhre, "Making of the Model," above at note 33 at 11–12; Cheffins, "Corporate Governance," above at note 21 at 731; See also, Jill E. Fisch, "Measuring Efficiency in Corporate Law: The Role of Shareholder Primacy" (2006) 31:3 *Journal of Corporation Law* 637–674 at 669.

35 Hardin, "Magic Frontier," above at note 32 at 2015; See also, Avery Katz, "Taking Private Ordering Seriously" (1996) 144:5 *University of Pennsylvania Law Review* 1745–1764; Morton Horowitz, "Law and Economics: Science or Politics" (1980) 8:4 *Hofstra Law Review* 905–912.

36 John J. Wallis and Douglass North, "Measuring the Transaction Sector in the American Economy, 1870–1970" in Stanley L. Engerman and Robert E. Gallman (eds.), *Long-Term Factors in American Economic Growth* (Chicago: The University of Chicago Press, 1992), pp. 95–162 at p. 121, Table 3.13.

37 Stanley Fischer, "Long-term Contracting, Sticky Prices and Monetary Policy: A Comment" (1977) 3:3 *Journal of Monetary Economics* 317–323 at 322 note 5.

38 Posner, *Economic Analysis*, above at note 33. See also, A. Mitchell Polinsky, *An Introduction to Law and Economics*, 2nd ed. (Boston: Little, Brown and Company, 1989) at pp. 27–36; Coleman, "A Critical Review," above at note 32 at 666; Carl J. Dahlman, "The Problem of Externality" (1979) 22:1 *The Journal of Law and Economics* 141–162 at 151.

39 Richard H. Pildes, "The Destruction of Social Capital through Law" (1996) 144:5 *University of Pennsylvania Law Review* 2055–2078; Frederick A. Hayek, "The Use of Knowledge in Society" in Paul S. Myers (ed.), *Knowledge Management and Organizational Design* (London: Routledge, 1996), pp. 7–16. See also, Mario J. Rizzo, "The Mirage of Efficiency" (1980) 8:3 *Hofstra Law Review* 641–658 at 658; Robert D. Cooter, "Decentralized Law for a Complex Economy: The Structural Approach to Adjudicating the New Law Merchant" (1996) 144:5 *University of Pennsylvania Law Review* 1643–1696 at 1646; Shahar Dobzinski, Noam Nisan and Sigal Oren, "Economic Efficiency Requires Interaction" (2014) 118 *Games and Economic Behavior* 589–608 at 590. See also, Bryce C. Tingle, "Returning Markets to the Center of Corporate Law" (2023) 48:4 *Journal of Corporation Law* 663–718 [Tingle, "Markets to the Center"].

40 R. H. Coase, *The Firm, the Market and the Law* (Chicago: The University of Chicago Press, 1988) at p. 7.

41 *Ibid* at pp. 7–8.

42 North, "Evolution of Markets," above at note 16 at 1.

43 Ronald J. Gilson, "Corporate Governance and Economic Efficiency: When do Institutions Matter?" (1996) 74:2 *Washington University Law Quarterly* 327–346 at 327. See also, Daniel R. Fischel, "The Corporate Governance Movement" (1982) 35:6 *Vanderbilt Law Review* 1259–1292 at 1262.

44 Robert B. Thompson, "Delaware, the Feds, and the Stock Exchange: Challenges to the First State as First in Corporate Law" (2004) 29:3 *Delaware Journal of Corporate Law*

779–804 at 791. See also, Willem J. L. Calkoen (ed.), *The Corporate Governance Review*, 10th ed. (London: Law Business Research Ltd., 2020) at p. 366; Marcel Kahan and Edward Rock, "Embattled CEOs" (2010) 88:5 *Texas Law Review* 987–1052.

45 William Easterly, "In Search of Reforms for Growth: New Stylized Facts on Policy and Growth Outcomes" (2019), *National Bureau of Economic Research, Working Paper No. 26318*, online: *NBER*, www.nber.org/papers/w26318 [Easterly, "In Search"]; Kevin B. Grier and Robin M. Grier, "The Washington Consensus Works: Causal Effects of Reform, 1970–2015" (2021) 49:1 *Journal of Comparative Economics* 59–72 [Grier and Grier, "Washington Consensus"]; Joshua C. Hall and Robert A. Lawson, "Economic Freedom of the World: An Accounting of the Literature" (2014) 32:1 *Contemporary Economic Policy* 1–19. See also, Virgil Henry Storr and Ginny Seung Choi, *Do Markets Corrupt our Morals?* (Cham, Switzerland: Springer International Publishing, 2019) at pp. 83–133.

46 Stephen M. Bainbridge, "Dodd-Frank: Quack Federal Corporate Governance Round II" (2011) 95:5 *Minnesota Law Review* 1779–1821; Roberta Romano, "Quack Corporate Governance" (2005) 28:4 *Regulation* 36–44; Roberta Romano, "The Sarbanes-Oxley Act and the Making of Quack Corporate Governance" (2005) 114:7 *Yale Law Journal* 1521–1611; Danielle A. Chaim, "The Corporate Governance Cartel" (2023), online: *SSRN*, https://ssrn.com/abstract=4324567 at 48.

47 Lynn A. Stout, "On the Rise of Shareholder Primacy, Signs of its Fall, and the Return of Managerialism (in the Closet)" (2013) 36:2 *Seattle University Law Review* 1169–1186 at 1180–1181 [Stout, "Shareholder Primacy"]. See also, Eric W. Orts, "Corporate Law and Business Theory" (2017) 74:2 *Washington and Lee Law Review* 1089–1118 at 1094.

48 For example, quasi-monopolies work better than simple versions of economic theory predicts: Megan McArdle, "The War of Amazon, Apple and Other Near-Monopolies," Bloomberg, October 1, 2015, online: www.bloomberg.com/opinion/articles/2015-10-01/the-war-of-amazon-apple-and-other-near-monopolies; Michael Hirsh, "Big Talk on Big Tech – But Little Action," *Foreign Policy*, April 6, 2021, online: https://foreignpolicy.com/2021/04/06/big-tech-regulation-facebook-google-amazon-us-eu/. Externalities are also much less of a problem than is generally assumed so long as market participants can act on adjusted expectations: Donald J. Boudreaux and Roger Meiners, "Externality: Origins and Classifications" (2019) 59:1 *Natural Resources* 1–34 at 24–28. Markets produce many different viable ways of dealing with transaction costs: Ronald J. Gilson, Charles F. Sabel and Robert E. Scott, "Contracting for Innovation: Vertical Disintegration and Interfirm Collaboration" (2009) 109:3 *Columbia Law Review* 431–502 at 494–501. Recent research supporting markets' resilience is provided by looking at the impact of the market-focused 1990s-era reforms often referred to as the "Washington Consensus": Grier and Grier, "Washington Consensus," above at note 45; Easterly, "In Search," above at note 45.

49 Philip Mirowski, "The Rise (and Retreat) of a Market: English Joint Stock Shares in the Eighteenth Century" (1981) 41:3 *The Journal of Economic History* 559–577 at 575.

50 *Ibid* at 576–577.

51 See, for example, *The Swinging Pendulum: Board Governance in the Age of Shareholder Empowerment – PwC's 2016 Annual Corporate Directors Survey*, PricewaterhouseCoopers International Limited (October 2016), online (pdf): www.pwc.com/us/en/corporate-governance/annual-corporate-directors-survey/assets/pwc-2016-annual-corporate-directors-survey.pdf at 4, 9, 10–11, 14, 18, 29, 33. An earlier study found that a variety of governance best practices supported by usually more than 75 percent of polled investors, failed to get support from even 25 percent of directors: *What Matters in The Boardroom: Director and Investor Views on Trends Shaping Governance and the Board of the Future,*

PricewaterhouseCoopers International Limited (2014), online (pdf): www.pwc.pl/pl/pdf/forum-rad-nadzorczych/pwc-what-matters-in-the-boardroom-director-investor-views.pdf.

52 See, for example, Silvia Ascarelli, "Corporate Europe Is Skeptical About Tougher Governance Codes," *The Wall Street Journal*, October 7, 2004, online: www.wsj.com/articles/SB109710683845238701; Beckey Bright, "Investors Are Skeptical of Success of Sarbanes-Oxley, Poll Finds," *The Wall Street Journal*, October 14, 2005, online: www.wsj.com/articles/SB112912865268466716.

53 Carol Liao, "A Canadian Model of Corporate Governance" (2014) 37:2 *Dalhousie Law Journal* 559–600.

54 See, for example, Comment letter from Tom Quaadman, Vice President of Center for Capital Markets Competitiveness, *Re: Proxy Advisory Services Roundtable File No. 4-670*, US Securities and Exchange Commission (February 24, 2014), online (pdf): www.sec.gov/comments/4-670/4670-12.pdf; Comment letter from Washington Legal Foundation, *Comments of the Washington Legal Foundation to the Securities and Exchange Commission Concerning Issues Raised at the Proxy Advisory Firm Roundtable (File No. 4-607)*, US Securities and Exchange Commission (January 10, 2014), online (pdf): www.sec.gov/comments/4-670/4670-11.pdf; Comment letter from Joan C. Conley, Senior Vice President and Corporate Secretary of NASDAQ OMX, *Re: Proxy Advisory Firm Roundtable (File Number 4-670)*, US Securities and Exchange Commission (December 4, 2013), online (pdf): www.sec.gov/comments/4-670/4670-8.pdf; Kerry Shannon Burke, "Regulating Corporate Governance Through the Market: Comparing the Approaches of the United States, Canada and the United Kingdom" (2002) 27:3 *Journal of Corporation Law* 341–380. See also, Sanjai Bhagat, Brain J. Bolton and Roberta Romano, "The Promise and Peril of Corporate Governance Indices" (2008) 108:8 *Columbia Law Review* 1803–1882.

55 David F. Larcker, Allan L. McCall and Gaizka Ormazabal, "Proxy Advisory Firms and Stock Option Repricing" (2013) 56:2–3 *Journal of Accounting & Economics* 149–169. See also, David F. Larcker, Allan L. McCall and Brian Tayan, *The Influence of Proxy Advisory Firm Voting Recommendations on Say-on-Pay Votes and Executive Compensation Decisions*, The Conference Board (March 2012), online (pdf): www.gsb.stanford.edu/sites/gsb/files/publication-pdf/cgri-survey-2012-proxy-voting_0.pdf at 4; Matt Bloom and George T. Milkovich, "Relationships Among Risk, Incentive Pay, and Organizational Performance" (1998) 41:3 *Academy of Management Journal* 283–297; Young H. Baek and Jose A. Pagan, "Executive Compensation and Corporate Production Efficiency: A Stochastic Frontier Approach" (2002) 41:1/2 *Quarterly Journal of Business and Economics* 27–41; David F. Larcker, Allan McCall and Gaizka Ormazabal, "Outsourcing Shareholder Voting to Proxy Advisory Firms" (2015) 58:1 *The Journal of Law and Economics* 173–204; David F. Larcker, Gaizka Ormazabal and Daniel J. Taylor, "The Market Reaction to Corporate Governance Regulation" (2011) 101:2 *Journal of Financial Economics* 431–448.

56 *U.S. Spencer Stuart Board Index 2020 Highlights*, Spencer Stuart (2020), online (pdf): www.spencerstuart.com/-/media/2020/december/ssbi2020/ssbi_2020_highlights.pdf at 3.

57 Harald Baum, "The Rise of Independent Director: A Historical and Comparative Perspective" (2017), *Max Planck Private Law Research Paper No. 16/20*, online: SSRN, https://ssrn.com/abstract=2814978 at 2; 2019 *U.S. Spencer Stuart Board Index*, Spencer Stuart (2019), online (pdf): www.spencerstuart.com/-/media/2019/ssbi-2019/us_board_index_2019.pdf at 15 [Spencer Stuart, *2019 Board Index*].

58 Spencer Stuart, *2019 Board Index*, above at note 57 at 15.

59 *Ibid*.

60 *Ibid* at 29, 30.

61 Ethan Klingsberg, Paul Tiger and Elizabeth Bieber, "A Look at the Data Behind Recent Poison Pill Adoptions" (April 24, 2020), *Harvard Law School Forum on Corporate Governance*, online: https://corpgov.law.harvard.edu/2020/04/24/a-look-at-the-data-behind-recent-poison-pill-adoptions/.

62 See, for example, 2019 *Canada Spencer Stuart Board Index*, Spencer Stuart (2019), online (pdf): www.spencerstuart.com/-/media/2020/canada-bi-2019/canada-bi-2019-final.pdf.

63 Robert B. Thompson, "Why New Corporate Law Arises: Implications for the 21st Century" in Steven Davidoff Soloman and Randall Thomas (eds.), *The Corporate Contract in Changing Times: Is the Law Keeping Up?* (Chicago: The University of Chicago Press, 2019), pp. 3–28.

64 Carol Liao, "A Critical Canadian Perspective on the Benefit Corporation" (2017) 40:2 *Seattle University Law Review* 683–716; Carol Liao, "Corporate Governance Reform for the 21st Century: A Critical Reassessment of the Shareholder Primacy Model" (2012) 43:2 *Ottawa Law Review* 187–232.

65 Brett H. McDonnell, "Benefit Corporations and Public Markets: First Experiments and Next Steps" (2017) 40:2 *Seattle University Law Review* 717–742 at 724–725.

66 Alana Semuels, "Rampant Consumerism Is Not Attractive. Patagonia Is Climbing to the Top – And Reimagining Capitalism Along the Way," *Time*, September 23, 2019, online: https://time.com/5684011/patagonia/; Dennis Lomonaco, "Be Nice or Leave: The Pragmatic Case for B-Corps," *Forbes*, January 22, 2018, online: www.forbes.com/sites/forbesagency council/2018/01/22/be-nice-or-leave-the-pragmatic-case-for-b-corps/?sh=70769b2d4621; Jena McGregor, "What Esty, Patagonia and Warby Parker Have in Common," *The Washington Post*, April 20, 2015, online: www.washingtonpost.com/news/on-leadership/ wp/2015/04/20/what-etsy-patagonia-and-warby-parker-have-in-common/.

67 Stephen M. Bainbridge, *The Profit Motive: Defending Shareholder Value Maximization* (Cambridge, UK: Cambridge University Press, 2023).

68 Rodney D. Chrisman, "LLCs Are the New King Of The Hill: An Empirical Study Of The Number Of New LLCs, Corporations, and LPs Formed in the United States Between 2004–2007 and How LLCs Were Taxed For Tax Years 2002–2006" (2009) 15:2 *Fordham Journal Corporate & Finance Law* 459–490 at 459–460, 468–485.

69 Paul M. Altman, Elisa Erlenbach Maas and Michael P. Maxwell, "Eliminating Fiduciary Duty Uncertainty: The Benefits of Effectively Modifying Fiduciary Duties in Delaware LLC Agreements," *American Bar Association – Business Law Today*, February 4, 2013, online: https://businesslawtoday.org/2013/02/eliminating-fiduciary-duty-uncertainty-the-benefits-of-effectively-modifying-fiduciary-duties-in-delaware-llc-agreements/.

70 Winnifred A. Lewis, "Waiving Fiduciary Duties in Delaware Limited Partnerships and Limited Liability Companies" (2013) 82:2 *Fordham Law Review* 1017–1052 at 1020 note 32.

71 Suren Gomtsian, "The Governance of Publicly Traded Limited Liability Companies" (2015) 40:1 *Delaware Journal of Corporate Law* 207–279.

72 *Ibid* (of the twenty public LLCs that existed in 2014, only three had eliminated the fiduciary duty and sixteen created conflict-of-interest rules for managers).

73 Craig Doidge, Andrew Karolyi and René M. Stulz, "The US Listing Gap" (2017) 123:3 *Journal of Financial Economics* 464–487 at 464.

74 Bryce C. Tingle and J. Ari Pandes, "Reversing the Decline of Canadian Public Markets" (2021) 14:3 *The School of Public Policy Publications* 1–57, online: https://journalhosting .ucalgary.ca/index.php/sppp/article/view/69444 at 9 [Tingle and Pandes, "Reversing the Decline"]; Bryce C. Tingle, J. Ari Pandes and Michael J. Robinson, "The IPO Market in Canada: What a Comparison with the United States Tells Us About a Global Problem"

(2013) 54:3 *Canadian Business Law Journal* 321–367 at 327–328 [Tingle, Pandes and Robinson, "IPO Market"].

75 Tingle and Pandes, "Reversing the Decline," above at note 74 at 5–6; John Kay, *The Kay Review of UK Equity Markets and Long-Term Decision Making* (London: Business Innovation Skills, 2012), online (pdf): https://assets.publishing.service.gov.uk/govern ment/uploads/system/uploads/attachment_data/file/253454/bis-12-917-kay-review-of-equity-markets-final-report.pdf at 24.

76 Jay R. Ritter, "Re-energizing the IPO Market" in Martin Neil Baily, Richard J. Herring and Yuta Seki (eds.), *Financial Restructuring to Sustain Recovery* (Washington, DC: Brookings Institution Press, 2013), pp. 123–146.

77 Haeringer, *Market Design*, above at note 2 (describing the need for market "thickness" at p. 4).

78 Tingle, Pandes and Robinson, "IPO Market," above at note 74; Tingle and Pandes, "Reversing the Decline," above at note 74.

79 Louis Daniel Wilson, "Can Regulatory Reform Reverse the Decline of Public Markets in Canada? Assessing the Factors Impacting Decisions by Corporate Leaders to Avoid Canadian Public Listings," PhD Dissertation, Western University (2020), online: https://ir.lib.uwo.ca/etd/6869; Tingle and Pandes, "Reversing the Decline," above at note 74; Tingle, Pandes and Robinson, "IPO Market," above at note 74; Tingle, "Markets to the Center," above at note 39.

80 See for example, Joseph A. McCahery and Erik P. M. Vermeulen, *Corporate Governance of Non-Listed Companies* (New York: Oxford University Press Inc., 2008) at p. 8 [McCahery and Vermeulen, *Non-Listed Companies*]; Jennifer S. Fan, "The Landscape of Startup Corporate Governance in the Founder-Friendly Era" (2022) 18:2 *New York University Journal of Law and Business* 317–390.

81 McCahery and Vermeulen, *Non-Listed Companies*, above at note 80 at p. 144.

82 Josh Lerner, Morten Sorensen and Per Strömberg, "Private Equity and Long-Run Investment: The Case of Innovation" (2011) 66:2 *The Journal of Finance* 445–477.

83 Viral V. Acharya et al., "Corporate Governance and Value Creation: Evidence from Private Equity" (2013) 26:2 *The Review of Financial Studies* 368–402.

84 David F. Larcker, Eric C. So and Charles C. Y. Wang, "Boardroom Centrality and Firm Performance" (2013) 55:2–3 *Journal of Accounting and Economics* 225–250.

85 Laura Field, Michelle Lowry and Anahit Mkrtchyan, "Are Busy Boards Detrimental?" (2013) 109:1 *Journal of Financial Economics* 63–82 at 67.

86 Lynn A. Stout, "The Mythical Benefits of Shareholder Control" (2007) 93:3 *Virginia Law Review* 789–810 at 802. See also, Richard J. Sandler and Joseph A. Hall, *Corporate Governance Practices in US Initial Public Offerings*, The Conference Board (April 2014), online (pdf): www.davispolk.com/files/sandler.hall_.directors.notes_.article.apr14.PDF at 3 [Sandler and Hall, *US IPOs*].

87 Charlie Weir, David Laing and Mike Wright, "Incentive Effects, Monitoring Mechanisms and The Market for Corporate Control: An Analysis of the Factors Affecting Public to Private Transactions in the UK" (2005) 32:5–6 *Journal of Business Finance and Accounting* 909–943. See generally, Xi Wu, "SEC Regulations and Firms," PhD Dissertation, New York University (2020), online: SSRN, https://ssrn.com/abstract=3625115.

88 See, for example, Dhruv Aggarwal et al., "The Rise of Dual-Class Stock IPOs" (2022) 144:1 *Journal of Financial Economics* 122–153; Paul Gompers, Joy Ishii and Andrew Metrick, "Incentives vs. Control: An Analysis of U.S. Dual-Class Companies" (2004), *National Bureau of Economic Research, Working Paper No. 10240*, online: NBER, www .nber.org/papers/w10240; Dorothy S. Lund and Elizabeth Pollman, "The Corporate

Governance Machine" (2021) 121:8 *Columbia Law Review* 2563–2634; Ofer Eldar, "Dual-Class IPOs: A Solution to Unicorn Governance Failure" (2023), *European Corporate Governance Institute – Law Working Paper No. 741/2023*, online: SSRN, https://ssrn.com/abstract=4647143.

89 Davis Polk, "IPO Governance Survey: Corporate Governance Practices in U.S. Initial Public Offerings (Excluding Controlled Companies)" (July 2018), online (pdf): www.davispolk.com/files/2018_non-controlled_ipo_survey.7.9.2018.pdf at 3 [Polk, "IPO Survey"].

90 *Ibid*; Stout, "Shareholder Primacy," above at note 47 at 1182.

91 Gladriel Shobe and Jarrod Shobe, "The Dual-Class Spectrum" (2022) 39:3 *Yale Journal on Regulation* 1343–1390 at 1359–1360, note 61; Gabriel Rauterberg, "The Separation of Voting and Control: The Role of Contract in Corporate Governance" (2021) 38:4 *Yale Journal on Regulation* 1124–1181.

92 *2018 United States Spencer Stuart Board Index*, Spencer Stuart (2018), online (pdf): www.spencerstuart.com/-/media/2018/october/ssbi_2018.pdf at 15 [Spencer Stuart, *2018 Board Index*].

93 Polk, "IPO Survey," above at note 89 at 2. Scott Guernsey et al., "Classified Boards: Endangered Species or Hiding in Plain Sight" (2022), online: SSRN, https://ssrn.com/abstract=4085735; This echoes the prevalence of poison pills among earlier generations of IPO companies: Michael Klausner, "Institutional Shareholders, Private Equity, and Antitakeover Protection at the IPO Stage" (2003) 152:2 *University of Pennsylvania Law Review* 755–784.

94 Spencer Stuart, *2018 Board Index*, above at note 92 at 15.

95 Polk, "IPO Survey," above at note 89 at 2; Sandler and Hall, *US IPOs*, above at note 86 at 4.

96 Coling J. Diamon, Michelle Rutta and Danielle Herrick, "Reminders for US Public Companies for the 2019 Annual Reporting and Proxy Season," *White & Case*, December 5, 2018, online: www.whitecase.com/publications/alert/reminders-us-public-companies-2019-annual-reporting-and-proxy-season.

97 Polk, "IPO Survey," above at note 89 at 15.

98 Kobi Kastiel and Yaron Nili, "The Corporate Governance Gap" (2022) 131:3 *Yale Law Journal* 782–860.

99 Stephen M. Bainbridge, *Mergers and Acquisitions*, 3rd ed. (New York: Foundation Press, 2012) at p. 56.

100 James L. Park, "Equity Issuance, Distress, and Agency Problems: The 20% Rule for Privately Issued Equity" (2014), *Korea University Business School Working Paper*, online (pdf): www.placementtracker.com/samplereports/Equity%20Issuance%20Distress%20and%20Agency%20Problems%20The%2020%20Rule%20for%20Privately%20Issued%20Equity.pdf; Jun-Koo Kang and James L. Park, "Private Placements of Equity and Firm Value: Value Enhancing or Value Destroying?" (2021) 56:6 *Journal of Financial and Quantitative Analysis* 2072–2102; Rob Brown and Howard W. Chan, "Rights Issues versus Placements in Australia: Regulation or Choice?" (2004) 22:5 *Company and Securities Law Journal* 301–312 at 304–310. See also, Michael Ewens, Kairong Xiao and Ting Xu, "Regulatory Costs of Being Public: Evidence from Bunching Estimation" (2021), *National Bureau of Economic Research, Working Paper No. 29143*, online: *NBER*, www.nber.org/papers/w29143.

101 Paul Mason et al., "Does Shareholder Voting Matter? Evidence from the Takeover Market" (2018) 53:1 *Wake Forest Law Review* 157–210; Franklin A. Gevurtz, "The Shareholder Approval Conundrum" (2019) 60:7 *Boston College Law Review* 1831–1892. See also, Yair Listokin, "Management Always Wins the Close Ones" (2008) 10:2 *American Law and Economics Review* 159–184.

PART III

Are Social Welfare Outcomes Any Different?

Wherein:

- Recalling the failures of corporate governance to improve shareholder wealth outcomes, we inquire whether we should expect anything different in relation to social welfare outcomes, such as improving the environment or advancing employee welfare.
- As managers are constrained by competitive markets, regardless of the corporate governance practices under which they labor, we inquire whether these market pressures realistically leave much room for pursuing social investments.
- We evaluate the merits of the current enthusiasm for using corporate governance channels to improve the world:
  - Do corporate governance practices designed to advance the interests of non-shareholder constituencies actually do so?
  - What does the available evidence tell us about the motivation of managers?
- We evaluate the current initiatives in the United States to require companies to supply environmental, social, and governance (ESG) disclosure:
  - Do our current levels of disclosure lead to better or worse decisions?
  - Do third-party ESG rating firms understand and accurately capture the ESG profile of the companies they evaluate?
  - Will shareholders understand and productively use ESG disclosure?

11

Achieving Social and Environmental Goals through Corporate Governance

In Chapter 8, we stepped back to contemplate the failure of agency cost theory's normative project. Every major attempt we've made to control managerial slacking and self-enrichment has either failed to produce results or backfired amazingly. There are many possible reasons for this unblemished record of failure: one-size-fits-all best practices ignore the circumstances of specific firms; focusing only on reducing agency costs ignores a great deal of other, often more important governance activities; shareholders and their tribunes (e.g., proxy advisors) don't have the resources or motivation to do a good job on governance; and managers do not systemically depart from pursuing the company's financial best interests because they and their companies are embedded in tough, competitive markets.

Many people these days have a very dim view of business and markets. Because they don't like either, they tend to lump them together. "Well of course he likes markets, he's in business." This is a profound mistake. Economists celebrate competitive markets; businesspeople try to escape them. Adam Smith famously observed, "[p]eople of the same trade seldom meet together even for merriment or diversion, but the conversation ends in a conspiracy against the publick, or in some contrivance to raise prices."[1] If that seems too fussy for you, we can appeal to Peter Thiel, who distilled Silicon Valley's collective wisdom into a single pithy sentence: "Only one thing can allow a business to transcend the daily brute struggle for survival: monopoly profits."[2]

In Chapter 9, we saw that most American public companies seem to be trapped in very competitive markets. On average, they make almost nothing over the costs of running their business. Subject to some measurement caveats, 96 percent of the public companies in the last century don't appear to have even covered the cost of their capital. This struggle to survive seems like unpromising ground to plant the hope that American businesses will take their eyes off staying solvent and shift them to something else entirely – something that actually conflicts with the profit-seeking work that fills their days.

In other words, this sounds like exactly the place we would expect to see the emergence of a group of reformers who have both a track record of knowing better than corporate executives and of confidently ignoring markets. Predictably, the corporate governance industry has duly produced a range of reforms designed to secure various social and environmental outcomes without much regard to the "business" part of "business corporations."

As we have seen, thirty-five US states have enacted constituency statutes that amend the fiduciary duty of corporate managers to permit them to take into account the interests of non-shareholder constituencies. In the Introduction, we saw that there have been calls for even more dramatic changes.

Elizabeth Warren and Bernie Sanders campaigned for the 2020 Democratic presidential nomination with competing proposals to overhaul American corporate governance.[3] Both, for example, propose to pass legislation imposing significant employee representation on boards of directors and altering the character of corporate fiduciary duties. The European Commission has proposed similar reforms, as well as adding sustainability as part of directors' duties.[4]

11.1 WHAT DO PEOPLE MEAN WHEN THEY TALK ABOUT ENVIRONMENTAL AND SOCIAL OUTCOMES?

There is more than the usual amount of confusion surrounding what companies are supposed to do besides pursue their financial interests and obey the law. A measure of the confusion is the explosion in terms describing what reformers would like to see. They would like to see the pursuit, not of "shareholder value," but "enlightened shareholder value." They advocate for "purpose-driven" companies, where "purpose" does NOT mean "making money." As we saw in the Introduction, there are many other terms, the most prominent of which are "corporate social responsibility" or "CSR" and "Environmental, Social, Governance" or "ESG." ("Sustainable" tends to get used a lot as well, but possibly because it is a rather long word that can't be compressed into a three-letter acronym, it isn't quite as common.) There is considerable conceptual confusion among these competing terms, which upon investigation does not seem entirely accidental.

Let's take as an example "enlightened shareholder value." This phrase was adopted with considerable fanfare in connection with reforms to the UK's Companies Act in 2006.[5] Presumably, it means something different from the plain "shareholder value" it replaced, but it is hard to pin down what this might be. The UK Companies Act requires directors to "promote the success of the company" for the benefit of their shareholders, but to take into account the long-term effects of their decisions, as well as the impact of those decisions on employees, suppliers, customers, "others," the environment, the community, and the company's reputation. Practically and conceptually, this seems no different from the shareholder wealth maximization norm that it purports to amend. Any business corporation, whether claiming to pursue "enlightened" shareholder value or not, must work very hard to attract and retain the loyalty of non-shareholder constituencies – employees, customers, suppliers, relevant communities, lenders, and others – as doing so is essential to carry out a company's profit-making activities. A good way of summarizing the situation is that the 2006 amendments to the Companies Act were a trick played on people who don't understand (or like) business.

A different kind of trick produced "ESG," the most common phrase in use in the United States to describe governance that promotes social and environmental outcomes. This trick was designed to permit institutional investment managers to invest in ways that might arguably violate their fiduciary duty to maximize returns on their funds. Law professor John Coffee explains:

> Conceptually, [lawyers] "rebranded" SRI [socially responsible] investing and converted it into ESG investing by asserting that consideration of the "governance factors" associated with public corporations would enable the fiduciary to identify superior investments and enhance risk-adjusted return.... This in turn enabled law firms to opine to their clients that ESG investing was fully compatible with the trustee's fiduciary obligations.[6]

This explains the weirdest aspect of ESG: how one criterion, "governance," that, as we have seen, has historically been focused on improving risk-adjusted shareholder returns, was incorporated into a conceptual unit that also contained social and environmental criteria focused on improving outcomes for *non-shareholder* constituencies. In this case, the trick was played on regulators and courts, but the outcome was the same: a conceptually confused phrase that could mean different things to different groups.

This deliberate confusion is not helpful for a book like this one, so we will try to be more precise in our terminology. To do this, it is necessary to consider what makes a decision made to advance a social or environmental goal different from a decision made to advance a profit-making goal, which only incidentally has positive environmental or social outcomes. A company can give employees a raise, but is that an investment to secure a more egalitarian society, or a necessity imposed by labor markets to prevent the best employees from leaving and working elsewhere?

In theory, almost any social objective can be justified as being in the long-term interests of a corporation.[7] Businesses will best prosper on a planet that is not impoverished by a climate crisis, as well as in stable communities with lower levels of inequality, a vibrant middle class, and a respect for fundamental human rights. The key question is: "How long term?" Not every activity taken to advance a social welfare objective is, in practice, justifiable as commensurate with shareholder value, "enlightened" or otherwise. In the long run, we are all dead, and this is also true of companies that must balance the return expected by certain long-term investments against the possibility that the company will no longer be around to enjoy the fruits of today's sacrifices.

The discount rate applied to most corporate investments, itself partly a function of the corporation's weighted average cost of capital, means that cash flows generated more than ten years or so in the future often have a small present value.[8] This in turn means that when the net present value of an extremely long-term investment is evaluated, it is frequently less than the returns on alternative, shorter-term investments. For example, in a recent paper, the finance scholar, Roberto Tallarita, shows that the discount rates used by investors "massively underestimate the social value of climate mitigation."[9] We might decry this fact, but that would probably be a mistake. Making investments in ways that generate the highest return for a firm (net of opportunity costs) is the essential mechanism that produces the wealth that makes modern life possible and generates the resources we require to deal with social problems.[10] In any event, as we will see in the next section, a corporation that consistently fails to make investments with the best risk-adjusted return will eventually go out of business.

In practice, deliberately ambiguous terms like "enlightened shareholder value" and "ESG" are rhetorical devices used to disguise the necessity for hard choices, in particular about the relevant time horizon and discount rate for corporate investments. The great economist Robert Merton called it "escap[ing] the dilemma by swift flight from it."[11]

In an effort to navigate the conceptual confusion, this chapter will use "True CSR" to describe social welfare-maximizing activities that have a lower expected return than the alternatives. In light of the previous discussion, we can see that the central distinction is not between actions that benefit shareholders and actions that benefit other constituencies (in other words, "shareholder" vs. "stakeholder"). Rather, the distinction is between investments made because they have a high net present value and investments made that are known to have a lower net present value than alternatives, and which thus reflect noncommercial motivations. These latter investments are what we mean when we talk about True CSR.[12]

As it happens, there is some empirical evidence that, at least in a general way, the "CSR" measured by various commercial rating schemes has some overlap with what I am calling "True CSR." Research on a large sample of firms in the period between 1992 and 2014 shows that the investments made by high CSR firms are less valuable, presumably because the firms choose not to pursue more accretive opportunities.[13] Similarly, market reactions to announcements of CSR investments are generally negative.[14] This decline in share price suggests the market believes corporate assets are being deployed to less efficient uses. Another study finds that increases in CSR ratings are associated with negative future stock returns and declines in firm return on assets.[15] Finance scholars also find evidence that SRI investors both expect and receive lower returns from investments designed to have a nonfinancial impact.[16] Summarizing the empirical literature on this topic, one group of scholars observe, "the evidence that socially responsible firms have lower discount rates, and thereby investors have lower expected returns, is stronger than the evidence that socially responsible firms deliver higher profits or growth."[17]

11.2 WHAT IF COMPANIES ARE EMBEDDED IN COMPETITIVE MARKETS?

Why is it difficult for companies to pursue what we are calling True CSR? It seems obvious that a company couldn't invest in negative-return True CSR projects without seriously imperiling its financial health, but what about profitable projects that fall into the category of "True CSR" just because they are less profitable than the alternatives? For example, what is so wrong about a power plant pursuing a profitable voluntary carbon capture and sequestration program, even though it would be more profitable to abandon the program? The answer to these questions involves the nature of corporate governance and the nature of competitive markets.

11.2.1 *Theory*

Corporate governance as a channel for real-world effects can be usefully contrasted with traditional top-down regulation, such as carbon taxes or carbon emission limits. Regulation is imposed in many different forms, but in all these forms, regulation differs from corporate governance initiatives in several respects, principally that regulation makes certain outcomes mandatory and imposes costs on the firm in the event it fails to abide by the regulations. Actions taken through the corporate governance channel, on the other hand, are discretionary, and there is no financial penalty associated with those actions, except those exacted by the market. This gives rise to the most salient fact about regulation: it usually impacts all the firms competing in a market in roughly the same way. On the other hand, social and environmental welfare objectives pursued voluntarily as a matter of corporate governance affect only the firm in question.

In a perfectly competitive market, no corporation can voluntarily increase its costs and remain in business if its competitors do not act similarly. In such a market, the price of goods sold is identical to their cost (which includes, of course, the cost of capital). Even if a market rewards the achievement of social objects by, say, paying a premium for electrical power with a lower carbon footprint, the corporation can only spend an amount on carbon reduction equal to the market premium it can extract from consumers. If the corporation asks consumers for more than this, then its competitors will offer their own power at lower prices and drive the corporation out of business. If the generous corporation keeps its power prices competitive, it will have to reduce what it pays to employees below market (in which case the employees will eventually leave) or it will have to reduce the return it provides the bank or other investors below market (in which case it will be unable to secure capital). In either event, a company engaging in social activities that are less profitable than the alternative (in other words, more expensive than the alternative) will eventually go out of business in a competitive market.

The way we acknowledge this basic truth of economic theory is that we generally do not expect companies in clearly competitive markets to unilaterally engage in acts of social responsibility. We do not, as Milton Friedman once pointed out, expect mom-and-pop corner stores to sell their food below cost to help those who shop there.[18] But there is a great gulf between these sorts of firms and our public corporations. How closely do our largest firms approach the ideal of perfect competition?

As we saw in Chapter 9, the average American has a greatly exaggerated notion of the profits made by companies after taxes. The best estimates of scholars are that widely held American companies on average make very little over their costs. While this is a conclusion that will seem immediately suspicious to some readers, it is supported by an easily ascertained phenomenon: in every public company in America, most of the people in that company spend nearly all their time working directly on profit-making activities. This appears to be a major concern for these people. How do we know? Because all of us would like to work less hard and to work on more pleasurable things, like giving away money. Instead, businesspeople find themselves working on very difficult things, like re-engineering production lines in factories.

The other fact that seems to suggest the finance researchers are correct is the sheer amount of anxiety in American executive suites. These are largely not occupied by smug plutocrats smoking cigars. Instead, their overall atmosphere, tangible on even a short visit, is a lurking worry about the future. Intel was riding very high at the time its CEO, Andy Grove, disclosed his personal motto: "Only the paranoid survive."[19] Since then, even with healthy doses of paranoia, Intel missed the shift to mobile computing, lost ground to its rivals in cutting-edge technologies like the chips that run artificial intelligence engines, and recently lost the title of the world's largest chipmaker.[20] Its once proud gross margin on sales has been sliding for over a decade. Business executives know this story as well as dozens of others. Even if things are good now, they know this can change fast in a competitive market.

You can't run a business for long in which, as Henry Manne puts it, "the marginal returns to the corporation are less than the returns available from some alternative expenditure."[21] In his survey of the literature on CSR and financial performance, Professor David Vogel points out that lists of the most socially responsible firms in the past would have included: (1) Atlantic Richfield (acquired by British Petroleum); (2) Control Data (after massive losses divided into two companies, neither of which engage in unusual levels of CSR); (3) Cummins Engine (forced by competition to abandon its generous employment practices); (4) Dayton-Hudson (barely survived a hostile takeover in the 1980s); (5) Levi-Straus (forced by declining sales in the 1990s to abandon its domestic manufacturing pledge); (6) Polaroid (filed for bankruptcy in 2001); (7) Chiquita Brands (declared bankruptcy in 2001); (8) The Body Shop (investor pressure resulted in changes to CSR approach and management); (9) Ben and Jerry's (a series of failures and management changes before being acquired by Unilever); and (10) Enron (bankruptcy and scandal) among others.[22] These companies didn't necessarily fail or suffer setbacks because of their commitments to social causes; they failed or suffered setbacks because succeeding year after year in competitive markets is hard.

Even if key markets were not competitive, the incentives of managers and companies would militate against True CSR expenditures. This book reflects the experience of its author that businesspeople, whether in board rooms or executive offices, are generally decent and sincere. They can generally be trusted when they say they care about things like global warming and LGBTQ+ issues. This chapter has merely been arguing that markets constrain managers in what they can do to unilaterally solve pressing social and environmental problems. Nevertheless, it would be foolish to ignore the fact that the limited amounts that might be spent on True CSR initiatives without weakening the company's competitive position are the very same amounts that could be spent to benefit the managers themselves.

We don't have to accept an extreme version of agency cost theory to anticipate that some of this discretionary surplus will be spent on above-market salaries, less work, and perquisites, rather than social objects. Henry Manne argues that "we should anticipate corporate managers utilizing the available funds for charitable purposes in about the same way that any wealthy individuals might be expected to contribute to charities."[23] In the US, one-third of the population does not give to charity, and total donations level off around 2 to 3 percent of income (1.44 percent of GDP).[24]

We always assume that managers will be generous in allocating corporate contributions to True CSR causes because it is "not their money," but this assumption seems questionable if we understand that the money for CSR initiatives doesn't come from the corporation or its shareholders; it comes in a way from the pool of money available to the managers themselves.

Another conflict with True CSR arises in relation to the corporation's own interests. Firms are inherently commercial entities. They have a financial interest in every transaction. Managers making decisions to engage in voluntary CSR expenditures will always be tempted to choose those expenditures that will most burnish the company's reputation. This will exert an almost gravitational pull to engage in those activities that have the highest profile and are the most relevant to current public concerns, rather than choosing activities most intrinsically connected to solving a social problem. This is why so many claims of hypocrisy, greenwashing, and woke-washing appear credible.[25] It is also why firms usually seem to address a social problem created by their activities only after it becomes a public relations issue.[26]

11.2.2 *Empirical Evidence*

There are several different possible approaches to empirically testing whether corporations can, in fact, engage in significant True CSR activities. Unfortunately, most of the energy over the past four decades has gone into looking at whether companies that rank highly according to some commercial CSR metric outperform their peers.[27] The object of this body of research is to demonstrate that there are advantages to companies engaging in CSR or, at least, that there are no disadvantages. A vast literature has accumulated on this topic and, as Professor Vogel observed, "[i]ts central conclusion can be easily summarized: at best, it is inconclusive."[28] A recent meta-analysis found that of 251 studies, 59 percent revealed a nonsignificant relationship between CSR and a corporation's financial results.[29] Looking at all the studies in aggregate, however, there appears to be "a mildly positive relationship between corporate social performance and corporate financial performance."[30] The improvement is so slight, however, that the researchers conclude, "[c]itizens looking … to cure society's pressing ills ought not to appeal to financial returns alone to mobilize corporate involvement."[31]

Unfortunately, even this pessimistic conclusion is unlikely to be true. The sorts of studies used in CSR research usually fail to distinguish between social expenditures made instrumentally to secure better competitive outcomes and those expenditures made as ends in themselves, with lower marginal returns than the alternatives. (These latter investments are the ones we have been calling "True CSR.") We know from the empirical literature that some expenditures included in CSR rating schemes enhance a firm's ability to recruit and retain employees, give it advantages in competing for customers, facilitate a reputation that protects the firm in emergencies, and generate the social license that permits it to operate without interference from the community or regulators.[32] As far back as 1883, an English court pointed out in relation to company-sponsored employee picnics: "The law does not say that there are to be no cakes and ale, but there are to be no cakes and ale except such as are required for the benefit of the company."[33] The CSR-financial performance literature tells us something we already knew, that some attention to non-shareholder constituencies is always essential to commercial success.

There are significant additional problems with these studies. The measures they use for "CSR" are often quite poor, including things like media ratings of admired companies and insiders' self-reported impressions.[34] Even worse, as we will see in Chapter 12, the various third-party rating schemes used by researchers as an alternative often provide conflicting judgments about companies, lacking both validity and predictive power. The causal direction of superior financial performance and social expenditures is a perennial issue, as well as the question of whether the connection between social expenditures and firm performance is being driven by some third variable such as a firm's size, location, or particular industry.[35] Finally, even what counts as financial performance is unclear as one survey of the literature found researchers were using seventy different ways of measuring it.[36]

While less extensive than the literature on financial performance, there is also a body of research that looks at CSR outcomes in relation to various corporate governance variables (such as the number of independent directors or whether the CEO is also chair of the board). These studies suffer from most of the same limitations as the financial performance literature.[37] The most significant is that once again, the corporate governance studies are unable to distinguish between investments ostensibly benefiting non-shareholder constituencies (but actually made with the aim of maximizing financial returns), from those investments made notwithstanding alternatives with higher net present values.

The more useful empirical approaches for the purpose of this chapter are studies that look inside firms to detect the motivations of corporate actors. Even better are those studies that look at behavior under different corporate governance regimes, including ones more friendly to non-shareholder stakeholders (and thus True CSR), to determine if corporate behavior changes. A third class of study looks at actual True CSR outcomes and analyzes whether they were produced by corporate governance channels or some other cause.

11.2.2.1 What Are the Motivations of Corporate Actors?

There is a lot of research that attempts to understand why corporate leaders do certain things; none of it supports the view that when acting in their professional roles, they are significantly committed to nonfinancial outcomes. Executive pay practices are almost exclusively concerned with economic performance. According to the Conference Board, only 2.6 percent of the Russell 3000 companies use any nonfinancial metric to award bonuses.[38] If we narrow our gaze just to the CEOs sitting on the board of the Business Roundtable when it issued its 2019 statement in support of CSR, only three of them had their pay even slightly linked to a quantified stakeholder metric.[39] In each of these cases, the percentage of the bonus connected to CSR outcomes was, in the words of researchers, "negligible."[40] America's companies may talk about the importance of CSR, but they pay their CEOs as if the only thing that matters is competitive success. The equity incentives historically promoted by the governance industry are actually negatively correlated with CSR.[41]

The arrival of the Covid pandemic provides a natural experiment for how corporations handle executive compensation. The pandemic provided managers with opportunities to show solidarity with their workers, communities, customers, and suppliers. Only 17 percent of the Russell 3000 decided to reduce executive compensation, and these companies were the ones that were most negatively financially impacted by the pandemic.[42] The voluntary salary reductions were related to financial performance, not some version of social solidarity. In fact, researchers found "companies with better ESG scores are *less likely* to make compensation changes, even when economic performance is held constant." They dryly conclude, "This finding is unexpected."[43]

The Business Roundtable statement on corporate governance has proven particularly useful for understanding how corporate managers treat non-shareholder constituencies. Researchers report many difficulties with accepting the statement as a guide to actual managerial motivation. One study finds that the signatories had higher rates of environmental and labor-related compliance violations than their peers.[44] These violations were not trivial. The Roundtable signatories were "more likely to have paid a settlement in lawsuits alleging workplace discrimination or wage theft" as well as paying more for environmental violations.[45] The signatory firms even pay their CEOs more than carefully matched peers.[46]

Only one of the forty-eight signatories that responded to researcher inquiries advised that the decision to sign the statement was approved by the board of directors.[47] The same researchers found that of the twenty companies represented on the Roundtable's board of directors, nineteen did nothing to change their governance guidelines to reflect the pro-CSR sentiments of the statement.[48] The one that did change their governance policies to include a reference to constituencies made it clear it was only to improve advancing "the interests of the Corporation's shareholders."[49] It is hard to take the Business Roundtable statement seriously if the companies, themselves, don't take it seriously.

For their part, shareholders apparently shrugged at the news. "An event study around the announcement of the BRT [Business Roundtable] suggests no stock price effect of signing, suggesting that the market viewed the BRT Statement as cheap talk rather than a commitment to change."[50] Investors were correct, as these BRT Statement signatories subsequent to Covid's impact paid out 20 percent more capital to shareholders than peer firms and were 20 percent more likely to announce employee layoffs or furloughs.[51]

Shareholder proposals on CSR issues make up a very large percentage of the total set of proposals made each year and they demonstrate a similar pattern of near-total irrelevance. In contrast to proposals made suggesting corporate governance changes, social issue proposals attract very little support.[52] In fact, 75 percent of these sorts of proposals receive less than 20 percent of favorable votes.[53] Looking at one class of successful CSR proposals, those that barely achieve majority support, Caroline Flammer finds evidence that these close-call proposals were the ones more closely tied to financial performance. They are more frequently found in what she terms "stakeholder-sensitive" industries, where corporate performance depends greatly on the relationship with customers and employees.[54] In other words, this class of successful "social" proposal appears to have nothing to do with True CSR, but with improving the firms' relationship with key groups.

Even when there are high levels of agreement in America about social outcomes, along with consumer boycotts, the evidence for True CSR is discouraging. Following the unprovoked Russian invasion of Ukraine, many companies left the Russian market. Researchers report, however, that the most likely companies to announce their withdrawal from Russia were the ones with the least revenue exposure to the country.[55] The decision to withdraw also tended to be associated with public boycott campaigns, and these boycott campaigns were aimed at the largest American companies, not the lower-profile companies that, it turns out, were most exposed to the Russian economy.[56] The researchers conclude, "[o]ur empirical analysis shows how – even in the presence of public consensus around a particular socially responsible action – the risk is that managers could engage in woke-washing and protect stakeholders only to the extent beneficial for shareholder value maximization."[57]

A final source of information about the motivations of corporate actors arises from surveys of corporate directors. Often, these studies find limited enthusiasm for CSR. PwC's 2020 Annual Corporate Directors Survey found that only 38 percent of board members think ESG issues have a financial impact on their companies.[58] It is important to keep in mind that "ESG" includes "governance," so who knows how much lower the number would be if directors were polled solely on less-remunerative "social" and "environmental" activities? It is suggestive that a team of researchers investigating the credentials of directors of the Fortune 100 companies found that only five of the 1,188 directors had relevant experience for "environmental" issues, and in relation to "social" issues, the number of directors with skills related to "human rights, human resource development, benefits and safety" was "negligible."[59] Other surveys find CSR programs are not managed at the top of the organization but, "initiated and run in an uncoordinated way by a variety of internal managers."[60]

The empirical research on corporate managers' motivations can be easily summarized: they are almost exclusively concerned with maximizing profitability. To the extent non-shareholder constituencies factor into their decisions, it is instrumentally, as members of the productive coalition that must be kept together for the corporation to achieve market success. Studies of how directors handle CSR show they weigh the costs and benefits of CSR investments and adopt those CSR practices that positively impact firm performance, just as economic theory would suggest.[61]

Of course, the failure of corporate leaders to act in accordance with the kind of True CSR promises made by the BRT Statement or in their annual reports may be due to cynical personal hypocrisy on the part of boards and executives rather than an inevitable consequence of the strong constraints of market competition, as this book has been arguing. The charge of hypocrisy is hard to credit, however, as it suggests an almost universal duplicity in this one area that is hard to reconcile with the high levels of social trust enjoyed by businesses relative to other institutions.[62] A simpler explanation would be that corporate leaders actually do strongly value various constituencies, but they are compelled to pursue competitive advantage. As we shall see, this view finds support in the other bodies of empirical research looking at CSR.

11.2.2.2 What Impact Do CSR-friendly Corporate Governance Regimes Have on Behavior?

One of the most prominent suggestions by governance reformers interested in increasing True CSR is to revise the corporate fiduciary duty to permit or require directors to take into account the interests of a broad range of constituencies. As we saw in Chapter 9, this reform has already occurred in many jurisdictions and there is no evidence that directors use this freedom from focusing on shareholder outcomes to change their behavior. They continue to run their companies, just as they did before, with a concern for maximizing their profitability, which primarily benefits shareholders.

Professors Bebchuk, Kastiel, and Tallarita recently looked at the contracts negotiated in over 100 different private equity acquisitions of public companies in constituency jurisdictions.[63] They were interested in discovering who benefitted from corporate leaders' bargaining activities. Freed from a shareholder primacy model of corporate duties, did managers concern themselves with their employees or the environment? What they found was that the usually long negotiations between the private equity funds and corporate managers resulted in sizeable premiums paid to shareholders and additional payments to the executives. What they did not find is much evidence that managers were bargaining on behalf of non-shareholder constituencies. "In particular, in ninety-seven percent of the transactions in the entire sample ... corporate leaders did not negotiate for any limitations of the buyer's post-deal freedom to fire employees and reduce employment. Indeed, some of the acquisition agreements explicitly endorse this unlimited post-deal freedom to fire."[64] None of the agreements imposed real constraints designed to protect the corporations' consumers, suppliers, creditors, or the environment. In keeping with what we saw in Chapter 9, changes to the fiduciary duty produced by constituency statutes have no effect.

Interestingly, the only changes to corporate behavior detectable in the studies around constituency statutes are ones that are directly related to improving the competitive performance of the affected corporations. These companies remain just as focused on delivering appealing returns to shareholders (visible, for example, in earnings management practices and the failure of a constituency state stock price discount to appear).[65] This does not mean, however, that corporate behavior remains unchanged. Rather, corporate managers apparently use the freedom provided by constituency statutes to get better deals from corporate lenders and customers, who may have less fear that their firm-specific investments will be expropriated by shareholders.[66] Using the enactment of constituency statutes as a natural experiment, researchers find they cause companies to expand their R&D activities, producing more patents per employee, and the quality of these patents increases, measured by the number of times these patents are cited.[67] (Increased R&D is frequently used as a proxy for long-term corporate planning by managers.[68]) In contrast to the predictions of both those who believe a stakeholder regime will lead to more True CSR investments and those agency cost story die-hards who believe it will result in more negligence and profusion, the average value of cash holdings for companies incorporated in constituency jurisdictions actually increases.[69] Improved outcomes for constituencies, such as employees, which might impair firm profitability, do not occur.[70]

In terms of other governance structures, we repeatedly find that increasing managers' freedom from shareholders does not alter managerial focus on optimizing the firm's financial performance. For example, one group of researchers looked at the impact of staggered boards on CSR.[71] Helpfully, they decomposed the measures of CSR into "positive CSR," which consists of investments in employees or the environment, and "negative CSR," which consists of the firm's involvement in some social or environmental controversy.[72] The most salient feature of staggered boards is that they provide corporate leaders with a significant degree of freedom from the shareholders, as these boards make both proxy campaigns and hostile takeovers exceptionally difficult. The study thus allows us to look in a general way at what effect leaving managers to their own devices has on their propensity to engage in True CSR. The researchers found that staggered boards invested in "positive CSR" in the same ways as companies without staggered boards, but that they used their freedom from shareholders to engage in activities that made them more likely to experience a "negative CSR" event. Since it is difficult to understand what these activities would be aimed at, other than enhancing corporate profits, it does not seem unreasonable to conclude that corporate leaders use the freedom granted by staggered board structures to compete more aggressively.

Similar results are reported by researchers looking at the impact of dual-class shares on environmental performance.[73] Dual-class shares generally provide managers with increased power relative to outside shareholders. As we would expect in light of the research we have encountered so far, dual-class share structures appear to be associated with worse environmental performance.[74] The most recent of these studies, "[u]sing a sample of 3,400 firm years from 2013 through 2016, … found that dual-class firms have lower CSR performance than their single-class counterparts and that this difference primarily relates to the social and environmental dimensions of CSR."[75]

As a whole, the evidence from empirical studies seems to suggest that managers use the freedom conferred by constituency statutes, staggered boards, and dual-class voting structures to focus on corporate strategies that involve less True CSR. Displacing shareholders from their usually central place in corporate governance, either by recasting the fiduciary duty or weakening their power to discipline managers, does not result in the increase in True CSR hoped for by corporate governance reformers. Even more importantly, the corporate governance structures we have looked at are the ones that are generally assumed to allow longer-term firm investments (that is why technology companies frequently use them), and yet they result in less, not more, CSR.[76]

11.2.2.3 Is Corporate Governance Responsible for Producing True CSR Outcomes?

Corporations engage in (usually well-publicized) CSR behaviors. There is a small body of research that attempts to understand what is driving these actions ostensibly taken against the corporation's financial self-interest. Generally, researchers find either that there is a clear ulterior motive to the social activity, which strongly suggests it is not True CSR, or that the investment was influenced by something other than corporate governance.

An example of "ulterior motive" research is a recent study that looked at political statements made over a five-year period in the past decade by the CEOs of the

S&P 500. It finds that Republican-leaning CEOs (measured by their personal donations to that party) "are 88 percent more likely to engage in activism [which has a liberal Democrat-slant] than their Democrat-leaning and neutral peers."[77] The researchers go on to note the obvious point: "If furthering their private political views were the dominant motive, the CEOs' political donations and public opinions should be aligned."[78] One possible motive for CEOs' strategic behavior can be discerned in the evidence that, following a Democrat-leaning initiative, there is a slight but material increase in the corporation's share price and an increase in its sales over the following quarter. The positive economic effects are not visible for Republican-leaning political activism.

A similar point is made by a couple of studies that look at the relationship between CSR expenditures and bad behavior. They find that corporations are more likely to make charitable donations or burnish their CSR credentials if they have a bad reputation.[79] Interestingly, this bad reputation can be the result of failures in areas of the business far removed from the social expenditures. For example, firms with weaknesses in corporate governance are more likely to advance CSR social objectives in the areas of the environment, community relations, and human rights.

Shareholders are one of the most prominent corporate governance channels claimed to be capable of producing True CSR. This expectation has been accompanied by a vast increase in ESG investment funds with explicit social purposes. The most recent research finds that the purchase of stock in a company by a fund self-identifying as socially responsible is not followed by any measurable change in that company's workplace safety, employee satisfaction, gender or racial board diversity, or levels of pollution.[80] The arrival of ESG funds in a corporation's capital stack does not lead to improvements in environmental or social responsibility. This is similar to the discovery decades ago that labor unions acting as activists were a "model for any large institutional investor attempting to maximize return on capital."[81] Direct employee ownership of companies also has little effect on the behavior of firms.[82]

For its part, as we have seen, shareholder activism rarely involves a nonfinancial object,[83] and a large body of research finds successful activist campaigns are associated with worse outcomes for non-shareholder constituencies: employees, customers, suppliers, and debtholders.

Probably the best example of the corporate governance channel failing to explain a positive social outcome is provided by worker representation on corporate boards. This is a very prominent proposed reform to North American corporate governance. On the surface, it is appealing because there is clear evidence that European workers in companies with these sorts of board arrangements are paid more and face less earnings risk.[84] However, this effect turns out to be entirely a function of these companies' larger size and higher unionization rate. When unionization and size are controlled for, the impact of the corporate governance channel – worker representation on boards – turns out to be nonexistent.[85] Several studies conducted over decades have found the same thing: the most dramatic step that is possible in corporate governance – placing a non-shareholder constituency on the board of directors itself – has no effect on the welfare outcomes of that constituency.[86] As economic theory would suggest, boards don't find themselves able to voluntarily produce much True CSR.

11.3 SUMMARY: WHY THIS MATTERS

Activists trying to reform corporate governance to advance important social and environmental objectives think that these reforms will really make a difference. Bernie Sanders and Elizabeth Warren are not proposing to put employees on the boards of directors of America's largest companies because they are hoping companies will improve the food in the corporate cafeteria or install a foosball table in the employee lounge. They are promoting corporate governance reform as a way to materially reduce income inequality and job insecurity. It doesn't matter that a company is slightly nicer to its employees if it continues to pursue efficiencies through automation and accessing cheaper international labor pools. The job assigned to corporate governance is to solve big social and environmental problems. We have seen that corporate governance is not up to this task.

Even if reformers were successful in creating effective governance reforms so that social outcomes actually displaced economic outcomes, it is not clear that we would be happy with the result. For one thing, the progressive causes celebrated by reformers are not the only ones occupying the field. Progressive causes rarely command the allegiance of more than a large minority of voters. The employees who stand to receive considerably more power in many American schemes of governance reform have tended, as a class, to support the political vision of the Republicans.[87] Individual retail shareholders apparently rank the environmental aspects of their investments as the least important consideration.[88] This helps us understand a final reason to worry if the governance reforms are successful. It would introduce our current polarized politics into one of the few remaining institutions that have mostly avoided being subsumed by this conflict. Ever since Voltaire's famous *Letters on the English*, it has been obvious that a narrow concern for commercial success has provided a way of getting along for people with strongly held conflicting political and religious opinions.[89] According to surveys, business corporations are currently the *only* trusted institution in the US.[90] They are also the one in which political and social conflict plays the smallest role – this is not likely a coincidence.

There is a large, modern social science literature that finds markets produce unrivaled levels of cooperative behavior and social trust.[91] Replacing the governance market with regulations designed to secure some *ex post* social welfare outcome may lead to declines in cooperation and trust that we can ill afford. The phenomenon of externally imposed rules crowding out pro-social motivations is reflected elsewhere in social science literature.[92] Imposing a social welfare-inflected reform to corporate governance might be worth considerable sacrifice, but not if the reforms are incapable from the outset of producing the desired outcomes.

NOTES

1 Adam Smith, *An Inquiry into the Nature and Causes of the Wealth of Nations* (London: W. Strahan and T. Cadell, 1776) at p. 160.
2 Peter Thiel, *Zero to One: Notes on Startups, or How to Build the Future* (New York: Crown Business, 2014) at p. 32.
3 US, Bill S.3348, Accountable Capitalism Act, 115th Congress, 2018; Bernie Sanders, "Corporate Accountability and Democracy," online: https://berniesanders.com/issues/corporate-accountability-and-democracy/.
4 Directorate-General for Justice and Consumers and EY, "Study on Directors' Duties and Sustainable Corporate Governance: Final Report" (July 2020), online: *Publications Office of the European Union*, https://op.europa.eu/en/publication-detail/-/publication/e47928a2-d2ob-11ea-adf7-01aa75ed71a1/language-en.
5 *Companies Act 2006*, 2006, c. 46.
6 John C. Coffee, Jr., "The Future of Disclosure: ESG, Common Ownership, and Systematic Risk" (2021) 2021:2 *Columbia Business Law Review* 602–650 at 632–633. See also, Max M. Schanzenbach and Robert H. Sitkoff, "Reconciling Fiduciary Duty and Social Conscience: The Law and Economics of ESG Investing by a Trustee" (2020) 72:2 *Stanford Law Review* 381–454 at 439; Susan N. Gary, "Best Interests in the Long Term: Fiduciary Duties and ESG Integration" (2019) 90:3 *University of Colorado Law Review* 731–802.
7 Paul Cox, Stephen Brammer and Andrew Millington, "An Empirical Examination of Institutional Investor Preferences for Corporate Social Performance" (2004) 52:1 *Journal of Business Ethics* 27–43 at 29; Alex Edmans, *Grow the Pie: How Great Companies Deliver Both Purpose and Profit* (Cambridge, UK: Cambridge University Press, 2020); Colin Mayer, *Prosperity: Better Business Makes the Greater Good* (Oxford: Oxford University Press, 2018).
8 Michael T. Jacobs and Anil Shivdasani, "Do You Know Your Cost of Capital?" (July-August 2012), *Harvard Business Review*, online: https://hbr.org/2012/07/do-you-know-your-cost-of-capital; Stephen A Ross et al., *Corporate Finance*, 8th Canadian ed. (Canada: McGraw-Hill Education, 2019) at pp. 176–177, 360; Niels Joachim Gormsen and Kilian Huber, "Corporate Discount Rates" (2023), *National Bureau of Economic Research Working Paper No.* 31329, online: *NBER*, www.nber.org/papers/w31329.
9 Roberto Tallarita, "The Limits of Portfolio Primacy" (2023) 76:2 *Vanderbilt Law Review* 511–569 at 518.
10 Tyler Cowan, *Stubborn Attachments: A Vision for a Society of Free, Prosperous, and Responsible Individuals* (San Francisco: Stripe Press, 2018).
11 Robert K. Merton, *Sociological Ambivalence and Other Essays* (New York: The Free Press, 1976) at p. 88.
12 This formulation of CSR is aligned with that used in the economics literature: Lucian A. Bebchuk and Roberto Tallarita, "The Illusory Promise of Stakeholder Governance" (2020) 106:1 *Cornell Law Review* 91–177 [Bebchuk and Tallarita, "Illusory Promise"]; Anjan V. Thakor and Robert E. Quinn, "The Economics of Higher Purpose" (2013), *European Corporate Governance Institute – Finance Working Paper No.* 395/2013, online: SSRN, https://ssrn.com/abstract=2362454 at 2; Rebecca Henderson and Eric Van den Steen, "Why Do Firms Have 'Purpose'? The Firm's Role as a Carrier of Identity and Reputation" (2015) 105:5 *American Economic Review* 326–330 at 327; Abagail McWilliams, Donald S. Siegel and Patrick M. Wright, "Corporate Social Responsibility: Strategic Implications" (2006) 43:1 *Journal of Management Studies* 1–18 at 1.

13 Avishek Bhandari and David Javakhadze, "Corporate Social Responsibility and Capital Allocation Efficiency" (2017) 43 *Journal of Corporate Finance* 354–377 [Bhandari and Javakhadze, "Capital Allocation"]. See also, Joscha Nollet, George Filis and Evangelos Mitrokostas, "Corporate Social Responsibility and Financial Performance: A Non-Linear and Disaggregated Approach" (2016) 52 *Economic Modelling* 400–407 [Nollet, Filis and Mitrokostas, "Disaggregated Approach"]; Sung C. Bae, Kiyoung Chang and Ha-Chin Yi, "Are More Corporate Social Investments Better? Evidence of Non-linearity Effect on Costs of US Bank Loans" (2018) 38 *Global Finance Journal* 82–96.

14 Philipp Krüger, "Corporate Goodness and Shareholder Wealth" (2015) 115:2 *Journal of Financial Economics* 304–329 at 313. See also, Gunther Capelle-Blancard and Aurélien Petit, "Every Little Helps? ESG News and Stock Market Reaction" (2019) 157:2 *Journal of Business Ethics* 543–565 [Capelle-Blancard and Petit, "Every Little Helps"].

15 Alberta Di Giuli and Leonard Kostovetsky, "Are Red or Blue Companies More Likely to Go Green? Politics and Corporate Social Responsibility" (2014) 111:1 *Journal of Financial Economics* 158–180.

16 Brad M. Barber, Adair Morse and Ayako Yasuda, "Impact Investing" (2021) 139:1 *Journal of Financial Economics* 162–185.

17 Bradford Cornell and Aswath Damodaran, "Valuing ESG: Doing Good or Sounding Good?" (2020), online: SSRN https://ssrn.com/abstract=3557432 at 22.

18 David Chan Smith, "How Milton Friedman Read His Adam Smith: The Neoliberal Suspicion of Business and the Critique of Corporate Social Responsibility" (2020), online: SSRN, https://ssrn.com/abstract=3674604 at 27.

19 Andrew S. Grove, *Only the Paranoid Survive: How to Identify and Exploit the Crisis Point that Challenge Every Business* (New York: Currency Doubleday, 1996).

20 Slejven Djurakovic, "Intel Can't Even Grow Profits During a Global Chip Shortage – Where Did it All Go Wrong?," *The Conversation*, January 28, 2022, online: https://theconversation.com/intel-cant-even-grow-profits-during-a-global-chip-shortage-where-did-it-all-go-wrong-175877.

21 Henry G. Manne and Henry C. Wallich, *The Modern Corporation and Social Responsibility* (Washington, DC: American Enterprise Institute for Public Policy Research, 1972) at p. 4 [Manne and Wallich, *Social Responsibility*].

22 David J. Vogel, "Is There a Market for Virtue? The Business Case for Corporate Social Responsibility" (2005) 47:4 *California Management Review* 19–45 at 36, 39–41 [Vogel, "Market for Virtue"].

23 Manne and Wallich, *Social Responsibility*, above at note 21 at pp. 20–21.

24 *Statistics on U.S. Generosity*, Philanthropy Roundtable, online: www.philanthropyround table.org/almanac/statistics-on-u-s-generosity/.

25 See, for example, Richard Dahl, "Green Washing: Do You Know What You're Buying?" (2010) 118:6 *Environmental Health Perspectives* A247–A252 (referencing TerraChoice Report which, after examining 2,219 products making green claims, the report found 98 percent of the products had indicia of greenwashing at A247); Mary-Hunter McDonnell and Brayden King, "Keeping Up Appearances: Reputation Threat and Prosocial Responses to Social Movements Boycotts" (2013) 58:3 *Administrative Science Quarterly* 387–419; Magali A. Delmas and Vanessa Cuerel Burbano, "The Drivers of Greenwashing" (2011) 54:1 *California Management Review* 64–87; Thomas P. Lyon and A. Wren Montgomery, "The Means and Ends of Greenwash" (2015) 28:2 *Organization and Environment* 223–249; Eun-Hee Kim and Thomas P. Lyon, "Greenwash vs. Brownwash: Exaggeration and Undue Modesty in Corporate Sustainability Disclosure" (2015) 26:3 *Organization Science* 705–723.

26 See, for example, the case of sweatshops: Denis G. Arnold and Laura P. Hartman, "Worker Rights and Low Wage Industrialization: How to Avoid Sweatshops" (2006) 28:3 *Human Rights Quarterly* 676–700; Benjamin Powell, "A Case Against Child Labor Prohibitions" (July 29, 2014) *Cato Institute – Economic Development Bulletin No. 21*, online: www.cato .org/economic-development-bulletin/case-against-child-labor-prohibitions;   Benjamin Powell and David Skarbek, "Sweatshop Wages and Third World Living Standards: Are the Jobs Worth the Sweat?" (2006) 27:2 *Journal of Labor Research* 263–274.

27 Gunther Capelle-Blancard and Stéphanie Monjon, "Trends in the Literature on Socially Responsible Investment: Looking for the Keys Under the Lamppost" (2012) 21:3 *Business Ethics: A European Review* 239–250 at 239.

28 Vogel, "Market for Virtue," above at note 22 at 29; See also, Joshua D. Margolis, Hillary Anger Elfenbein and James P. Walsh, "Does it Pay to Be Good? A Meta-Analysis and of the Relationship Between Corporate Social and Financial Performance" (2009), online: SSRN, https://ssrn.com/abstract=1866371 [Margolis, Elfenbein and Walsh, "Does it Pay"]; *"Honey, I Shrunk the ESG Alpha": Risk-Adjusting ESG Portfolio Returns*, Scientific Beta Publication (April 2021), online (pdf): https://cdn.ihsmarkit.com/www/ pdf/0521/Honey-I-Shrunk-the-ESG-Alpha.pdf at 7; Hoje Jo and Maretno A. Harjoto, "The Causal Effect of Corporate Governance on Social Responsibility" (2012) 106:1 *Journal of Business Ethics* 53–72 at 53 [Jo and Harjoto, "Causal Effect"]; Inah Bassey Okpa et al., "Implications of Environmental, Social and Governance Dimensions of CSR Practice on Firms' Profitability, Value and Cash Flows in the UK" (2019) 21:5 *Journal of Business and Management* 1–10 at 2; Bhandari and Javakhadze, "Capital Allocation," above at note 13 at 355.

29 Margolis, Elfenbein and Walsh, "Does it Pay," above at note 28 at 21.

30 *Ibid* at 23. See also, Nollet, Filis and Mitrokostas, "Disaggregated Approach," above at note 13; Philipp Schreck, "Reviewing the Business Case for Corporate Social Responsibility: New Evidence and Analysis" (2011) 103:2 *Journal of Business Ethics* 167–188; Markus Kitsmueller and Jay Shimshack, "Economic Perspectives on Corporate Social Responsibility" (2012) 50:1 *Journal of Economic Literature* 51–84.

31 Margolis, Elfenbein and Walsh, "Does it Pay," above at note 28 at 34.

32 *2019 Survey on Shareholder Versus Stakeholder Interests*, Stanford Graduate School of Business, online (pdf): www.gsb.stanford.edu/sites/default/files/publication-pdf/survey-shareholder-versus-stakeholder-interests-2019.pdf; Kristin B. Backhaus, Brett A. Stone and Karl Heiner, "Exploring the Relationship between Corporate Social Performance and Employer Attractiveness" (2002) 41:3 *Business & Society* 292–318; Caroline A Bartel, "Social Comparisons in Boundary-spanning Work: Effects of Community Outreach on Members' Organizational Identity and Identification" (2001) 46:3 *Administrative Science Quarterly* 379–413; Sanker Sen and Chitra Bhanu Bhattacharya, "Does Doing Good Always Lead to Doing Better? Consumer Reactions to Corporate Social Responsibility" (2001) 38:2 *Journal of Marketing Research* 225–243; Karen E. Schnietz and Marc J. Epstein, "Exploring the Financial Value of a Reputation for Corporate Social Responsibility During a Crisis" (2005) 7:4 *Corporate Reputation Review* 327–345; Peter Williams, Alison Gill and Ian Ponsford, "Corporate Social Responsibility at Tourism Destinations: Toward a Social License to Operate" (2007) 11:2 *Tourism Review International* 133–144; Stephen M. Bainbridge, "Making Sense of the Business Roundtable's Reversal on Corporate Purpose" (2021) 46:2 *Journal of Corporation Law* 285–318 at 317; Kee-Hong Bae et al., "Does Corporate Social Responsibility Reduce the Costs of High Leverage? Evidence from Capital Structure and Product Market Interactions" (2019) 100 *Journal of Banking and Finance* 135–150 at 135.

33 Hutton v. West Cork Rly Co (1883) 23 Ch. D. 654.
34 Margolis, Elfenbein and Walsh, "Does it Pay," above at note 28 at 29; Vogel, "Market for Virtue," above at note 22 at 30–31; Tessa Hebb, Heather Hachigian and Rupert Allen, "Measuring the Impact of Engagement in Canada" in Tessa Hebb (ed.), *The Next Generation of Responsible Investing: Advances in Business Ethics Research* (New York: Springer, Dordrecht, 2011), vol. 1, pp. 107–125 at pp. 121–122.
35 Margolis, Elfenbein and Walsh, "Does it Pay," above at note 28 at 29; Jo and Harjoto, "Causal Effect," above at note 28 at 53.
36 Vogel, "Market for Virtue," above at note 22 at 30.
37 Tanusree Jain and Dima Jamali, "Looking Inside the Black Box: The Effect of Corporate Governance on Corporate Social Responsibility" (2016) 24:3 *Corporate Governance: An International Review* 253–273 at 268.
38 Matteo Tonello, *CEO and Executive Compensation Practices: 2019 Edition*, The Conference Board (November 6, 2019), online: www.conference-board.org/topics/ceo-executive-compensation/ceo-executive-compensation-practices-2019 at 27.
39 Bebchuk and Tallarita, "Illusory Promise," above at note 12 at 150–151. See also, David I. Walker, "The Economic (In)significance of Executive Pay ESG Incentives" (2022) 27:2 *Stanford Journal of Law, Business and Finance* 318–352.
40 Bebchuk and Tallarita, "Illusory Promise," above at note 12.
41 Michael Mayberry, "Good for Managers, Bad for Society? Causal Evidence on the Association between Risk-taking Incentives and Corporate Social Responsibility" (2020) 47:9–10 *Journal of Business Finance and Accounting* 1182–1214.
42 Amit Batish et al., "Sharing the Pain: How Did Boards Adjust CEO Pay in Response to COVID-19?" (September 2020), *Stanford Closer Look Series – Corporate Governance Research Initiative*, online: www.gsb.stanford.edu/faculty-research/publications/sharing-pain-how-did-boards-adjust-ceo-pay-response-covid-19.
43 *Ibid* at 2.
44 Aneesh Raghunandan and Shiva Rajgopal, "Do the Socially Responsible Walk the Talk?" (2022), online: SSRN, https://ssrn.com/abstract=3609056 at 2 [Raghunandan and Rajgopal, "Walk the Talk"].
45 *Ibid.*
46 *Ibid.*
47 Lucian Bebchuk and Roberto Tallarita, "'Stakeholder' Capitalism Seems Mostly for Show," *The Wall Street Journal*, August 6, 2020, online: www.wsj.com/articles/stakeholder-capitalism-seems-mostly-for-show-11596755220.
48 Bebchuk and Tallarita, "Illusory Promise," above at note 12 at 134–135.
49 Lucian Bebchuk and Roberto Tallarita, "Was the Business Roundtable Statement Mostly for Show? – (2) Evidence from Corporate Governance Guidelines" (August 18, 2020), *Harvard Law School Forum on Corporate Governance*, online: https://corpgov.law.harvard.edu/2020/08/18/was-the-business-roundtable-statement-mostly-for-show-2-evidence-from-corporate-governance-guidelines/.
50 Raghunandan and Rajgopal, "Walk the Talk," above at note 44 at 2–3. See also, Capelle-Blancard and Petit, "Every Little Helps," above at note 14.
51 Jerry Useem, "Beware of Corporate Promises," *The Atlantic*, August 6, 2020, online: www.theatlantic.com/ideas/archive/2020/08/companies-stand-solidarity-are-licensing-themselves-discriminate/614947/.
52 Geeyoung Min and Hye Young You, "Active Firms and Active Shareholders: Corporate Political Activity and Shareholder Proposals" (2019) 48:1 *The Journal of Legal Studies* 81–116 at 108–109.

53 *Ibid* at 109; Caroline Flammer, "Does Corporate Social Responsibility Lead to Superior Financial Performance? A Regression Discontinuity Approach" (2015) 61:11 *Management Science* 2549–2568 at 2552 [Flammer, "Superior Performance"]; Eugene F. Soltes, Suraj Srinivasan and Rajesh Vijayaraghavan, "What Else Do Shareholders Want? Shareholder Proposals Contested by Firm Management" (2017), *Harvard Business School Accounting and Management Unit Working Paper*, online: SSRN, https://ssrn.com/abstract=2771114 at 25.

54 Flammer, "Superior Performance," above at note 53 at 2550.

55 Anete Pajuste and Anna Toniolo, "Corporate Response to the War in Ukraine: Stakeholder Governance or Stakeholder Pressure?" (2022), *European Corporate Governance Institute – Finance Working Paper No. 839/2022*, online: SSRN, https://ssrn.com/abstract=4183604.

56 *Ibid.*

57 *Ibid* at 47.

58 *Turning Crisis into Opportunity: PwC's 2020 Annual Corporate Directors Survey*, PricewaterhouseCoopers International Limited (2020), online (pdf): www.pwc.com/us/en/services/governance-insights-center/assets/pwc-2020-annual-corporate-directors-survey.pdf at 8.

59 *Ibid*; Tensie Whelan, "Boards Are Obstructing ESG – At Their Own Peril" (January 18, 2021), *Harvard Business Review*, online: https://hbr.org/2021/01/boards-are-obstructing-esg-at-their-own-peril at 2–3.

60 Kasturi Rangan, Lisa Chase and Sohel Karim, "The Truth About CSR" (January-February 2015), *Harvard Business Review*, online: https://hbr.org/2015/01/the-truth-about-csr at 43.

61 Peter Iliev and Lukas Roth, "Director Expertise and Corporate Sustainability" (2023), online: SSRN, https://ssrn.com/abstract=3575501 at 5.

62 *Edelman Trust Barometer* 2022, Edelman (2022), online (pdf): www.edelman.com/sites/g/files/aatuss191/files/2022-01/2022%20Edelman%20Trust%20Barometer%20FINAL_Jan25.pdf at 5 [Edelman, *Trust Barometer*].

63 Lucian A. Bebchuk, Kobi Kastiel and Roberto Tallarita, "For Whom Corporate Leaders Bargain" (2021) 94:6 *Southern California Law Review* 1467–1560.

64 *Ibid* at 1518.

65 K. J. Martijn Cremers, Scott B. Guernsey and Simone M. Sepe, "Stakeholder Orientation and Firm Value" (2019), online: *American Economic Association*, www.aeaweb.org/conference/2019/preliminary/paper/9ZHrGSE9 at 32; Douglas Cumming, Bryce C. Tingle and Feng Zhan, "For Whom (and For When) is the Firm Governed? The Effect of Changes in Corporate Fiduciary Duties on Tax Strategies and Earnings Management" (2021) 27:5 *European Financial Management* 775–813. See also, notes 66–68 below (no effect on relative market valuations).

66 Huasheng Gao, Kai Li and Yujing Ma, "Shareholder Orientation and the Cost of Debt: Evidence from State-Level Adoption of Constituency Statutes" (2021) 56:6 *Journal of Financial and Quantitative Analysis* 1908–1944; Bo Becker and Per Strömberg, "Fiduciary Duties and Equity-Debtholder Conflicts" (2012) 25:6 *The Review of Financial Studies* 1931–1969; Bill B. Francis et al., "The Effect of State Antitakeover Laws on the Firm's Bondholders" (2010) 96:1 *Journal of Financial Economics* 127–154; Jagadison K. Aier, Long Chen and Mikhail Pevzner, "'Debtholders' Demand for Conservatism: Evidence from Changes in Directors' Fiduciary Duties" (2014) 52:5 *Journal of Accounting Research* 993–1027; Ling Cen, Sudipto Dasgupta and Rik Sen, "Discipline or Disruption? Stakeholder Relationships and the Effect of Takeover Threat" (2016) 62:10 *Management Science* 2820–2841; William C. Johnson, Jonathan M. Karpoff and Sangho Yi, "The Bonding Hypothesis of Takeover Defenses: Evidence from IPO Firms" (2015) 117:2

Journal of Financial Economics 307–332 at 329; Po-Hsuan Hsu et al., "Do Constituency Statutes Really Benefit Customers?" (2020), online: www.readcube.com/articles/10.2139% 2Fssrn.3622817.

67 William W. Bratton, "The Separation of Corporate Law and Social Welfare" (2017) 74:2 *Washington and Lee Law Review* 767–790.

68 Rafael Corredoira et al., "The Changing Nature of Firm R&D: Short-Termism & Technological Influence of US Firms" (2021), *Working Paper – Harvard Business School*, online (pdf): www.hbs.edu/faculty/Shared%20Documents/conferences/strategy-science-2021/15_Rachelle%20Sampson_The%20Changing%20Nature.pdf; Anne Marie Knott, "The Real Reasons Companies Are So Focused on the Short Term" (December 13, 2017), *Harvard Business Review*, online: https://hbr.org/2017/12/the-real-reasons-compa nies-are-so-focused-on-the-short-term; Erin Smith, "How Short-Termism Impacts Public and Private R&D Investments" (June 7, 2016), *Bipartisan Policy Center*, online: https:// bipartisanpolicy.org/blog/how-short-termism-impacts-innovation-investments/.

69 Rajib Chowdhury, John A. Doukas and Jong Chool Park, "Stakeholder Orientation and the Value of Cash Holdings: Evidence from a Natural Experiment" (2021) 69 *Journal of Corporate Finance* 102029.

70 Jitendra Aswani et al., "The Cost (and Unbenefit) of Conscious Capitalism" (2022), online: SSRN, https://ssrn.com/abstract=3926335.

71 Charles P. Cullinan, Lois Mahoney and Pamela B. Roush, "Entrenchment vs Long-Term Benefits: Classified Boards and CSR" (2019) 10:1 *Journal of Global Responsibility* 69–86.

72 *Ibid* at 74.

73 Paul Seaborn, Tricia D. Olsen and Jason Howell, "Is Insider Control Good for Environmental Performance? Evidence from Dual-Class Firms" (2020) 59:4 *Business and Society* 716–748 [Seaborn, Olsen and Howell, "Insider Control"]; Charles P. Cullinan, Lois B. Mahoney and Linda Thorne, "CSR Performance: Governance Insights from Dual-class Firms" in Charles Richard Baker (ed.), *Research on Professional Responsibility and Ethics in Accounting* (Bingley, UK: Emerald Publishing Limited, 2020), vol. 23, pp. 23–46 at p. 26 [Cullinan, Mahoney and Thorne, "CSR Performance"].

74 Seaborn, Olsen and Howell, "Insider Control," above at note 73 at 719.

75 Cullinan, Mahoney and Thorne, "CSR Performance," above at note 73 at p. 28.

76 See, for example, Van Thuan Nguyen and Li Xu, "The Impact of Dual Class Structure on Earnings Management Activities" (2010) 37:3–4 *Journal of Business Finance and Accounting* 456–485; Daniel Ferreira et al., "Shareholder Empowerment and Bank Bailouts" (2013), *European Corporate Governance Institute – Finance Working Paper No.* 345/2013, online: http://eprints.lse.ac.uk/56083; Ronald W. Masulis, Cong Wang and Fei Xie, "Agency Problems at Dual-Class Companies" (2009) 64:4 *The Journal of Finance* 1697–1727; Vijay Govindarajan, "Should Dual-Class Shares Be Banned?" (December 3, 2018), *Harvard Business Review*, online: https://hbr.org/2018/12/should-dual-class-shares-be-banned; Oliver Hart and Luigi Zingales, "Companies Should Maximize Shareholder Welfare Not Market Value" (2017), *European Corporate Governance Institute – Finance Working Paper No.* 521/2017, online: SSRN, https://ssrn.com/abstract=3004794; Kosmas Papadopoulos, "Dual-Class Shares: Governance Risks and Company Performance" (June 28, 2019), *Harvard Law School Forum on Corporate Governance*, online: https:// corpgov.law.harvard.edu/2019/06/28/dual-class-shares-governance-risks-and-company-performance/; Rani Molla, "More Tech Companies Are Selling Stock That Keeps Their Founders In Power," *Vox*, April 11, 2019, online: www.vox.com/2019/4/11/18302102/ipo-vot ing-multi-dual-stock-lyft-pinterest; Jerry Davis, "The Simple Reason Tech CEOs Have So

Much Power," *Fast Company*, April 3, 2021, online: www.fastcompany.com/90620747/
dual-class-voting-tech-ceo-power.

77 Swarnodeep Homroy and Shubhashis Gangopadhyay, "Strategic CEO Activism in
Polarized Markets" (2023) *Journal of Financial and Quantitative Analysis* 1–74 at 28–29.

78 *Ibid* at 4. See also, Jacob Hacker and Paul Pierson, "Conflicted Consequences" (July 21,
2020), *Center for Political Accountability*, online (pdf): https://politicalaccountability.net/
hifi/files/Conflicted-Consequences.pdf.

79 Matthew Kotchen and Jon J. Moon, "Corporate Social Responsibility for Irresponsibility"
(2012) 12:1 *The B.E. Journal of Economic Analysis and Policy* 55; Alan Muller and Roman
Kräussl, "Doing Good Deeds in Times of Need: A Strategic Perspective on Corporate
Disaster Donations" (2011) 32:9 *Strategic Management Journal* 911–929.

80 Davidson Heath et al., "Does Socially Responsible Investing Change Firm Behavior?"
(2023) 27:6 *Review of Finance* 2057–2083. See also, Bryce C. Tingle, "What Do We Know
About Shareholders' Potential to Solve Environmental and Social Problems?" (2023)
Georgia Law Review.

81 Stewart J. Schwab and Randall S. Thomas, "Realigning Corporate Governance:
Shareholder Activism by Labor Unions" (1998) 96:4 *Michigan Law Review* 1018–1094 at
1020.

82 Steve Sleigh, "The Real World of Employee Ownership" (Book Review) (2002) 5:1
University of Pennsylvania Journal of Labor and Employment Law 215–220.

83 Hadiye Aslan, "A Review of Hedge Fund Activism: Impact on Shareholders and
Stakeholders" (2021), online: SSRN, https://ssrn.com/abstract=3785292.

84 Christine Blandhol et al., "Do Employees Benefit from Worker Representation on
Corporate Boards?" (2021), *National Bureau of Economic Research Working Paper No.*
28269, online: *NBER*, www.nber.org/papers/w28269.

85 *Ibid.*

86 *Ibid*; Gary Gorton and Frank A. Schmid, "Capital, Labor, and the Firm: A Study of
German Codetermination" (2004) 2:5 *Journal of the European Economic Association*
863–905; Simon Jäger, Benjamin Schoefer and Jörg Heining, "Labor in the Boardroom"
(2021) 136:2 *The Quarterly Journal of Economics* 669–725; Simon Jäger, Shakked Noy and
Benjamin Schoefer, "What Does Codetermination Do?" (2022) 75:4 *ILR Review* 857–890
at 866.

87 Toni Monkovic, "Why Does Education Translate to Less Support for Donald Trump?,"
The New York Times, November 1, 2016, online: www.nytimes.com/2016/11/02/upshot/
why-does-education-translate-to-less-support-for-donald-trump.html; Gerald F. Seib,
"Republicans Unveil Policies to Match 'Working-Class Party' Claim," *The Wall Street
Journal*, April 12, 2021, online: www.wsj.com/articles/republicans-unveil-policies-to-
match-working-class-party-claim-11618237594; Thomas Frank, *What's the Matter with
Kansas? How Conservatives Won the Heart of America* (New York: Henry Holt and
Company, 2004).

88 Gary Mottola et al., "Investors Say They Can Change the World, if They Only Knew
How: Six Things to Know About ESG and Retail Investors" (March 2022) *FINRA Investor
Education Foundation – Consumer Insights: Money & Investing*, online (pdf): www.finra
foundation.org/sites/finrafoundation/files/Consumer-Insights-Money-and-Investing.pdf.
See also, Lydia Saad, "Where U.S. Investors Stand on ESG Investing," Gallup, February
23, 2022, online: https://news.gallup.com/poll/389780/investors-stand-esg-investing.aspx;
Stefano Giglio et al., "Four Facts about ESG Beliefs and Investor Portfolios" (2023),
National Bureau of Economic Research Working Paper No. 31114, online: *NBER*, www
.nber.org/papers/w31114.

89 De Voltaire, *Letters Concerning the English Nation*, 2nd ed. (London: C. Davis, 1741); Nathan B. Oman, *The Dignity of Commerce: Markets and the Moral Foundations of Contract Law* (Chicago: The University of Chicago Press, 2016) at pp. 63–65; Nathan B. Oman, "Markets as a Moral Foundation for Contracts" (2012) 98:1 *Iowa Law Review* 183–230 at 195.

90 Edelman, *Trust Barometer*, above at note 62 at 5.

91 Bryce C. Tingle, "Returning Markets to the Center of Corporate Law" (2023) 48:4 *Journal of Corporation Law* 663–718.

92 See, for example, Matthias Sutter, Stefan Haigner and Martin G. Kocher, "Choosing the Carrot or the Stick? Endogenous Institutional Choice in Social Dilemma Situations" (2010) 77:4 *The Review of Economic Studies* 1540–1566; Marco A. Janssen et al., "Effect of Rule Choice in Dynamic Interactive Spatial Commons" (2008) 2:2 *International Journal of the Commons* 288–312 at 308. See also, Elinor Ostrom, "A Behavioral Approach to the Rational Choice Theory of Collective Action" (1998) 92:1 *American Political Science Review* 1–22. The findings on the effect of regulation on social behavior is analogous to the findings about the impact of financial incentives on pro-social actions: Uri Gneezy and Aldo Rustichini, "A Fine is a Price" (2000) 29:1 *The Journal of Legal Studies* 1–17 at 3; Carl Mellström and Magnus Johannesson, "Crowding Out in Blood Donation: Was Titmuss Right?" (2008) 6:4 *Journal of European Economic Association* 845–863 at 857; Dan Ariely, *Predictably Irrational: The Hidden Forces that Shape Our Decisions* (New York: HarperCollins Publishers, 2008) at p. 71.

12

Shareholders and ESG Disclosure

The law school experience holds many unpleasant shocks, but the worst is the sheer amount of reading students are expected to do. In keeping with their chosen profession, law students complain a lot to anyone who will listen, and they receive several sorts of replies. The first comes from fellow students, and it more or less amounts to, "Listen, only a fool does all the readings. You should just read summaries of the materials prepared by previous generations of students instead of the materials themselves." This is a very helpful (and popular) piece of advice. The second comes from lawyers in practice who say something along the lines of, "Have you found someone to give you a summary of the readings yet?"

Almost the only voices raised in favor of reading all the class materials are the professors. They usually say something like, "Well, there is a lot of reading, but if you do all of it, you will not necessarily do better on the exams, but you will, in an ineffable but beautiful way, become more sophisticated in your handling of legal argument." Of course, the students have usually stopped listening after "you won't do better on exams," and they probably rightly conclude that the professors have the weaker case. (The professors' claims are similar to Lionel Trilling's amusing summary of arguments in favor of studying English in university: "Certain good things happen if we read literature."[1])

This fascinating sociological drama is relevant to the hottest current topic in corporate governance: expanding corporate disclosure obligations to include social and (especially) environmental outcomes. There is already a vast amount of disclosure produced by public corporations. In fact, corporations are required to produce so much information that virtually no one familiar with the materials generated by public companies actually believes our disclosure rules are accomplishing their goals.[2] To the extent humor exists in the practice of securities law, it derives almost exclusively from the fact that no one reads the registration statements, circulars, and other legal detritus that collectively, and often individually, run to hundreds of pages and cost hundreds of thousands of dollars to prepare. (The exception, of course, are financial statements, which tend to be read carefully.)

Even in the normally disconnected academy (I say this with love!) many professors are aware of the reality: "Documents are often too long and convoluted to be of much use to the ordinary investor."[3] Or, as Professor Barbara Black trenchantly observed, in light of the length and complexity of current corporate disclosure, reading it "would be a waste of investors' time."[4] The SEC, itself, periodically reflects on whether disclosure requirements have become self-defeating, though this self-reflection does not rise to formal expression very often.[5] (One assumes doubts about the usefulness of the disclosure that makes up so much of the SEC's work hovers like an existential hole in the SEC offices, a not-quite ignorable presence infecting the people who work there with the kind of despair Kierkegaard called "the sickness unto death." Thank heavens so many SEC employees are eventually saved by finding meaning in their future investment banking jobs.)

On top of the question of whether investors actually read and understand the disclosure, there is a relatively well-known body of empirical research that convincingly demonstrates that the quality of people's decisions goes down as the quantity of information available to them increases.[6] In other words, the massive amount of corporate disclosure is probably making markets less efficient.[7]

This is the unpromising ground on which advocates of environmental and social disclosure have chosen to plant their hopes. Since the 2008 financial crisis, academics have flooded the usual forums with proposals concerning ways that shareholder power might improve various social and environmental outcomes. As one observer notes, "climate change and sustainability disclosure has especially gripped the imagination of legal scholars."[8] Academics are not alone with this idea. The SEC and other securities commissions around the world have announced disclosure initiatives in relation to certain ESG matters, particularly carbon emissions. Meanwhile, institutional investors purporting to invest according to ESG criteria have grown from managing 1 percent of mutual fund assets in 2014 to administering more than one-third of all American assets under management today.[9] Branding oneself as an ESG (or "sustainable" or "impact") fund has provided a tremendous marketing advantage over the past decade. The corporate governance industry has taken note, and various third parties (including proxy advisors) have created an array of reporting standards and rating schemes to assist investors in allocating capital according to ESG criteria.

This book began in a campus movie theater with a student – as a joke – predicting that a ridiculous scheme of Wile E. Coyote was finally going to work. In that spirit, I would like to assure the reader that this time the corporate governance industry has nailed it. America will definitely see improvement in welfare outcomes thanks to enhanced ESG disclosure. If, as we have seen throughout this book, corporate governance reforms have failed to deliver improved financial results, something that shareholders, managers, and anyone interested in the ongoing survival of a company all want, and which does not involve the complex balancing of competing and incommensurate ends, then securing desirable environmental and social outcomes will definitely be quite easy. All we need is more mandatory disclosure.

12.1 WHO WILL USE THE DISCLOSURE?

As we saw in Chapter 11, "ESG" includes "governance," which ostensibly is about improving the risk-adjusted financial performance of a corporation, but in practice that part of "ESG" is ignored, and "ESG" has really become about improving outcomes for non-shareholder constituencies: the "E" and the "S" part of the acronym. That is how we will be using the term in this chapter.

To evaluate the merits of the current plans to solve climate change and other intractable problems through corporate governance channels, it is necessary to evaluate which constituency will use the disclosure to push change on the corporation. There are four possibilities: (1) consumers of the corporation's products and services; (2) employees; (3) third-party advocacy organizations; or (4) shareholders.

Really, the only realistic agent for change making use of this disclosure is the shareholders, particularly the institutional shareholders that own over three-quarters of the shares in US public companies.[10] Consumer boycotts of socially underperforming companies require considerable effort; they are rare, their success is not assured, and most corporations are not consumer-facing.[11] In the case of employees, they have been unable to halt the decline in labor's share of national income over the past several decades, so it is hard to believe that outside a few high-tech industries where specialized human capital is vital, employees will be able to fundamentally alter corporate behavior in other areas.[12] As we saw in Chapter 11, even when European corporate law places employee representatives on the board of directors, the best evidence is that they are unable to use this uniquely powerful corporate governance channel to produce better wages or job security.

Third-party environmental organizations are limited in number, limited in resources, and lack any power under corporate law. As we saw in Chapters 5 and 11, when these social and environmental advocacy organizations purchase shares in a company to enable themselves to bring shareholder proposals, those proposals are almost inevitably defeated. These proposals are also noteworthy for being deliberately weak and ineffectual, doubtless to attract elusive shareholder support.

In contrast, shareholders are given a privileged position in firm governance as a matter of corporate and securities law. They appear (!) focused on corporate governance outcomes already, and they are sufficiently concentrated that they are easier to mobilize than thousands of preoccupied ordinary consumers. Finally, the managers of institutional investors are sophisticated enough to, in theory, read, process, and come to accurate conclusions about the complex disclosure provided on social and environmental issues. For these reasons, most advocates of ESG disclosure assume shareholders will be its primary consumers.

The rest of this chapter will point out that the overwhelming body of evidence suggests that: (1) it is very hard for shareholders to know about the social and environmental impacts of their portfolio companies; (2) very hard for them to find out about the viable alternatives available to individual companies; and (3) very hard to productively intervene in corporate strategy using the tools they are given by the legal system.

12.2 THE SITUATION OF SHAREHOLDERS WITH REGARDS TO ESG

As we have seen (particularly in Chapters 5 and 6), institutional shareholders do not do well at firm-specific governance. Most fund managers find themselves embedded in competitive markets in which funds flow to the most successful performers. This means fund managers compete to generate relative returns measured against either competitors or certain benchmark indices. Even professional investors managing "trapped" money, such as public pension fund managers, are regularly evaluated on the basis of their performance relative to other investment funds or market indices.

Firm-specific interventions do not improve the relative performance of a fund because the individual company in question is almost always held by competitor funds and included in the relevant indices. This is why investment fund managers are invariably chosen for skills that do enhance funds' relative performance: competence in picking stocks and trading them, rather than other skills more relevant to corporate governance or ESG. For example, in relation to ESG, as of 2019, Blackrock employed only forty-five "stewardship personnel" to oversee ESG matters for an estimated 11,246 portfolio companies.[13] Vanguard and State Street employ less than half as many ESG specialists for even larger portfolios.

Fund managers' pay and career prospects are not the only reasons firm-specific governance initiatives are rarely undertaken. Funds also often compete on the basis of their costs, and so most funds do not have enough money to engage in the kind of detailed, firm-specific analysis and effort needed to productively engage with a particular firm's governance. As well, the effects of governance initiatives are uncertain (anyone who claims otherwise is a charlatan) and usually play out over a time period that is much longer than the time horizons that concern professional fund managers. (The average holding period for shares on the NYSE these days is about six months.[14])

Even with hundreds of pages of disclosure (most of it unread), shareholders of public companies typically lack the detailed information about portfolio companies that would allow them to evaluate the merits of, for example, R&D initiatives with environmental implications or the green credentials of alternative suppliers. (They don't even know the identity of alternative suppliers.) Professional fund managers also rarely have relevant experience operating or governing business corporations, disadvantaging them when it comes to judging corporate operating decisions.

The final, sort of obvious point to make about shareholders is that relatively few of them decide to invest their money in stocks for reasons unrelated to making money. Even with the absolute best environmental intentions in the world, fund managers are also going to care about generating appealing returns in their funds.

We know this theoretical point about shareholders seeking to maximize returns is true, as we have given shareholders an increasing amount of power in corporate governance over the past three decades. During this time, corporate retained earnings in America have declined from an average of 50 to 60 percent in 1962 to 3 percent in 2002. Shareholders in the US have withdrawn more money from public companies than they have invested[15] until "[t]here is little question that public equity largely has disappeared as a significant form of permanent capital."[16]

We have repeatedly seen in this book that where corporations gain relatively more independence from institutional shareholder influence, the evidence is that at least some non-shareholder constituencies benefit, as these corporations pay more tax (as a result of deploying less aggressive tax avoidance strategies),[17] they get better deals from lenders (as the risk of expropriation by shareholders declines),[18] they are more likely to have stronger relationships with important customers, suppliers, or strategic partners,[19] they engage in less risky behavior (which means they make lower profits but are more likely to survive a crisis),[20] they spend more on corporate social responsibility,[21] and they invest more in longer-term projects.[22] As we saw in Chapter 5, the most notable shareholder interventions (by activist investors) are generally about financial engineering moves designed to increase short-term payouts to shareholders, often by transferring wealth from stakeholders like employees and debt holders.

We have also seen that as shareholders gain increasing power, the compensation arrangements of companies are altered so that executive pay closely tracks fluctuations in shareholder welfare. Several recent papers even argue that the growth of institutional shareholder power has had a direct effect on increasing inequality by holding down non-executive employee wages.[23]

It should be noted that this is not a uniquely American phenomenon – the result, say, of Delaware's fiduciary duty regime. The growth in shareholder power over the past thirty years occurred throughout the developed world and the results were essentially the same.[24] The European Commission's recent report on sustainable corporate governance found:

> Evidence collected over the 1992–2018 period shows that there is a trend for publicly listed companies within the EU to focus on short-term benefits to shareholders rather than on the long-term interests of the company. Data indicate an upward trend in shareholder pay-outs, which increased fourfold, from less than 1% of revenues in 1992 to almost 4% in 2018. Moreover, the ratio of CAPEX and R&D investment to revenues has been declining since the beginning of the 21st century.[25]

It is impossible, of course, to conclusively demonstrate a causal connection between these trends in corporate behavior and the rise of shareholder influence. However, it is clear that: (1) the trends are closely matched; (2) we would expect a causal relationship based on a simple assessment of the interests of institutional asset managers; and (3) at the very least, the rise of shareholder power did not prevent a worsening of corporate outcomes for non-shareholder constituencies. In fact, as we shall see, the evidence is weak that shareholders – even those who are branded as ESG funds – meaningfully pursue social and environmental objectives unrelated to marketing or fund financial performance.

In short, most of the available evidence seems to suggest shareholders generally care about financial returns. This cannot be controversial.

12.3 WHAT ABOUT SYSTEMIC STEWARDSHIP?

Lots of people interested in ESG know that, at least to some degree, shareholders aren't incentivized or able to engage in many firm-specific governance activities. These people suggest, as an alternative, that since many investment funds "own" the market (either as a function of scale or internal mandate), perhaps these funds do have an incentive to reduce ESG risk across the economy.[26] Index funds, which are unable to sell the shares of companies with significant ESG risk, are a particular source of optimism.

The problem with these sorts of arguments is that just because a problem is systemic, doesn't mean the solution is systemic. The analogy with corporate governance is useful: a systemic problem (managerial agency costs) produced systemic solutions (independent directors, the use of equity incentives, etc.), which turned out to have, on average, no effect whatsoever on the problem at hand and might have created new ones. It is likely that the only effective solutions to systemically problematic managerial self-interest are a series of idiosyncratic, firm-specific measures. That is what a lot of the empirical evidence we have reviewed in this book suggests anyway.

There are good reasons to believe that there are also no practical solutions to social and environmental problems that are easily generalizable to heterogeneous companies. There are only a few current strategies available to ESG funds, and later in the chapter, we will see that there is little evidence investors are able to either use them consistently or that when used, these strategies produce better social and environmental outcomes.

A simple illustration of the problem is provided by a recent study that found "the majority of this recent green patenting is not driven by highly rated ESG firms – firms that are commonly favored by ESG funds – but instead by firms that are explicitly excluded from ESG funds' investment universe."[27] These excluded companies not only produce more environmentally beneficial patents, but the patents they produce are significantly higher quality. In fact, these low-rated companies are "significantly more likely to produce 'blockbuster' green patents than other firms."[28] Any shareholder investment and engagement protocol that depends on evaluating the R&D initiatives of various companies, regardless of their ESG credentials, requires precisely the careful attention and engagement with the idiosyncratic activities of specific companies that this book suggests is unlikely.

A second problem with the "systemic" argument is that arresting climate change is only one of many corporate welfare outcomes desired by society. Employees want good-paying, stable employment. Lenders (as we have seen, the real contributors of capital to public firms) desire to be repaid. Governments need tax revenue. Consumers need products and services. Future generations will surely have an interest in innovation and economic growth. Even if we assume systemic solutions to climate change are available to shareholders, society has an interest in the impact of these solutions on other constituencies and the other things society wants from corporations.

Most people involved with firms do not "own" the market like an index fund. The vast majority of the people involved in a corporation, like retail investors, employees, suppliers, and customers, have an interest in decision-making that respects the specific circumstances of "their" firm and that is designed to facilitate its unique flourishing. Surely their interests must be considered if government regulation is being enlisted to assist institutional shareholders in imposing solutions that, at best, might reduce undiversifiable portfolio risk.

The third problem with systemic risk arguments is that they fail to connect the (assumed) long-term risk reduction benefits of social and environmental engagement to the (actual) short-term benefit to investment fund managers of maximizing relative portfolio returns. As one group of scholars correctly observes, "[t]here is a broad consensus in the conceptual literature that many of the financial gains from improved social performance accrue in the long run."[29] Even if ESG initiatives reduce systemic risk, the incentives for conscientiously pursuing ESG goals are still much lower than the incentives we have already discussed to improve the short-term relative financial performance of the fund.

The fourth problem with the systemic risk argument is that it doesn't appear to reflect what actually happens when investors incorporate ESG information into their decision-making. A recent survey found, for example, that "ESG investors tend to prefer analysis on individual companies over industry level analysis."[30] This is precisely what we would expect if reducing risk in the long term was less important than outperforming competitors in the short to medium term. The researchers summarize the attitude of institutional investors: "ESG integration is much like traditional active management based on fundamental investing, in the sense that it is characterized by a strong need for company specific information."[31]

The final problem is that, as we will see, there have been multiple long-term studies looking at the impact of the usual measures of ESG on firm risk; they generally find no evidence for the claimed connection.

12.4 HOW DO ESG FUNDS BEHAVE?

So much for the theory, how do funds that describe themselves as concerned with environmental and social issues actually behave? A recent survey of institutional fund managers found that "the use of ESG information is driven primarily by financial rather than ethical motives."[32] Researchers find that the managers of many types of investment funds tend to use third-party ESG ratings rather than actually reading companies' ESG disclosure, which "suggests that the managers are constrained in their resources."[33] Strangely, however, these same respondents did not believe ESG investing necessitated additional resources. The only thing that explains these apparently divergent observations is that fund managers have a general reluctance to spend resources on ESG.

Another way of examining investor incentives is by looking at whether managers are prepared to sacrifice portfolio returns for ESG benefits. There are many theoretical arguments that fund managers should be prepared to do so, given their clients' stated concern for environmental and social outcomes. However, a great empirical study conducted under real market conditions finds that "the greenium, or the premium that green assets trade to otherwise identical non-green securities, is precisely equal to zero."[34] Other studies find infinitesimal greeniums over limited time periods.[35] This is in line with a recent survey by the State Treasurer's Office of California that elicited a unanimous response by managers that "their firms would not accept a lower yield for a green bond."[36]

It should come as no surprise, therefore, that empirical studies repeatedly find that ESG-branded investment funds do not, on average, hold more environmentally and socially responsible companies than conventional funds.[37] Many researchers find ESG funds hold portfolio companies with *worse* track records for compliance with labor and environmental laws, relative to non-ESG funds.[38] A typical finding is that ESG funds' investments on average "exhibit worse performance with respect to carbon emissions, in terms of both raw emissions output and emissions intensity."[39] A recent survey among investment managers who claim to actively integrate ESG factors into their investment process showed many of them did not buy or sell a single share in a given year due to ESG-related information.[40] Indeed, another study found a company's addition or deletion from an ESG index (and thus the ESG funds that follow the index) was almost completely unrelated to its actual history of environmental and labor violations.[41]

The way ESG managers build their portfolios seems to support the argument of this chapter that their primary motivation is to generate superior relative financial returns. This means their ESG rhetoric is, in practice at least, likely little more than a fund marketing strategy. Tellingly, new ESG funds start by owning high social responsibility companies for the first two years, but once the funds are established, there is a steep decline in the environmental and social quality of portfolio companies in subsequent years.[42] This is not a function of changes in the companies but of managers' altering their investment behavior, presumably once the fund's "brand" has been established.

If we look at the way shareholders vote their shares, we find a similar picture of disengagement with environmental and social concerns. In 2019, investor support for shareholder proposals on ESG matters reached a new record, but it was on average only 29 percent of the votes cast at the meeting.[43] Active investment managers who sign the UN's Principles of Responsible Investment actually vote less on environment related issues after signing.[44]

Voting is the easiest and cheapest form of shareholder engagement and so it is telling, for example, that America's largest and oldest ESG fund "has voted against almost all environmental resolutions over the past fourteen years. The same is true of other socially conscious resolutions, including board diversity."[45] Because index funds cannot sell bad actors, it has been hoped they would instead use their voting power to advance ESG causes, but the three biggest index fund groups are actually less likely to support ESG proposals than other institutional investors.[46] (This is another blow to the theory that systemic risk will lead to systemic engagement.)

12.5 IS THERE A LINK BETWEEN ESG INVESTING AND FUND RETURNS?

It is very hard to make sense of all this fund behavior if ESG investing is, in fact, connected to higher risk-adjusted returns. This connection is essential to the argument that investment fiduciaries are permitted to invest in ways that support the interests of non-shareholder constituencies. It is also key to many of the arguments that shareholders are a viable source of support for social and environmental initiatives. But it amounts to saying that institutional fund managers, the most sophisticated parties in our financial markets, have not, until recently, understood key factors to generate investment returns. Why haven't they been "ESG" before now? Why do they seem reluctant to be ESG now, even if their brand is ESG? Why do regulators feel they need to get involved?

Even if we assume that for a long period investors didn't understand the importance of stakeholders or social license in the performance of portfolio companies, many of them do now.[47] In theory, it takes a relatively small group of investors to spot a way companies are systematically being overvalued (or undervalued) to sell (or buy) the shares of those companies until the pricing error is corrected.[48] In other words, the opportunity for ESG investing to generate abnormal returns lasts just as long as it takes for market prices to adjust to new understandings about the importance of ESG. There is, in fact, evidence that returns to some types of ESG investing existed through the 1990s before disappearing early this century.[49]

This problem does not go away if risk reduction is the rationale for ESG investing. If, for example, a particular company has a history of bad ESG practices, perhaps this means it has a higher risk of negative outcomes. In theory, this company should trade at a discount to its peers because of this risk. This does not mean, however, that an investor who buys the company will do worse with that investment than if the investor bought one of its peers. Because the investor acquired its shares at a discount, the investor's risk-adjusted returns should be identical to those it would have received by buying undiscounted stock in one of the better-behaved peer companies. Indeed, there is a chance that, as the company's bad behavior makes it riskier, the investor may receive a premium.[50]

As we would expect, researchers find that bad environmental performers trade at prices that more or less reflect the economic losses imposed by regulators.[51] The market appears to price the cost of bad ESG performance accurately. As well, one of the rare studies looking explicitly at risk found that, as theory would predict, "the risk/return trade-off is such that no clear utility gain or loss can be realized by investing in firms characterized by different levels of social and environmental performance."[52]

Notwithstanding these theoretical points, the literature on the performance of ESG investments is vast. Since the turn of the century, three-quarters of all academic papers on ESG investing have dealt with the financial performance issue.[53] There are many meta-studies attempting to summarize literally hundreds of empirical studies.[54] Unfortunately, it is impossible to draw any definite conclusions from all this work. As a literature review observed after analyzing the meta-studies, "to date the relationship between social responsibility and returns has not been conclusive."[55] Another team or researchers reviewed over 1,100 primary peer-reviewed papers and concluded, "the financial performance of ESG investing has on average been indistinguishable from conventional investing."[56]

Studies on ESG investing often use ESG ratings and, as we will see, there is considerable evidence that these rating schemes are invalid. There are some studies, however, that use real-world measures of environmental and social performance rather than depending on artificial third-party ESG ratings. In general, these studies fail to find that environmental and social considerations produce superior investment returns. For example, a couple recent papers have found that firms with more carbon-intense business models earn significantly higher returns.[57] (Another study merely found no connection between greenhouse gas emissions and stock and bond returns.[58]) Scholars looking at market reactions to ESG news stories found there was a very small reaction to negative events and no market reaction to positive ESG events.[59] A similar study found that corporate announcements of positive CSR initiatives are followed by a slight decline in share price.[60]

Similar results come from papers that concentrate on the ways different types of ESG funds assemble their portfolios. Dual-objective venture capital funds (also known as "impact" funds) are focused on investing in private companies that will generate positive environmental and social outcomes; these funds appear to earn lower rates of return on their investments than traditional venture capital funds.[61] A study looking at portfolios that exclude companies on the basis of fourteen potentially controversial issues (such as adult entertainment, gambling, fur, and weapons) found that "controversial investments generally yield positive abnormal returns, and that screening produces suboptimal financial performance."[62]

ESG rating of the funds, themselves, is a fairly recent phenomenon. Morningstar only began offering its "five globes" rating scheme in 2016. As we would expect, given the lack of a clear case for ESG investment returns elsewhere in the empirical literature, highly rated ESG funds do not appear to generate better financial performance than low-rated funds.[63] Last year Vanguard, one of the "big-three" index fund managers withdrew from ESG investing commitments on the grounds that, "our research indicates that ESG investing does not have any advantage over broad-based investing."[64]

12.6 INVESTORS DON'T BOTHER GETTING ACCURATE ESG DATA

Investors mostly depend on third-party ESG ratings.[65] They lack the time and resources to analyze companies' ESG performance, so they use ESG ratings in much the same way that they rely on proxy advisory firms to analyze corporate governance issues. This once again creates a market made up of only agents, in which the actual parties with an interest in the market – companies and the human beneficiaries of investment funds – are excluded. As we found with proxy advisors in Chapter 7, this market of agents working for agents generates simply terrible ESG advice.

The most important fact about ESG ratings is that they are invalid. There is no room for doubt on this point in the relevant empirical literature. Over a dozen studies have compared corporate ESG ratings and found wide variation in the way the same company is rated by different ESG data providers.[66] The lack of correlation and consistency between rating firms suggests the ESG data from these firms is not reliably telling us much about the ESG qualities of the subject corporations. Correlation among credit rating agencies is 99 percent (meaning they rate the same company identically 99 percent of the time).[67] Correlations among ESG rating firms are usually below 50 percent.[68] This is not a problem that the industry is getting closer to solving. Disagreement among ESG data intermediaries over the performance of a given company has been increasing over time.[69]

Another way of measuring the validity of the ESG data provided to investors is by looking at how well it predicts future performance. Once again, the ESG ratings are poor guides to the things we care about in the real world. The companies at the center of the largest corporate scandals of the past two decades have often been highly ranked on ESG measures: Enron, WorldCom, Adelphia, Healthcare, BP, and Shell. Empirical studies find that ESG intermediaries' measurements of "environmental strengths" do a poor job of predicting future pollution and compliance violations.[70] High ESG ratings are unconnected with labor-related issues and enforcement actions.[71] Instead, high ethical and social scores are actually connected with aggressive accounting policies and earnings management.[72] High ESG ratings, and particularly the "social" aspects of those ratings, are positively correlated with future corporate scandals.[73] Companies with high ESG ratings pay their executives in the same ways and in the same amounts as other companies, but when Covid hit, they were *less likely* to reduce CEO and director pay even as they laid off employees.[74]

There is also a more limited body of research on the impact of ESG ratings on firm risk. (This is particularly relevant to the "systemic stewardship" claim on behalf of ESG funds.) A long-term (eighteen-year) study of highly rated ESG companies found "a negative but insignificant relationship between the various corporate social strengths and systemic financial risk."[75] This was true when the rated ESG components were considered individually and in aggregate. A recent examination of ESG funds found their methods of portfolio selection actually exposed them to *more* investment risk, as it led them to be overweight in small issuers, volatile tech companies, and firms that are abnormally susceptible to changes in inflation, interest rates, and – amazingly – oil prices.[76]

The heavy reliance of institutional investors on the work of third-party ESG advisory firms is strong evidence that those investors are more concerned with keeping overhead low and achieving strong relative returns rather than effecting meaningful ESG reforms. It isn't as if these ESG rating failures are unknown.[77] They are widely reported in the financial press,[78] by securities regulators,[79] and even in communications from ESG asset managers themselves.[80]

12.7 EVALUATING ESG IS HARD

Like corporate governance generally, figuring out a company's ESG issues and merits is very hard. A nonexhaustive list of the difficulties includes:

- Unlike most relevant financial aspects of a business, ESG involves elements that are either impossible to quantify or that are too complex to quantify.[81]
- Many ESG factors are purely subjective, such as employee happiness and being a good member of the community. There is a large empirical literature that finds low validity in these sorts of management system measurements.[82] For example, unions and management disagree on how often they meet and whether work has become more intense.[83] Employees fail to agree on the human resource management practices in place at their firms.[84]
- Many ESG factors are incommensurate, even across a single dimension. Taking worker welfare as an example, in 2000, Exxon Mobil was rated highly because of its strong retirement benefits program, but it had also been involved in major controversies about health and safety issues.[85] Does it treat employees well or not?
- ESG factors are incommensurate across dimensions.[86] How does positive performance in one dimension, such as the environment, relate to negative performance in other dimensions, such as treating the workforce poorly? Bloomberg's ESG data covers 120 different indicators; how are these to be weighted and balanced?[87] In one example of this problem, as the war in Ukraine began, it was discovered that ESG funds had been preferentially investing in Russian oil and gas operations because of their lower per barrel carbon emissions.[88] Does

supporting the Putin regime (which depends on Russia's oil industry) feel like those funds got ESG right?

- ESG involves constituencies whose interests often conflict over the usual time-frame for business decision-making: shareholders, workers, lenders, customers, communities, suppliers, and the environment. How are these conflicts to be factored into evaluating a firm's performance?

- ESG requires nuanced value judgments. Many ESG funds avoid companies active in the arms trade. Should this include firms that make radar systems for the military? Or provide logistical support to the armed forces? Or who (like Walmart) only *sell* guns, rather than *manufacture* them? These types of questions ramify across an ESG portfolio and are much harder to solve than the simple question of whether a business' risk-adjusted returns merit an investment (and most active managers don't even manage to succeed at this consistently).[89]

- One value judgment that deserves specific attention is whether it is the absolute externalities produced by a company that matters or its relative production of externalities. Is it carbon use adjusted for size that matters or total carbon emissions? (As it happens, large companies tend to receive better ESG scores than smaller companies, notwithstanding shareholder engagement with a large company is likely to produce greater total reductions in emissions.[90])

- Another value judgment that deserves specific attention is whether we focus on the ESG performance of the company in question or include the ESG performance of its customers or suppliers? Companies (and their shareholders) often have little knowledge or power over firms in their supply or customer chains. The food production industry scores very well on emissions if we only look at the industry itself; if we look at emissions from third parties who supply the food production industry with materials or who buy the food and waste from the industry, then it becomes one of the worst emitting industries in the economy.[91]

- Disclosure, generally, seems poorly suited to providing a basis for ESG decision-making. ESG is so complex that it takes considerable effort and time to understand disclosure. Since we know that decision-making quality *declines* as the amount of disclosure increases, it is not a surprise that a study finds that more ESG disclosure is associated with larger disagreements between ESG rating firms.[92]

- ESG decisions must take into account the cost and viability of various alternative ESG-relevant strategies or investments, but securities disclosure is almost always about what the company is doing, not about hypothetical possibilities. (Disclosure about possible futures and predicted results carry a risk of lawsuits.)

- The most useful ESG information for shareholders would be details around ESG strategies, innovations, and the results of a firm's experiments to improve outcomes. Unfortunately, this is exactly the same kind of information that is also most helpful to a company's competitors in their own ESG efforts. To the extent regulators require this sort of disclosure of proprietary information, they create incentives for public companies to refrain from pioneering new innovations, as disclosure will enable their competitors to achieve the same outcomes more efficiently by avoiding the expense of research and experiments, as well as the losses produced by mistakes.[93] In the same way that executive pay disclosure probably helped increase executive pay, corporate ethics disclosure resulted in watering down ethical codes, and anti-corruption disclosure may have hurt the developing countries it was trying to help, public disclosure is well understood as reducing the returns to innovation.[94] At the very least, this means companies will work hard to avoid making public the kind of proprietary information shareholders would find most useful in appraising ESG activities.[95]

- Relatedly, ESG information can only come from the issuers themselves. The ambiguities, commensurability issues, missing hypotheticals, and value judgments contained in the disclosure will generally be resolved by a company in whatever ways make itself look best. As this ESG disclosure may impact a firm's cost of capital, the attitude of its employees and customers, and the company's regulatory future, it is probably the duty of management (as well as being in their own interests) to put the company's best foot forward.[96] (Along these lines, several amusing studies find that firms falling short of earnings expectations or releasing negative news about litigation are more likely to cite social and environmental achievements in their public announcements.[97])

In summary, ESG factors are often subjective, nonquantifiable, incommensurate between themselves, poorly suited to disclosure regimes, and vary according to competing plausible value judgments. It should not be surprising that the third-party intermediaries offering to make sense of corporate ESG data for shareholders come to different conclusions.

12.8 SHAREHOLDER GOVERNANCE TOOLS ARE POORLY SUITED TO ESG INTERVENTIONS

One of the themes of this book is that it is not just a lack of information and poor incentives that prevent institutional investors from playing the expanded role in corporate governance we hoped for them. It is also a problem that the tools shareholders are given by corporate law are both too limited and too crude.

Directors and officers of a corporation may advance ESG goals by engaging in operational fine-tuning or testing possible improvements with small-scale experiments. Their tools for addressing ESG issues are suited to the task. In contrast, shareholders have only very blunt mechanisms for making changes: interventions (such as shareholder proposals and proxy fights) or dropping a firm from their portfolio. These are binary decisions. Should the shareholder invest their resource-constrained time and money in a company? To make these decisions, shareholders need a straightforward identification of which companies merit either an ESG intervention or a refusal to purchase their shares. In other words, the corporate governance tools of shareholders are also responsible for driving the need for the deeply flawed and overly simplistic ESG ratings.

12.8.1 *Negative Screening or Divestment*

Selling or refusing to purchase the shares of companies with poor ESG track records is the most common ESG investing strategy today.[98] It is popular with investors because it is easy, and compared with various types of shareholder engagement, it is cheap. Of course, it depends on actually knowing who the bad ESG performers are, and as we have seen, shareholders do not know this. However, they may feel they can at least identify the bad industries (this is the point when negative screening turns into divestment).[99] To get some idea of how coarse negative screening is in practice, one group of scholars found negative screening for carbon emissions was only applied to companies in three industries: oil and gas, utilities, and automotive.[100] This means negative screening was not used in relation to companies in all other industries, regardless of those companies' total emissions or relative emission intensity.

The goal of negative screening or divestment is to get corporations, or entire sectors of the economy, to change their behavior by applying pressure to their share price and thus their cost of capital. In theory, this should be impossible. Unlike other goods and services, the value of a corporate share is not derived from the intersection of supply and demand but from the risk-adjusted future cash flows of the corporation.[101] If demand for hula hoops declines, the price of hula hoops will decline as well, and so manufacturers will make fewer hula hoops. In the graph familiar to all "Econ 101" students, the demand curve for hula hoops slopes downward. Stocks, on the other hand, derive their value from the cash flows of the underlying business. Their demand curve is a horizontal line. Stated simply, undervalued companies tend not to remain undervalued for long, as less socially engaged investors buy the companies' shares until their price once again reflects the expected gain from holding the shares.

Even if the market came to somehow consistently misvalue a firm's risk-adjusted cash flows, all that would occur is that disfavored assets would migrate to the private market. Already, nearly 60 percent of corporate carbon emissions in the world are generated by private state-owned companies.[102]

Many divestment campaigns or negative screens simply target companies whose core activities generate adverse social and environmental outcomes. There is nothing those companies can do to meet shareholder demands. An oil company cannot stop looking for new hydrocarbon reserves, investing in new projects, or stop producing oil. The only option available to oil company managers is to simply ignore this segment of shareholder opinion.

Most of the empirical research on the impact of negative screens on corporate behavior has been conducted in connection with the divestment campaign against companies doing business in apartheid-era South Africa. It seems to vindicate economic theory. First, the divestment campaign had no impact on the price of affected companies' shares.[103] Second, the share prices of companies that announced they were leaving South Africa *declined* relative to companies that refused to leave, reflecting market expectations that departure was politically – not financially – motivated.[104] Third, qualitative assessments of the impact of the divestment campaign conclude it had little impact on corporate behavior – or the decisions of South African political leaders.[105]

12.8.2 *Positive Screening*

The idea behind positive screening is that ESG investors will preferentially buy high-performing ESG companies, lowering the cost of capital of those companies. This will encourage the development of ESG-friendly business plans as well as advantage socially responsible companies relative to their less responsible competitors. In other words, the ESG funds will pay a premium to own the shares of socially responsible companies, accepting, in consequence, lower portfolio returns. (Of course, the frequently mentioned marketing claim that ESG investing will produce higher returns is incompatible with the strategy of paying extra to own ESG stocks.)

There are studies claiming that companies scoring highly according to an ESG rating scheme find it easier to raise capital[106] and possibly benefit from a lower cost of capital.[107] However, it is difficult to understand how these empirical findings are compatible with the research, discussed earlier, that finds investment managers do not sacrifice returns in their ESG investments. One likely explanation is that the research on positive screening uses the same ESG ratings that we know are invalid. In contrast, the research on fund manager attitudes and the absence of a "greenium" for ESG securities do not depend on these problematic ESG ratings.[108]

It is also hard to reconcile the claim that ESG companies enjoy lower costs of capital with common sense. How could a set of companies consistently enjoy higher share prices relative to their risk adjusted financial cash flows than their peers? Any non-ESG investor could sell shares of the high-ESG companies and buy shares of their undervalued competitors until the arbitrage opportunity disappeared. Three well-respected law and finance professors at Stanford summed up the theoretical situation as follows: "When can investments or divestments in public capital markets have an impact by affecting the behavior of portfolio companies directly through purchasing company securities? *The answer is virtually never*."[109] We saw in relation to the South Africa divestment campaign that markets were relatively efficient in pricing corporate cash flows, regardless of the behavior of some investors. It is unclear how positive screening today could produce very different results.

The mechanism through which positive screening supposedly operates is facilitating a lower cost of capital for strong ESG companies. Obviously, this mechanism only operates for those companies that raise capital through the issuance of new shares.[110] These financings would, presumably, be conducted at a substantial premium to the market; the premium represents the subsidy given to the company by ESG investors. However, experienced finance scholars are unaware of any instance of this premium being paid.[111] (In contrast, there is plenty of evidence for premiums in private markets, where there is no secondary market in a company's shares, and thus no arbitrage opportunities, so financings can be priced to include an ESG premium through negotiations between the company and private "impact" investors.[112])

There are other significant barriers to effective positive screening. Positive screening requires investors to know a lot more details about companies – their plans, operations, customers, and suppliers – than negative screening. As we have already seen, there is little evidence that public shareholders have the necessary information to make these kinds of decisions.

For example, as noted earlier, some of the very same energy companies targeted for negative screening (and thus unlikely to benefit from positive screening) turn out to be the ones producing the most valuable and important green patents. The largest reduction of carbon emissions in the world occurred in the United States as a result of the fracking industry, allowing natural gas to be produced so cheaply that it supplanted coal as a power source in many parts of the country.[113] This transition occurred despite the explicit lack of support for these energy firms by ESG investors.

It is unlikely that public market institutional shareholders, who only seem to manage negative screening on the basis of what industry a company belongs to, have sufficient information and resources to identify the companies most likely to advance ESG objectives. Anecdotally, most positive screens discussed by ESG funds also seem to depend mainly on the broad industry a firm belongs to, such as electric vehicles or alternative energy. This ignores most of the companies that matter (because it ignores most companies) and it seems likely to continually produce rude surprises when shareholders learn, for instance, that companies in these favored industries have their own serious environmental issues.[114] Even if firm-specific analysis was possible for institutional investors, it is hard to see how positive screening would have any effect on public firms because of the presence of arbitrageurs. The Stanford professors put it this way: "treat the presence of any public equities in a self-styled impact fund as the thirteenth strike of the clock, which calls the others into question."[115]

12.8.3 *Shareholder Engagement*

If investor purchase and selling decisions seem unlikely to materially impact corporate ESG performance, the use of the powers provided to shareholders by corporate and securities laws might seem more promising. They permit firm-specific interventions and, at least in theory, are much more finely calibrated than simply giving a thumbs up or down on a company (or, in practice, an entire industry), which is all positive and negative screening can do.

The evidence around shareholder engagement in ESG matters is discouraging. The highest-profile (and arguably most successful) climate change engagement by a shareholder so far is Engine No. 1's successful proxy battle against Exxon in the spring of 2021. This was widely seen as a major triumph for ESG advocates as a great deal of the rhetoric around the dispute dealt with Exxon's lack of plans to transition away from its current business.[116] However, as many have reported, the substance of Engine No. 1's argument was that Exxon had been financially underperforming as a result of an undisciplined capital allocation strategy.[117] This key observation was wrapped up in some ESG rhetoric, connecting Exxon's relatively disappointing financial performance to Exxon's failure to prepare for a carbon-less future.[118] The nature of this connection was notably never spelled out. Chevron and Shell have outperformed Exxon, but is it because of the ESG steps they have taken? Engine No. 1's presentation is silent on this point outside of arguing Exxon needs to invest in fields with a lower production cost per barrel. This is a strange sort of ESG concern: "we need to find more profitable oil reserves" isn't exactly a message to warm environmentalists' hearts. In any event, no one could seriously suggest that Exxon's financial performance issues over the past decade have been caused by widespread decarbonization, because oil demand has only increased over that time.[119]

Engine No. 1 actually had no concrete suggestions about what Exxon could do to reduce its emissions profile or prepare for a carbon-less future. For those familiar with the materials generated by activist shareholders in proxy contests, the most interesting thing about Engine No. 1's presentation is how closely it hews to the traditional playbook.[120] Almost all of its presentation is on financial underperformance, supported by corporate governance arguments (misaligned incentives, directors with a poor record of value creation in other businesses). The only new thing is the occasional and vague allusion to the need for energy transition and decarbonization. These ESG appeals no doubt helped it secure support, particularly from index funds, but there is little evidence they are more than window dressing.[121] As we saw in Chapter 6, activist funds have historically used claims of corporate governance failures in a similar fashion.

Some of the most useful data we have on shareholder engagement with ESG issues arises from studies on shareholder proposals. We have a long history of proposals driven by ESG concerns, so we are not dependent on anecdotal evidence. As well, shareholder proposals have historically been the only way shareholders got to vote on ESG matters. As we saw in Chapter 6, outside of a narrow circle of "gadflies" and some union pension funds, institutional investors don't bring proposals. When ESG shareholder proposals are brought, institutional shareholders almost never support them.[122] Over a three-year period, of the 633 ESG proposals brought to vote in the companies making up the Russell 3000, just 2.5 percent received enough votes to pass.[123] The amount of ESG shareholder proposals has actually been declining over the period that ESG marketing language from investment funds has been increasing.[124]

Very similar to the deliberately ineffective voting strategies we saw in Chapter 5, at least two empirical studies have discovered evidence that ESG investment funds "vote in favor of E&S [environmental & social] shareholder proposals when they are unlikely to pass, but they vote against them when their vote is likely to be pivotal."[125]

Of the ESG proposals that are brought, 40 percent are withdrawn in a typical year (compared to only 10 percent of governance proposals).[126] It is unlikely that these ESG proposals are withdrawn because of meaningful concessions by corporate management, as there is no evidence of consequent amendments to the corporation's articles or bylaws, which would make the ESG concessions binding on management and which are visible to the public.[127] If we look at the climate change proposals filed in 2020, we find that only sixteen were voted on, and of the sixteen that were voted on, fifteen asked for more corporate disclosure, and one was for the creation of a climate-risk board committee.[128] These cannot be understood as meaningful attempts to drive ESG change in the minuscule number of firms impacted.

For their part, corporate managers themselves seem to believe that shareholder engagement is mostly about financial performance. A group of scholars looked at so-called "close call" votes on shareholder proposals.[129] These are votes that either only slightly pass the 50 percent requirement for adoption or that slightly fail to reach this level. The assumption in these types of studies is that whether a proposal in this group fails or not is random. The ones that fail can therefore usefully be used as controls to evaluate the impact of a proposal that passes. The scholars found that companies that had a shareholder proposal pass, "experience significantly slower growth in goodness [ESG] scores than firms in which the proposals narrowly fail."[130] In other words, when shareholders successfully engage with managers, managers respond by cutting back on ESG initiatives. Managers could be wrong about what will improve their relationship with activist shareholders, but it seems unlikely.

Most ESG investors emphasize that they engage informally with corporate managers to improve performance; this activity, of course, would not be reflected in the kinds of studies we have been discussing. Fortunately, a very recent study allows us to see the impact of informal ESG engagement by looking at how corporate behavior changes following an influx of ESG capital.[131] Eschewing the usual ratings because of concerns about their validity, the study looks at employee satisfaction (using data from Glassdoor), workplace safety (using data from the Occupational Safety and Health Administration), and pollution (using data from the Environmental Protection Agency). At this point, it should be no surprise that the researchers conclude, "we find no evidence that SRI [socially responsible investment] funds have any impact on corporate [ESG] conduct."[132]

12.9 SUMMARY

One of the things parole boards consider when deciding to release an inmate is their behavior in prison. If the inmate has gotten into a lot of fistfights in prison, it seems likely that they will get into a lot of fistfights if they are sent back home. We call these kinds of individuals "recidivists," even if they promise to go straight and devote themselves to correcting injustices and lowering carbon emissions.

There is nothing in this chapter that we have not seen already in this book. The focus on ESG is new, but the governance tools are precisely the same: shareholder voting and activism, corporate disclosure, third-party rating firms, blithe disregard for markets, slightly different (but still independent!) boards of directors. If these governance practices have not materially improved corporate pay and performance – things that are much easier – then why would we expect them to work on ESG? If investors are both ignorant and irrational in the course of corporate governance activities intended to improve their financial returns, it seems unlikely that a material change will occur simply because we have given them a much, much more challenging and politicized task.

We didn't introduce all our best practices at once forty years ago and then step back to watch what happened. We have been progressively adding governance practices, shifting power to shareholders, generating new norms. The problems with our governance regime detailed in this book are *much worse* than they were ten years ago, and the same could be said about the preceding ten years, and the ten years before that. Our corporate governance regime has not only been failing, it has been getting stronger. This chapter merely suggests it is not yet time to let the corporate governance regime, pumped up by daily workouts in the prison yard and radicalized by association with various bad actors, escape its current bounds and venture out into broader society.

NOTES

1 Nathan Heller, "The End of the English Major," *The New Yorker*, February 27, 2023, online: www.newyorker.com/magazine/2023/03/06/the-end-of-the-english-major.
2 See, for example, Jeffrey N. Gordon, "The Rise of Independent Directors in the United States, 1950–2005: Of Shareholder Value and Stock Market Prices" (2007) 59:6 *Stanford Law Review* 1465–1568; Henry T. C. Hu, "Illiteracy and Intervention: Wholesale Derivatives, Retail Mutual Funds, and the Matter of Asset Class" (1996) 84:7 *Georgetown Law Journal* 2319–2380 at 2376–2377; Steven L. Schwarcz, "Rethinking the Disclosure Paradigm in a World of Complexity" (2004) 2004:1 *University of Illinois Law Review* 1–38; Tamar Frankel, "The Failure of Investor Protection by Disclosure" (2013) 81:2 *University of Cincinnati Law Review* 421–442.
3 Susanna Kim Ripken, "Paternalism and Securities Regulation" (2015) 21:1 *Stanford Journal of Law, Business and Finance* 1–56 at 46.
4 Barbara Black, "Behavioral Economics and Investor Protection: Reasonable Investors, Efficient Markets" (2013) 44:5 *Loyola University Chicago Law Journal* 1493–1508 at 1506.

5   US Securities and Exchange Commission, "Disclosure to Investors: A Reappraisal of Federal Administrative Practices Under the 1933 and 1934 Acts" (New York: Commerce Clearhousing, 1969); US Securities and Exchange Commission, "Report of the Task Force on Disclosure Simplification" (March 5, 1996), online: www.sec.gov/news/studies/smpl.htm.

6   Omri Ben-Shahar and Carl E. Schneider, *More than You Wanted to Know: The Failure of Mandated Disclosure* (Princeton: Princeton University Press, 2014); Troy A. Paredes, "Blinded by the Light: Information Overload and its Consequences for Securities Regulation" (2003) 81:2 *Washington University Law Quarterly* 417–486 [Paredes, "Blinded"]; Susanna Kim Ripken, "The Dangers and Drawbacks of the Disclosure Antidote: Toward a More Substantive Approach to Securities Regulation" (2006) 58:1 *Baylor Law Review* 139–204.

7   Steven M. Davidoff and Claire A. Hill, "Limits of Disclosure" (2013) 36:2 *Seattle University Law Review* 599–638 at 609–623; Paredes, "Blinded," above at note 6 at 440–443.

8   Brandon D. Stewart, "Shining Some Sunlight on Mandatory Corporate Climate-Related Disclosure" (2021) 17:1 *McGill Journal of Sustainable Development Law and Policy* 34–71 at 70.

9   *2020 Report on US Sustainable and Impact Investing Trends*, US SIF: The Forum for Sustainable and Responsible Investment (November 16, 2020), online (pdf): www.ussif.org/files/Trends/2020_Trends_Highlights_OnePager.pdf; Greg Iacurci, "Money Invested in ESG Funds More than Doubles in a Year," CNBC, February 11, 2021, online: www.cnbc.com/2021/02/11/sustainable-investment-funds-more-than-doubled-in-2020-.html; Sara Bernow, Bryce Klempner and Clarisse Magnin, *From "Why" to "Why Not": Sustainable Investing as the New Normal*, McKinsey & Company (October 2017), online (pdf): www.mckinsey.com/~/media/mckinsey/industries/private%20equity%20and%20principal%20investors/our%20insights/from%20why%20to%20why%20not%20sustainable%20investing%20as%20the%20new%20normal/from-why-to-why-not-sustainable-investing-as-the-new-normal.pdf?shouldIndex=false.

10 Jonathan Lewellen and Katharina Lewellen, "Institutional Investors and Corporate Governance: The Incentive to Increase Value" (2018), online (pdf): *Dartmouth College*, https://faculty.tuck.dartmouth.edu/images/uploads/faculty/katharina-lewellen/Institutional_incentives_5_2018.pdf at 1.

11 Philippe Delacote, "On the Sources of Consumer Boycotts Ineffectiveness" (2009) 18:3 *The Journal of Environment and Development* 306–322; Jean-Robert Tyran and Dirk Engelmann, "To Buy or Not to Buy? An Experimental Study of Consumer Boycotts in Retail Markets" (2005) 72:285 *Economica* 1–16.

12 *The Labour Share in G20 Economies*, International Labour Organization, Organisation for Economic Co-operation and Development (February 26, 2015), online (pdf): www.oecd.org/g20/topics/employment-and-social-policy/The-Labour-Share-in-G20-Economies.pdf; James Manyika et al., *A New Look at The Declining Labor Share of Income in The United States*, McKinsey Global Institute (May 2019), online (pdf): www.mckinsey.com/~/media/mckinsey/featured%20insights/employment%20and%20growth/a%20new%20look%20at%20the%20declining%20labor%20sh"re%2'of%20income%20in%20the%20united%20states/mgi-a-new-look-at-the-declining-labor-share-of-income-in-the-united-states.pdf.

13 Lucian Bebchuk and Scott Hirst, "Index Funds and the Future of Corporate Governance: Theory, Evidence, and Policy" (2019) 119:8 *Columbia Law Review* 2029–2146 at 2077.

14 Justin Fox and Jay W. Lorsch, "What Good Are Shareholders?" (2012) 90:7/8 *Harvard Business Review* 48–57 at 51 [Fox and Lorsch, "What Good"]. See also, Roger M. Barker and Iris H.-Y. Chiu, *Corporate Governance and Investment Management: The Promises*

and Limitations of the New Financial Economy* (Cheltenham, UK: Edward Elgar Publishing Limited, 2017).

15 William Lazonick, "Profits Without Prosperity: Stock Buybacks Manipulate the Market and Leave Most Americans Worse Off" (2014) 29:1 *Harvard Business Review* 1–18; Lawrence E. Mitchell, "Whose Capital; What Gains?" (July 2012) 49 *Issues in Governance Studies at Brookings*, online (pdf): www.brookings.edu/wp-content/uploads/2016/06/Whose-Capital-What-Gains.pdf [Mitchell, "What Gains?"].

16 Mitchell, "What Gains?," above at note 15 at 3. See also, Fox and Lorsch, "What Good," above at note 14 at 50; Mark J. Roe, "Looking for the Economy-Wide Effects of Stock Market Short-Termism" (2021) 33:4 *Journal of Applied Corporate Finance* 76–86.

17 Douglas Cummings, Bryce C. Tingle and Feng Zhan, "For Whom (and For When) is the Firm Governed? The Effect of Changes in Corporate Fiduciary Duties on Tax Strategies and Earnings Management" (2021) 27:2 *European Financial Management* 775–813; Inder K. Khurana and William J. Moser, "Institutional Shareholders' Investment Horizons and Tax Avoidance" (2013) 35:1 *Journal of the American Taxation Association* 111–134; C.S. Agnes Cheng et al., "The Effect of Hedge Fund Activism on Corporate Tax Avoidance" (2012) 87:5 *The Accounting Review* 1493–1526.

18 Bryce C. Tingle, "Two Stories about Shareholders" (2021) 58:1 *Osgoode Hall Law Journal* 57–108 at 96; Huasheng Gao, Kai Li and Yujing Ma, "Stakeholder Orientation and the Cost of Debt: Evidence from State-level Adoption of Constituency Statutes" (2021) 56:6 *Journal of Financial and Quantitative Analysis* 1908–1944.

19 William C. Johnson, Jonathan M. Karpoff and Sangho Yi, "The Bonding Hypothesis of Takeover Defenses: Evidence from IPO Firms" (2015) 117:2 *Journal of Financial Economics* 307–332 at 329.

20 Nadia Saghi-Zedek and Amine Tarazi, "Excess Control Rights, Financial Crisis and Bank Profitability and Risk" (2015) 55 *Journal of Banking and Finance* 361–379 at 371; Reint Gropp and Matthias Köhler, "Bank Owners or Bank Managers: Who is Keen on Risk? Evidence from the Financial Crisis" (2010), *Centre for European Economic Research Discussion Paper No. 10-013*, online: SSRN, https://ssrn.com/abstract=1589511. See also, Alan Dignam, "The Future of Shareholder Democracy in the Shadow of the Financial Crisis" (2013) 36:2 *Seattle University Law Review* 639–694 at 643–658.

21 Ing-Haw Cheng, Harrison Hong and Kelly Shue, "Do Managers Do Good with Other People's Money?" (2023) 12:3 *The Review of Corporate Finance Studies* 443–487 at 446–447 [Cheng, Hong and Shue, "Other People's Money"].

22 Caroline Heqing Zhu, "The Preventive Effect of Hedge Fund Activism: Investment, CEO Compensation and Payout Policies" (2013) 17:3 *International Journal of Managerial Finance* 401–415; John C. Coffee, Jr. and Darius Palia, "The Wolf at the Door: The Impact of Hedge Fund Activism on Corporate Governance" (2016) 41:3 *Journal of Corporation Law* 545–608; Ian D. Gow, Sa-Pyung Sean Shin and Suraj Srinivasan, "Activist Directors: Determinants and Consequences" (2014), online: SSRN, https://ssrn.com/abstract=4321778; K. J. Martijn Cremers and Simone M. Sepe, "Board Declassification Activism: Why Run Away from the Evidence?" (2017), online: SSRN, https://ssrn.com/abstract=2991854. See also, K. J. Martijn Cremers and Simone M. Sepe, "Board Declassification Activism: The Financial Value of the Shareholder Rights Project" (2017), online: SSRN, https://ssrn.com/abstract=2962162; Joern H. Block, "R&D Investments in Family and Founder Firms: An Agency Perspective" (2012) 27:2 *Journal of Business Venturing* 248–265 at 249; Pavlos E. Masouros, *Corporate Law and Economic Stagnation: How Shareholder Value and Short-Termism Contribute to the Decline of the Western Economies* (The Netherlands: Eleven International Publishing, 2013)

[Masouros, *Stagnation*]; Caroline Flammer and Aleksandra J. Kacperczyk, "The Impact of Stakeholder Orientation on Innovation: Evidence from a Natural Experiment" (2016) 62:7 *Management Science* 1982–2001.

23 Anna Stansbury and Lawrence H. Summers, "The Declining Worker Power Hypothesis: An Explanation for the Recent Evolution of the American Economy" (Spring 2020) *Brookings Papers on Economic Activity* 1-96 at 3; Antonio Falato, Hyunseob Kim and Till M. von Wachter, "Shareholder Power and the Decline of Labor" (2022), *National Bureau of Economic Research Working Paper No. 30203*, online: NBER, www.nber.org/papers/w30203.

24 Masouros, *Stagnation*, above at note 22.

25 Directorate-General for Justice and Consumers and EY, *Study on Directors' Duties and Sustainable Corporate Governance: Final Report*, Publications Office of the European Union (July 2020), online: https://op.europa.eu/en/publication-detail/-/publication/e47928a2-d20b-11ea-adf7-01aa75ed71a1/language-en at vi.

26 Jeffrey N. Gordon, "Systematic Stewardship" (2022) 47:3 *Journal of Corporation Law* 627–674.

27 Lauren Cohen, Umit G. Gurun and Quoc H. Nguyen, "The ESG-Innovation Disconnect: Evidence from Green Patenting" (2022), *National Bureau of Economic Research Working Paper No. 27990*, online: NBER, www.nber.org/papers/w27990 at 2.

28 *Ibid* at 3.

29 Paul Cox, Stephen Brammer and Andrew Millington, "An Empirical Examination of Institutional Investor Preferences for Corporate Social Performance" (2004) 52 *Journal of Business Ethics* 27–43 at 29. See also, Elisabeth Albertini, "Does Environmental Management Improve Financial Performance? A Meta-analytical Review" (2013) 26:4 *Organization and Environment* 431–457 at 437 [Albertini, "Environmental Management"].

30 Emiel van Duuren, Auke Plantinga and Bert Scholtens, "ESG Integration and the Investment Management Process: Fundamental Investing Reinvented" (2016) 138 *Journal of Business Ethics* 525–533 at 531 [van Duuren, Plantinga and Scholtens, "ESG Integration"].

31 *Ibid* at 529.

32 Amir Amel-Zadeh and George Serafeim, "Why and How Investors Use ESG Information: Evidence from a Global Survey" (2018) 74:3 *Financial Analysts Journal* 87–103 at 92; Tim Quinson, "Why the Biggest U.S. ESG Fund has No Direct Renewable Holdings," Bloomberg News, March 3, 2021, online: www.bloomberg.com/news/articles/2021-03-03/biggest-esg-fund-has-no-direct-renewable-holdings-green-insight-kltcg25d   [Quinson, "Biggest ESG Fund"].

33 van Duuren, Plantinga and Scholtens, "ESG Integration," above at note 30 at 529.

34 David F. Larcker and Edward M. Watts, "Where's the Greenium?" (2020) 69:2–3 *Journal of Accounting and Economics* 101312 at 2, 4 [Larcker and Watts, "Greenium"].

35 John Carmichael and Andreas C. Rapp, "The Green Corporate Bond Issuance Premium" (2022), *International Finance Discussion Paper No. 1346*, online: SSRN, https://ssrn.com/abstract=4194858 at 3. See also, Matt Levine, "Which 20% of a Picture of a Dog?," *Bloomberg*, September 10, 2021, online: www.bloomberg.com/opinion/articles/2021-09-09/twenty-percent-of-a-picture-of-a-dog (reporting that the greenium in Europe is an insignificant 0.02 percent).

36 John Chiang, California State Treasurer, *Growing the U.S. Green Bond Market, Volume 1: The Barriers and Challenges* (January 23, 2017), online (pdf): www.treasurer.ca.gov/greenbonds/publications/reports/1.pdf at 14. See also, Vitaly Orlov, Stefano Ramelli and Alexander F. Wagner "Revealed Beliefs about Responsible Investing: Evidence from Mutual Fund Managers" (2023), *Swiss Finance Institute Research Paper No. 22-98*, online: SSRN, https://ssrn.com/abstract=4296497 (fund ownership by managers is negatively correlated with sustainability performance); Austin Moss, James P. Naughton and Clare Wang, "The Irrelevance of ESG Disclosure to Retail Investors: Evidence from

Robinhood" (2022), online: SSRN, https://ssrn.com/abstract=3604847; Quinn Curtis, Mark C. Weidemaier and Mitu Gulati, "Green Bonds, Empty Promises" (2023), *Virginia Public Law and Legal Theory Research Paper No. 2023–14*, online: SSRN, https://ssrn .com/abstract=4350209 (the "green" promises in these bonds are vague, unenforceable and have been getting weaker over time with investors' tacit permission).

37 Sebastian Utz and Maximillian Wimmer, "Are They Any Good at All? A Financial and Ethical Analysis of Socially Responsible Mutual Funds" (2014) 15 *Journal of Asset Management* 72–82; Hao Liang, Lin Sun and Melvyn Teo, "Greenwashing: Evidence from Hedge Funds" (2021), *Singapore Management University Working Paper*, online: https://ink.library.smu.edu.sg/lkcsb_research/6737/; Aneesh Raghunandan and Shivram Rajgopal, "Do Socially Responsible Firms Walk the Talk?" (2020), online: SSRN, https://ssrn.com/abstract=3609056 at 37; Soohun Kim and Aaron Yoon, "Analyzing Active Managers' Commitment to ESG: Evidence from United Nations Principles for Responsible Investment" (2023) 69:2 *Management Science* 741–758 [Kim and Yoon, "Active Managers"]. See also, Quinson, "Biggest ESG Fund," above at note 32.

38 Aneesh Raghunandan and Shiva Rajgopal, "Do ESG Funds Make Stakeholder-Friendly Investments?" (2022) 27:3 *Review of Accounting Studies* 822–863 [Raghunandan and Rajgopal, "Do ESG Funds"]; Rajna Gibson Brandon et al., "Do Responsible Investors Invest Responsibly?" (2022) 26:6 *Review of Finance* 1389–1432; Kim and Yoon, "Active Managers," above at note 37.

39 Raghunandan and Rajgopal, "Do ESG Funds," above at note 38 at 824; Patrick Bolton and Marcin Kacperczyk, "Do Investors Care About Carbon Risk?" (2021) 142:2 *Journal of Financial Economics* 517–549 at 520 [Bolton and Kacperczyk, "Carbon Risk"].

40 van Duuren, Plantinga and Scholtens, "ESG Integration," above at note 30 at 528–529.

41 Raghunandan and Rajgopal, "Do ESG Funds," above at note 38.

42 Maximillian Wimmer, "ESG-persistence in Socially Responsible Mutual Funds" (2013) 3:1 *Journal of Management and Sustainability* 9–15.

43 Cydney Posner, "How Do the Largest Fund Families Vote on Shareholder Proposals Related to ESG?," *JD Supra*, March 2, 2020, online: www.jdsupra.com/legalnews/blog-how-do-the-largest-fund-families-90960/ [Posner, "Largest Fund Families"].

44 Kim and Yoon, "Active Managers," above at note 37.

45 Gita R. Rao, "A Surprise About Some ESG Funds – They Actually Vote Against Environmental and Socially Conscious Resolutions," *Market Watch*, December 18, 2020, online: https://www.marketwatch.com/story/a-surprise-about-some-esg-funds-they-actually-vote-against-environmental-and-socially-conscious-resolutions-11608306020 [Rao, "Surprise"].

46 Posner, "Largest Fund Families," above at note 43; Caleb N. Griffin, "Environmental and Social Voting at the Big Three," The Columbia Law School's Blog on Corporations and the Capital Markets, June 16, 2020, online: https://clsbluesky.law.columbia.edu/2020/06/16/environmental-and-social-voting-at-the-big-three/ [Griffin, "Environmental and Social Voting"].

47 There were 27,500 newspaper articles about ES investing between 1982–2009: Gunther Capelle-Blancard and Stéphanie Monjon, "Trends in the Literature on Socially Responsible Investment: Looking for the Keys Under the Lamppost" (2012) 21:3 *Business Ethics: A European Review* 239–250 at 241 [Capelle-Blancard and Monjon, "Under the Lamppost"].

48 Eugene F. Fama and Kenneth R. French, "Disagreement, Tastes, and Asset Prices" (2007) 83:3 *Journal of Financial Economics* 667–689; Henri Servaes and Ane Tamayo, "The Role of Social Capital: A Review" (2017) 33:2 *Oxford Review of Economic Policy* 201–220 at 215.

49 Arian Borgers et al., "Stakeholder Relations and Stock Returns: On Errors in Investors' Expectations and Learning" (2013) 22 *Journal of Empirical Finance* 159–175; Jeroen

Derwall, Kees Koedijk and Jenke Ter Horst, "A Tale of Values-driven and Profit-seeking Social Investors" (2011) 35:8 *Journal of Banking and Finance* 217–2147; Gerhard Halbritter and Gregor Dorfleitner, "The Wages of Social Responsibility – Where Are They? A Critical Review of ESG Investing" (2015) 26 *Review of Financial Economics* 25–35 at 31 [Halbritter and Dorfleitner, "Wages"].

50 For example, researchers have found premiums associated with owning so-called "sin" stocks (alcohol, gaming, and tobacco): Harrison Hong and Marcin Kaperczyk, "The Price of Sin: The Effects of Social Norms on Markets" (2009) 93:1 *Journal of Financial Economics* 15–36 [Hong and Kaperczyk, "Price of Sin"]; Lasse Heje Pedersen, Shaun Fitzgibbons and Lukasz Pomorski, "Responsible Investing: The ESG-Efficient Frontier" (2021) 142:2 *Journal of Financial Economics* 572–597 [Pedersen, Fitzgibbons and Pomorski, "Responsible Investing"].

51 Jonathan M. Karpoff, John R. Lott, Jr. and Eric W. Wehrly, "The Reputational Penalties for Environmental Violations: Empirical Evidence" (2005) 48:2 *The Journal of Law and Economics* 653–675. But see, Simon Gloßner, "The Price of Ignoring ESG Risks" (2018), online: *Semantic Scholar*, www.semanticscholar.org/paper/The-Price-of-Ignoring-ESG-Risks-Glossner/e973c8c07b60d1a4b9d7b337af045ccec3c579d5 (finding the market fails to fully incorporate the consequences of bad behavior).

52 Ioannis Oikonomou, Chris Brooks and Stephen Pavelin, "The Impact of Corporate Social Performance on Financial Risk and Utility: A Longitudinal Analysis" (2012) 41:2 *Financial Management* 483–515 at 512 [Oikonomou, Brooks and Pavelin, "Risk and Utility"]. But see, Emirhan Ilhan, Zacharias Sautner and Grigory Vilkov, "Carbon Tail Risk" (2021) 34:3 *The Review of Financial Studies* 1540–1571 (finding carbon emissions may increase risk as reflected in out-of-the-money put option prices).

53 Capelle-Blancard and Monjon, "Under the Lamppost," above at note 47 at 245.

54 These studies include: Donna J. Wood and Raymond E. Jones, "Stakeholder Mismatching: A Theoretical Problem in Empirical Research on Corporate Social Performance" (1995) 3:3 *The International Journal of Organizational Analysis* 229–267; Moses L. Pava and Joshua Krausz, "The Association Between Corporate Social-Responsibility and Financial Performance" (1996) 15 *Journal of Business Ethics* 321–357; Joshua D. Margolis and James P. Walsh, "Misery Loves Companies: Rethinking Social Initiatives by Business" (2003) 48:2 *Administrative Science Quarterly* 268–305; Marc Orlitzky, Frank L. Schmidt and Sara L. Rynes, "Corporate Social and Financial Performance: A Meta-analysis" (2003) 24:3 *Organization Studies* 403–441; Andreas G. F. Hoepner and David G. McMillan, "Research on Responsible Investment: An Influential Literature Analysis Comprising a Rating, Characterisation, Categorisation and Investigation" (2009), online: *SSRN*, https://ssrn.com/abstract=1454793; Albertini, "Environmental Management," above at note 29; Christophe Revelli and Jean-Laurent Viviani, "Financial Performance of Socially Responsible Investing (SRI): What Have We Learned? A Meta-Analysis" (2015) 24:2 *Business Ethics: A European Review* 158–185; Jan Endrikat, Edeltraud Guenther and Holger Hoppe, "Making Sense of Conflicting Empirical Findings: A Meta-analysis Review of the Relationship Between Corporate Environmental and Financial Performance" (2014) 32:5 *European Management Journal* 735–751; Timo Busch and Gunnar Friede, "The Robustness of the Corporate Social and Financial Performance Relation: A Second-order Meta-analysis" (2018) 25:4 *Corporate Social Responsibility and Environmental Management* 583–608.

55 Miriam von Wallis and Christian Klein, "Ethical Requirement and Financial Interest: A Literature Review on Socially Responsible Investing" (2015) 8:1 *Business Research* 61–98 at 80. See also, Capelle-Blancard and Monjon, "Under the Lamppost," above at note 47 at 247; Halbritter and Dorfleitner, "Wages," above at note 49 at 25; Joscha Nollet, George Filis and Evangelos Mitrokostas, "Corporate Social Responsibility and Financial

Performance: A Non-Linear and Disaggregated Approach" (2016) 52 *Economic Modelling* 400–407; Pedersen, Fitzgibbons and Pomorski, "Responsible Investing," above at note 50; Oikonomou, Brooks and Pavelin, "Risk and Utility," above at note 52 at 483; Stephen J. Fowler and Chris Hope, "A Critical Review of Sustainable Business Indices and Their Impact" (2007) 76:3 *Journal of Business Ethics* 243–252 at 244. Investment results outside of America seem broadly similar: Benjamin R. Auer and Frank Schuhmacher, "Do Socially (Ir)responsible Investments Pay? New Evidence from International ESG Data" (2016) 59 *The Quarterly Review of Economics and Finance* 51–62; Florencio Lopez-de-Silanes, Joseph A. McCahery and Paul C. Pudschedl, "ESG Performance and Disclosure: A Cross-Country Analysis" (2020) *Singapore Journal of Legal Studies* 217–241.

56 Ulrich Atz et al., "Does Sustainability Generate Better Financial Performance? Review, Meta-analysis, and Propositions" (2023) 13:1 *Journal of Sustainable Finance and Investment* 802–825 at 802.

57 Bolton and Kacperczyk, "Carbon Risk," above at note 39 at 520. See also, Shaojun Zhang, "Do Investors Really Care About Carbon Risk?" (2023), *Hong Kong Institute for Monetary and Financial Research (HKIMR) Research Paper AP No. 1/2023*, online: SSRN, https://ssrn.com/abstract=4372589.

58 Wei Dai and Philipp Meyer-Brauns, "Greenhouse Gas Emissions and Expected Returns" (2022), online: SSRN, https://ssrn.com/abstract=3714874.

59 Gunther Capelle-Blancard and Aurélien Petit, "Every Little Helps? ESG News and Stock Market Reaction" (2019) 157:2 *Journal of Business Ethics* 543–565. See also, Nahoko Mitsuyama and Satoshi Shimizutani, "Stock Market Reaction to ESG-Oriented Management: An Event Study Analysis of Disclosing Policy in Japan" (2015) 35 *Economics Bulletin* 1098–1108.

60 Philipp Krüger, "Corporate Goodness and Shareholder Wealth" (2015) 115:2 *Journal of Financial Economics* 304–329 [Krüger, "Corporate Goodness"].

61 Brad M. Barber, Adair Morse and Ayako Yasuda, "Impact Investing" (2021) 139:1 *Journal of Financial Economics* 162–185.

62 Pieter Jan Trinks and Bert Scholtens, "The Opportunity Cost of Negative Screening in Socially Responsible Investing" (2017) 140 *Journal of Business Ethics* 193–208 at 194 [Trinks and Scholtens, "Opportunity Cost"]. See also, Doron Avramov et al., "Investment and Asset Pricing with ESG Disagreement" (2020), online: SSRN, https://ssrn.com/abstract=3684979 at 2; Hong and Kaperczyk, "Price of Sin," above at note 50; Pedersen, Fitzgibbons and Pomorski, "Responsible Investing," above at note 50.

63 Samuel M. Hartzmark and Abigail B. Sussman, "Do Investors Value Sustainability? A Natural Experiment Examining Ranking and Fund Flows" (2019) 74:6 *The Journal of Finance* 2789–2837 at 2793.

64 Chris Flood et al., "Vanguard Chief Defends Decision to Pull Asset Manager Out of Climate Alliance" (Feb 20, 2023) *Financial Times*, online: www.ft.com/content/9dab65dd-64c8-40c0-ae6e-fac4689dcc77.

65 David F. Larcker et al., "ESG Ratings: A Compass without Direction" (2022), *Rock Center for Corporate Governance at Stanford University Closer Look Series*, online: SSRN, https://ssrn.com/abstract=4179647 at 2.

66 See, for example, Feifei Li and Ari Polychronopoulos, "What a Difference an ESG Ratings Provider Makes!" (January 2020), *Research Affiliates*, online: www.researchaffiliates.com/publications/articles/what-a-difference-an-esg-ratings-provider-makes; Florian Berg, Julian F. Kölbel and Roberto Rigobon, "Aggregate Confusion: The Divergence of ESG Ratings" (2022) 26:6 *Review of Finance* 1315–1344 at 1321 [Berg, Kölbel and Rigobon, "Aggregate Confusion"]; Halbritter and Dorfleitner, "Wages," above at note

49; Gregor Dorfleitner, Gerhard Halbritter and Mai Nguyen, "Measuring the Level and Risk of Corporate Responsibility – An Empirical Comparison of Different ESG Rating Approaches" (2015) 16 *Journal of Asset Management* 450–466 at 465 [Dorfleitner, Halbritter and Nguyen, "Measuring the Level"]; "The ESG Data Challenge" (March 2019), online (pdf): *State Street Global Advisors*, www.ssga.com/investment-topics/environmental-social-governance/2019/03/esg-data-challenge.pdf [SSGA, "Data Challenge"]; Arthur Hughes, Michael A. Urban and Dariusz Wójcik, "Alternative ESG Ratings: How Technological Innovation Is Reshaping Sustainable Investment" (2021) 13:6 *Sustainability* 3551; Doron Avramov et al., "Sustainable Investing with ESG Rating Uncertainty" (2022) 145:2 *Journal of Financial Economics* 642–664 at 643; Rajna Gibson Brandon, Philipp Krueger and Peter Steffen Schmidt, "ESG Rating Disagreement and Stock Returns" (2021) 77:4 *Financial Analysts Journal* 104–127 [Gibson Brandon, Krueger and Schmidt, "Rating Disagreement"]; Lies Bouten et al., "CSR Performance Proxies in Large-Sample Studies: 'Umbrella Advocates', Construct Clarity and the 'Validity Police'" (2018), online: *SSRN*, https://ssrn.com/abstract=3107182; Dane M. Christensen, George Serafeim and Anywhere Sikochi, "Why is Corporate Virtue in the Eye of the Beholder? The Case of ESG Rating" (2022) 97:1 *The Accounting Review* 147–175 at 157 [Christensen, Serafeim and Sikochi, "Corporate Virtue"]; Elroy Dimson, Paul Marsh and Mike Staunton, "Divergent ESG Ratings" (2020) 47:1 *The Journal of Portfolio Management* 75–87.

67 Berg, Kölbel and Rigobon, "Aggregate Confusion," above at note 66 at 1320.

68 *Ibid.*

69 Christensen, Serafeim and Sikochi, "Corporate Virtue," above at note 66 at 157.

70 Aaron K. Chatterji, David I. Levine and Michael W. Toffel, "How Well Do Social Ratings Actually Measure Corporate Social Responsibility?" (2009) 18:1 *Journal of Economics and Management* 125–169 [Chatterji, Levine and Toffel, "How Well"]; Aaron K. Chatterji et al., "Do Ratings of Firms Converge? Implications for Managers, Investors and Strategy Researchers" (2016) 37:8 *Strategic Management Journal* 1597–1614; Natalia Semenova and Lars G. Hassel, "On the Validity of Environmental Performance Metrics" (2015) 132:2 *Journal of Business Ethics* 249–258; James E. Mattingly and Shawn L. Berman, "Measurement of Corporate Social Action: Creating Taxonomy in the Kinder Lydenburg Domini Ratings Data" (2006) 45:1 *Business and Society* 20–46; Raghunandan and Rajgopal, "Do ESG Funds," above at note 38.

71 Raghunandan and Rajgopal, "Do ESG Funds," above at note 38.

72 See, for example, Vassiliki Grougiou et al., "Corporate Social Responsibility and Earnings Management in US Banks" (2014) 38:3 *Accounting Forum* 155–169 at 156; Jennifer Martínez-Ferrero, Shantanu Banerjee and Isabel María Garcia-Sánchez, "Corporate Social Responsibility as a Strategic Shield Against Costs of Earnings Management Practices" (2016) 133 *Journal of Business Ethics* 305–324 [Martínez-Ferrero, Banerjee and Garcia-Sánchez, "Strategic Shield"]; Diego Prior, Jordi Surroca and Josep A. Tribó, "Are Socially Responsible Managers Really Ethical? Exploring the Relationship Between Earnings Management and Corporate Social Responsibility" (2008) 16:3 *Corporate Governance: An International Review* 160–177; Rim Makni Gargouri, Ridha Shabou and Claude Francoeur, "The Relationship Between Corporate Social Performance and Earnings Management" (2010) 27:4 *Canadian Journal of Administrative Sciences/Revue Canadienne des sciences de l'administration* 320–334 [Gargouri, Shabou and Francoeur, "The Relationship Between"].

73 Christina Kjaer and Tom Kirchmaier, "Deceived by 'S': Corporate Scandals and ESG" (2023), online: *SSRN*, https://ssrn.com/abstract=4428468.

74 Amit Batish et al., "Sharing the Pain: How Did Boards Adjust CEO Pay in Response to COVID-19?" (2020), *Rock Center for Corporate Governance at Stanford University Closer*

Look Series: Topics, Issues and Controversies in Corporate Governance No. CGRP-86, online: SSRN, https://ssrn.com/abstract=3682766.

75 Oikonomou, Brooks and Pavelin, "Risk and Utility," above at note 52 at 505.

76 Derek Horstmeyer, "The Surprising Risks of Investing in ESG Funds," *The Wall Street Journal*, September 16, 2021, online: www.wsj.com/articles/risks-of-esg-funds-11631539404.

77 *Rate the Raters 2020: Investor Survey and Interview Results*, SustainAbility (March 2020), online (pdf): www.sustainability.com/globalassets/sustainability.com/thinking/pdfs/sustainability-ratetheraters2020-report.pdf.

78 See, for example, James Mackintosh, "Is Tesla or Exxon More Sustainable? It Depends Whom You Ask," *The Wall Street Journal*, September 17, 2018, online: www.wsj.com/articles/is-tesla-or-exxon-more-sustainable-it-depends-whom-you-ask-1537199931; Robin Wigglesworth, "Rating Agencies using Green Criteria Suffer from 'Inherent Biases,'" *Financial Times*, July 20, 2018, online: www.ft.com/content/a5e02050-8ac6-11e8-bf9e-8771d5404543; Jon Sindreu and Sarah Kent, "Why It's So Hard to be an 'Ethical' Investor," *The Wall Street Journal*, September 1, 2018, online: www.wsj.com/articles/why-its-so-hard-to-be-an-ethical-investor-1535799601; Kate Allen, "Lies, Damned Lies and ESG Rating Methodologies," *Financial Times*, December 5, 2018, online: www.ft.com/content/2e49171b-a018-3c3b-b66b-81fd7a170ab5.

79 Commissioner Hester M. Peirce, *Scarlet Letters: Remarks before the American Enterprise Institute*, US Securities and Exchange Commission (June 18, 2019), online: www.sec.gov/news/speech/speech-peirce-061819.

80 SSGA, "Data Challenge," above at note 66.

81 Daniel Cash, "Can Regulatory Intervention Save the Sustainability Rating Industry?" (2021) 42:1 *Business Law Review* 13–25.

82 Chatterji, Levine and Toffel, "How Well," above at note 70 at 164.

83 Adrienne E. Eaton, "The Survival of Employee Participation Programs in Unionized Settings" (1994) 47:3 *ILR Review* 371–389; Francis Green, "Why Has Work Effort Become More Intense?" (2004) 43:4 *Industrial Relations: A Journal of Economy and Society* 709–741.

84 Chatterji, Levine and Toffel, "How Well," above at note 70 at 164.

85 Oikonomou, Brooks and Pavelin, "Risk and Utility," above at note 52 at 490.

86 Gibson Brandon, Krueger and Schmidt, "Rating Disagreement," above at note 66 at 105.

87 Krüger, "Corporate Goodness," above at note 60 at 305; Bradford Cornell and Aswath Damodaran, "Valuing ESG: Doing Good or Sounding Good?" (2020), online: SSRN, https://ssrn.com/abstract=3557432 at 3.

88 Ian Vandaelle, "'Shocking': ESG Funds Piled into Russian Oil Over Canadian Energy," Bloomberg, March 1, 2022, online: www.bnnbloomberg.ca/esg-funds-missing-the-mark-on-social-and-governance-cibc-analysts-1.1740710 (citing a report from CIBC Capital Markets).

89 There is relatively little disagreement that active managers generally fail to beat the market. See, for example, Martin J. Gruber, "Another Puzzle: The Growth in Actively Managed Mutual Funds" (1996) 51:3 *The Journal of Finance* 783–810 at 787; Javier Gil-Bazo and Pablo Ruiz-Verdú, "The Relation between Price and Performance in the Mutual Fund Industry" (2009) 64:5 *The Journal of Finance* 2153–2183.

90 Dorfleitner, Halbritter and Nguyen, "Measuring the Level," above at note 66 at 460; Samuel Drempetic, Christian Klein and Bernhard Zwergel, "The Influence of Firm Size on the ESG Score: Corporate Sustainability Ratings Under Review" (2020) 167 *Journal of Business Ethics* 333–360; Bolton and Kacperczyk, "Carbon Risk," above at note 39 at 519; Chatterji, Levine and Toffel, "How Well," above at note 69 at 165.

91   Bolton and Kacperczyk, "Carbon Risk," above at note 39 at 525. See also, Elena Escrig-Olmedo et al., "Rating the Raters: Evaluating How ESG Rating Agencies Integrate Sustainability Principles" (2019) 11:3 *Sustainability* 915.

92   Christensen, Serafeim and Sikochi, "Corporate Virtue," above at note 66 at 164. See also, Jinji Hao, "Disclosure Regulation, Cost of Capital, and Firm Values" (2023), online: SSRN, https://ssrn.com/abstract=4393031.

93   Sergio Gilotta, "Disclosure in Securities Markets and the Firm's Need for Confidentiality: Theoretical Frameworks and Regulatory Analysis" (2012) 13:1 *European Business Organization Law Review* 45–88; Luigi Zingales, "The Future of Securities Regulation" (2009) 47:2 *Journal of Accounting Research* 391–425 at 394; Wolfgang Schön, "Corporate Disclosure in a Competitive Environment – The Quest for a European Framework on Mandatory Disclosure" (2006) 6:2 *Journal of Corporate Law Studies* 259–298 at 294–296.

94   Bryce C. Tingle, "Corporations on the Couch: Is Therapeutic Disclosure a Kind of Madness?" (2022) 22:3 *UBC Law Review* 745–801. See also, Matthias Breuer, Christian Leuz and Steven Vanhaverbeke, "Reporting Regulation and Corporate Innovation" (2022), *National Bureau of Economic Research Working Paper No. 26291*, online: NBER, www.nber.org/papers/w26291; Tomasz Obloj and Todd Zenger, "The Influence of Pay Transparency on (Gender) Inequity, Inequality and the Performance Basis of Pay" (2022) 6:5 *Nature Human Behaviour* 646–655.

95   Hans B. Christensen, Luzi Hail and Christian Leuz, "Mandatory CSR and Sustainability Reporting: Economic Analysis and Literature Review" (2021) 26:3 *Review of Accounting Studies* 1176–1248.

96   Martínez-Ferrero, Banerjee and Garcia-Sánchez, "Strategic Shield," above at note 72 at 306; Gargouri, Shabou and Francoeur, "The Relationship Between," above at note 72. See also, Thomas P. Lyon and A. Wren Montgomery, "The Means and End of Greenwash" (2015) 28:2 *Organization and Environment* 223–249; Christopher Marquis, Michael W. Toffel and Yanhua Zhou, "Scrutiny, Norms, and Selective Disclosure: A Global Study of Greenwashing" (2016) 27:2 *Organization Science* 483–504; Eun-Hee Kim and Thomas P. Lyon, "Greenwash vs. Brownwash: Exaggeration and Undue Modesty in Corporate Sustainability Disclosure" (2015) 26:3 *Organization Science* 705–723; Marcus J. Milne, "Phantasmagoria, Sustain-a-babbling in Social and Environmental Reporting" in Lisa Jack, Jane Davison and Russell Craig (eds.), *The Routledge Companion to Accounting Communication* (London: Routledge, 2013), pp. 149–167.

97   Ryan Flugum and Matthew E. Souther, "Stakeholder Value: A Convenient Excuse for Underperforming Managers?" (2023), online: SSRN, https://ssrn.com/abstract=3725828; Daewoung Choi et al., "The Mitigation of Reputational Risk via Responsive CSR: Evidence from Securities Class Action Suits" (2021), online: SSRN, https://ssrn.com/abstract=3807643.

98   Trinks and Scholtens, "Opportunity Cost," above at note 62 at 193.

99   The main divestment targets these days are the energy companies: See, for example, Dennis Halcoussis and Anton D. Lowenberg, "The Effects of the Fossil Fuel Divestment Campaign on Stock Returns" (2019) 47 *The North American Journal of Economics and Finance* 669–674; Irene Henriques and Perry Sadorsky, "Investor Implications of Divesting from Fossil Fuels" (2018) 38 *Global Finance Journal* 30–44; Callum Macpherson, "The Potential Impact of Investor Fossil Fuel Divestment Behaviour on Oil Prices" (2019), online: SSRN, https://ssrn.com/abstract=3382739.

100   Bolton and Kacperczyk, "Carbon Risk," above at note 39 at 548.

101   See, for example, Richard A. Brealey and Stewart C. Myers (eds.), *Principles of Corporate Finance*, 11th ed. (New York: McGraw-Hill Education, 2013) at pp. 80–84.

102 Paul Griffin, *The Carbon Majors Database: CDP Carbon Majors Report* 2017, CDP Worldwide (July 10, 2017), online (pdf): https://cdn.cdp.net/cdp-production/cms/reports/documents/000/002/327/original/Carbon-Majors-Report-2017.pdf?1501833772 at 10.

103 Laurian Casson Lytle and O. Maurice Joy, "The Stock Market Impact of Social Pressure: The South African Divestment Case" (1996) 36:4 *The Quarterly Review of Economics and Finance* 507–527 at 519 [Lytle and Joy, "Divestment Case"]; Siew Hong Tech, Ivo Welch and C. Paul Wazzan, "The Effect of Socially Activist Investment Policies on the Financial Markets: Evidence from the South African Boycott" (1999) 72:1 *The Journal of Business* 35–89 at 79 [Tech, Welch and Wazzan, "Socially Activist"]; Wallace N. Davidson III, Dan L. Worrell and Abuzar El-Jelly, "Influencing Managers to Change Unpopular Corporate Behavior through Boycotts and Divestitures: A Stock Market Test" (1995) 34:2 *Business and Society* 171–196 at 190 [Davidson, Worrell and El-Jelly, "Influencing Managers"]. See also, Jonathan Berk and Jules H. van Binsbergen, "The Impact of Impact Investing" (2022), *Stanford University Graduate School of Business Research Paper*, online: SSRN, https://ssrn .com/abstract=3909166.

104 Lytle and Joy, "Divestment Case," above at note 103.

105 Davidson, Worrell and El-Jelly, "Influencing Managers," above at note 103 at 171; Tech, Welch and Wazzan, "Socially Activist," above at note 103 at 35; Paul Lansing and Sarosh Kuruvilla, "Business Divestment in South Africa: In Who's Best Interest" (1988) 7:8 *Journal of Business Ethics* 561–574 at 573. See also, Samuel M. Hartzmark and Kelly Shue, "Counterproductive Sustainable Investing: The Impact Elasticity of Brown and Green Firms" (2023), online: SSRN, https://ssrn.com/abstract=4359282.

106 Beiting Cheng, Ioannis Ioannou and George Serafeim, "Corporate Social Responsibility and Access to Finance" (2014) 35:1 *Strategic Management Journal* 1–23.

107 Dan S. Dhaliwal et al., "Voluntary Non-Financial Disclosure and the Cost of Equity Capital: The Initiation of Corporate Social Responsibility Reporting" (2011) 86:1 *The Accounting Review* 59–100; Sadok El Ghoul et al., "Does Corporate Social Responsibility Affect the Cost of Capital?" (2011) 35:9 *Journal of Banking & Finance* 2388–2406; Sudheer *Chava*, "Environmental Externalities and Cost of Capital" (2014) 60:9 *Management Science* 2223–2247.

108 Larcker and Watts, "Greenium," above at note 34.

109 Paul Brest, Ronald J. Gilson and Mark A. Wolfson, "Essay: How Investors Can (and Can't) Create Social Value" (2018) 44:2 *Journal of Corporation Law* 205–232 at 217 (emphasis in original) [Brest, Gilson and Wolfson, "Social Value"].

110 Shaun William Davies and Edward Dickersin Van Wesep, "The Unintended Consequences of Divestment" (2018) 128:3 *Journal of Financial Economics* 558–575 at 571.

111 Brest, Gilson and Wolfson, "Social Value," above at note 109 at 219.

112 See Bryce C. Tingle, "What Do We Know About Shareholders' Potential to Solve Environmental and Social Problems?" (2023) 58:1 *Georgia Law Review* 169–247.

113 David Blackmon, "Like That Cleaner Air You're Breathing? Fracking Says, 'You're Welcome!,'" *Forbes*, September 5, 2018, online: www.forbes.com/sites/david blackmon/2018/09/05/like-that-cleaner-air-youre-breathing-fracking-says-youre-welcome/?sh=412b40836610.

114 Theocharis Tsoutsos, Niki Frantzeskaki and Vassilis Gekas, "Environmental Impacts from the Solar Energy Technologies" (2005) 33:3 *Energy Policy* 289–296; Rahman Saidur et al., "Environmental Impact of Wind Energy" (2011) 15:5 *Renewable and Sustainable Energy Reviews* 2423–2430; Victoria Flexer, Celso Fernando Baspineiro and Claudia Inés Galli, "Lithium Recovery from Brines: A Vital Raw Material for Green Energies

with a Potential Environmental Impact in its Mining and Processing" (2018) 639 *Science of the Total Environment* 1188–1204.

115   Brest, Gilson and Wolfson, "Social Value," above at note 109 at 231.

116   See, for example, Matt Phillips, "Exxon's Board Defeat Signals the Rise of Social-Good Activists," *The New York Times*, June 9, 2021, online: www.nytimes.com/2021/06/09/busi ness/exxon-mobil-engine-no1-activist.html.

117   *Reenergize ExxonMobil: Summary Investor Presentation*, Engine No. 1 (May 2021), online (pdf): https://reenergizexom.com/documents/Investor-Presentation-Summary-May-2021.pdf.

118   *Ibid* at 6 and 7.

119   *World Oil Supply and Demand*, 1971–2020, International Energy Agency (October 22, 2022), online: www.iea.org/data-and-statistics/charts/world-oil-supply-and-demand-1971-2020.

120   David Nicklaus, "Exxon Board Fight Wasn't About Being Woke. It Was About Poor Performance," *St. Louis Post-Dispatch*, June 4, 2021, online: www.stltoday.com/busi ness/subscriber/nicklaus-exxon-board-fight-wasnt-about-being-woke-it-was-about-poor-performance/article_53207bb5-a365-5642-b347-39ff623c030a.html.

121   *Ibid*; Bernard S. Sharfman, "The Illusion of Success: A Critique of Engine No. 1's Proxy Fight at Exxon Mobil" (2021–2022) 12 *Harvard Business Law Review Online* 1–21.

122   Geeyoung Min and Hye Young You, "Active Firms and Active Shareholders: Corporate Political Activity and Shareholder Proposals" (2019) 48:1 *The Journal of Legal Studies* 81–116 at 109; Griffin, "Environmental and Social Voting," above at note 46; Rao, "Surprise," above at note 45; Tao Li, S. Lakshim Naaraayanan and Kunal Sachdeva, "Conflicting Objectives of ESG Funds: Evidence from Proxy Voting" (2023), online: SSRN, https://ssrn.com/abstract=3760753.

123   Alex Knowlton, *No Support for ESG Proposals? Leverage Voting Power Elsewhere*, Equilar (February 5, 2018), online (blog): www.equilar.com/blogs/357-how-to-gain-support-for-esg-proposals.html.

124   *Shareholder Proposal Developments During the 2020 Proxy Season*, Gibson Dunn (August 4, 2020), online (pdf): www.gibsondunn.com/wp-content/uploads/2020/08/shareholder-proposal-developments-during-the-2020-proxy-season.pdf [Gibson Dunn, *2020 Proxy Season*].

125   Davidson Heath et al., "Does Socially Responsible Investing Change Firm Behavior?" (2023) 27:6 *Review of Finance* 2057–2083 at 2060 [Heath et al., "Socially Responsible"]; Roni Michaely, Guillem Ordonez-Calafi and Silvina Rubio, "Mutual Funds' Strategic Voting on Environmental and Social Issues" (2023), *European Corporate Governance Institute –Finance Working Paper No. 774/2021*, online: SSRN, https://ssrn.com/abstract=3884917.

126   Sarah C. Haan, "Shareholder Proposal Settlements and the Private Ordering of Public Elections" (2016) 126:2 *Yale Law Journal* 262–345 at 301, note 146.

127   *Ibid* at 302.

128   Gibson Dunn, *2020 Proxy Season*, above at note 124 at 13 (one of the fifteen categorized as requesting more corporate disclosure "requested the company adopt quantitative company-wide GHG goals.").

129   Cheng, Hong and Shue, "Other People's Money," above at note 21.

130   *Ibid* at 447.

131   Heath et al., "Socially Responsible," above at note 125.

132   *Ibid* at 2081. See also, Dhruv Aggarwal, Lubomir Litov and Shivaram Rajgopal, "Big Three (Dis)Engagements" (2023), *Northwestern Law & Econ Research Paper No. 23-17*, online: SSRN, https://ssrn.com/abstract=4592727.

13

Where Do We Go from Here?

There is something heroic about Wile E. Coyote. He has grit. In fact, he may be the most resilient figure in American popular culture: no one has failed – or suffered – more than him, but he never gives up; he is always ready to try something new. At the same time, this makes him a tragic figure: his resilience and cock-eyed optimism are the very things that prevent him from realizing the futility of his campaign against the Road Runner. Because of this tragic flaw (in the Aristotelian sense), he is consigned to a Sisyphean hell, condemned to forever repeat a pointless task that always ends in failure.

The good news about corporate governance is that I don't think we are collectively made of the stuff of Wile E. Coyote. We are simply, in the aggregate, not heroic in the way he is. As a result, I feel confident that at some point we will stand on a desert mesa watching the Road Runner speeding out of sight and collectively decide to move to the city and get into another line of work.

The most amazing thing about the modern corporate governance regime is how firmly it has retained its grasp on the imagination of investors, lawyers, regulators, and academics. For example, reviewing the vast literature on board independence and firm performance, one group of scholars notes that "[a]t least two levels of consistency are present in all of these reviews and discussions. First, they provide no evidence of systemic relationships between these variables. Second, most of the authors have not forsaken their commitment to affirm these relationships."[1]

Why have we persisted over forty years to follow (admittedly plausible) theories that have consistently failed to generate the expected results? One cause may be that most of the people actively engaged in discussions of corporate governance are not familiar with the bodies of research bearing on, for example, the agency cost story's track record or the impact of independence on firm performance. Each of these professionals has a busy life, and combing through academic journals is not part of it. They probably don't feel the lack.

Another cause may be that we want to do something when a large organization creates a problem. We want to believe (and politicians need to show) that we can do something to ensure incompetence, dishonesty, fraud, and recklessness will never happen again. Simply shrugging and saying something like "people are occasion-ally greedy idiots" is too passive. The fact that our legal and regulatory system often has trouble putting greedy idiots into jail or getting them to personally pay for the messes they make only puts more pressure on us to instead propose yet another reform to corporate governance.

Finally, it is in a lot of groups' interests to keep the corporate governance industry humming along: proxy advisors, ESG rating agencies, investment fund managers with marketing strategies, public pension fund managers with political masters, activist hedge funds seeking support for their short-term financial maneuvers, pro-fessional advisors on governance (lawyers, accountants, consultants), executive compensation consultants, media outlets, think-tanks, governance and disclosure professionals in companies, and academics needing something new to write about. This is very much a nonexhaustive list.

Regulators and politicians also want something like the modern corporate gov-ernance project to remain on the scene. Corporate governance reforms are useful as a way for politicians, regulators, and other powerful parties to seem to be doing something about a problem, without actually impacting the real interests of those who benefit from our current economic arrangements. Legislative interventions in the wake of massive corporate failures over the past two decades have usually seen the adoption of governance structures that: (1) were already present and in place in the badly behaved companies; (2) had significant empirical evidence they were ineffec-tive; and (3) were preceded by well-known corporate law scholars making the first two points in articles with "quack corporate governance" in their titles.[2]

If the modern governance project does not provide us with one-size-fits-all prac-tices to improve the things we care about – profits, probity, the environment, jus-tice – then a lot of people are going to have to find something more productive to do. On the plus side, like Wile E. Coyote, this will mean abandoning a project that mostly just wastes money and effort while doing nothing to prevent the bird from running around the desert. Just imagine how much more fulfilling Wile E. Coyote will feel his life in the city to be, once he has begun an ISO 9001 compliant com-petitor to Acme Corp.

In some ways, therefore, it is helpful that the corporate governance industry has set its sights on our pressing social and environmental problems. This book has gen-erally talked about the waste of time and resources created by a governance system that fails to deliver much in the way of financial benefits. But, let's face it, most peo-ple don't care much about economic efficiency (though they really should). They do care, however, about things like pollution, income inequality, global warming, and their conception of justice. If we are wasting our time with corporate gover-nance solutions to these problems, that will matter to *everyone*.

It would be nice, though, to not have to wait until the American public generally concludes corporate governance has failed in the social and environmental tasks we are setting for it. We would save the time, energy, and resources social reformers are putting into ESG projects. We would also save America from another depressing example of institutional failure.

In the long run, America will probably survive more cynicism and a few dejected environmentalists quitting jobs in the ESG disclosure departments of oil companies. The consequences of damaging our public markets, however, are more severe. The rise of the modern corporate governance project has coincided with an unprecedented decline in our public markets. There is a great deal of debate about the reasons for this, but the fact is that thirty years ago, corporate managers wanted to go public. It was a way for them to break free of the strict oversight imposed by venture capital and other investors, a chance for them to build a great American institution, a chance for them to make even more money, a chance for them to burnish their reputation and maybe become famous. Now, if you talk to entrepreneurs, they are desperate to avoid the public markets – even though this means selling their companies, losing their jobs, and seeing their vision for the business extinguished as it becomes a division of a larger company. When entrepreneurs are asked why they avoid public markets, their answer usually touches on some aspect of the modern corporate governance regime. Public markets seem not to be worth the hassle, the risk to one's reputation, the loss of control over governance, the second-guessing by the ignorant and self-righteous, or the simple inability to run their company as they believe it must be run if it is to continue to flourish. As Professor Steven Kaplan observes succinctly, "We've made it miserable to be a public company."[3]

Public markets matter. They are the only place where companies can be built over the very long term. Private equity funds have five- or seven-year investment horizons, and their investment strategies often involve heaping precarious amounts of debt on portfolio companies. This is not a viable multi-decade strategy for most businesses, which must accommodate downturns and failures as a natural part of competing in tough markets. The stability (really, solvency) provided by the locked-in equity of the public markets has historically been very important in creating and scaling up new American businesses. If entrepreneurs want to avoid the public markets like the plague (and most of them do), then the only other way for them to provide an exit for their investors is to sell their business to a larger company – snuffing out a potentially great new American institution.

One understudied thing about Wile E. Coyote is his ability – for a while – to literally walk on air. In keeping with the rules of classical tragedy, this superiority over the rest of us signals his greatness. In some of the cartoons, he can, especially if he is running or assisted by roller skates, travel some distance horizontally through the ether – until he looks down. Then he falls (usually while looking at the camera in weary resignation). It is time for all of us involved in various ways in the corporate governance project to look down. We have been running on air, buoyed only by our frantic, delusional confidence for too long. It's time we came back to Earth.

What can practically be done about the governance mess we have made? What follows is a nonexhaustive list. It may not even be the best list. Each of the possibilities below has received favorable attention at different times by the SEC, business groups, or American lawmakers. They may all require considerable refinement, but they should serve as reassurance that we are not helpless about the current state of corporate governance and that we can land safely on solid ground.

- Proxy advisors, which are the de facto regulators of modern corporate governance practices, must have their power reduced. This book is full of evidence that their prescriptions for executive pay and governance structures are failures. Though the proxy firms are unaccountable to anyone besides their disengaged institutional investor clients, this list contains, among its other recommendations, several possible ways their impact on corporate governance could be ameliorated. The case has been made elsewhere, at length, that there is systemic underproduction of high-quality governance advice in the proxy advice market and that regulatory attention is therefore warranted.[4]
- Require proxy advisors to provide companies with the right to challenge their recommendations in the very document the proxy advisors send to their clients. The SEC could go further and hold proxy advisors liable for material errors of fact or negligent errors of judgment in their recommendations. Investors rely on advisors' voting advice; why should those advisors enjoy immunity from the standards that apply to the voting recommendations of other parties?
- Remove the various legislative and regulatory rules that impose corporate governance structures on firms. There may be some governance structures that are strongly supported by empirical studies, but this should be required before anything is imposed on companies. This sounds like an anodyne recommendation, but it would mean, for example, removing mandatory board and audit committee independence requirements.
- Hold shareholders accountable for living up to their marketing representations. If a fund says it is concerned with environmental and social problems, or if it says it is focused on governance, there should be repercussions if these representations turn out to be false. Investors rely on these representations when deciding where to put their money. Institutional fund managers are sophisticated enough that we can hold them liable for fraud.
- Make it clear that institutional investors do not have a legal obligation to vote – provided they inform their investors. If they do vote, they must demonstrate they are demonstrating the care a reasonable person would if voting on their own behalf, and there must be a mechanism for them to be held accountable if they demonstrably fail to devote the resources to vote wisely. Many institutions that vote in apparent lockstep with proxy advisors' recommendations claim the recommendations are only one factor they take into account when coming to an independent decision. They should show their work.
- If a disclosure requirement has been imposed on issuers to advance some corporate governance object beyond reasonably informing the shareholders about

a matter in front of a shareholder meeting, the disclosure should be eliminated. The traditional "materiality" tests should once again be the touchstone for disclosure. Only a minority of the things that we presently require to be disclosed are actually "material" as that term has traditionally been defined in legislation and the courts. Investors need more guidance from companies about what matters, rather than being confronted with massive piles of paper containing undifferentiated information, much of it unimportant.

- More generally, the SEC needs to admit the reality that there is too much disclosure required of companies. It is not helping investors and it is a tremendous burden on companies. We have lots of data about the limitations of disclosure, particularly once it increases to a certain volume. Everyone knows we have long since passed this point in our public markets. Management should be held accountable if it fails to provide material information, but they should once again be permitted to choose what information is material. Shorter, more relevant, and focused disclosure will help shareholders inform themselves about the important issues.
- Even the most basic mandatory reporting framework imposed on companies, the GAAP metrics, no longer provides a strong correlation with stock prices.[5] For example, in the booming economy prior to Covid, nearly half of American companies reported losses in their financial statements. There are serious scholars suggesting there is room for more bargaining and experimentation between corporate constituencies even around the accounting rules that will most usefully disclose the performance and thus governance of different types of companies.[6]
- The strong bias of regulation should be to encourage the experimentation and bargaining that this book points out characterizes private market corporate governance. At the beginning of our governance experiment, we assumed shareholders were terribly vulnerable to imperial managers, so regulation was needed. Even if that was true then (and there are grounds for suspicion), it is demonstrably not true now. Managers have adopted – often voluntarily – pretty much every governance practice demanded by shareholders. Just look at the sheer amount of purely voluntary ESG disclosure companies have come to provide over a very short period. This means that regulation needs to become about permitting flexibility and enforcing bargains. It should be focused on facilitating *ex ante* negotiations and experimentation, not attractive *ex post* outcomes. Modern corporate governance has proved utterly inept at getting the latter.
- Activist shareholders should be required to disclose the long-run operational outcomes experienced by those companies whose boards they have joined or replaced. Yale professor Jeffrey Sonnenfeld has several very amusing studies showing, for example, how poorly the companies targeted by activist investor Nelson Peltz perform after he or his team join the board.[7] Sonnenfeld also

has data showing that some executives targeted by activist funds have much better track records at creating value for investors than the funds themselves.[8] We have seen that underperformance is the statistically most likely outcome of activist interventions. Shouldn't shareholders have the track record of those soliciting their votes? Isn't this one of the most relevant facts for investors considering how to vote?

- Organizations holding *de minimis* levels of stock should be permitted to bring only one or two shareholder proposals a year. Right now, what happens is that a small number of gadflies are responsible for the vast majority of shareholder proposals. These proposals almost always fail, and they represent a dead loss of considerable corporate resources. They generally reflect the latest governance fad and almost never show any understanding of the particular circumstances of the targeted companies. This is a waste of time, energy, and money.
- State legislatures should regularly require an independent accounting of the impact of public funds' activist campaigns. Public investment funds like CalPERS generate a disproportionate number of corporate governance engagements. Funds like these have incentives to please the politicians that retain them and have comparatively less concern about the beneficiaries of the funds because those beneficiaries are locked in. To the extent that third-party studies have been performed about the outcomes of these public fund-specific engagements with portfolio companies, these studies suggest the interventions are either ineffective or value-destroying.[9] Legislatures have a responsibility to oversee public investment funds, and part of this surely includes inquiring about the longer-term financial outcomes of the funds' activism.
- Given the failure of various attempts to measure governance and use it to rank or rate companies, regulators should be clear with investment funds that funds cannot rely on governance rating measures in making investment decisions. Fund managers are fiduciaries, and it is a scandal if they are making decisions based on these absurd third-party assessments of governance quality. The same is even more true of fund managers making use of the deeply flawed ESG ratings surveyed in Chapter 12.
- Return the business of setting pay structure and totals to the market. Mandatory pay disclosure rules should be abandoned to give directors more flexibility to try innovative and firm-specific pay practices. Shareholders will be able to successfully demand the pay information they need. Removing the details about pay will prevent proxy advisors and the small number of one-size-fits-all pay experts from mandating rigid pay practices across all companies. As a side benefit, since executives, themselves, have clearly been the main beneficiaries of our pay disclosure rules, eliminating them may go some way to eventually reducing the upward trajectory of executive compensation in America.
- Congress should remove the tax incentives that encouraged the growth in performance and equity-linked pay over the last three decades. Leave it to the

directors and managers to negotiate what they believe is the right mix of instruments and incentives to go into executive pay packages.

- Remove the obstacles to punishing bad corporate actors individually and in person. Considerable political and public pressure would be taken off corporate governance as a regulatory intervention if the rules that are supposed to impose discipline on bad behavior were working properly.
- Regulate environmental and social harms directly. It hurts companies and the country to pretend that businesses in competitive markets can voluntarily and unilaterally start investing their resources in lower marginal return ways than their competitors. As disappointing as it sounds, politics, not end runs through the executive branch, is the only way to get real progress on our very real problems.

While it isn't part of the list of possible reforms to our corporate governance situation, this book and various other publications like it, are attempts to help solve the corporate governance mess we are in. This book has been written to loosen the grip of some of the stories that have held our imaginations over the past forty years: that executives as agents are unreliable, that shareholders are a solution to governance weakness, that the focus of regulation should be on outcomes rather than facilitating a marketplace, that the various governance practices we have tried are working, and that competitive markets and the actual business of corporations can be ignored as unimportant for corporate governance. We have received the hard lessons; it is time we heed them.

NOTES

1 Dan R. Dalton et al., "The Fundamental Agency Problem and Its Mitigation: Independence, Equity, and the Market for Corporate Control" in James P. Walsh and Arthur P. Brief (eds.), *The Academy of Management Annals* (New York: Lawrence Erlbaum Associates, 2007), vol. 1, pp. 1–64 at p. 11.
2 Roberta Romano, "Quack Corporate Governance" (2005) 28:4 *Regulation* 36–44; Stephen M. Bainbridge, "Dodd-Frank: Quack Federal Corporate Governance Round II" (2011) 95:5 *Minnesota Law Review* 1779–1821.
3 Hal Weitzman, "Is the US Economy 'Going Dark'?" (May 30, 2023), *Chicago Booth Review*, online: www.chicagobooth.edu/review/is-us-economy-going-dark#:~:text="The%20fact%20 that%20more%20capital,Herren%20Lee%20in%20October%202021.
4 Bryce C. Tingle, "The Agency Cost Case for Regulating Proxy Advisory Firms" (2016) 49:2 *UBC Law Review* 725–787.
5 Israel Klein, "Voting on Reporting" (2022) *Journal of Corporation Law*, forthcoming, online: SSRN, https://ssrn.com/abstract=4078226; See also, Baruch Lev and Feng Gu, *The End of Accounting and the Path Forward for Investors and Managers* (Hoboken: John Wiley & Sons, Inc., 2016).
6 *Ibid.* See also, Roberta Romano, *The Advantage of Competitive Federalism for Securities Regulation* (Washington, DC: The AEI Press, 2002) at pp. 12–42.
7 Jeffrey Sonnenfeld, "Demystifying Nelson Peltz's Track Record of Investment Underperformance: And Not Just Peltz: Activist Investment Returns Significantly Trail the S&P 500 Across the Board," online (pdf): *Yale School of Management*,

https://yale.app.box.com/s/rmfa6of2q4mc578v5s8nvntz3x6ox2im [Sonnenfeld, "Demystifying"]; Jeffrey Sonnenfeld and Steven Tian, "The Last Flicker of the Candle as Peltz Melts," Fortune, January 19, 2023, online: https://fortune.com/2023/01/19/nelson-peltz-disney-bob-iger-board-performance-track-record-analysis-sonnenfeld-tian/.

8 Sonnenfeld, "Demystifying," above at note 7.

9 Michael P. Smith, "Shareholder Activism by Institutional Investors: Evidence from CalPERS" (1996) 51:1 *The Journal of Finance* 227–252; Willard T. Carleton, James M. Nelson and Michael S. Weisbach, "The Influence of Institutions on Corporate Governance through Private Negotiations: Evidence from TIAA-CREF" (1998) 53:4 *The Journal of Finance* 1335–1362 at 1351–1353; Tracie Woidtke, "Public Pension Fund Activism and Firm Value: An Empirical Analysis," September 2015, online (pdf): *Manhattan Institute – Legal Policy Report*, https://media4.manhattan-institute.org/pdf/lpr_20.pdf at 5; Vinod Venkiteshwaran, Subramanian R. Iyer and Ramesh P. Rao, "Is Carl Icahn Good for Long-term Shareholders? A Case Study in Shareholder Activism" (2010) 22:4 *Journal of Applied Corporate Finance* 45–57 at 51.

Index

activist board nominees, 107, 124, 127, 175
activist investors, 28, 122–125, 127, 262, 293.
  See also shareholder activism
agency cost theory, 9, 13, 20–21, 24–26, 38,
  48, 70–71, 77, 81, 94, 119, 129, 169–180,
  182–187, 195–196, 198, 214–216, 235, 241,
  246, 289
analyst forecasts, 107, 125, 175
astrophysics
  elephant, 215
  turtle, 215
attitudes of directors and managers towards
  corporate governance, 8, 28, 103, 155, 157,
  187, 199, 201, 220–221, 245
audit committee, 42–43, 102, 179, 292

Bainbridge, Stephen, 15, 206, 225, 228, 230, 232,
  252, 295
Bebchuk, Lucian, 14–16, 61–62, 67–68, 85,
  89, 126, 138, 140–141, 188–189, 246, 250,
  253–254, 278
benefit corporation, 221
Berle, Adolph, 18–19, 193
best practices, 21, 24–26, 30, 37–38, 41, 43–44,
  47–49, 56, 58–59, 61, 63–64, 70–71, 73–74,
  79, 81–82, 84, 101, 108, 145, 150, 173, 177,
  185–186, 215, 277
board committees, 41, 44, 58, 179, 221, 276
box-checking, 29, 150, 156, 201. *See also* one-size-
  fits-all governance
Business Roundtable statement, 7, 243–245
butt dial, 23

Cadbury Committee, 37, 215. *See also* best
  practices
Caplan, Bryan, 96, 99, 111–112
carbon emission and pollution, 7, 25, 42, 239,
  248, 259, 265, 268–270, 272, 274–275,
  277, 290

CEO
  equity ownership, 72, 74, 80, 129, 180
  impact on performance, 77
  pay, 3, 40, 70–72, 77, 82–83, 176, 182, 185, 244.
    See also executive compensation
  turnover, 11, 78, 130, 133, 153
CEO duality, 46–47, 180. *See also* separating
  CEO and chair roles
cheap shots
  Charlie Brown, 205
  FTX, WeWork, Theranos, 222
  Hollywood, 22, 199
  Jeffrey Epstein, 37
  Nazis, 193
  Supreme Court of Canada, 197–198
  vampire squid, 201
Cheffins, Brian, 30–31, 33, 49, 187, 194, 205,
  226–227
children, nimble fingers of, 210
civic voting, 93, 96–98, 110
Coase, Ronald, 19, 30, 217, 227
Coffee, John, 65, 95, 111, 115–116, 124, 135–138, 188,
  237, 250, 279
compensation committee, 3, 12, 41, 44, 81, 151, 179
compensation consultant, 3–4, 81
comply or explain, 37, 63–64, 186
constituency, 19, 21, 25, 82, 94–95, 128, 145,
  149, 171, 196, 198, 212–213, 236, 238,
  242–243, 245–246, 249, 260, 262, 270.
    See also stakeholders
constituency statutes, 196, 236, 246–247
consumer boycotts, 244, 260
corporate governance, history, 71, 144, 169,
  194, 213
corporate governance, staffing, 156
corporate governance, waivers, 197, 206
corporate governance costs, 8, 10, 12, 20, 83–84,
  95, 290–291, 294
corporate paranoia, 203, 240

corporate profitability, 106, 120, 123–124, 132, 202–203, 235, 239–240, 245–246

corporate structure, 20–21, 24, 26–27, 29, 49, 64, 80, 105, 108, 110, 150, 157, 185, 195, 211, 213–215, 220–223, 246–247, 290, 292

cost of capital, 202–203, 237, 239, 271–274

costs of corporate governance, 77

Coyote, Wile E., 1, 3–8, 259, 289–291

CSR (corporate social responsibility), 7, 236, 238–249, 262, 267

disclosure, 1–5, 8, 10, 57, 74, 143–144, 176, 181, 201, 213, 258–261, 265, 270–271, 276–277, 291–294

diversity, 12, 39, 44–45, 212, 248, 266

divestment, 272–273, 275

Dodd, Merrick, 18–19, 193

Dodd–Frank, 3–6, 96, 153

dual-class shares, 23, 175–176, 195, 213, 223–224, 247

Easterbrook, Frank, 192, 206, 214–215, 219, 221, 226

efficiency, 20, 29, 46, 203, 215–218, 238, 249, 259, 290

E-Index, 61–63, 130, 186

Eisenberg, Melvin, 22, 31, 194, 205

employee representation on boards, 236, 248–249, 260

employees, 7, 17–18, 21, 25, 27, 58, 64, 71, 84, 95, 124, 149, 156, 170, 182, 184, 203–204, 212–213, 236–237, 239, 242, 244, 246, 248–249, 260, 262, 264, 268–269, 271

Engine No.1, 275

enlightened shareholder value, 236–238

Enron, 29, 40, 44, 57, 72, 76, 178, 195, 240, 268

environmental outcomes, 236–237, 247, 249, 258–259, 263, 265, 267, 272

ESG (environmental, social, and governance), 7–8, 10, 59–60, 236–238, 243, 245, 248, 254, 258–261, 263–277, 291, 293

ESG ratings (rankings), 8, 59–60, 186, 241–242, 259, 263, 265, 267–273, 294

event studies, 104, 121, 196, 244

executive compensation, 1–6, 8–11, 24, 26, 29, 39, 44–46, 70–71, 73–74, 78–84, 109, 123, 130, 133, 153, 155, 177–179, 181–182, 185, 201, 204–205, 210, 224, 243, 262, 268, 294

Exxon, 269, 275. *See also* Engine No.1

Fama, Eugene, 19, 30–31, 46, 53, 177, 179, 190–191, 194–195, 202, 205, 209, 281

fiduciary duties, 95, 100, 144, 148, 195–198, 221, 236–237, 245–247, 262, 292

financial restatements, 2, 43, 59, 76, 102, 176, 182, 186

Fischel, Daniel, 175, 189, 192, 206, 214–215, 219, 221, 226–227

Fischer, Stanley, 113, 217, 227

Frankenstein, 18–19, 23. *See also* Fronckensteen

fraud, 29, 37, 40, 42–44, 47, 57, 74, 76, 102, 179, 181–182, 194, 215, 289, 292

Friedman, Milton, 240

Fronckensteen, 19

GAAP, 293

gardening practices, 12–13

Gilson, Ronald, 15, 105, 111, 115–116, 134, 170, 184, 187, 192, 205, 218, 227–228, 287–288

G-Index, 61–63, 130, 186

Glass Lewis, 2, 62, 119, 144–146, 155–156, 160. *See also* proxy advisors

governance industry, 6–7, 9, 22–25, 28–29, 38, 41–42, 44, 46–47, 56, 58, 71–75, 77–80, 83–84, 94–96, 104, 119, 172, 181, 204, 214, 219, 223–224, 236, 243, 259, 290

governance ratings (rankings), 57–60, 62–65, 143, 153–154, 186, 294

hedge funds, 107, 122–126, 221. *See also* shareholder activism

Hunger Games, 70. *See also* Piketty, Thomas

hybrid board, 147. *See also* activist board nominees

Icahn, Carl, 109, 117, 296

impact funds, 267, 274

independent directors, 25–26, 38–44, 49, 56, 58, 80, 107, 119, 147, 154–155, 178–180, 185, 219–220, 277, 292

Indian Independence movement, 4

inequality, 7, 70, 71, 237, 249, 262, 290

initial public offering
nonconforming governance structures, 48, 109, 223–224
reluctance to go public, 222, 224, 291

institutional shareholders
behavior, 63, 79, 82, 95, 100, 103, 108–109, 120, 178, 261
dependence on third parties for governance activities, 56, 94–95, 143–144, 149–150, 265, 268–269, 294
ESG behavior, 261, 264–266, 269, 274–275
impact on companies, 10, 63, 79, 94, 108–109, 120, 173, 262, 294
incentives, 95, 101, 103, 108, 120, 143–144, 147, 173, 261, 290, 294
staffing, 95, 261

voting, 29, 95, 100–101, 108–109, 275. *See also* shareholder voting

voting policies, 3–4, 39, 82, 177

interlocking directorships, 12, 48, 223

ISS, 2–3, 25, 38, 47, 56, 58–59, 64, 74, 101, 119, 143–148, 153–160. *See also* proxy advisors

Jensen, Michael, 20, 22, 24, 31, 46, 53, 70, 74, 87, 90, 139, 169, 171, 179–181, 187, 190–191, 194

Kahan, Marcel, 8, 16, 109, 114, 117, 120, 133, 135, 140, 160–161, 163, 174, 188, 228

Larcker, David, 51, 54–55, 65–66, 68–69, 86, 89, 91–92, 111, 115–117, 133, 137–140, 142, 146–147, 161–164, 187, 192, 205, 229, 231, 280, 283, 287

law and economics, 19–20, 217

loyalty of managers, 9, 13, 19–20, 182, 194–197, 199. *See also* fiduciary duties

Manne, Henry, 139, 226, 240–241, 251

market for corporate control, 62, 118, 127, 129–133, 175, 183–185. *See also* takeovers

markets
benefits, 9–10, 93, 201, 210, 218, 291
business, 9–10, 17, 201–202, 211, 235
governance (private), 18, 27–28, 222, 293
governance (public), 18, 27, 204, 211–215, 218–220, 222–224, 291, 293
labor, 10, 169, 204, 212, 237, 249, 294
public, 9–11, 27, 30, 83, 100, 128, 204, 220–224, 291

Martin, Roger, 76, 89

Masouros, Pavlos, 119, 133, 279–280

maximizing shareholder value, 7, 58, 133, 196, 198–199, 216, 236, 243–244, 262

Means, Gardiner, 193

measuring corporate governance, 3, 9, 56–58, 60–65, 77, 121, 126, 130, 144, 148, 153–156, 158, 177, 179, 186, 242, 268–269, 294

Meckling, William, 20, 22, 24, 31, 70, 169, 171, 180, 187, 191, 194

Miller, Merton, 19, 30, 194–195, 205

monitoring board, 9

motivation of managers, 72–74, 76–77, 84, 152, 182, 198–199, 205, 241, 243, 245–247

North, Douglass, 214, 217, 226–227

one-size-fits-all governance, 9, 41, 84, 120, 150, 152, 156, 185, 187, 204, 220–221, 224, 235, 290, 294. *See also* best practices

overboarded directors, 47–48, 223

Palia, Darius, 86, 115–116, 124, 135–138, 188, 191, 279

patents, 47, 132, 185, 246, 263, 274. *See also* research and development

pay practices
crudeness, 83, 182, 294
equity incentives, 5–6, 26–28, 58, 72–76, 78–80, 82–84, 176–177, 180–182, 243
impact on taxes, 2, 5, 79, 294
pay-for-performance, 3, 6, 72–79, 82, 84, 177, 180–182

philosophers, irrelevant references to, 12, 193

Piketty, Thomas, 70, 77, 85, 89

poison pills, 26, 62–63, 110, 130–132, 174, 184, 220

polls, 28, 201. *See also* attitudes of directors and managers towards corporate governance

positive screening, 273–275

Posner, Richard, 217, 227

potatoes, 22

private companies, 27, 30, 221–223, 272. *See also* markets, governance (private)

private equity, 30, 82–83, 123, 177, 222, 246, 291. *See also* shareholder influence

proxy access, 96, 110, 174

proxy advisors
assumptions, 56, 72–73, 94, 147–153
bias, 147, 290
influence, 2, 57, 79, 119, 143, 145–146, 292
market for proxy advice, 95, 143–145, 159–160, 268
mistakes, 64, 156–159, 292
moustache-twirling, 146
staffing, 156
voting guidelines, 3, 26, 38, 47–48, 75, 82, 96, 143, 146–147, 150–156, 158, 177

proxy fight, 9, 12, 106, 108, 118, 122, 175, 203, 271, 275. *See also* shareholder activism

recessions, 29, 76, 79, 203

Reddy, Bobby, 176, 189–190

research and development, 30, 40, 47, 74, 124, 132, 169–170, 173, 176, 181, 185, 199, 219, 246, 261–263, 271

Rock, Edward, 8, 16, 21, 31, 109, 114, 120, 133, 135, 174, 188, 228

Rose, David, 200, 208

Runner, Road, 1, 3–5, 8, 289

Sanders, Bernie, 236, 249–250

Sarbanes–Oxley, 2, 5–6, 42–43, 222

separating ceo and chair roles, 12, 26, 39, 46, 179–180, 185, 223

shareholder activism, 106–107, 118–119, 122, 127, 131, 149, 175, 203, 248, 277

shareholder engagement, 266, 270, 272, 274–276
shareholder influence, 83, 94, 178, 185, 262
shareholder proposals, 39, 96, 108, 110, 118,
    120–122, 148, 174, 244, 260, 265, 271,
    275–276, 294
shareholder voting
  activist campaigns, 105, 108, 122–126, 132, 175,
    204, 247–248, 294
  attempts to avoid, 119, 223–224
  ESG, 265–266, 277
  majority voting, 26, 103–105, 110, 157, 174,
    220, 223
  rational ignorance and irrationality, 9, 93–94,
    97, 100, 102, 108, 111, 277
  say-on-pay, 3, 5, 83, 96, 153, 178
  uncontested elections, 101–102
  value given to voting rights, 93, 96, 99–100,
    111, 173
short-slate, 147. *See also* activist board nominees
Simple Agreement for Future Equity (SAFE), 28
Smith, Adam, 193, 235
Smith, Gordon, 213, 225
social outcomes, 8, 10, 236–237, 239, 244, 248–249,
    258–259, 263, 265, 267, 272
Somin, Ilya, 98, 112

Sonnenfeld, Jeffrey, 293, 295–296
staggered boards, 26, 96, 130–132, 184, 195, 220,
    223–224, 246–247
stakeholders, 7, 25, 196–198, 243–244, 262, 266
stock options, 26, 56, 71–72, 74, 79, 83, 152, 181,
    205, 220
Stout, Lynn, 30, 76, 88, 138–139, 207–208, 218,
    228, 231–232
Strine, Leo, 5, 15, 123, 133, 135, 138, 173, 188
surveys, 80, 158–159, 220, 245, 249, 265
sustainability, 7, 39, 57, 236, 259
systemic governance, 263–264, 266, 269

takeover defenses, 61, 63, 127–132, 183–184
takeovers, 9, 47, 72, 118, 127–130, 132, 180, 183–185,
    196, 203–204, 247
Tallarita, Roberto, 238, 246, 250, 253–254
Thiel, Peter, 235, 250
transaction costs, 203–204, 216–218
trust, 6, 8, 17, 29, 76, 129, 193, 199–201, 212, 214,
    245, 249

Vogel, David, 240, 242, 251–253

Warren, Elizabeth, 7, 15, 236, 249

For EU product safety concerns, contact us at Calle de José Abascal, 56–1°, 28003 Madrid, Spain or eugpsr@cambridge.org.

www.ingramcontent.com/pod-product-compliance
Ingram Content Group UK Ltd.
Pitfield, Milton Keynes, MK11 3LW, UK
UKHW021108100725
460633UK00016B/210